DISRUPTION TO DIVERSITY

EDINBURGH DIVINITY 1846–1996

DISRUPTION
TO DIVERSITY

EDINBURGH DIVINITY
1846–1996

Edited by

David F. Wright
Gary D. Badcock

T&T CLARK
EDINBURGH

T&T CLARK LTD
59 GEORGE STREET
EDINBURGH EH2 2LQ
SCOTLAND

First published 1996

ISBN 0 567 08517 1

British Library Cataloguing-in-Publication Data
A catalogue record for this book is available from the British Library

Typeset by Waverley Typesetters, Galashiels
Printed and bound in Great Britain by Hartnolls Ltd, Bodmin

Contents

Introduction

NEW COLLEGE – THE BUILDING

O PINIONS HAVE long been divided over the architectural merits of New College, this 'grimy frown on the Mound'[1] overlooking Princes Street in the heart of Edinburgh. John Ruskin thought the design of its towers incomprehensible,[2] and a recent chairman of the Royal Fine Art Commission for Scotland has commented on this 'undistinguished building'.

> Its chief fault seems to be that it is on a scale too small for either its architectural pretensions or for the splendid site which it occupies at the head of the Mound . . . Its main recommendation is, perhaps, that it is not too prominent.[3]

Other commentators, however, regard it, together with the classical galleries at the foot of the Mound, as providing 'a spectacular entry into the Old Town'; 'the exterior is purely scenographic and it most elegantly turns the corner'.[4]

Edinburgh residents quite commonly identify the edifice as the Church of Scotland's Assembly Hall, which in reality shelters, hidden from view, behind New College.[5] Such confusion, however, is not wholly incongruous, for New College was founded as a church college,

---

[1] CES 320; 'Within the collegiate quadrangle thunders a Bible-brandishing bronze of John Knox.'

[2] See Watt 17–18.

[3] Youngson (1966), 280–1.

[4] CES 780; Gow (1984), 54.

[5] For years the local Edinburgh telephone directory carried a sketch of the College frontage on its cover, describing it as the Assembly Hall. The Assembly Hall, designed by David Bryce, was built 1858–9; Gifford (1984), 185; Pinkerton and Windram (1983), 92. When the possibility was mooted in 1950 that the United Nations Organisation

and the University of Edinburgh's Faculty of Divinity, which the building has housed since the 1930s, has always been closely associated with the national Church, as have the other three Scottish Divinity faculties, at St Andrews, Aberdeen and Glasgow.

The foundation stone of the New College was laid by its distinguished first Principal, Thomas Chalmers, 150 years ago on 3 June 1846.[6] The circumstances that brought it into being and the lofty aspirations that inspired its formative years are skilfully surveyed by Professor Stewart J. Brown in the second chapter of this volume. The new institution was the creation of the Free Church of Scotland, formed in 1843 from the division in the established Church known as the Disruption. The story, then, of Divinity in Edinburgh over the last century and a half begins in ecclesiastical Disruption, an event of high principle and high tragedy that left the new Free Church without access to the University Divinity faculties for the education of its future ministers. New College was the first of the Divinity halls founded by the Free Church to meet this need.[7] It was up and running in other premises in Edinburgh before 1843 was out. Professors and students finally took possession of their grand new building on the Mound in November 1850.[8]

TRADITION AND CONTEXT

New College remained an independent church institution for some eight and a half decades – from its beginnings to 1900 as a Free Church College and then from 1900 until the church Union of 1929 as a United Free Church College. It was not until January 1935 that the negotiations and legislation entailed by that Union (which reconstituted the national Church of Scotland by the merger of the United Free Church and the existing Church of Scotland) finally brought about the marriage of New College with the University's Faculty of Divinity in the New College building.[9] The dual identity of the resulting College-cum-Faculty (which it shares with the other Scottish Divinity faculties and

might meet in Edinburgh, an offer was made of the use of the Assembly Hall and much of New College. The Faculty and Senate resolved that they and the students could manage for a term 'in the top flat of the College'.

[6] See Watt 1–5. The location of the stone is no longer precisely known.

[7] Had the debate not gone the other way, it might have been the only Free Church college; see pp. 44–5.

[8] Watt 43–52. The professors' opening lectures can be found in Cunningham (1851).

[9] Watt 131–52.

which still represents one of their claims to distinctiveness among theological schools in the United Kingdom) is sensitively mapped by Professor Bill Shaw in chapter 9, and also touched on in David Wright's survey of the wider Edinburgh scene in chapter 13. They will repay careful reading, for the question how a single institution can be both a Church of Scotland College and a University Faculty is frequently asked with some puzzlement. The answer is best approached from a historical perspective.

Yet if the New College Divinity Faculty has been part of the University of Edinburgh only since 1929 – or more accurately, only since the Universities (Scotland) Act of 1932 – it is entirely proper that this sesquicentennial history should encompass also the activities of the continuing University Faculty of Divinity in Old College on South Bridge between the Disruption of 1843 and the enlargement of the Faculty and its relocation to New College at the top of the Mound, a relocation completed in January 1935. Hence the several chapters in Part II of this book trace the development of the disciplines of theological study in both Old and New College from the Disruption onwards (with the exception of the more recent emergence of Religious Studies). Their authors deploy their diverse skills and methods in pursuing both trajectories within a single narrative.

The appropriateness of this comprehensive embrace rests on several considerations. The New College drew half its initial teaching complement – Principal Thomas Chalmers and Professor David Welsh – from the University Faculty, so denuding the latter as to leave it temporarily reduced to one professor. As Stewart Brown's account of 'The Disruption and the Dream' reveals, Chalmers and others soon espoused a vision of the new institution as a Free Christian university. If such ambitions had before long to yield to more modest reality, the New College enterprise continued to bear the contours of the academic rock whence it was hewn; it was essentially a University Divinity Faculty in exile. So many features of its life, from the spread of its disciplines to its international relations (on which Dr Andrew Ross's sketch of the 'Student Kaleidoscope' in chapter 11 throws much light), reveal that it was not a narrowly denominational seminary. No less than the continuing University Faculty, New College claimed to represent the mainstream Scottish Reformed theological tradition reaching back to the Reformation – a tradition whose salient features are here sketched in a characteristically vigorous essay by Professor Tom Torrance.

Furthermore, the theological worlds of the University Faculty and New College were never completely insulated from each other, though this is an impression one might gather at times from Hugh Watt's centenary history of New College. As early as 1865 a Principal of the Free Church College – R. S. Candlish – was awarded an Honorary D.D. by the University. Three New College professors were similarly honoured in the next few years, including A. B. Davidson in 1868, even before he officially succeeded 'Rabbi' Duncan in the chair of Old Testament.[10] Ministers in Free Church congregations had been similarly honoured by Edinburgh University from 1849, when Thomas Guthrie of St John's Free Church in the city was made a D.D. And this was at a time when several years saw no D.D.'s awarded at all.[11]

A teaching post in New College was no bar to a University appointment. Patrick MacDougall moved from the chair of Moral Philosophy in New College to the University chair in 1853, and A. C. Fraser transferred from one chair of Logic to the other in 1856. Institutional links between the University Faculty of Divinity and New College are scarcely in evidence during the nineteenth century, although we may be sure that their teachers read each other's writings and interacted with each other in sundry ways.[12] In 1904, for example, when the New College building was returned to the continuing Free Church by the remarkable House of Lords adjudication against the claims of the new United Free Church, the University promptly offered the homeless staff and students both teaching accommodation and Library

[10] Others were George Smeaton in 1869 and James MacGregor in 1871. W. G. Blaikie, Professor from 1868, had received a D.D. in 1864 while minister of Pilrig Free Church in Edinburgh.

[11] *A Catalogue of the Graduates in the Faculties of Arts, Divinity, and Law, of the University of Edinburgh* (Edinburgh, 1858), 252–3; three D.D.'s were awarded in 1843, two in 1847, five in 1849, three in 1854, three in 1855. The Disruption itself seems not to have been the cause, for none was granted between 1827 and 1836 or between 1839 and 1843.

[12] Relations between the two prior to 1900, at all levels, merit further investigation. From a quick collation of lists of B.D. graduates published annually in the University *Calendar* and of Hugh Watt's typescript list of students who matriculated at New College, it is clear that New College students gained the University's B.D. degree in good numbers from 1871. Of fourteen graduating that year, eight had studied at New College. Probably the first to do so were Edgar Williams and Thomas Young in 1869, although Young was admitted to the Church of Scotland the same year (*FES* VI, 192). According to the *Calendar* of 1864–5 (p. 158), the B.D. 'fell into disuse' in 1843, thanks no doubt to the effects of the Disruption on the Faculty of Divinity. Following the enabling recommendation of a University Commission in 1862, the B.D. was reintroduced,

access.[13] Behind such generosity lay some history of cordiality between Old and New College. From the University side it had included for a generation or more a liberal approach to the opening up of the B.D. degree to other than Church of Scotland students.[14] The experience of sharing premises during 1904–6 (the United Free Church resumed possession of New College at the beginning of 1907)[15] must have eased the way for the sharing of teaching that took place during the First World War in 1916–18 – an 'amalgamation' (as Hugh Watt calls it) designed to release professors for war duties.[16] Such close co-operation in turn prepared the ground for the more significant and lasting joint enterprise of the Postgraduate School of Theology begun in 1919.[17]

So for a cluster of reasons, to have told the story of New College prior to the 1929 Union without taking in also the Divinity Faculty in Old College would have seriously narrowed the perspective. But the clinching consideration must be the intellectual attractiveness and personal achievements of several University professors in their own right (even though collectively over the whole period the Old College Faculty scarcely matched New College's distinction): Robert Lee, whose influential liturgical innovations in Greyfriars Kirk are sympathetically recorded here by John O'Neill alongside his lively lecturing on the New Testament; A. H. Charteris, the versatile initiator of so many lasting ventures in Church and University that he achieves a mention in the chapters on both New Testament and Practical Theology; John Patrick, that *rara avis* of Scottish theology, a patristic scholar of note; W. P. Paterson, a fascinatingly eclectic divine 'as concerned for praxis as he was for theory', as George Newlands portrays him; the learned Robert Flint, Fellow of the British Academy and defender of a robustly modern faith (he wrote a work on *Socialism* as early as 1894) but 'almost

---

with the first examinations taking place in November 1864 and March 1865, and the first degrees awarded in 1866. It was now open to candidates who had completed the theological curriculum of churches other than the Church of Scotland and hence not in the University Faculty, but all such candidates must have attended 'during at least one Session, two at least of the classes of the Theological Faculty of this University'. So from 1868–9, if not earlier, some New College students also took some theological classes in the University.

[13] See pp. 173–4. New College Settlement in the Pleasance became meanwhile the College's temporary base; Watt 96.

[14] Watt 96; *DSCHT* 281.

[15] Watt 97–101.

[16] Watt 107–8.

[17] See p. 175; Turner (1933), 71–3; Watt 109–13.

invisible as a man' (Newlands); A. R. S. Kennedy, holder of the chair of Hebrew until his seventy-ninth year and a very early President of the Society for Old Testament Study; and James Mackinnon, whose tenure of the professorship of Ecclesiastical History raised the discipline to a new height of distinction in the University.

THE BUILDING IN LOCAL CONTEXT

The building whose 150th birthday has occasioned this volume has been a property of elastic proportions. In his chapter on New College Library, John Howard notes its move in 1936 from what is now the Martin Hall (named after Alexander Martin, Principal of New College at the time of the Union in 1929 and a major facilitator of the Union from the United Free Church side)[18] to its present premises, on the eastern flank of the New College quadrangle complex. They had been built originally as a church to house the Free High congregation, which was formed at the Disruption by withdrawal from St Giles.[19] Later the United Free High, and then in 1929 simply the High Church, the congregation was transported in 1935 to become the new Reid Memorial parish church in south Edinburgh. The building it vacated on the Mound was skilfully adapted to serve the needs of a Library – though this is a task at which its Librarians have never ceased to struggle.

At the time, the property immediately to the west of the College, then known as Lister House, was also considered as a possible home of the relocated Library – either itself or a new construction on the site.[20] These buildings further up the slope of Mound Place, to the right of the College as you face the entrance arch, are older than New College by over half a century.[21] They are all that remains from the clearance required to make space for the new College. They have been linked with the College in various ways for various periods of time. In the 1840s they were identified simply as 1 and 2 Mound Place. The College janitor was one of the residents in number 2 for some years, and later the Revd Harry Miller lived in number 1 during his first years as Warden of New College Settlement in the Pleasance (of which more may be learned from David Lyall's chapter).

In 1887, 2 Mound Place became University Hall, Scotland's first student residence, set up by Patrick Geddes, then a lecturer in Botany.

[18] *DSCHT* 549.
[19] Watt 170; Dunlop (1988), 274–5.
[20] Watt 14, 169–70; Pinkerton and Windram (1983), 84.
[21] For what follows see Pinkerton and Windram (1983), 76–88.

This pioneering enterprise stimulated similar ventures elsewhere in the city, including a residence for Church of Scotland Divinity students and probationers opened in 14 George Square in 1895. When University Hall extended into Ramsay Garden (on the right of the steep lane skirting the west side of the College), Geddes no longer needed 2 Mound Place, and for a few years around the turn of the century it became the New College students' residence. For unknown reasons, the United Free Church leased it back to Geddes in 1903, and it resumed its role as part of University Hall. (The dates of 1887 and 1903 around the front door still mark Geddes' two associations with the building.) It was renamed Lister House, after the one-time Edinburgh professor of surgery who pioneered antiseptics. During 1914–20 it again became New College Residence, but then until 1952 housed women students, latterly under the aegis of the Church of Scotland Committee on Social Service.

The women's hostel closed in 1952 for essential rehabilitation and the property was transferred to New College. The cost of upgrading and restoring it was met, with difficulty, from several sources, including the sale of 22–24 Chalmers Street, which had taken over from 14 George Square as the Divinity Students Residence, and part of the sale of New College Settlement in the Pleasance. The refurbished New College Residence opened in August 1954, accommodating some forty to fifty students. (The hostel had since 1927 incorporated the upper floors of 1 Mound Place; below was the Alexandra Hostel of the Scottish Girls Friendly Society.)

New College Residence survived until 1973, when structural weaknesses threatened the edifice's future. It had been purchased by the University in 1964, following the ceding of New College itself to the University by the Church of Scotland. From 1969 it no longer served Divinity students alone. In stages it had been incorporated into the emerging Mylne's Court complex of University halls of residence encircling New College to the west and the south.

After the 1973 closure, plans to use the building or the site for Faculty purposes (a chapel, additional teaching rooms, etc.) came to nothing, and instead it received an expensive and sensitive internal reconstruction before re-opening as Patrick Geddes Hall in November 1978.[22]

As one of the University's student residences, Patrick Geddes Hall no longer has any special relationship to the Divinity Faculty. Its span

---

[22] On Patrick Geddes (1854–1932), botanist, discoverer of chlorophyll, town-planner and visionary, see *CSE* 414; Boardman (1978).

of existence as New College Residence, 1954–73, will recall a host of varied – and not always apocryphal – memories for a generation of students. The Warden was sometimes resident and sometimes not, and the post was commonly held by a member of Faculty. The late Dr Ian Moir was non-resident Warden. A more determinative figure in students' lives was the Matron, a position occupied for several years prior to the 1973 closure by Miss C. E. Mackenzie, who commanded fear and affection in roughly equal proportions.

The Ramsay Lane wing of New College began life in 1837 as the Tolbooth Parish School. The Tolbooth Church, immediately behind the Assembly Hall at the back of the College, was built 1839–44 to serve both the Tolbooth congregation and the meetings of the General Assembly of the Church of Scotland. It fulfilled the latter role until 1929, and the former, through several unions and changes of name, until 1981. The united charge of Greyfriars, Tolbooth and Highland Church formed in 1979 remains the parish church of New College. David Lyall's chapter records the University Missionary Society's responsibility for the Tolbooth ministry in the 1870s. The future use of the Tolbooth building, still owned by the Church of Scotland, is uncertain, but its commanding spire, framed by the towers of New College, attracts almost every tourist's camera.[23]

After its incorporation into New College, the rooms in the Ramsay Lane wing have undergone repeated changes of use, without ever truly endearing themselves to students and staff. The topmost floor has successively provided for elocution and badminton, the Baillie and Mackintosh Libraries of the Divinity and Dogmatics Departments, and now undergraduate and postgraduate computer workshops. In such metamorphoses lurks a parable of New College's developing culture. Nowadays there is no space even for table-tennis.

At the summit of Ramsay Lane, on the corner of Castlehill, stands the Outlook Tower. The Camera Obscura on its top storey is a magnet for visitors to Edinburgh. After the University acquired the property in 1964, some possibilities emerged of the use of part of the premises by the Faculty. Nothing came of these, but for a couple of years New College ran the Camera Obscura on behalf of the University – and at a profit![24]

The University's involvement in the creation of a complex of student halls of residence around New College began in 1960, when New

[23] See Gifford (1984), 192, 169–70; Dunlop (1988), 94–5, 106.
[24] Pinkerton and Windram (1983), 96–7; Gifford (1984), 192.

College Senate bought the northern part of Mylne's Court from the Free Church for £2,000 – giving the University time to raise funds for its redevelopment. The building had so deteriorated as to be in danger of incurring a demolition order. Part of it, once restored, was to be used as an extension to New College Library, and part also to house New College students. The University was already engaged in discussions with the Church about the future of New College itself, which issued in a decision of the General Assembly in 1961 to transfer both New College and Mylne's Court to the ownership of the University.[25]

Thus began the story of conservation and adaptation of historic buildings in the immediate vicinity of New College that brought great credit on the University. The result was the group of student residences in use today and known collectively as Mylne's Court. A key element in its development was the recruitment of New College's Rainy Hall to be the dining-hall for the new student population, and the construction of a state-of-the-art kitchen suite to service it.

The Rainy Hall was not part of the original New College, but was built in 1900 to mark the jubilee of the College's opening in 1850. It was to bear the name of Robert Rainy, Principal of New College since 1874 and Moderator of the first General Assembly of the United Free Church in 1900. It is perhaps the nearest thing Edinburgh possesses to an Oxbridge college dining-hall. The Common Hall was now freed to serve as a general reading-room, and a clutch of other changes of accommodation also took effect.[26] Over the ensuing decades the Rainy Hall played host to a varied menu of activities. Until the Library's transfer to the old High Church in 1936 freed the Martin Hall for this purpose, lectures, public meetings and social events were held in the Rainy Hall. Later it provided ancillary space for the General Assembly or for Festival productions mounted in the Assembly Hall. Its ambience made it an ideal venue for re-enacting medieval banquets.

Yet it was as the refectory for the New College community that it was built and that it will live long in communal and individual memories. College lunch was never, to be sure, a *cordon bleu* occasion; by many accounts, it survived only by a shared resolve to enjoy oneself despite the gruel, and rumours abounded about the unnameable horrors to be encountered in the Dickensian kitchens. (A student boycott of

[25] Pinkerton and Windram (1983), 68–70; *NCB* 1:1 (Easter 1964), 13–15.

[26] Watt 83–4; Pinkerton and Windram (1983), 92–6. On the Common Hall as the location of College dinner since it began in 1872, see Watt 74–7.

Rainy Hall lunch was once organised by James Weatherhead, later dignified as Principal Clerk and Moderator of the Church of Scotland's General Assembly and a D.D. of the University.) The new facilities to serve Mylne's Court residents opened in 1969 represented a great leap forward, and New College lunch picked up more than the crumbs from the new refectory-type tables. But with the expansion and diversification of the student body, lunch attendance fell away in the 1980s. The reasons were many; more meetings were held in the lunch hour, some students found even the subsidized cost too high, increased teaching loads tempted staff to seek peace and quiet elsewhere, and the cohesiveness of a community centrally committed to church ministry was eroded.

The tastes of students in the halls changed also, and self-catering became the flavour of the month. In 1995 the University closed and stripped the Rainy Hall kitchen, unable to justify the expense of upgrading it to satisfy statutory regulations. And so the Hall reverted to the sole use of the Faculty. The University's Students Association is providing a catering service that is certain to be closely responsive to student needs.

By the terms of the agreement ceding the New College building to the University in 1961, the Church of Scotland retained the right to use the Rainy Hall and other rooms during the General Assembly. It was partly in order to improve the Assembly Hall's ancillary accommodation and to make it more attractive to external hirers that the Church shared with the University the cost of converting much of the Common Hall space to new uses in 1992. Nonagenarian former Dean and Principal Norman Porteous declared open the new Baillie lecture room, and four seminar rooms – named Mackinnon, Porteous, Blackie and Mackintosh (this last later switched with the Oldham Room) after distinguished professors of the several theological disciplines. At the same time William Manson's name was assigned to the New Testament seminar room. A more extensive internal reconstruction had taken place during 1973–5, converting the under-utilised examination rooms on the top floor into offices, inserting a lift and creating a new entrance and spacious reception area. The original internal configuration of much of the west side of the quadrangle was altered out of all recognition.[27]

A building of New College's vintage – over-generously endowed with corridors and staircases, and inhospitable to the disabled – cannot

[27] *NCN* 3 (June 1975), 1, 8; 4 (Dec. 1975), 1.

hope to satisfy perfectly the demands of an institution of higher education approaching a new millennium. Yet for all its limitations, its ample walls enclose so numerous and varied a complex of rooms that it can confidently claim to be second to none among theological institutions in Britain in the range and comprehensiveness of its provision. For worship, for example (discussed here in Gary Badcock's final chapter), it offers not only the Martin Hall, with organ and impressive mosaic cross, but also the quiet of the Sanctuary under the Library. Nor is adaptation at an end. Perhaps the computers that have gobbled up so much square-footage in recent years will one day calculate the ideal distribution of available space to recognised uses. That will be a miracle indeed.

Scarcely a hundred metres to the east of New College stands the Free Church College. Its proximity, yet separateness, is a reminder of unhealed rifts within Scottish Presbyterianism, as well as of the history that gave birth to New College. The story of the Free Church College for much of the twentieth century is deftly sketched in the chapter by Donald MacLeod.

STUDENT GROWTH

The student body to be accommodated in New College's network of rooms at the end of the twentieth century has never been so large.[28] Stewart Brown's chapter registers the extraordinary early growth of student numbers, reaching in 1850–1 a total of 257 that placed the College among the biggest theological schools in the West. From that peak they settled between 100 and 150 for most of the rest of the century, rising towards 175 in the 1880s. The Church Union of 1900 caused a momentary upsurge but a longer-term fall to below 100. After the recovery from the First World War figures rose steadily into the 160s in the years preceding the Second World War. The post-1929 merger of University Faculty and Church College provided only a minor fillip to enrolments. On the eve of the Second World War, of 169 students fifty-one were postgraduates.

By the early 1960s, the student community was in the 200s. In 1974 it reached 300 for the first time, with 160 B.D. candidates, a score on the infant Religious Studies programme, almost forty non-graduating students and seventy-five postgraduates. But it was not until the end of

[28] The figures that follow are based on Watt 273–5, and on College Handbooks for the last three decades.

the 1980s that the total reached that level again. (In the interval, vacillating government policies and the imposition of 'full-cost' fees for international students had taken their toll.) By the mid-1990s numbers had soared well above 500: the B.A./M.A. (Religious Studies) enlisted more than the B.D. (with some 300 undergraduates in all), non-graduating students came mostly from continental Europe (about thirty), and postgraduates neared 200. The developments charted in Duncan Forrester's chapter and in the latter pages of David Lyall's account of Practical Theology's expansion largely explain the boom in graduate studies.

The sharp diversification of constituencies that has accompanied growth of these proportions has inevitably raised hard questions and created a measure of unease in the New College community. The issues are entered into by more than one contributor to this collection of essays – by Bill Shaw, Frank Whaling and David Wright, and not least helpfully by Gary Badcock in his concluding chapter. How best may New College not so much retain as build on its identity within the Reformed tradition of divinity in an era of religious and cultural pluralism? No easy answers are on offer, but the question is squarely addressed with encouraging confidence.

THEY ALSO SERVE

Behind the core activities of teaching, learning and researching in a Divinity Faculty of the size and complexity of New College, in its sole-occupancy building and its subtle Church-relatedness, stand a body of support staff without whom the academics could scarcely function. They cannot all be named, except representatively, *pars pro toto*. They have fulfilled a great variety of roles: tutors in theological German, such as Rudolf Ehrlich, an Edinburgh minister who had fled Nazi Germany and was a powerful theologian in his own right, and Duncan Shaw, church historian, Moderator and for many years Secretary of the University's General Council of Graduates; part-time lecturers in specialisms ancillary to Practical Theology – church music, for example, taught by Herrick Bunney, the distinguished long-serving organist of St Giles, and hospital chaplaincy, where Stewart McGregor of the Royal Infirmary has instilled practical wisdom for more than two decades; and the Fulton lecturers in elocution, including during 1925–30 one Alastair Sim, whose distinctively lugubrious features, later made famous by the Ealing film comedies, are already recognisable in the photograph in Hugh Watt's history,[29] and for a much longer period, 1949–81, Miss Evelyn Balfour Brown, a highly qualified lady of refined distinction, whose farewell tribute in *New College Bulletin* was headed, in those gloriously free pre-PC days but with real affection, '. . . and who will guard the church's diaphragm now?'[30]

Where would the College have been without the warders, janitors and servitors who secured the ramparts and delivered the mail? I remember in the 1960s Mr William Jeromson, whose passion for a tidy quad extended to washing Faculty members' cars. The cleaners have inevitably remained largely unknown down the generations, but not so the catering staff, for students and other staff alike have known where their best interests lay. Ruling the roost at coffee and lunch for many years was Mrs Jessie Cooper, whose warm memories of New College burn brightly in her retirement. And then the secretaries, indispensable still in the era of information technology, which threatens to turn us all into our own secretaries. Not so long ago every Department of the Faculty had its own secretary, a state of affairs that would have puzzled earlier generations as much as it is the envy of the present Faculty. When Miss Erna R. Leslie, M.A., B.Com. joined the College in 1935 she was not only secretary to the Principal and Dean but also sole Library Assistant – and sole secretarial support for the rest of the teaching staff. She carried the administrative load on her own until Edith Murray (later Mrs Edith Robertson) was appointed in 1950 as secretary to John Baillie as Principal and Dean. Both retired in 1971.[31] There were few things that they did not know about the College, and few services they did not render it. Miss Leslie, who spoke German fluently, was especially welcoming to German students, for whose benefit she left a generous bequest in her will. The running of the postgraduate studies office largely fell to her also, in which role she was succeeded in 1971 by Mrs Linda Stupart, who fills it still today. Senior administrative support was first provided in 1970 with the

[29] Watt, facing 225, 256. The entry on Sim in the *Dictionary of National Biography* describes the Fulton lectureship as 'His first connection with the stage'! While holding it he founded his own School of Drama and Speech Training. He was Rector of Edinburgh University 1948–51 (elected by a greater majority than any of his predecessors), and delivered his rectorial address in 'the inimitable Sim manner; the clipped words, the sardonic intonation, the crocodile smile'. The University made him an Honorary LL.D. (1951), and he died in 1976.

[30] *NCB* 12 (Sept. 1981), 6.

[31] On Miss Leslie, *NCB* 6:2 (Aut. 1971), 4–5, and *NCB* (Aut. 1989), 3, 8; on Mrs Robertson, *NCB* 6:2 (Aut. 1971), 5 and *NCB* 5 (July 1976), 9.

appointment of Miss Jean Ewan, who served until 1983. Miss May Hocking, secretary to the Ecclesiastical Historians since 1978 (and to others also latterly), has greatly helped with the production of this volume, and in many other ways. She and her colleagues on the secretarial front, Miss Margaret Rankin and Mrs Julie McCormick, who joined the staff in 1975 and 1979 respectively, and Mrs Anne Fernon (née Burns), first in 1972, have provided a human and humane point of contact between Faculty and Department and the burgeoning student population of recent years.

NOT FORGETTING ALUMNI/AE

In North America, a theological school of New College's international distinction would operate a well-founded alumni/ae office. Since 1906, New College Union has linked together former students once or twice a year, chiefly in Scotland and mostly ministers of the Church (United Free or Church of Scotland). It has had only seven secretaries in that time. Its list of presidents is a veritable roll of honour for New College's twentieth-century history.[32] The Union has been the source of numerous benefactions to the College, especially the Library, and it must be our common concern that its future role extend to encompass the loyalties of a far more diverse body of graduates.

Since 1964, the resources of New College Senate have financed the publication every year, and for a short period twice a year, of *New College Bulletin* (or some such title). It has been an enormously variable entity – in size, format, content and readability. Greater consistency is a high desideratum, but few other sectors of the University can claim so unbroken a means of contact with alumni/ae for so long, and for this a debt is owed to a succession of imaginative – and unremunerated – editors. Special mention is merited for the bumper issue of September 1983, which was part of the Faculty's contribution to the 400th anniversary of the foundation of the University. In preparation for the sesquicentennial in 1996, superhuman efforts have tracked down hundreds of hitherto missing former students. Their total is nearing three thousand, and others still lost are surely yet to be found.

Copies of the *Bulletin* are dispatched in bulk across the Atlantic for mailing in the USA and Canada by our 'American desk'. This was located for many years in Wooster College, Ohio, in the person first of Buck Smith and then over a long span of Gordon Tait. It was a

---

[32] Watt 129–30; *NCB* 1:1 (Easter 1964), 31–5.

great joy to us all when the University awarded Gordon an Honorary Fellowship of the University in 1991, as he handed over the 'American desk' to Barbara and Fraser MacHaffie of Marietta College in the same state. The Faculty owes an immeasurable debt to the *pietas* of these wonderfully supportive graduates in the States – year on year mailing out the *Bulletin*, updating addresses and channelling back news (and also gifts, either through the British Schools and Universities Foundation or directly to the Faculty).

A recent innovation in our attempts to keep in touch with alumni/ ae has been the hosting of a New College reception in the USA during the massive November jamboree of the Society of Biblical Literature and American Academy of Religion. Similar reunions have been held in different parts of the world – in Australia, in Hungary, but chiefly in North America – when Faculty members have been on sabbatical leave or travelling for lectures or conferences. Former students in Northern Ireland have assembled at a Scottish breakfast during the Presbyterian Church's Assembly. And more recently still, in 1995 the Faculty has launched its own journal, whose title, *Studies in World Christianity: The Edinburgh Review of Theology and Religion*, indicates its global embrace and distinctive local vantage-point. Professor James Mackey occupies the editor's chair, and Edinburgh University Press is the publisher, in association with Orbis Books, Maryknoll, NY.

OF BOOKS AND PUBLISHERS

The bibliography in this volume could not hope to provide an exhaustive listing of the works of Edinburgh's academic divines over 150 years, such as Hugh Watt provided in his centenary chronicle. The inventory of Tom Torrance's monographs would alone fill several pages.[33] But the bibliography given here contains more than the items referred to by the contributors to the volume. It thus aims to give a representative picture of the works published in theology and religion by the teachers in the College and Faculty over this span. The reader who leafs through it will gather a fair impression of the range and interest of Edinburgh Divinity's contribution to the desks and libraries of the theological world.

[33] For a bibliography, incomplete even when published, see Torrance, I. R. (1990). A select bibliography of George Anderson's works will be found in *Vetus Testamentum* 32 (1982), 125–8 and in Auld (1993), 21, and of John McIntyre's in Badcock (1996).

In turn, no account of the study of theology and religion in Edinburgh over the past 150 years can fail to take note of the contribution of publishing houses. In every generation, it seems, publishers have come and gone.[34] Two firms eminent in religious publishing in Edinburgh in the nineteenth century are now based elsewhere – A. & C. Black and Thomas Nelson. Oliver & Boyd, the first publisher of the *Scottish Journal of Theology*, and of the new translation of Calvin's New Testament commentaries edited by D. W. and T. F. Torrance, flourished in the mid-twentieth century but is no more. St Andrew Press, the Church of Scotland's publishing arm, became known the world over for William Barclay's Daily Study Bible on the New Testament – completed by a set of volumes on the Old Testament edited by John Gibson of New College. More traditional fare, especially reprints of older Reformed classics, has been served up by the Banner of Truth Trust, located in Edinburgh since 1973.

But no firm comes close to the record of achievement of T&T Clark, which began publication in 1821 and is still going, as strong as ever, as we approach the twenty-first century.[35] In recent decades it has passed through the hands of a series of larger companies, but a management buy-out in 1991 regained its independence, and it forges ahead in its twin fields of law and theology. It now publishes the *Scottish Journal of Theology*, alongside the evergreen resort of ministers needing to preach but too busy to read books, the *Expository Times*. The latter, begun in 1889, was one of the many ventures of that editor supreme, James Hastings, whose biblical dictionaries can still be consulted with profit.[36] His *Encyclopaedia of Religion and Ethics* (13 vols, 1908–26) remains in demand across the world. All of these were published by T&T Clark, who added to their reference list in 1993 the *Dictionary of Scottish Church History and Theology*.

Translation series have been another of the house's strong suits – from the Ante-Nicene Christian Library (in later reprints the Ante-Nicene Fathers), the Works of St Augustine (edited by Marcus Dods of New College) and the Calvin Translation Society series of Calvin's commentaries, letters and treatises, to the Foreign Theological Library (180 vols, 1846–91), Karl Barth's *Church Dogmatics* and other works, and a similar Catholic enterprise, Hans Urs von Balthasar's *The Glory of the Lord* (1982–91). Other important series have been the International

---

[34] *DSCHT* 684–6.
[35] Dempster (1992).
[36] *DSCHT* 394–5.

Critical Commentary and the International Theological Library (both with Scribners of New York), and for lay use the Bible Class Handbooks initiated *c.*1879.

A feature of T&T Clark's policy has been to keep books in print long-term. One way to get a bird's-eye view of Scottish theology – both what it consumed, especially from the continent, and what it produced – over a wide time-span was to peruse T&T Clark's catalogues, for they used to list all the items ever published, whether still in print or not. The firm's nourishing of the lifeblood of Edinburgh divinity has been unparalleled, and it is entirely fitting that this commemorative volume should come forth from its expert and sympathetic press.

SOME STONES UNTURNED

Much must remain unrecorded, such as the successions of distinguished scholars who have graced the endowed lectureships held in Edinburgh – the Giffords (famed in all the world, and once in the Faculty's gift but now under University-wide aegis), the Gunnings (the most distinguished lectureship appointed by the Faculty alone), the Cunninghams and the Warracks (both featuring in the 1996 celebrations), the Croalls, and the Chalmers, preserving the name of New College's founding Principal.[37] Nor is there space to trace the fortunes of the Edinburgh Theological Club from 1886 until its demise in 1991. Its meetings (held in New College since 1936) continued unbroken through both World Wars. In its day it gathered as eminent and ecumenical a body of theological *periti* as one could find meeting regularly anywhere. The full summaries of papers in its more recent minute books must tell an eloquent tale of shifting interests and fashions. The Scottish Church History Society has met regularly in New College since 1922, maintaining in its *Records* the most significant periodical publication in its field.

Our special overseas links might have merited fuller attention – with the Hungarian Reformed community, going back almost to the beginning of New College,[38] with the Stift in Tübingen, the longest-lived of our annual student exchange schemes, with other European

---

[37] Basic information on all these lectureships will be found in *DSCHT*.

[38] An unpublished paper of 1989 by Richard Hörcsik, archivist at the Sarospatak Academy and later a member of the Hungarian Parliament, sketches the history of the Hungarian scholarship, which goes back to 'Rabbi' John Duncan who had served in the Church of Scotland's Jewish mission in Budapest.

institutions such as Strasbourg under ERASMUS auspices, with Princeton Theological Seminary and Union Theological Seminary, New York, with the very different Department of Religion in Dartmouth College, Hanover, New Hampshire, with Waldensian and Czech brethren, and most recently, through the Centre for the Study of Christianity in the Non-Western World, with Yale and Accra in Ghana – and most points East and West. Beyond peradventure, no single volume could begin to do justice to the extraordinarily rich and far-flung constituency of our former students furth of Scotland – even if Martin Luther King failed to turn up after being accepted for doctoral study by Professor O. S. Rankin. As an editor knows only too well, you cannot win them all.

David Wright

We wish to express warm gratitude to the Carnegie Trust for the Universities of Scotland and to the Drummond Trust (3 Pitt Terrace, Stirling) for generous grants towards the costs of publishing this volume. For invaluable help in ironing out some of its wrinkles and smoothing its asperities, we thank especially Professor John McIntyre, Professor David Fergusson and Professor Stewart J. Brown. Malcolm Kinnear's assistance in proof-reading has been much appreciated.

The Editors

Abbreviations

AFCS   *Annals of the Free Church of Scotland*, 2 vols, ed. W. Ewing (Edinburgh, 1914)

CES   *Collins Encyclopedia of Scotland*, ed. John Keay and Julia Keay (London, 1994)

CTPI   Centre for Theology and Public Issues

DNB   *Dictionary of National Biography*, ed. L. Stephen, S. Lee *et al.* (London, 1885–)

DSCHT   *Dictionary of Scottish Church History and Theology*, organ. ed. N. M. de S. Cameron; gen. eds, D. F. Wright, D. C. Lachman, D. E. Meek (Edinburgh, 1993)

EB   *Encyclopedia Britannica*, 11th edn, 29 vols (Cambridge, 1910–11)

FES   *Fasti Ecclesiae Scoticanae*, ed. Hew Scott *et al.*, 2nd edn (Edinburgh, 1915–)

FUFCS   *The Fasti of the United Free Church of Scotland, 1900–29*, ed. J. A. Lamb (Edinburgh, 1956)

NCB   *New College Bulletin*

NCN   *New College News*

RS   Religious Studies

RSCHS   *Records of the Scottish Church History Society*

SJT   *Scottish Journal of Theology*

UF, UFC   United Free, United Free Church

UP, UPC   United Presbyterian, United Presbyterian Church

Watt   Hugh Watt, *New College Edinburgh, A Centenary History*, with a section on the Library by A. Mitchell Hunter (Edinburgh, 1946)

Contributors

GRAEME AULD: an alumnus of New College who returned to lecture in Old Testament in 1972 and was appointed to a personal chair of Hebrew Bible in 1995. Previously Assistant Director of the British School of Archaeology in Jerusalem, and subsequently its home Secretary, Graeme laboured as Editor of the Society for Old Testament Study's essential *Book List* during 1987–92. His research expertise has focused on Joshua–Kings, and their inter-related literary and textual (Hebrew and Greek) development. He was Dean of the Faculty during 1993–6. He edited a Festschrift in honour of Professor George Anderson – *Understanding Poets and Prophets* (1993).

GARY BADCOCK: hails from Newfoundland, where he graduated in philosophy at Memorial University, St John's, before travelling to New College for the B.D. He stayed on to earn a doctorate for a thesis on modern Trinitarian theology (1991), and was appointed to a lectureship in Aberdeen. He returned to Edinburgh in 1993 as Meldrum Lecturer in Dogmatic Theology. He edited a collection of John McIntyre's writings entitled *Theology after the Storm* (1996), and has written a theology of the Holy Spirit called *Light of Truth and Fire of Love*. Gary served as a lay minister in Canada and has a particular concern for worship in the New College community.

STEWART J. BROWN: holder of the chair of Ecclesiastical History since 1988. A graduate of the Universities of Illinois and Chicago, he taught previously at Northwestern University and the University of Georgia. Author of a major biography on Thomas Chalmers, and co-editor of the indispensable *Scottish Historical Review*, he lectures and writes not only on the Scottish churches since the Reformation but also on issues of church and society throughout Britain and Ireland over the last three centuries.

ALEC CHEYNE: held the chair of Ecclesiastical History in succession to J. H. S. Burleigh from 1964 to 1986, and latterly also the Principalship of New College (1984–6). He presided over a significant expansion of his Department (with a trio of long-serving lecturers it was known as the Cheyne gang) and set his Faculty colleagues a daunting example of excellence in lecturing – 'meticulous in detail, deft in touch, lucidity itself in phrasing' (Alan Lewis). The same qualities distinguish his authoritative account of *The Transforming of the Kirk: Victorian Scotland's Religious Revolution* (1983), as well as lengthy essays on Donald and John Baillie, Thomas Chalmers and other eminent Scottish church theologians.

DUNCAN FORRESTER: holder of the chair of Christian Ethics and Practical Theology since 1978, and creative initiator of the Centre for Theology and Public Issues. Formerly a missionary in India (he has written extensively on the caste system) and chaplain and lecturer at Sussex University, Duncan was Principal of New College 1986–96, and assumes the Deanship of the Faculty in 1996. He has published prolifically on Christian attitudes to public policy issues. He is a member of the Center of Theological Inquiry in Princeton.

JOHN HOWARD: became New College's first professional Librarian in 1965, remaining in charge of the Library until 1987, when he assumed responsibility for Special Collections (chiefly manuscripts and rare books) as Sub-Librarian in the main University Library. He retired in 1995. It is largely to John Howard's leadership that we owe the modern face of New College Library. He transformed the acquisition and lending systems, and relocated and refurbished the whole stock of over 200,000 books. A leading figure in the Association of British Theological and Philosophical Libraries, he edited its *Bulletin* from the early 1970s to 1987. He has been Chairman of the Edinburgh Bibliographical Society, and has written for journals and reference works in his professional field. He is an active member of St Mary's Episcopal Cathedral in Edinburgh.

DAVID LYALL: bringing to his post as Senior Lecturer in Christian Ethics and Practical Theology many years of experience as chaplain of Edinburgh's Western General Hospital (and three years teaching at St Andrews), David serves as Associate Dean of the Faculty. He has edited *Contact*, played a leading role in international conferences on pastoral care and counselling, and now co-ordinates the M.Th. in Ministry, as well as teaching in medical and family ethics. His most recent work is *Counselling in the Pastoral and Spiritual Context* (1995).

DONALD MACLEOD: a native of the Isle of Lewis who has been Professor of Systematic Theology in the Free Church of Scotland College, New College's near neighbour on 'Presbyterian Ridge', since 1978. For his first couple of years he combined his teaching with continued charge of Partick Highland Free Church in Glasgow. Donald edited the *Free Church Monthly Record* during 1977–90, earning a reputation as one of Scotland's sharpest commentators on the religious scene. A brilliant wordsmith in Gaelic and English, able to preach and lecture with powerful fluency without a note, he has taught in New College on Scottish theology, on which his expertise is unrivalled.

GEORGE NEWLANDS: a B.D. of New College who went on to lecture at Cambridge before assuming the chair of Divinity at Glasgow in 1986. He subsequently served as Dean of Divinity there and latterly as Principal of Trinity College. He is also convener of the Church of Scotland's Panel on Doctrine. After a grounding in patristics, George's interests have focused increasingly on contemporary theology. He has written a *Theology of the Love of God* (1980) and an ambitious essay in systematics, *God in Christian Perspective* (1994).

JOHN O'NEILL: an Australian Presbyterian who taught at Westminster College, Cambridge, for many years, and has been Professor of New Testament at Edinburgh since 1985. Prolific author (most recently of *Who Did Jesus Think He Was?*, 1995), iconoclast of critical consensus, enthusiastic promoter of both discipline and Department, relentless emender of texts – John has stamped his distinctive mark on the teaching of New Testament in the Faculty. Among his innovations is a Monday morning seminar which attracts serving ministers and others in healthy numbers.

ANDREW ROSS: has held a teaching post in the History of Missions in the Department of Ecclesiastical History since 1966, after eight years' service in Malawi. A man of many parts – unrivalled raconteur, soccer enthusiast, champion of black Africa and confidant of prominent politicians – he was Principal of New College and Dean of Divinity through six demanding years (1978–84). His teaching has ranged widely over America and Africa – especially race and slavery. In 1994 Edinburgh University Press (and Orbis, Maryknoll, NY) published *A Vision Betrayed*, his account of the Jesuit missions to Japan and China 1542–1742.

BILL SHAW: trained as a lawyer before studying Divinity and hence qualified to bear an enormous burden over many years in the running of College and Faculty, latterly as Principal and Dean 1974–8. In 1979 he was appointed Professor of Divinity at St Andrews – subsequently becoming Principal and Dean there too! Bill joined the Department of Divinity in Edinburgh in 1961. His countless roles in Church, University and community have demonstrated remarkable versatility – expert squash players, observer at Vatican II, interpreter of process thought, resourceful troubleshooter and conciliator, and sensitive teacher of Divinity amid the challenges of modern thought.

THOMAS F. TORRANCE: the best known of the Faculty's twentieth-century theologians, Professor of Christian Dogmatics 1952–79. Translator of Barth, founding editor of the *Scottish Journal of Theology* and author of a stream of books still flowing strongly in his retirement. Much honoured throughout the world, he was Moderator of the General Assembly of the Church of Scotland in 1976 and recipient of the Templeton Prize in 1978. Edinburgh University is to make him an honorary D.D. in 1996 at a special graduation to mark the 150th anniversary of the New College building.

FRANK WHALING: an English Methodist minister, graduate of Cambridge and Harvard Universities and missionary in India, he has borne the main burden of the Religious Studies teaching programme since joining the Department of Divinity (as it then was) in 1973. Promoted to a Readership in 1994, with a formidable publication list to his credit, he has commended himself to a generation of students by the warmth and fluency of his lecturing. Religious Education in schools, harmonious inter-faith dialogue in the local community and the vision of a global theology have all benefited from his efforts. Indian religion continues to be his leading research interest.

DAVID WRIGHT: appointed to the Department of Ecclesiastical History in 1964, after studying at Cambridge and Oxford. Originally an early church historian, he later trespassed into the Reformation. He was also the chief editor of the *Dictionary of Scottish Church History and Theology* (T&T Clark, 1993). Augustine, Bucer and Calvin engage his scholarly energies, and he has written extensively on the Fathers' use of the Reformers and on baptism. The Faculty's first lay Dean (1988–92), he is a Church of Scotland elder.

PART I

From Reformation to New College

Chapter 1

From John Knox to John McLeod Campbell: A Reading of Scottish Theology

Thomas F. Torrance

THE REFORMATION

THE THEOLOGY of the Church of Scotland has seen changes and modifications over the centuries, but affecting them all was the original mould contributed by John Knox and the Scots Confession of 1560.[1] In contrast to other Reformation confessions it gave primary importance to the missionary calling of the church. 'And this glad tydings of the kingdom shalbe preached throught the hole world for a witness to all nations and then shall the end come' (Matthew 24:14, cited on the title-page). The missionary task to which the Reformers devoted themselves was the proclamation of 'the sweet savour of the Evangel' to people in Scotland, the origin of our 'home mission'.

John Knox, the minister of Edinburgh, was essentially a preacher-theologian. He did not intend to be a theologian, but the desperate earnestness with which he took his calling demanded theological earnestness. His was a theology in the service of evangelism and preaching, in which 'arguments and reasons serve only instead of handmaids, which shall not command but obey Scripture pronounced by the Voice of God'.[2]

In this Reformation theology there took place a fundamental transition from the medieval set of mind, away from an abstract theology of logically ordered propositions, to a dynamic theology oriented, not

[1] Ed. Henderson (1937).
[2] Knox (1846–64), V, 61; also VI, 175ff., 205, 425, 559.

1

primarily to the salvation of the individual soul, but to the nation as a whole. It involved a radical change in the doctrine of God, marked by the place given to the Holy Trinity in the first article of the Confession. As there is no other content to the doctrine of God but the Father, the Son and the Holy Spirit, Trinitarian teaching was woven into the doctrinal substance of subsequent articles. Throughout, however, the immediate centre of focus was upon Jesus Christ himself.

Two main features of this Reformation theology may be noted. The first is the emphasis on the dynamic intervention of God in the history of his people. The effect of this upon Scottish theology, at least during the Reformation period, was to give it a narrative, 'salvation-history', form.[3] Characteristic of this understanding of God was the combination of judgment and mercy in God's action, but behind all proclamation of divine judgment, which we find especially in Knox, there is equally a passionate pleading with the nation on behalf of the divine mercy, coupled with a vivid trust in divine providence.

Everything is made by God to serve the operation of the ordinance of divine grace of which the Scriptures tell us in the long history of Israel. The essential pattern which the ordinance of grace assumed is revealed supremely in the incarnation of God's beloved Son in Jesus Christ, and in the life and mission of the Kirk, but continues to be manifested in the Church as the messianic community continually called into being from death to life, and marvellously preserved from age to age.

The Mediator

The second feature of Reformation theology to note is its focus on the Mediator. If that doctrine of God provided the overarching perspective within which all John Knox's thought moved, the inner heart of his faith and message was found in the doctrine of the mediatorship of Jesus Christ, which had a prominent place in the Reformation catechisms of John Craig (minister in Edinburgh's Canongate and Knox's colleague in St Giles) and John Davidson (who ministered both in and near Edinburgh). As with Calvin, so with the Scots Confession and these catechisms, classical patristic Christology was acknowledged in undiminished fullness: but the characteristic emphasis was upon the role of Christ's humanity united to his Deity[4] – Jesus Christ is Advocate, Mediator, Interpreter, Priest, High Priest, Intercessor – that is a constant

---

[3] Cf. Macleod, J. (1943).
[4] Knox (1846–64), III, 96.

2

refrain in Knox's writings, as in the liturgical and confessional documents of the Scottish Reformation which he had a hand in composing.

This doctrine of the Mediator carried with it a stress upon the actual humanity of Christ. In the doctrine of justification Knox rarely spoke of justification by faith, but rather of justification through the blood of Christ, thereby indicating the objective nature of the saving act of Christ's humanity, his active obedience in life, death, passion and resurrection.[5] In the thought of John Knox an important place was given to the ascension as well as the resurrection, for it has to do with the appearance of Christ in his humanity in our place before the Father. The mediatorial work of Christ is not restricted to his earthly life and passion, but has to do with his intercessory presence and activity as the risen and ascended man at the right hand of the Father.

The doctrine of the Mediator was closely linked to the doctrine of Christ's union with us and our union with him, 'the blessed conjunction' or 'fraternity' which he has established with us in the incarnation.[6] Christ's saving work was fulfilled in the inner depths of our human nature, so that through his union with us and our union with him, what he has done for us, in our name, in our person, and in our stead, is an act in which we may share and claim as our very own. Justification is no external forensic transaction, but involves a 'blessed conjunction' in which Christ takes what is ours, sanctifies and regenerates it in himself, and we receive what is his as we participate in that renewed new humanity through baptism and the Lord's Supper and the communion of the Spirit.[7]

In the Scots Confession the 'wondrous conjunction betwixt the Godhead and the manhood of Christ Jesus' is traced back to 'the eternal and immutable decree of God from which all our salvation springs and depends' (art. 7). This is followed by an article headed 'Election' in which predestination is given a Christological explanation, for while it proceeds from the eternal decree of God from which all salvation springs, it assumes in time the form of the hypostatic union of God and humanity, two perfect natures united in the one person of the Mediator by whom we are saved and redeemed. A lengthy account of this was given in Knox's work *On Predestination*, in which 'that joyfull

---

[5] Scots Confession, art. 8; *Book of Common Order*, in Knox (1846–64), VI, 364.

[6] Scots Confession, 7, 8, 11, 21; *Book of Common Order*, in Knox (1846–64), VI, 366f.

[7] Scots Confession, 15, 21; *Book of Common Order*, in Knox (1846–64), VI, 364. See especially the Treatise by Balnaves on justification, edited by Knox (1846–64), III, 12ff., 23f., 449f., 455, 461ff., 477f., 494f., 513f.

Atonement made betwene God and man by Christ Jesus, by his death and resurrection and ascension' is traced back to its eternal ground in the infinite goodness and grace of God. Predestination was expounded in such a way as to show that 'no portion of man's salvation consists within himself, to the end that the whole praise of our redemption may be referred back to Christ Jesus alone'.[8] Its concern is with the objectivity of the grace of God in which faith attributes everything to God and nothing to ourselves, with weight laid on the unconditional love of God on which our salvation rests.

Woven into John Knox's doctrine of election, however, and constituting its real heart, are the mediatorial life and work of Christ Jesus. What he did on our behalf he did not just as Son of God but as man, 'that he mycht offer sacrifice'. The focus was upon the priesthood of the human Jesus. For John Knox this was what the Reformation was really about, whether in the understanding of salvation, in the eucharistic rite, or in the conception of the ministry. 'Christ is the right hand by whom we offer anything to the Father', cited from Ambrose.[9] For Knox personally this was of special significance for the relation between the eucharist and prayer. As Christ is the only High Priest, and as it is by his right hand that we offer anything to God, our prayer in his name at the eucharist is gathered up by Christ into his own vicarious prayer and offered by him to the Father. Hence it is in prayer and intercession at the eucharist that Knox saw the true 'priestly character' of the ministry, when we pray in Christ's name, involving not only prayer of thanksgiving but also the prayer of intercession in Christ which is linked through the eternal Spirit to the heavenly intercession of Christ before the presence of the Father.

It should be added that this stress on intercession, as upon our oneness with Christ and with one another at the Supper, carried with it, in Knox's mind, deep concern for the poor. This flows from 'the action' (or *actio gratiarum*, the Latin for the Greek *eucharistia*) which belongs to the eucharistic worship and life of the members of the body of Christ.

THE OLDER SCOTTISH TRADITION

The theologians who followed Knox laid considerable stress on the sovereignty and grace of God, but they did not understand grace in the causal Augustinian/Thomist sense of Roman theology. They thought

[8] Knox (1846–64), V, 23–30.
[9] Knox (1846–64), III, 97.

of election as taking place in Christ and as bound up with adoption more than with eternal decrees. However, a rationalistic form of Calvinism arose which left its mark on Scottish theology. Aristotelian philosophy and Ramist dialectics were introduced into Scottish universities, which, with the doctrine of limited atonement canonised by the Synod of Dort and the formalisation of federal theology, affected the development of Reformed theology. A bifurcation developed between evangelical and rationalist forms of Calvinism.

On the one hand, central place was given to the mediatorial work of Christ, of union and communion with him through the Holy Spirit, and or participation in his saving and sanctifying humanity. The atonement had to do not only with the act of God in Christ, but with the whole course of his life and obedience from his birth to his death and resurrection. If by his sacrificial death on the cross Christ saves us from actual sins, through his conception and birth of the Virgin Mary he saves us from our original sin. It was on this Christological and soteriological ground that Robert Bruce expounded his doctrine of the sacraments in his famous sermons in St Giles, Edinburgh.[10]

On the other hand, there took place a movement of thought in which the biblical concept of the covenant was split into a covenant of nature and works and a covenant of grace, on which a contractual form of law was superimposed, giving law priority over grace. As Robert Rollock, first Principal of Edinburgh University, wrote:

> The covenant of God generally is a promise made under some condition. And it is twofold; the first is the covenant of works; the second is the covenant of grace . . . The covenant of works, which may be called a legal or natural covenant, is founded in nature . . . The ground of the covenant of works was not Christ, nor the grace of God in Christ; but the nature of man.

In it there was no mediator between God and humanity. Here the biblical one-way notion of covenant was changed into a two-way conditional contract, the fulfilment of which depends on the completion of certain stipulations.[11]

This bifurcation in theology was very marked in the difference between the federal Calvinism of Samuel Rutherford, George Gillespie (of Greyfriars and St Giles, Edinburgh), David Dickson (sometime

---

[10] *Sermons upon the Sacrament of the Lords Supper* (? 1591), ed. Torrance, T. F. (1958B), and his sixth Sermon on Isaiah 38 in Bruce, R. (1591).
[11] Rollock (1844–9), I, 34.

Professor of Divinity at Edinburgh) and James Durham, and the teaching of Calvin and the Scots Confession which continued to have their place in the parishes of the Kirk. There were mediating Calvinists, however, who sought to preserve a more Christocentric emphasis concerned with the interrelation of the incarnation and atonement, like Robert Boyd (briefly Principal of Edinburgh University) and Hugh Binning, who advocated a biblically-grounded Christocentric theology in which grace was given priority over law.

John Forbes of Corse (1593–1648)

Special mention must be made of John Forbes of Corse, the most learned theologian Scotland produced between the Reformation and the Disruption. He was a mild Calvinist, and stood close to Bruce, Boyd and Binning, without adhering to federal theology. He upheld the Trinitarian and Christological teaching of the ancient Catholic church and was an irenical thinker with deep sacramental and practical concern for the life and mission of the Kirk. His great work published at Amsterdam in 1645 was entitled *Instructiones Historico-Theologicae de Doctrina Christiana*. This was a contribution of monumental importance to the history of theology, for in bringing together the interpretations of the Scriptures, the teaching of the orthodox Fathers, and the ecumenical councils, Forbes laid the foundation for Christian dogmatics, and initiated the pursuit of Reformed patristics.

Two other theologians left their mark upon the latter half of the seventeenth century, Samuel Rutherford (who was briefly a regent in Edinburgh University) and James Fraser of Brea.

Samuel Rutherford (1600–61)

Rutherford's theology was governed by rigid forensic and logically necessary relations on the one hand, and by a concentration on particular election and redemption on the other hand. His writings manifest a passionate devotion to Christ crucified and a spiritual inwardness expressed in language indebted to the Song of Solomon.[12] In presenting his federal theology in a more popular form Rutherford often spoke of the personal relation of the believer to Christ in terms of a marriage contract, but no less frequently adopted the language of the market and commerce in which he described the covenant of grace as a 'striking hands' with God and of its saving benefits as a 'bargain' purchased through the blood of Christ. It was this more popular presentation of

---

[12] See particularly Rutherford, S. (1863).

federal theology that was taken up by David Dickson and James Durham in *The Sum of Saving Knowledge,* which was disseminated throughout the Kirk, giving rise to a rather moralistic understanding of the gospel.

In his federal framework of thought, Rutherford operated with two covenants, the covenant of nature and works contracted by God with Adam and the covenant of grace contracted by God and Christ on behalf of the elect. Christ himself, the Mediator who is God and man in one person, is 'the substantial covenant', who is offered in the gospel to sinners on the condition of 'saving and true faith', in which they go out of themselves to Christ and rest on him alone. The atonement was conceived in juridical terms: we are saved by an act of God through the instrumentality of Christ as Mediator in fulfilment of an eternal contract between him and the Father.

Rutherford's doctrine of double predestination was not grounded in the incarnate person of Christ, but in a contractual relation between him and God, which limited the extent of the atonement. He rejected the idea that the gospel is to be preached to the heathen, for redemption applies only to those for whom it is bought, and to no others.[13] In his *Communion Sermons,* on the other hand, Rutherford could declare: 'We are said in Scripture "to be reconciled unto God" and not God to be reconciled unto us. His love is everlasting . . . so that sin could not change God's mind.'[14] However, he was not consistent, for with him the atoning satisfaction made by Christ was purchased from the Father only for the elect, so that a sufficient act of redemption by Christ on the cross had to be necessitarian in its actuality and limited in its application. This teaching gave rise to troubled reaction among people whose hearts cried out for assurance of salvation.

James Fraser of Brea (1638–98)

James Fraser was a staunch covenanter who lived within the prevailing Calvinist tradition, but took care to interpret the Scriptures out of themselves and declined to subordinate them to that tradition. He was thus at odds with the interpretation of the covenant of grace in contractual terms, which he felt ran counter to the teaching of the gospel.[15] It was this which led him to produce one of the most impressive works in Scottish theology on the gospel of grace and the evangelical nature of faith, which he wrote when a prisoner on the Bass Rock, *A*

[13] Rutherford, S. (1655), 17.
[14] Rutherford, S. (1877), 236.
[15] Fraser, J. (1721), 15.

Treatise on Justifying Faith. In it Fraser showed that it is not faith which justifies us but Christ in whom we have faith; and argued that Christ died for all people, and not for a limited number.

Fraser claimed that contemporary divinity was 'much altered from what it was in the primitive reformers' time', and called theologians to return to 'the good old paths'.[16] He admitted that 'to affirm that Christ died for all is contrary to the Current of the most godly and judicious Protestant Divines, and contrary to our Confession of Faith',[17] but with them, he insisted. 'the doctrine of the First Reformation had been overthrown and condemned, and a new notion of faith given'.[18]

Fraser's main concern was with the infinite love of God in Christ as the one Mediator between God and humankind. It is in the whole Christ, from his birth to his resurrection presented to us in the gospel account of God's love for all humankind, that the salvation of humanity is to be considered rather than in the abstract with reference to election and reprobation.[19] Fraser spoke frequently about 'the all sufficiency of Christ to save to the uttermost', for it is in Christ's obedient life and death, and God's good-will toward sinners incarnated in him, that believing faith rests. The glad tidings of the gospel do not depend on any conditions at all, for remission of sins is declared absolutely and offered freely through Christ to faith.[20]

While faith rests on Christ's reconciling life and death, it is grounded on the fact that God 'did not spare his only Son but freely delivered him up for us all. How shall he not with him freely give us all things?'[21] Of supreme importance here, as Fraser saw it, is the fact of Christ's perfect obedience and sacrifice of himself, which he offered up through the eternal Spirit in atoning satisfaction. He regarded this satisfaction, however, as flowing ultimately from 'God's good-will to sinners', not as fulfilling a legal requirement on the part of God, but as deriving from the infinite love of God.[22]

Like Calvin, Fraser rejected the idea that 'Christ died sufficiently for all, and efficaciously only for the elect'.[23] It is on the ground of the

[16] Fraser, J. (1749), 43.
[17] *Ibid.*, 250, also 292.
[18] *Ibid.*, 292.
[19] *Ibid.*, 75.
[20] *Ibid.*, 84ff.
[21] *Ibid.*, 125ff., 2 Cor. 5:20 and Rom. 8:32–4.
[22] Cf. *ibid.*, 216, 236.
[23] *Ibid.*, 162. See Calvin, *Concerning the Eternal Predestination of God* IX, 5, tr. by J. K. S. Reid (1964), 148.

universal all-sufficiency of Christ's atoning sacrifice that the gospel of redemption is rightly and freely offered to all. Christ laid down his life absolutely, and so when it is said that he tasted death for everyone, 'this is absolutely said and meant'.[24] Christ really died for all those he is said in Scripture to have died for – he tasted death for every person.[25] On the other hand, it must be said that although Christ died for all, this does not mean that all are necessarily saved.[26] Fraser made a point of saying that there is 'no certain or physical connexion between the death of Christ and salvation, so as for all whom Christ died should be saved'.[27] Thus Fraser rejected the scholastic way of thinking in terms of logico-causal relations, in accordance with which it was argued that if Christ died for all people, all would have to be saved, and if some people are finally damned, Christ could not have died for them.

THE WESTMINSTER TRADITION

The Westminster Confession of Faith was the product mainly of Anglican and Puritan Calvinists. After it was adopted by the General Assembly of the Church of Scotland in 1647, along with the Larger Catechism and the Shorter Catechism, it has ever since remained its principal subordinate doctrinal standard. The theology of the Westminster standards certainly made a magnificent as well as a lasting impact on Scottish life and thought, particularly through their combination of a high theology with worship and the glorification of God. It imparted an awesome sense of the sovereign majesty of God to Presbyterian worship.

The framework in which the Confession was formulated was that of seventeenth-century federal theology, combined with a way of thinking in terms of primary and secondary causes, and a medieval conception of the *ordo salutis*. This gave the Confession and Catechisms a legalistic character in which doctrinal statements were formalised with 'almost frigidly logical definition'.[28]

The Confession begins with a long chapter on the Holy Scripture as 'the rule of faith and life'. This marks out sharply the difference between the Reformed Church and the Roman Church. However, by giving

[24] Fraser, J. (1749), 183, also 215.
[25] *Ibid.*, 216–338, where Fraser answers objections against a universal sufficient redemption.
[26] *Ibid.*, 202.
[27] *Ibid.*, 146f., 219.
[28] Mitchell (1886), xxvii.

the doctrine of Holy Scripture priority of place over the fundamental doctrines of the gospel, it gave biblical statements the character of canonical propositions from which the other doctrines may be logically derived. This was rather different from the Scots Confession, in which biblical statements point away from themselves to divine truth which by its nature cannot be contained in finite forms of speech and thought.[29]

This separation between the biblical form and the evangelical substance of the faith was made acute by the following chapter on God and the Holy Trinity, in which an abstract account is given of *what* God is apart from *who* God is, to which two sentences on the Holy Trinity were appended. Priority was thus given to the absolute sovereignty of God over his Trinitarian nature as an eternal consubstantial communion of divine persons, who are God, and whose Being is love. It cannot be said that the Confession of Faith presents a properly Christian doctrine of God, one made known to us through Christ and his gospel. In line with this the Confession devotes a chapter to God's eternal 'decrees' which governs the following chapters on creation, providence, the fall of man and woman, sin and punishment, and God's covenant with humanity – all before one on Christ the Mediator!

In the chapter on election there is no hint of the biblical principle governing salvation history – the election of one for the many – either in respect of Israel or Christ. In its teaching about God's predestination the emphasis is laid on its partitive and particularist character, with explicit statements that while some are predestinated to everlasting life, others are foreordained to everlasting death. On the other hand, it states that those who are predestinated to life, God 'has chosen in Christ unto everlasting glory out of his mere free grace and love'. This note reflects a milder form of Calvinism than sometimes preceded it on the continent or often followed it in Scotland.

Covenant
The idea that the relations between God and humankind are governed 'by some voluntary condescension on God's part, which he has been pleased to express by way of covenant' had both a disadvantage and an advantage. On the one hand, through the notion of a covenant of works, it not only altered the biblical notion of law and covenant, but built into the background of Westminster theology a concept of contractual law that gave a forensic and conditional slant even to the

[29] Cf. Calvin's account of biblical statements as referring beyond themselves to God's eternal truth, *Institutes*, 'Prefatory Address to the King of France'.

presentation of the truths of the gospel. On the other hand, the primary place given to the covenant of grace directed the focus of attention upon the fact that God calls people into fellowship with himself, addresses them personally and asks for their response in worship and love. The doctrine of election rightly entailed a view of grace as objective and unconditional, but the conception of double predestination was evangelically unfortunate. It introduced a deep-seated uncertainty into faith which was not adequately met by the later chapter 'Of Assurance of Grace and Salvation'.

In the fine chapter 'Of Christ the Mediator' we are given the evangelical heart of the Confession, with attention given to the hypostatic union and the three-fold office of Christ as Prophet, Priest and King, the Head and Saviour of the Church. Weight is also laid on the perfect obedience and sacrifice of Christ which through the eternal Spirit he offered to his Father. One misses here, however, the place given to the redemptive activity of the incarnate Son in the whole course of his life and ministry from his birth to his resurrection, and within the whole movement of atoning mediation and reconciliation, and also the blessed exchange effected through Christ's identification with us in our sin and poverty that was so important for evangelical Calvinism. The Westminster Catechisms have more to say about the humiliation Christ suffered for our sakes in his birth, life, temptations, his subjection to the law, his ministry in the form of a servant, and his death and burial, which are more biblical and more in line with Calvin's teaching about the vicarious humanity of Christ in the form of a servant.

According to the Confession the Lord Jesus through his perfect obedience and self-sacrifice fully satisfied the justice of his Father and 'purchased reconciliation' for us. This implies a transactional notion of atoning satisfaction in fulfilment of a divine requirement, on the ground of which the Father was induced to reconcile us. At this important point the Confession departs from the teaching of the New Testament in which there is no suggestion that reconciliation was bought from God; but it also departs from the teaching of Calvin about 'the love of God the Father which goes before and anticipates our reconciliation in Christ'.[30] The truth of the prevenient love and grace of God in Christ was one of the primary principles of the Reformation.

A problem in the Westminster Confession here arises from the fact that the chapter on the Mediator is preceded by those on providence and God's covenant in which use is made of a rational framework of

[30] John Calvin, *Institutes* 2:16:3–4.

God's relation to the world in terms of 'first cause' and 'second causes'. Along with the two-way contractual and conditional nature of the covenant of grace as well as of works, this helped to project into the Westminster tradition of Scottish theology a logico-causal understanding of the activity of God in redemption as well as in creation. This implied that if Christ died for all people, then all people must be saved; but also that if some people are damned, Christ could not have died for them. It was a logico-causal nexus of this kind that displaced in the relation of the atoning sacrifice of Christ to sinners the kind of divine activity by the Holy Spirit revealed in the Virgin Birth of Jesus and his resurrection from the dead. It is highly significant that the Confession does not have an article on the Holy Spirit or indeed on the gospel of God's infinite love savingly incarnate in Jesus and proclaimed to all people alike, an omission that was made good by American Presbyterians in their edition of the Westminster Confession of Faith.[31] The same grave omission is found in the Westminster Catechisms.[32]

Moralism

The lack of a Christocentric framework results in a doctrine of sin and its judgment involving a moralistic notion of what is called 'total depravity'. If Christ died for us, not in a partial but in a total way, then the whole of our being comes under the judgment of the Cross, our good as well as our evil; it is in that theological light that a proper understanding of what the Confession calls 'total depravity' is to be understood, not on moralistic grounds.

This way of thinking is evidently implied by the Confession in its article on justification by faith. While faith is regarded as the passive instrument of justification, the accounting and acceptance of persons as righteous is not on account of anything wrought in them or done by them, but 'for Christ's sake alone, and not by imputing faith itself to them as their righteousness, but by imputing the obedience and satisfaction of Christ alone unto them'. The Confession goes on to say, however, that faith, thus receiving and resting on Christ and his righteousness, is 'the alone instrument of justification; yet it is not alone in the person justified, but is ever accompanied with all the other saving graces, and it no dead faith, but works, by love'. This is in line with the chapters on 'Saving Faith' and 'Repentance unto Life'. As

[31] See Hendry (1960), 117ff., 121ff.
[32] See my introduction in Torrance (1959), xcvff.

expounded by Scots theologians in this Westminster tradition this gave rise to two problems.

On the one hand, while this is followed by chapters on adoption and sanctification through the activity of the Holy Spirit, the notion of justification is construed mainly in terms of a forensic 'imputation', while union with Christ is understood as a 'judicial' union, which must then be cultivated and deepened in a spiritual and sanctifying way through the help of 'indwelling grace' (a Roman idea!). On the other hand, within the contractual framework of the covenant, this concept of imputed righteousness rested on a notion of atonement in which 'Christ Jesus, by his obedience and sacrifice of himself which he through the eternal Spirit once offered up unto God, has fully satisfied the justice of the Father'. Thus justification was regarded not only as the justification of the sinner but as the justification of the law of God. This way of regarding the satisfaction of divine justice and the justification of God's eternal law as inducing divine favour toward sinners, had the effect of imprinting on Westminster theology a rather harsh view of God. Moreover, this notion of justification as a legal fulfilling of the contractual requirement of the covenant in respect of God's eternal law had a moralising effect upon the life and theology of the Kirk, which was particularly evident in the overwhelming attention given to the law, in comparison to the gospel, and to a detailed fulfilment of divine commandments, in the Westminster Larger Catechism.

The Confession had a high doctrine of the church, which along with the chapter 'Of the Communion of Saints', continued the teaching of John Calvin in offering a theological account of the church as the body of Christ, realistically understood in its union with him. The Church was identified with the kingdom of the Lord Jesus Christ, the house and family of God, through which men and women are ordinarily saved and union with which was held to be essential to their best growth and service. 'To this catholic and visible Church Christ has given the ministry, oracles and ordinances of God, for the gathering and perfecting of the saints, in this life, to the end of the world, and by his own presence promises to make them effectual thereunto.' It was in these terms as well as in terms of the one covenant of grace which, with different administrations and sacraments, spanned the whole life of the people of God from Old Testament to New Testament times, that formulation was given to the ordinances of baptism and the Lord's Supper, in and through which Christ effectually applies and communicates his redemption to all for whom he died, interceding for them and revealing to them the mysteries of salvation.

THE PRESBYTERIAN TRADITION:
THOMAS BOSTON (1676–1732)

Thomas Boston, a graduate of Edinburgh, is particularly significant in Scottish theology, for the divergence between federal Calvinism and evangelical Calvinism ran through the middle of his thought. He was a parish minister and a fine scholar whose thinking was influenced both by 'the old ways' and by the Westminster tradition. He was troubled by the un-evangelical, legalist strain in contemporary Calvinism, and had 'no great fondness' for the conditional notions of grace.[33]

In his early ministry he came across *The Marrow of Modern Divinity*, in which evangelical teaching about the gospel of free grace was presented within the federal system. Under its influence he tried to work out a way of accommodating his preaching of the gospel with the Westminster Confession of Faith. On the one hand he held steadily to the doctrines of limited election and atonement, but on the other hand he tried to be faithful to the teaching of the Gospels. He often cited John 3:16, and other statements about Christ as the Saviour of the world, the one Mediator between God and humankind who gave his life a ransom for all. How was he to preach the gospel of free grace, although Christ only died for the elect? His general approach was more Christocentric than that of the Westminster tradition, and his doctrine of the covenant was more Christological. It is only through Christ that we can have an 'eye to God'.

For Boston, 'union with Christ' was a real union with the 'whole Christ' in his death and resurrection, not just a 'judicial relation' brought into line with a merely forensic notion of justification as imputation. Real union with Christ is grounded in the 'personal' or hypostatic union in him of divine and human natures.[34] Through union with him all benefits of the covenant of grace are given to elect believers. This helped to give both justification and sanctification objective and Christological depth.

Brief attention may be given to Boston's doctrines of the incarnation, the atonement, and the covenant of grace.

[33] Boston (1852), 156.
[34] Boston (1848–52), I, 398f., 544ff., also VIII, 177ff.

The Incarnation

Boston's doctrine of Christ was cast in the mould of the Nicene and Athanasian theology. He presented his doctrine of Christ from the soteriological perspective of 'the wonderful love and grace of God in sending his Son to be the Redeemer of sinful men'. However, he qualified that by saying that in his love God freely sent his only begotten Son to be 'the Redeemer of an elect world'. He was unable to correlate a notion of particular predestination and redemption with 'the matchless love of the Son of God to poor sinners'.[35]

His account of the incarnation is superb.[36] He laid great emphasis upon the truth that divine and human natures are hypostatically united in the one person of Christ without division and without change. He recalled how Athanasius regarded the burning bush as a type of Christ's incarnation. As the bush was not consumed by the divine fire, so the human nature of Christ was not consumed by his divine nature.[37]

Boston thought of the assumption of our human nature from the Virgin Mary in such a way as to redeem and sanctify it. In explaining this, Boston turned to the teaching of St Paul: 'God sending his own Son in the likeness of sinful flesh, and for sin, condemned sin in the flesh.' He understood that to mean that, in the very act of assuming 'sinful flesh', far from sinning in it Christ condemned sin in the flesh, and sanctified it, that we sinners may be sanctified, body, soul and spirit, in him.[38] Like Calvin, Boston thought of Christ as paying the price of our redemption from his very birth, and of the birth of Jesus of the Virgin Mary as itself a saving and sanctifying event.

> Behold the wonderful love of God the Father, who was content to degrade and abase his dear Son, in order to bring about the salvation of sinners. How astonishing is it, that he should send his only-begotten Son to assume our nature, and bear that dreadful wrath and punishment that we deserved![39]

The Atonement

Boston expounded his doctrine of atonement in terms of the priesthood, oblation and intercession of Christ the incarnate Mediator in which he

[35] Boston (1848–52), I, 396f.
[36] *Ibid.*, 339–43.
[37] *Ibid.*, 393–8.
[38] *Ibid.*, 308.
[39] *Ibid.*, 400–3.

adapted language taken from the ceremonial law of the Old Testament about expiatory sacrifice.

> As the Mediator of the Covenant it behoved Christ to deal with both parties, in order to bring them together. God was offended with our sin and guilt; and therefore for us he behoved to be a Priest, to satisfy law and justice, and intercede for our pardon.[40]

'God was to be propitiated that so he might pardon man.'[41] 'It was to satisfy divine justice, and reconcile us to God. The grand design and intendment of this oblation was to atone, pacify, and reconcile God, by giving him a full and adequate satisfaction for the sins of the elect world', and thereby to 'purchase reconciliation' for us with God.[42]

Boston emphasised the fact that Christ suffered not just in a true body but in a reasonable soul, thereby rejecting any element of Apollinarian as well as docetic heresy in his doctrine of atonement.[43] This implied that the atoning passion took place in the inner being of the incarnate Mediator, God and man in one person, but what of its bearing upon his inner relation as human being with God himself?

In recalling Paul's statement that 'God spared not his own Son' (Romans 8:32), Boston did not think of that as revealing the self-sacrificing love of the Father, but as indicating

> the strictness and severity of divine justice, that required satisfaction equivalent to the desert of sin . . . The fountain of divine mercy stopt its course, and would not let out one drop to Christ in the day of his extreme sorrow and suffering . . . O the inflexible severity of divine justice![44]

Boston did not think of God as reconciling us to himself but as being propitiated and reconciled to us by the blood of Christ, and failed to see that in the Bible God was never held to be the object of atoning or propitiating sacrifice. And yet it was the gospel offer of saving grace made unconditionally to the world, that Boston was so concerned to proclaim. As a pastor he could say to his congregation

---

[40] *Ibid.*, 406.

[41] *Ibid.*, 442.

[42] Boston overlooks the fact that nowhere in the New Testament is reconciliation said to be 'purchased' from God, although it is said that the church was bought by God's blood (Acts 20:28).

[43] Boston (1848–52), I, 394–6.

[44] *Ibid.*, 464.

'Think not that Christ is more willing to save you than the Father is. The will of Christ, his Father and Spirit are one . . . Behold the matchless love of the Father to lost sinners of Adam's race, 1 John III:1. The whole contrivance sprang from free grace.'[45]

The Covenant of Grace

Boston rejected the contemporary notion of a 'covenant of redemption' as unbiblical, and identified it with the one covenant of grace embodied in Christ.[46] However he still adhered to the so-called 'covenant of works', a binding contract made by God with Adam and the human race.[47] This was of evangelical importance for Boston, for it was through the vicarious obedience of Christ in fulfilling all the conditions of that covenant with humankind, and through his substitutionary sacrifice on the cross in bearing the punishment of our sin, thereby satisfying the justice of God and appeasing his wrath, that Christ was able to offer the gospel freely to 'mankind sinners' without conditions, for all the conditions have already been fulfilled completely by him.

Since Christ has fulfilled all the conditions of the covenant, the gospel of saving grace can be offered freely to sinners so that though they are summoned to believe in Christ and repent, neither faith nor repentance can be regarded in a conditional way.[48] Properly regarded faith follows upon the offer of grace, and repentance comes after the forgiveness of sins and does not precede it. This was the doctrine of 'two forms of repentance', 'repentance of the law' and 'repentance of the gospel', taught by Calvin.[49] Since Christ is himself the covenant of grace, it is through union with him made effectual by the Holy Spirit that saving faith and evangelical repentance are really possible.

Attention should be drawn to the eschatological strand that ran through Boston's preaching and teaching which struck deeply into the very heart of people's need and gripped their souls when facing up to the thought of death and the final judgment. Boston gave special place to this in *Human Nature in its Fourfold State*, in which he also directed his readers to 'the mystical union between Christ and believers' which

[45] *Ibid.*, 324.

[46] *Ibid.*, 233.

[47] *Ibid.*, 229.

[48] See Boston's notes on the *Marrow of Modern Divinity* 2.3.4. in Boston (1848–52), VII, 278ff.

[49] John Calvin, *Institutes* 3:3:4; cf. 3:3:1–3.

persists through death right into eternity. That combination made this work the most published, the most widely read, and probably the most influential book in Scottish theology.

EIGHTEENTH-CENTURY PRESBYTERIANISM

The deep tensions in Scottish theology came to the surface in two controversies early in the eighteenth century, over the alleged antinomianism and universalism of the teaching of *The Marrow of Modern Divinity*, and over the alleged rationalism and Socinianism of Professor John Simson of Glasgow. They anticipated problems which were to continue to trouble theology, and lay at the root of the divisions that kept on breaking out within the Kirk.

The eighteenth century saw a remarkable renaissance in literature, which made a considerable impact on Scottish thought. Theological questioning, counter-questioning and defensive reaction took place when traditional hyper-Calvinist structures, centring on the absolute sovereignty of God rather than on his infinite love, were under pressure from a fuller understanding of the gospel, but also from brilliant developments in the Scottish Enlightenment.

The Marrow Controversy

In the *Marrow* controversy Calvinists who recognised 'the good old ways of the Reformers' found themselves trapped between a rigid adherence to the Westminster theology and a more evangelical way of understanding the teaching of the Bible. The controversy was precipitated by a republication of *The Marrow of Modern Divinity*, when several of its tenets were condemned by the General Assembly of the Church of Scotland in 1720.[50] This prompted Thomas Boston and a group of evangelical Calvinists (among whom were two Edinburgh graduates Ralph and Ebenezer Erskine) to make a theological presentation of their case to the General Assembly in 1722,[51] but without avail.[52] The basic point of difference was made clear in the Assembly's condemnation of what it called 'an universal redemption

---

[50] *Acts of the General Assembly of the Church of Scotland*, Sess. 9, May 20, Edinburgh, 1720.

[51] Sess. 9, May 20, 1720 and Sess. 10, May 21, 1722.

[52] See the Appendix to Boston's edition of the *Marrow*, in Boston (1848–52) VII, 465–99; and also *A Full and True State of the Controversy Concerning the Marrow of Modern Divinity, as debated by the General Assembly, and several ministers in the year 1720 and 1721* (Glasgow, 1773).

as to purchase'. When applied to all people this could only mean, in the Assembly's view, a doctrine of universal atonement and redemption, which the supporters of *The Marrow* like Thomas Boston resolutely denied.[53] Behind that decision lay the fact that in practice the Scriptures had come to be interpreted in strict accord with the formulations of the Confession of Faith, which were regarded as exact transcripts of biblical doctrines. This was more of a problem for the evangelical divines, in their commitment to the gospel of salvation by grace alone and in their concern more with the saving person of Christ than formal doctrine. Nevertheless they tried to take more seriously the command of Christ to go into all the world and preach the gospel.

The Simson Case

In the Simson controversy adherence to the Westminster Confession brought to light other problems, not least its necessitarian idea of God together with the view of nature enshrined in the notion of the covenant of works grounded not on Christ but on nature, and a Nestorian – even Arian – tendency in the notion of an absolute God behind the back of the incarnate Christ. John Simson, Professor of Divinity in Glasgow University, was twice accused of various heresies, mainly Socinianism and Arianism. His rather ambiguous views were not unconnected with the moralistic teaching about the light of nature, with the general framework of first and second causes in the Westminster Confession, and not least with the rather deterministic doctrine of God and what Simson called 'omnipotent grace'. This laid him open to the rationalism and determinism of the English Deists like John Locke and Samuel Clarke. Although he was not a rationalist, he stood for a religion of reason rather than a religion of experience.

Enlightenment and Realism

After the Toleration Act of 1712 a broader and more urbane outlook began to come over Scotland which made itself felt in Scottish thought. During the decades known as the Scottish Enlightenment a new outlook in theology asserted itself, for not a few ministers became deeply interested in the scientific advance that began with Isaac Newton, and was carried on in Scotland notably by Colin MacLaurin (1698–1746), who was the son of a minister and the brother of another. On

---

[53] Boston's edition of the *Marrow*, in Boston (1848–52), VII, 262f.

Newton's recommendation he was appointed to the chair of Mathematics at Edinburgh, where he made distinguished contributions in mathematics and physics for which he was honoured by the Royal Society in London and the French Academy. This was the century of Francis Hutcheson, Adam Smith, David Hume and James Watt, which in 1783 saw the foundation of the Royal Society of Edinburgh 'For the Advancement of Learning and Useful Knowledge'. As with the foundation of the Royal Society of London, ministers joined with scientists, mathematicians and philosophers in the establishment of its counterpart in Edinburgh, some of whom made outstanding contributions to British philosophy and science.

Particular mention must be made of the paradoxical contribution of Edinburgh's David Hume (1711–76), whose critical philosophy did much to undermine the rationalism of the hyper-Calvinists, and helped theologians of the Kirk to break free from the non-biblical and non-evangelical presuppositions in which they had been caught up. Reference must also be made to Thomas Reid (1710–96), a minister who succeeded Adam Smith as Professor of Moral Philosophy in Glasgow. He laid the foundations for a realist epistemology which had a big impact on Reformed theology. His ideas were developed by the Edinburgh Professor Sir William Hamilton (1788–1856) in a way that was to influence the devout James Clerk Maxwell in the next century, who, according to Einstein, did more than anyone else to change the rational structure of science. Maxwell began as a student in Edinburgh.

It is difficult to estimate the full impact of the critical attack on rationalism and the return to a realist way of thinking, which had a better reception from the Moderate than the Evangelical wing of the Kirk, but perhaps its most important effect was the way in which it made room for a fresh understanding of the gospel by freeing it from the rigid framework of rationalist Calvinism. Churchmen now felt more free to follow a straightforward interpretation of biblical passages about the unrestricted nature of the redemption of humankind by Christ, and the unconditional offer of the gospel to all people even beyond the supposed limits of the covenant of grace.

Moderates and Evangelicals
Due to the problematic course of Scottish theology in the eighteenth century, although there were some outstanding churchmen, no

outstanding theologians were found in the leadership of the Kirk, apart from some able theologians of the hyper-Calvinist school. In the main it was the double contribution of the Moderates and Evangelicals that gave the Scottish theology its character, in which philosophical, theological, liturgical and evangelical concern presented a uniform face in their more urbane adherence to the Confession of Faith and in their concern for Christian learning in the universities and in the schools.

It is perhaps in the Kirk of the Greyfriars in Edinburgh that we get our clearest glimpse of the relation between the Moderates and the Evangelicals, in the way in which William Robertson (1721–93) the Moderate and John Erskine (1721–1803) the Evangelical shared the ministry for forty years. Both adhered strictly to the West-minster standards, but they also shared in a common liturgical interest and in regular parish work with its care for the poor. There were divergences between Evangelicals and Moderates in their party adherence in the General Assembly, but it was in preaching that the contrast between them was greatest. What really divided the Moderates and the Evangelicals was not Westminster theology, but the issues of lay patronage and Kirk discipline through the General Assembly which were eventually to play a role in the Disruption.

Foreign Missions

William Robertson and John Erskine both held that the proclama-tion of the gospel should be carried to the heathen world. On the whole, the Kirk was too tied to the narrow outlook on the world that stemmed from the rigid principles of its Westminster tradition, but along with the wider horizon opened up through colonial expansion and overseas trade, a change began to take place in the conscience of the Kirk. This was due to a large extent to a fresh approach to the Scriptures, and not least as a result of the evangelical preaching of people like George Whitefield and Robert and James Haldane, which was most notable in Secession congregations. Then in 1796 a debate took place in the General Assembly in which the whole question of missionary activity at home and abroad was raised, when the door for foreign missions was not closed but left open, with the decision that the General Assembly 'will embrace with thankfulness any future opportunity of contributing by their exertions to the propagation of the Gospel'.

EARLY NINETEENTH-CENTURY THEOLOGY:
JOHN McLEOD CAMPBELL (1800–72)

The outlook of theology in the early decades of the nineteenth century may be indicated by reference to two prominent churchmen, George Hill (1750–1819) of St Andrews, a Calvinist theologian who put law before grace, and Thomas Erskine (1788–1870) of Linlathen, an evangelical lawyer who put grace before law. For Hill God is reconciled only on the ground of satisfaction made by vicarious punishment to the divine Lawgiver; for Erskine God cannot be spoken of as being reconciled, but only as he who was in Christ reconciling the world to himself. For Hill the grace connected with salvation is confined only to those whom God has chosen, but for Erskine it is freely and unconditionally offered to all. The basic issue had to do with the concept of God: what kind of God is spoken of in the gospel? That was the question with which the General Assembly of the Church of Scotland was faced in 1831.

John McLeod Campbell, the profoundest theologian in the history of Scottish theology since the Reformation was charged by the General Assembly in May 1831 with teaching doctrine contrary to the Confession of Faith and the Catechisms of the Church of Scotland. He was deposed from the ministry on account of his belief in 'the doctrine of universal atonement and pardon, as also the doctrine that assurance is of the essence of faith and necessary for salvation'. Both the Moderates and the Evangelicals combined to condemn McLeod Campbell. But Thomas Chalmers, Professor of Divinity at Edinburgh, sat silent all through the Assembly debate, without saying a word, and declined to vote against McLeod Campbell. He realised, as he wrote later, that in regard to the Kirk's attitude to 'the universality of the Gospel', 'there must be a sad misunderstanding somewhere'.[54]

The act of the 1831 Assembly was undoubtedly of crucial importance for Scottish theology, for it had to do with the contradictions in the theology of the Kirk which required to be resolved. The prevailing legalistic framework of thought made it difficult for people to interpret many passages of Holy Scripture without unnatural violence. That was happening with some of the great gospel passages in the New Testament such as John 3:16, 1 John 1:2, 1 Timothy 2:4f., Hebrews 2:9, 17–19, in order to bring them into line with the accepted doctrine of particular redemption.

---

[54] Chalmers (1849), I, 404 ('On the Universality of the Gospel').

What had gone wrong? James B. Torrance (who taught for many years in New College) has put his finger on the problem in his introduction to the new edition of McLeod Campbell's great work, *The Nature of the Atonement.*

> Campbell saw that fundamental to the whole issue was the doctrine of God. Instead of thinking of God as the Father, who loves all humanity, and who in Christ gives us the gift of sonship and who freely forgives us through Jesus Christ, they thought of God as One whose love is conditioned by human repentance and faith, and whose forgiveness had to be purchased by the payment of the sufferings of Christ on behalf of the elect. 'Instead of resting in the character of God as revealed in Christ, they looked upon the death of Christ as so much suffering – the purchase money of heaven to a certain number, to whom it infallibly secured heaven.'[55] They saw a contract-god who needs to be conditioned into being gracious.[56]

A New Framework

Faced with this state of affairs McLeod Campbell felt that a decisive shift had to be made to another framework of thought appropriate to God's self-revelation in Christ and to the nature of the atonement understood in its own light. This was a methodological decision not to separate method and content, which his contemporaries did not appreciate, for they still tried to understand his theology within the parameters of their own rationalistic Calvinism, and their customary belief that the Westminster Confession was an exact and complete transcript of scriptural doctrine.

McLeod Campbell held firmly to 'the Catholic and Reformed' doctrine of the atonement. In Jesus Christ his incarnate Son, God himself has come among us as the one Mediator between God and humankind, to be one with us and one of us in such way as to appropriate our actual human nature, and make our life and death under divine judgment his own, in order to pay our debt and make reparation which we are unable to do, to substitute himself for us in such a way as to bear upon and in himself the righteous wrath of God against our sin, to suffer the penalty of death which is the wages of sin, and through offering himself in body and soul without spot or blemish in sacrifice to God to make atonement for our sin

[55] Campbell (1873A), 25.
[56] Torrance, J. B. (1996), 4.

and thus on our behalf to satisfy the holiness and righteousness of the Father.[57]

McLeod Campbell did not expound this view of atonement in abstract terms but in personal terms of the filial relation between the Son and the Father.[58] Atonement has to be understood in recognition of the fact that out of his infinite love God sent his Son to be the propitiation for our sins, that God was in Christ reconciling the world to himself, and therefore that 'if God provides the atonement, then forgiveness must precede the atonement; and the atonement must be the form of the manifestation of the forgiving love of God, not its cause'.[59] While the ultimate ground of atonement is in God,[60] Jesus Christ is himself propitiation.[61]

Incarnation and Atonement

Instead of beginning, then, with the eternal decrees of God and the reign of law, McLeod Campbell turned to the incarnation in which God has revealed himself in his Son Jesus Christ as the God who is love. It was not just to the incarnation itself that he turned, but to the incarnation in its relation to the atonement, and thus to the atonement as developed in the incarnation.[62] It is, then, in the light of the actual life and work of the incarnate Son of the Father that the atonement is to be understood.

In giving the interrelation between the Father and the incarnate Son central significance for his understanding of the atonement, McLeod Campbell had to take with the utmost seriousness the incarnate being of the Mediator as God and man indissolubly united in one person, and think out the nature of the atonement as the propitiating love of God the Father actualised within the life and death of Christ, through whom alone we are given access to God the Father. This is an atonement which God in his grace freely provides in order to reconcile us to himself, not one which makes God gracious.

---

[57] See particularly Campbell (1886), 98ff., 122ff., 248ff., 258ff.

[58] Campbell (1886), 59ff., 139ff., 150ff. This registers a return to John Knox's doctrine of God's fatherly love; see *The Biblical Doctrine of Baptism* (Church of Scotland Special Commission; Edinburgh, 1958), 12.

[59] Campbell (1886), 16.

[60] *Ibid.*, 286.

[61] *Ibid.*, 16f., 170f. See Calvin, *Institutes* 2:16:3–4; Augustine, *Homilies on St John's Gospel* 110:6.

[62] Campbell (1886), xviff.

Thus conceived, the intrinsic nature of the atonement is to be under-stood as essentially moral and spiritual as well as physical.[63] It was not just an external transaction, but the unitary divine-human movement of propitiation fulfilled within the mediatorial person and obedient life of Christ from his birth of the Virgin Mary to his death and resurrection. McLeod Campbell could not forget that Christ is God and man, God himself come among us as human, and acting personally in our human existence precisely as God incarnate, so that he thought of atonement as taking place at once within the filial relations of the incarnate Son to the Father, and in the depths of Christ's divine humanity. Hence he thought of Christ as vicariously bearing in himself the righteous judgment of God against sin, not just physically but spiritually and morally. As the one Mediator between God and man who is both God and man, he bore in himself the righteous wrath of the Father and in our name confessed our sin – a confession, made with his whole incarnate being, which was, in McLeod Campbell's words, 'a perfect Amen in humanity to the judgment of God on the Sin of man'.[64] Far from being subjective, this vicarious 'Amen' was one acted out objectively in the whole course of Christ's vicarious life from his birth to his death, in which he bore our sin, condemned it in the flesh he assumed from us, and offered himself in sacrifice to the Father.[65]

It is important to note that the 'perfect Amen' in which Christ confessed our sin, and in which he yielded himself in body and soul to the inflictions of the Father, was yielded out of the ontological depths of his sinless humanity and in his inseparable relation to sinners, thereby acknowledging and receiving in our place and in our stead the judicial condemnation of God upon us and absorbing it in himself.[66] As James Orr pointed out,[67] it would be a serious error to think of this 'Amen' as a mere ideal realisation of what God's wrath toward sin is, for it was yielded 'under the actual pressure of the judgment which that wrath inflicts'. It was not a subjective but a real 'Amen', yielded out of the midst of Christ's vicarious death as well as his life.

McLeod Campbell took seriously the teaching of St Paul in the opening verses of Romans 8: 'What the law could not do, in that it was weak through the flesh, God sending his own Son in the likeness

---

[63] See the note to Chapter VI, Campbell (1886), 342–4.
[64] *Ibid.*, 117.
[65] Cf. Campbell (1873B), 101.
[66] Campbell (1886), 118.
[67] Orr (1897), 313.

of sinful flesh, and for sin, condemned sin in the flesh.'[68] He did not hold this to mean that in becoming one with us and one of us in our fallen humanity Christ himself became a sinner, but the very reverse, that in assuming what was ours he condemned sin in the flesh, sanctified and redeemed it, and so paid the price of our redemption from the beginning of his incarnate entry into our Adamic existence and all through his incarnate life among sinners.

Following the great Athanasius, who regarded the incarnate mediatorial and priestly office of Christ as one in which he ministered the things of God to humanity and the things of humanity to God,[69] McLeod Campbell thought of Christ as dealing with men and women on the part of God, and as dealing with God on the part of men and women, not as two activities but as one seamless activity within his incarnate person.[70] Like Athanasius, therefore, he thought of atonement as taking place within the incarnate constitution of the Mediator who is of one and the same being as God the Father.

Within the strictly Christological and soteriological frame of thought the classical notions of penalty and satisfaction have a much deeper and fuller meaning than they had in a federal Calvinism. Thus the term 'penal' which McLeod Campbell used frequently has to be understood in a spiritual and moral way, not simply in a physical way as the external infliction of divine judgment which in his death on the cross Christ bore in our place. His vicarious penal sufferings were certainly physical, but they had to do above all with what he bore for us and on our behalf agonisingly in the depths of his 'divine humanity' – 'the sorrows of the man of sorrows'.[71] The penal infliction which Christ endured in our nature, for us and in our place, he endured in his soul as well as his body.

Sacrifice of the Father

Something else must be said. The redemptive activity of Christ in our place and on our behalf was fulfilled in his inseparable oneness with the Father, in such a way that the Father did not hold himself aloof from the humiliation and passion of Christ but identified himself with it, and took it upon his own heart and shared it to the full. Behind the

---

[68] *Ibid.*, 109; Romans 8:3.

[69] Athanasius, *Against the Arians* 4:6 (McLeod Campbell does not actually cite this passage).

[70] Campbell (1886), 111ff.

[71] *Ibid.*, 111–18.

sacrifice of Christ was the sacrifice of the Father, who did not spare his own Son but delivered him up for us all. That ultimate oneness between the Father and the Son must surely obtain even in Christ's atoning identification with us in our sin and in his bearing with us God's (and his own) judgment upon our sin. It is that identification of God incarnate with us which was inexpressibly present in the 'Amen' to God actualised in the Saviour's vicarious submission, contrition and confession which McLeod Campbell sought to express by the term 'perfect repentance' (prompted by the hypothetical use of 'equivalent sorrow and repentance' by Jonathan Edwards). The all-important truth to be noted here is that the ultimate objective ground of Christ's vicarious life, suffering and sacrifice, lies in God himself who so loved us that he did not withhold his only-begotten Son but gave him to be our Saviour, and in him gave us himself. However unsatisfactory the idea of 'perfect repentance' used in this vicarious way may be, it was meant to indicate the profound truth that when sinners confess their sins, all too unworthily, the gospel tells them that Christ has already answered for them, and that God in Christ has already accepted them, so that sinners do not rest on any repentance of their own, but on what Christ had already offered to the Father not just in their stead but on their behalf.

We must return again to the relation between incarnation and atonement upon which McLeod Campbell laid such stress, for the atonement cannot be understood apart from the oneness of Christ with us in which he made our sin and our death, our poverty and our misery, our indebtedness to God, his own. It was through this oneness with us that the incarnate Son of God penetrated into the inner depths of our alienation from God, and brought his holy condemnation and atoning activity to bear upon us at the very root of our sinful existence, that is, even of our original sin. That is what the atonement conceived as an external legal transaction could not do; at the best it could only deal with actual sins. As McLeod Campbell understood it, the incarnate activity of Christ in his oneness with us in our fallen human existence reached forward into the atonement with both retroactive and prospective effect, retroactively penetrating into the depths of our sin and guilt and undoing them, but prospectively translating us from imprisonment in our mortal existence into the new life of the risen Jesus. This understanding of the ontological interrelation between the incarnation and the atonement reinforced the message of the gospel that the forgiving love of God precedes the atonement, and that the atonement is the supreme manifestation of the love of God in which it is ultimately grounded. It was this biblical and evangelical conviction that radically altered the fundamental conception of God which McLeod Campbell had inherited from his Calvinist tradition, and led him to say calmly and frankly to the General Assembly 'I hold and teach that Christ died for all men.'

Chapter 2

The Disruption and the Dream: The Making of New College 1843–1861

Stewart J. Brown

THE NEW COLLEGE in Edinburgh was a product of religious conflict and of the zeal aroused by that conflict. It emerged out of the Disruption of 1843, when over a third of the ministers and perhaps half the lay membership left the established Church of Scotland in protest against what they perceived as state efforts to undermine the Church's spiritual independence and integrity. Against all odds, the outgoing clergy and laity formed the Free Church of Scotland as a new national Church, free from state connection and acknowledging only the headship of Christ. Amid the idealism and fervour aroused by the Disruption, the struggling Free Church founded New College as an institution for educating not simply a learned ministry, but a new Scottish Christian leadership, who would guide the nation through a new Reformation, reasserting the spiritual independence of the Church and elevating the religious and moral conditions of the Scottish people. For a time, New College was envisaged as a free university, a citadel of conscience which would stand against the system of patronage and privilege that for centuries had enabled the Crown and members of the gentry and aristocracy to dominate the religious and intellectual life of the nation.

This chapter will explore the establishment and early development of New College under its first two Principals, Thomas Chalmers and William Cunningham – the one a liberal evangelical social theologian with strong roots in the Scottish Enlightenment, the other a conservative Calvinist historical theologian. Under the leadership of these two men, between 1843 and 1861, New College developed the distinctive features – a well-defined curriculum centred on five core departments, an emphasis on biblical languages and literature, and a strong social commitment – that would characterise it for the next century and a half. It began to develop an international reputation as a centre of Reformed scholarship, forming a vital link between Reformed communions on the European continent and in North America.

THE NON-INTRUSION CONTROVERSY AND THE DISRUPTION OF 1843

The Disruption of 1843 was probably the most important event in the history of nineteenth-century Scotland and a major episode in the history of the modern Western Church.[1] It emerged out of a prolonged conflict between the Church of Scotland and the British state – a conflict which centred on the procedures for appointing ministers to parish churches, and particularly on the thorny issue of patronage, which had troubled the peace of the Scottish Church since the Reformation. Patronage was a property right, a development of the medieval Church. It permitted the founders of a new church, and their heirs, to present an ordained priest to the living. At the Scottish Reformation in 1560, the Reformers had endeavoured to replace patronage with a form of congregational election of ministers. The Crown and landed classes, however, had fought to retain patronage, viewing it as a means of settling family members or supporters in parish livings and of exercising a degree of control over the pulpits of Scotland. Patronage came to symbolise the struggle between those who believed that the voice of the godly in local congregations, regardless of their wealth or social status, should prevail in the Church, and those who supported the dominance of the landed élites, as persons of education, culture and political influence. Although the Scottish parliament largely abolished patronage after the Revolution of 1688, this decision was reversed shortly after the act of union of 1707 by the newly formed British parliament, which restored patronage in 1712, against the wishes of the large majority in the Scottish Church. The supporters of the popular rights of congregations soon found themselves under overwhelming pressure from the landed classes and the Crown's political managers in Scotland. Some left the national Church of Scotland rather than submit to having patrons' candidates 'intruded' into their churches,

[1] For recent accounts of the Disruption, see Henderson (1943), Watt (1943B) and Brown, S. J. (1982).

and several sizeable secession denominations emerged by the end of the eighteenth century. Others remained within the national Church, and organised themselves into a Popular party to defend the rights of the congregations.

During the early nineteenth century, the position of the Popular party in the Church was greatly strengthened by two movements which had been growing in influence during the previous fifty years. The first was the Evangelical movement, with its emphasis on a vital, heart-felt religion, the centrality of conversion, the authority of Scripture and the importance of mission. The second was the movement for democratic reform, with its emphasis on representative government and equality of opportunity through the extension of popular education – which was, in turn, strongly influenced by the Scottish philosophy of common-sense with its stress on the intellectual capacities of the common people. During the 1820s, the Popular, or Evangelical party as it was increasingly known, revived the anti-patronage campaign and called for additional parish churches and schools to provide for the religious and educational needs of the growing population, especially in the new industrial towns and cities. In 1843, the Evangelical party, now led by the celebrated preacher, theologian and political economist, Thomas Chalmers, gained a majority within the General Assembly of the Church of Scotland. The Evangelical-dominated General Assembly of 1834 passed the Veto Act, which restricted the operation of patronage by giving male heads of family the right to veto a patron's presentee if they were dissatisfied with him for any reason. The common-sense of parishioners, Chalmers maintained, could be trusted to guard against improper appointments. In the same year, the General Assembly began a Church extension campaign, aimed at erecting hundreds of new parish churches and schools through private contributions. Church leaders asked only that the state provide a partial endowment for the new churches, to enable them to provide religious services for the poor who could not afford to contribute to the stipends of the minister and schoolmaster. Under Evangelical influence, the Church of Scotland was revitalised as a force for the religious and moral education of the Scottish people. Evangelical confidence in the potential of the Scottish people was rewarded. Private giving to the Church's educational, philanthropic and evangelical work increased fourteen-fold between 1834 and 1839, and some two hundred new churches were built or begun.[2]

[2] Buchanan, R. (1852), I, 230; Hanna (1849–52), IV, 87.

The British state, however, declined to support the Evangelical campaign. In 1838, the Whig government announced that it would not provide partial endowments for the new parish churches which had been built through private effort. In the same year, the Court of Session, the highest civil court in Scotland, declared the Church's Veto Act to be an illegal encroachment on the property rights of patrons – a decision upheld by the House of Lords the following year. The civil courts began instructing presbyteries to ordain patrons' candidates as ministers in parish churches, regardless of the desires of the parishioners. When presbyteries refused to 'intrude' unpopular patrons' presentees into churches, they were threatened with civil penalties, including fines and imprisonment. Many in the Church were prepared to submit to civil authority. The majority of the Evangelical party, however, refused to submit, insisting that the intrusion of unpopular patrons' candidates into parish livings was an affront to congregations and would undermine the influence of the national Church in the more democratic age. Further, they argued, the ordination of parish clergy was a spiritual function, over which the civil power could have no authority. For the Church to accept state control over its spiritual functions would be to relinquish its spiritual independence and cease to be a Church of Christ. When Parliament rejected the Evangelical appeals for legislative redress, a considerable body of ministers and lay members, under the leadership of Chalmers, William Cunningham and Robert Smith Candlish, resolved to leave the established Church. For decades, Chalmers had argued that only an established national Church could command the resources required for the religious and moral instruction of the whole Scottish people. By 1843, however, he was prepared to sacrifice the establishment for what he viewed as the higher principle of the Church's spiritual independence.

The mass exodus took place in May 1843, and the outgoing ministers and laity now formed themselves into the Free Church of Scotland. Their aim was to create a free national Church, with a parochial organisation that would offer religious observances and instruction to the whole people of Scotland, free of control by the state or aristocratic patrons. Perhaps half the membership of the state Church entered the Free Church and there were soon over 700 congregations requiring ministers and places of worship. A considerable number of these congregations were in poorer rural districts, especially the Highlands, where many landowners viewed the Free Church as a radical movement which challenged the existing social order. Critics confidently predicted that the Free Church could not collect the necessary money or stand out for long against the combined hostility of the landlords and the British government.

THE FREE CHURCH EDUCATIONAL IDEAL

The critics, however, failed to account for the religious fervour roused by the Disruption. For those who had gone out, the Disruption marked a new Reformation which would both restore the Scottish Church's spiritual independence and purity of doctrine, and liberate Scottish moral and intellectual life from aristocratic patronage and state-supported privilege. On 20 May 1843, the new Free Church General Assembly appointed an Education Committee under the convenership of David Welsh, former Professor of Church History at the University of Edinburgh. Welsh's committee presented its first report to the Assembly only five days later, on 25 May. The report offered two sets of recommendations – the first regarded as essential, and the second as desirable.[3] First, as an essential requirement, the committee called for the immediate establishment of a college in Edinburgh, which would continue the training of those divinity students who had joined the Free Church and provide theological courses for new students intending the Free Church ministry. The minimum college requirements were defined as the appointment of four professors, the procurement of a lecture hall and the establishment of a library. The college was to be organised immediately, with an eye to beginning instruction in early November 1843.

The second set of recommendations called for the development of a Free Church national system of education, including primary schools in every parish, grammar schools in every major town and three universities. The aim was to achieve the ideal of the sixteenth-century Scottish Reformers, as expressed in the *First Book of Discipline* – educating each individual up to that person's potential, regardless of ability to pay. This reflected the Disruption emphasis on the independence and intellectual potential of the common people. Welsh assured the Assembly that

> by a well-organised system of superintending and reporting, the gifts and graces of all – of each individual, from the highest to the humblest classes of society, would be duly appreciated. Where, in the remotest parish, the

[3] *Proceedings of the General Assembly of the Free Church, May 1843*, 113–18; Dunlop (1846), 113.

child of the humblest peasant or artisan gave promise of talents that fitted him for more extensive usefulness than his birth seemed to indicate, opportunities might be afforded for his attending the grammar school most nearby situated.

From there, if the young person demonstrated ability, 'he might be advanced to a university; and here, after full proof, a suitable career should not fail to be opened'.[4] To be sure, the committee did not envisage full equality of opportunity, as there was no conception of girls continuing to grammar school and university. But within the context of the time, the education report was a powerful expression of the ideal of the democratic intellect.

With the approval of the Assembly, the Education Committee proceeded rapidly to implement the first set of recommendations, those calling for the founding of a theological college in Edinburgh. During the summer it appointed four professors. Two of them were former theological professors at Edinburgh University who had joined the Free Church. The famed Thomas Chalmers, who had resigned his chair of Theology at Edinburgh University at the Disruption, was appointed Principal and Senior Professor of Theology. David Welsh, the former Professor of Ecclesiastical History at Edinburgh University, was appointed Professor of Church History. For the chair of Hebrew and Old Testament, the Committee selected John Duncan, a respected scholar of ancient and Semitic languages, who had been serving with the Church of Scotland mission to the Jews in Pest (Budapest).[5] Finally, William Cunningham, an Edinburgh clergyman who had established a reputation as a formidable controversial author and speaker during the Non-Intrusion conflict, became Junior Professor of Theology. He was then sent for several months to the United States, to study at first hand 'some of the most eminent of the American Theological Institutions' as well as to seek financial contributions for the Free Church.[6] It was agreed he would begin his duties in the session 1844–5. All four men held conservative Reformed theological beliefs combined with a grounding in the common-sense of the Scottish Enlightenment, issuing in a respect for the Scottish tradition of a learned ministry.

The Education Committee purchased rooms at 80 George Street, in Edinburgh's New Town, and set up a library there with the help of

[4] *Proceedings . . . Free Church, May 1843*, 115–16.
[5] Brown, D. (1872), 352–3.
[6] Rainy and Mackenzie (1871), 203.

donations of money and books. The college opened for its first session in November 1843 with 168 students, including about 100 students who had begun their divinity studies before the Disruption.[7] David Welsh took the leading role in the early development of the College, and devoted particular attention to the building up of the library. He was, however, also seriously ill, having suffered a heart attack in 1838, and he was rapidly weakening under the strain.

THOMAS CHALMERS AND THE FREE CHRISTIAN UNIVERSITY

During its first session, of 1843–4, New College was a modest theological hall, with only four professors and a small library, and it followed the patterns of theological education then prevailing in the Scottish universities.[8] For many in the Free Church, this was all that was required. They looked to the example of other unendowed dissenting churches, such as the United Secession Church, which maintained only small theological halls, often staffed by professors who also served as ministers of neighbouring congregations.[9] Others, however, recalled the ideal of a Free Church national system of education as presented in the Education Committee's report of May 1843, and dreamed of a greater future for the College – perhaps as the first of the Free Church universities which the Committee had envisaged as the pinnacle of a new national educational system.

Contributing to this larger vision of New College was the expectation that the established Church would insist on the enforcement of religious tests and drive Free Church members out of Scottish university chairs and teaching posts. Following the Disruption, Free Church academics, such as John Fleming, Professor of Natural Philosophy at King's College, Aberdeen, experienced pressure from the college authorities to resign their posts.[10] In 1844, moreover, the established Presbytery of St Andrews began legal proceedings for the ejection of David Brewster from the Principalship of the United College of St Andrews University, because of his membership in the Free Church.[11] Some began to look upon New College as a possible haven for professors threatened with

[7] Watt, 273; Brown, T. (1893), 328.
[8] Watt, 11.
[9] Gibson, J. (1850), 28–9; Gray (1850), 1–9.
[10] Duns (1859), lxxxiii–iv.
[11] *The Grievance of University Tests, as Set Forth in the Proceedings of St Andrews* (Edinburgh, 1845), 21–35; Gordon, M. M. (1869), 174–5.

dismissal for their conscientiously-held principles. In a pamphlet published in 1843, the philosopher and linguist, John Stuart Blackie, who was not a member of the Free Church, called on the Free Church to respond to persecution by forming a free university in Scotland. 'If these men drive Free Church professors out', Blackie advised the Free Church leaders, 'take your students along with them, and build a College for yourselves. You will perform an essential service to Scotland, and reap no small glory to yourselves, by erecting a Free University in this country, founded on the broad and deep principles of humanity and fraternity; a University with religion and with Christianity, but without monopoly and without tests.'[12] By late 1844 and early 1845, many perceived New College as the beginning of a great free Christian university, destined not only to prepare a learned Free Church ministry, but to advance Christian scholarship across a range of disciplines and to educate leaders in politics and the professions.

One who embraced this vision was Thomas Chalmers, Scotland's celebrated theologian and political economist, and Principal of New College. For the first year and a half after the Disruption, Chalmers had been absorbed in the task of developing a system for the maintenance of the Free Church clergy and had little time for College affairs. From the beginning of 1845, however, he turned his attention to the College. The death of David Welsh, his friend and long-time colleague, in January 1845, created a gap in the College leadership which Chalmers now felt called to fill.[13] In 1845–6, moreover, Chalmers became absorbed by what he perceived as growing infidelity in the continental universities, and the need for Scottish Christians to prepare themselves for an onslaught of dangerous new theological and philosophical forces.[14] For Chalmers, New College was not only destined to be a free university for Scotland, championing the principles of spiritual independence, evangelical religion and the democratic intellect; it was also called upon to lead the defence of the Reformed faith against the forces of modern biblical and historical scholarship and transcendental philosophy.[15] Under Chalmers' guidance, New College embraced in 1846 a series of proposed developments intended to make it one of the best equipped theological halls in the world.

---

[12] Blackie (1843), 35; Fraser, A. C. (1905), 126.

[13] Hanna (1849–52), IV, 423–4.

[14] Hanna (1849–52), IV, 429–33; Fraser, A. C. (1905), 131–2; Chalmers (1847).

[15] 'Report of the New College Committee', in *Proceedings . . . Free Church, 1846*, 20.

THE CORE CURRICULUM

The first group of innovations involved the development of a formal curriculum, through which students would progress in a set order over the course of four years, gaining a sound knowledge of what were perceived as the core theological disciplines. Prior to the Disruption, the theological hall at the University of Edinburgh had consisted of only three professors – in Divinity, Hebrew and Church History. The Professors of Divinity and Church History had each offered one series of lectures which they completed over a period of four years. This meant that students in a given year might find themselves joining the third or fourth session of Divinity or Church History and then completing the earlier parts of the course in their final years of study. The system, in short, failed to recognise that the subjects should be presented to students in a set order. The curriculum, moreover, had provided little formal study of the Bible. The Professor of Hebrew gave instruction in that language, but there was little systematic exegesis of the Old and New Testaments. Years before, in 1828, Chalmers had outlined a programme of reforms in theological education in his evidence before a Royal Commission appointed to visit the Scottish universities. Neglected by the British government, Chalmers' proposals of 1828 now became the inspiration for the New College curriculum.[16]

Chalmers' curricular plans centred on the creation of five chairs of theology – Systematic Theology, Apologetics and Practical Theology, Church History, Hebrew and Old Testament, and New Testament Exegesis – instead of the three chairs in the older universities.[17] Under his plan, each professor would teach two classes each in his subject – a junior and a senior class. Students would then progress through a defined four-year programme of study, which would include two years of study in each of the core disciplines. The curriculum also included a new focus on the study of the Bible. Chalmers had long maintained that students should not be admitted to theological study without a knowledge of Latin, Greek and the elements of Hebrew, and he advocated the introduction of a German-style gymnasium in major towns around the country, in order to prepare the students in these languages.[18] By entering college with a sound grounding in Greek and

[16] Hanna (1849–52), IV, 416–22; Buchanan, J. (1849), 14–15.
[17] For an early expression of the developing New College curriculum, see 'Report of the New College Committee', in *Proceedings . . . Free Church, 1846*, 15–30.
[18] *Ibid.*, 17–19.

Hebrew, students could proceed immediately to advanced exegesis of the Scriptures in the original languages. This, Chalmers argued, would prepare New College students to respond effectively to the challenges to the traditional faith coming from continental biblical scholarship.[19]

In addition to the theological curriculum, New College also took steps to provide instruction in a full range of Arts subjects. To begin, New College appointed professors in three disciplines – Moral Philosophy, Logic and Natural Science. Natural Science became a required part of the theological curriculum, to be taken during the first year.[20] This reflected the tradition of natural theology – still strong in British religious thought – which viewed the harmony in the natural realm as evidence of a benevolent Creator, supplementing scriptural revelation. Chalmers was himself a leading natural theologian, who in 1831 had published one of the celebrated Bridgewater Treatises in natural theology.[21] There was also a belief that Christian ministers had to be prepared to respond to the radical new ideas of biological development, as expressed in the *Vestiges of the Natural History of Creation*, published anonymously in 1844. Indeed, the first Professor of Natural Science, John Fleming, referred directly to the *Vestiges* in the debate concerning the founding of the chair in the General Assembly of 1845.[22] The chairs of Moral Philosophy and Logic would assert the claims of Scottish common-sense philosophy against continental philosophy.[23] From the beginning, many non-divinity students enrolled in the Arts classes; indeed, of the approximately 440 students attending classes at New College in 1846, over 200 were Arts students.[24] In addition to the three Arts subjects there were plans to establish chairs of Latin, Greek and Mathematics, with other chairs to follow.[25] It was a time of rising aspirations. The young Free Church philosopher, Alexander Campbell Fraser, was persuaded to accept the professorship of Logic in 1846 by the vision of New College as a 'great free university, founded on the broad and deep principles of humanity in union with Christianity'.[26]

[19] *Ibid.*, 20.
[20] *Ibid.*, 19.
[21] Chalmers (1833).
[22] Baxter (1993), 105–8.
[23] 'Report of the New College Committee', in *Proceedings . . . Free Church, 1846*, 20.
[24] *Ibid.*, 16–17.
[25] Watt, 27–9.
[26] Fraser, A. C. (1905), 127.

Finally, New College sought to encourage the highest standards of scholarship within a competitive atmosphere. A start was made in 1845 with the introduction of a system of competitive bursaries. The money was raised largely through the efforts of J. M. Hog of Newliston.[27] In the past, bursaries had generally been awarded to students on the basis of financial need, or according to often arbitrary criteria set by the donors. The New College bursaries, however, were to be awarded only after competitive examination, as 'rewards of merit'. During the first year of the scheme, in 1845–6, a total of forty scholarships were awarded, with the values ranging from £12 to £15 each per annum. About 100 students presented themselves in Edinburgh at the end of October and sat a series of examinations, with the papers set by New College professors.[28] The competitive examinations were modelled on those at the Oxford and Cambridge colleges, and their aim was 'to hold forth such rewards and such stimulus as might act throughout and on the whole body of our students, and thus evoke the rising energies of the Hall wherever they might be found'.[29]

DREAMS IN STONE:
THE CITADEL ON THE MOUND

With proposals for the expanded professoriate and curriculum came plans for a new building, which would express the aspirations of the College. The rooms at 80 George Street could not be expected to house a great university and in May 1844 the General Assembly approved a proposal to collect money for erecting 'a college which would be a credit to the Church'.[30] Soon after this decision the College committee managed to purchase, at a bargain price of £10,000, a site on the Mound, in the centre of the city. One of David Welsh's last acts had been to raise a substantial sum for the proposed college building. Impressed by the contributions of the lower and middle classes for the erection of new Free churches and schools, Welsh had agreed to approach upper-class Free Church members, inviting donations of £1,000 each for the college building. Before being forced by failing health to give up the work in November 1844, he had collected

---

[27] Watt, 39–40.
[28] 'Report of the Bursary Committee, in *Proceedings . . . Free Church, 1846*, 7–13.
[29] 'Report of the New College Committee', in *Proceedings . . . Free Church, 1846*, 25.
[30] Brown, T. (1893), 329.

£19,000 and another £2,000 was subscribed soon after his death, making a total of £21,000. The highly successful Free Church fund-raiser, John MacDonald, minister of Blairgowrie, raised a further £10,000 by early 1845. The Free High Church congregation in the Old Town, moreover, agreed to share the costs of the site, in return for including the church among the College buildings.[31] The College Committee commissioned the celebrated Edinburgh architect, William Henry Playfair, to design the buildings. Playfair's plan, as presented to the General Assembly in May 1846, was for three quadrangles, each at a different level, rising from the level of the Mound to that of the Castle Hill, and providing accommodation for a full university. The first quadrangle would provide the public face for the building, so that if the Free Church later decided to restrict itself to theological education, the first quadrangle would itself 'form an entire and elegant edifice'.[32] At a time when many Free Church congregations were still worshipping in temporary accommodation, often rented rooms in back closes, Church leaders felt it was all the more important that New College should be an imposing edifice, set in a prominent part of the capital, as an expression of the permanence and confidence of the Free Church. Playfair designed the building so that, viewed from Hanover Street, its two towers would frame exactly the massive tower of the historic Tolbooth Church, creating a sense of continuity with the past. Two of the proposed three quadrangles were never constructed, but the first quadrangle was begun in 1846 and completed in 1850, its distinctive towers soon becoming a familiar landmark on the Mound overlooking the New Town.

THE SOCIAL MISSION

Thomas Chalmers laid the foundation stone in a public ceremony on 3 June 1846. In his speech defining the mission of New College, he emphasised its national responsibilities, and especially its duty to work for the improvement of the condition of the poor. At a time when the Free Church was being condemned in many circles as a political movement aimed at the overthrow of the existing social hierarchy, and when landowners were often refusing to provide the Free Church with sites for churches, Chalmers denied that the aim of New College was to sow social dissension or class envy. Although not revolutionary

[31] *Proceedings . . . Free Church, 1846*, 154–6.
[32] 'Report of the Building Committee', in *Proceedings . . . Free Church, 1846*, 5–6.

in a political sense, however, New College was to have a strong social commitment, preparing leaders who could conduct a ministry among the poor and marginalised in Scottish society, as well as to defend the faith among the educated classes. 'The youth who frequent our classes', Chalmers insisted,

> will with all earnestness and emphasis be told, that the Christian minister is a man of no rank, because a man of all ranks; and that although he should have an education which might qualify him for holding converse with princes and peers, it is his peculiar glory to be a frequent visitant of the poor man's humble cottage, and to pray by the poor man's dying bed. Heaven grant that the platform of humble life may be raised immeasurably higher than at present . . . Let kings retain their sceptres, and nobles their coronets, – what we want is a more elevated ground-floor for our general population.[33]

Chalmers' speech has been criticised for its acceptance of the social inequalities in early Victorian society.[34] He was, to be sure, a man of his time, and perceived social inequality as inevitable. But what was significant was Chalmers' insistence that the social mission was fundamental to New College. It is worth noting that in the summer of 1844, at the same time that Chalmers assumed active leadership in the College, he also began a model home mission operation in the West Port, then one of the most impoverished and crime-ridden districts of the city.[35] He appointed a salaried missionary and recruited an agency of voluntary workers, who were each assigned a specific neighbourhood and instructed to visit the families there on a regular basis, offering moral advice, encouraging church attendance, getting children into school and assisting the unemployed to find work. Chalmers and the agency also established day and evening schools, infant schools, Sunday schools, reading rooms, lending library, savings bank and bathing and laundry facilities, and worked for improved sanitation. The aim was to create a Christian community in the West Port, and to develop programmes for home mission for the Free Church and other denominations to follow. Chalmers began recruiting New College students as visitors in January 1845. Early student workers included John Mackintosh, the 'earnest student', a brilliant and idealistic Free Church candidate whose promise was cut short by early death, and

---

[33] 'Proceedings at the Laying of the Foundation Stone of the New College', in *Proceedings . . . Free Church, 1846*, 33–4.

[34] See, for example, Smith, D. C. (1987), 3–4.

[35] For the West Port mission, see Brown, S. J. (1978).

William Tasker, a New College student worker who became the first full-time minister of the West Port Free Church.[36] After December 1847, the New College Missionary Society concentrated its efforts on the West Port, gradually extending their voluntary social work to the Cowgate, the Infirmary and other parts of the city by the early 1850s.[37]

By May 1847, four years after the Disruption, a free university was emerging. By now eight professors had been appointed, five in Theology and three in Arts. A comprehensive curriculum had been developed, emphasising both natural theology and the systematic study of the Bible in the original languages. Further, there was a library with over 13,000 volumes, and a natural history museum, and an imposing new building was rising on the Mound. Student numbers were high – 168 Free Church divinity students in 1843–4; 165 in 1844–5; 190 in 1845–6 and 178 in 1846–7, with additional divinity students from Ireland – making it the largest unendowed theological hall in Great Britain, and probably in the English-speaking world.[38] After 1846, moreover, there were an estimated 200 Arts students each year. All this had been achieved at a time of dramatic growth and heavy financial demands on the Free Church as a whole. Between 1843 and 1848, Free Church members had, through voluntary giving, built an estimated 730 churches and over 400 manses, established over 500 parish schools, founded two Normal schools for teacher training, provided a decent minimum stipend to all the ministers and assumed the support of all but one of the pre-Disruption overseas missionaries. With the beginning of the devastating famine in Ireland and the Scottish Highlands and Islands in 1845, the Free Church had given more in famine relief than any denomination in Scotland. It was a time of dreams and unprecedented sacrifice and seemingly limitless possibilities. Such heroic efforts, however, could not be sustained indefinitely.

DOGMATISM AND REALISM: THE CUNNINGHAM YEARS

Thomas Chalmers died of heart failure at the end of May 1847, almost a year to the day after he had laid the foundation stone of New

[36] Macleod, N. (1854), 100, 119–22; Jolly (1880), 9–18.
[37] Watt, 115–16.
[38] *Ibid.*, 88. The largest theological halls in the United States in 1840 were Andover, with five professors and 153 students, Princeton with four professors and 100 students, and Union, New York, with four professors and ninety students; Miller (1990), 201–2.

College. His death was a serious blow to the developing College. While he had lived, he had inspired the Free Church with his vision for New College, and had commanded the influence and authority within the Free Church to ensure consensus for his ideal. There had been general agreement that resources should be invested to make New College a free Christian university. Following his death, however, this vision for New College was increasingly challenged.

Chalmers was succeeded as Principal by William Cunningham, who also held the chair of Church History. Cunningham would lead the College for the next fourteen years, a time of diminishing resources and often bitter controversy. He was a formidable man – large, powerfully built, possessing a body of considerable knowledge, a sharp and logical mind, decided convictions and an abiding sense of self-righteousness. His theological beliefs consisted of a narrow and rigid scholastic Calvinism, including a belief in predestination. He had an almost pathological hatred for Roman Catholicism and a contempt for Anglicanism.[39] His classes in Church History focused on historical theology and especially theological controversies, while he used history as an apologetic tool for his Calvinist beliefs.[40] He seemed to perceive the Free Church of Scotland as a small bastion of Reformed truth surrounded by the corruption and errors of an expansive Anglicanism and Roman Catholicism, as well as by the dangers of biblical scholarship and infidel philosophy. Despite his strict theological views, many students found him an attractive teacher, with clear and forceful lectures, an ability to arouse student interest and a warm manner in personal contacts. He was a demanding scholar, setting high standards of the amount of reading required for the 'decent and respectable' knowledge of theological literature expected in a minister.[41] His commitment to the study of early Church history won admiration from even so unlikely a figure as John Henry Newman.[42] He had a deep sense of duty both to New College and to the Presbyterian ideal of a learned clergy.[43] But he also lacked the broad-minded vision of Chalmers and his enthusiasm for the idea of a free university.

[39] Rainy and Mackenzie (1871), 493–9.
[40] *Ibid.*, 226–33; Riesen (1979), 140–1.
[41] Rainy and Mackenzie (1871), 223–4; Dods, d.1935 (1910), 73–5.
[42] Barbour (1923), 195.
[43] Cunningham (1848), 9–14.

THE COLLEGES CONTROVERSY

Shortly after Chalmers' death and Cunningham's appointment as Principal of New College, the Free Church leadership was bitterly divided by what became known as the Colleges controversy.[44] At the Disruption, there had been no consensus in the Free Church that resources should be concentrated on only one college at Edinburgh. In its first report in May 1843, the Education Committee had raised the prospect of at least three colleges, in Edinburgh, Aberdeen and Glasgow. In October 1845, a professor was appointed in Aberdeen to teach theology to students preparing for the Free Church ministry, although the Aberdeen students were also required to complete their final year of study at the Edinburgh college. By the session 1847–8, there were thirty-one theological students at Aberdeen.[45] During Chalmers' last years, there had been general agreement that the development of a theological hall at Aberdeen, and perhaps at Glasgow, would come only after the college at Edinburgh had been fully established. After Chalmers' death in 1847, however, there were calls in the north and west of Scotland for the additional halls to be established immediately. Motions to this effect were brought before the General Assembly of May 1848, where there was a long and acrimonious debate.[46] Cunningham vehemently opposed the proposals for developing additional colleges. In the event, he and his supporters gained a narrow victory in the debate, but at the cost of personal estrangements, including a break between the two Free Church leaders, Cunningham and Candlish. The defeated party, moreover, did not accept the vote of 1848 as a decisive expression of the will of the Church, and they continued to campaign for the additional colleges.

The supporters of college extension argued against what they perceived as an excessive and dangerous centralisation of Free Church educational provision in Edinburgh, which would give too much influence to the New College professors and have the effect of excluding many promising candidates for the ministry in the north and west of the country who were unable to afford the cost of moving to Edinburgh for the academic session. As a national Church, it was incumbent on the Free Church to respect the aspirations of the different regions,

[44] For a full discussion of the Colleges controversy, see Rainy and Mackenzie (1871), 330–79.
[45] Gray (1850), 18.
[46] *Proceedings . . . Free Church, 1848*, 111–59.

recognising that Aberdeen and Glasgow had long traditions of theological education. 'Are the people of the Free Church', asked one critic, 'to have their choice of ministers so narrowed that there shall be only one [type] turned out of the Edinburgh manufactory, made to order?'[47] For Cunningham and his supporters, however, college extension threatened the efforts to create a fully-equipped theological college, with a full complement of professors and a comprehensive curriculum. New College, they argued, was already struggling to meet the heavy costs of the building and the new chairs. Diffusion of resources among three colleges would force New College to curtail its development. It was significant that Cunningham based his arguments on New College as a theological college and seemed now to accept that the university was beyond the resources of the Free Church. Cunningham carried on the struggle to halt both the further development of the Aberdeen college and the plans for a Glasgow college, but with diminishing success. Supporters of the Aberdeen college appointed additional professors and erected a building by 1849.[48] There was little will in the general Assembly to abolish what had already been created at Aberdeen or to discourage the efforts in Glasgow that led to the founding in 1856 of what much later became known as Trinity College.[49]

INAUGURATION OF THE NEW BUILDING

In 1850, while the Colleges controversy continued to simmer, the New College students and professors finally moved into the Playfair buildings on the Mound in Edinburgh. For the first time, the College had the space it needed to put its curricular plans into full operation, as well as to house adequately the library and the natural history museum. To mark the inauguration of the new buildings, Cunningham and the other New College professors presented a series of public lectures on 6–8 November 1850. Each professor introduced his discipline and his methods of instruction, and the lectures were subsequently published together in a volume.[50] Three themes seem to emerge from these lectures. The first is the importance given to the study of the Old and New Testament in their original languages. The approach to the

---

[47] Gibson, J. (1850), 21.
[48] Candlish (1849), 10–11.
[49] Mechie (1956), 13–16.
[50] Cunningham (1851).

Scriptures was, to be sure, a conservative one, embracing belief in the direct verbal inspiration and infallibility of every text.[51] At the same time, however, the professors insisted upon a careful and methodical study of the Bible, which had been lacking in the Scottish theological halls prior to the Disruption. This emphasis on biblical exegesis would remain a distinctive feature of New College, and would lead in time to the more advanced critical scholarship of A. B. Davidson and Marcus Dods. Secondly, the addresses convey a picture of a New College which was narrowing its focus to theological study, and turning away from the perception of itself as a university. Cunningham's address as Principal made no mention of the Arts chairs or Arts subjects; he defined New College as a 'theological seminary' with a 'theological curriculum'.[52] The introductory addresses by the three Arts professors were relegated to the end of the proceedings and the back of the volume. Finally, the addresses as a whole reflected the conservative Reformed theology that characterised the Disruption fathers and Cunningham in particular. However, even here, there was a recognition that the Westminster Confession of Faith was neither complete nor infallible, and that the study of theology must be a lifetime pursuit of an ever-receding goal. 'The farther you advance', James Buchanan, the Professor of Systematic Theology, assured his audience, 'the field will be seen still stretching onward before you; the higher you rise, the horizon will seem to widen around you; and never, while your minds are finite, and God infinite, will you exhaust theology.'[53]

A STUDENT'S PERSPECTIVE IN THE 1850s

The unpublished autobiography of one former New College student provides a detailed view of student life in the later 1850s.[54] Alexander Ross came from a farming background in Aberdeenshire, and after a career as a schoolteacher and study at Aberdeen University, he sat the examination for a New College bursary and gained a scholarship worth £15 per annum, enabling him to matriculate in November 1856. With the other students, he paid a general fee of between £4 and £5 to John Laing, the New College Librarian, which covered his College costs, including class fees, and in return he received his general admission

---

[51] Cheyne (1983), 7–9; Drummond and Bulloch (1975), 251–2.
[52] Cunningham (1851), 39–58.
[53] *Ibid.*, 100.
[54] MacMillan (1988).

ticket. As required, Ross followed the defined curriculum. During his first year, he enrolled in James Bannerman's junior course on Apologetics and Practical Theology, and John Fleming's course on Natural Science. He should have also taken John Duncan's junior course in Hebrew and Old Testament, but because he had serious deficiencies in Hebrew, he was required to take the foundation Hebrew course, which was taught at an early morning hour by Theodore Meyer, a converted German Jew. In his second year, he enrolled in James Buchanan's junior course in Systematic Theology, William Cunningham's junior Church History, Duncan's junior Hebrew and Old Testament, George Smeaton's junior New Testament and a course on elocution, taught by a Mr Calvert. He also joined the Theological Society, though he was unhappy with the meetings, as he felt some students called attention to themselves 'by borrowing from German writers of doubtful character, and also speaking nonsense, with disregard to Scripture and common sense'. In his third session, he completed Buchanan's senior Systematic Theology, Cunningham's senior Church History, and Duncan's senior Hebrew and Old Testament. Finally, in his fourth session, he completed Bannerman's senior Apologetics and Practical Theology, Smeaton's senior New Testament, while he repeated Cunningham's Church History. During the four years, he completed six long essays, and a number of shorter essays, and at the close of his final session he sat for thirteen examination papers – four in Theology, two in Church History, two in Biblical exegesis, two in Greek, one in Latin, one in Hebrew and one in Natural Science.

Ross was conservative in his theology, and among his professors he not surprisingly gravitated to Cunningham, claiming that he learned more from Cunningham 'than from all the professors put together'. He admitted that John Duncan was a 'very great scholar and a deeply experienced Christian', but added that he was a man of extreme mood swings and 'could not be said to have taught us Hebrew'. Buchanan's Systematic Theology courses he liked because of their comprehensive and conservative character, though he acknowledged that Buchanan, a popular preacher, tended to be diffuse. He did not care for George Smeaton's New Testament courses, as he felt Smeaton was overly influenced by German critical scholarship. 'Scotchmen', Ross observed, 'should be able to produce theology directly from the Scriptures and their own experience and observation, without spending their time and energies on tomes of admittedly questionable character.' He found Fleming's Natural Science course useful, especially for its training in

Baconian scientific method. '"First catch your hare and then proceed to make your soup", and such like common sayings he repeated to impress on us the necessity of discovering the facts, before forming our theories.' Ross completed his course in 1860, and then emigrated to Canada, where he had a long and rewarding career as a Presbyterian minister. He had received a thorough theological education, which reflected the New College roots in both the Scottish common-sense tradition and the evangelical biblical tradition. On the whole, his conservative theological leanings had been confirmed and strengthened by his experiences. At the same time, however, it is significant that this conservative student was also uncomfortable with some of what he found and that advanced biblical scholarship from the continent was making its way into New College student societies and even some courses.

THE PASSING OF THE DISRUPTION FATHERS

In the mid-1850s, the vision of New College as the beginning of a great free Christian university finally came to an end. Two factors in particular lay behind this. The first was the Colleges controversy. As the colleges developed at Aberdeen and Glasgow, there was a growing feeling in the Free Church that the three colleges should be treated equally, and should offer approximately the same academic programme. As the Free Church could not afford to build and maintain three universities, it seemed sensible to concentrate on theological education at the three sites. As we have seen, Cunningham seemed to have taken this view from the beginning of the controversy. Secondly, in 1853 parliament abolished religious tests for non-theological chairs in the Scottish universities. Thus, there was no longer a need to provide separate chairs for Free Church Arts professors while the Free Church could now safely permit their students to take Arts courses in one of the Scottish universities.[55] Patrick MacDougall, the New College Professor of Moral Philosophy, had been presented by the Town Council to the chair of Moral Philosophy of the University of Edinburgh in 1850, and with the abolition of the religious test he was able to take up the post in 1853.[56] By 1856, Alexander Campbell Fraser, the New College professor of Logic, was having difficulties with Cunningham and the theological conservatives at New College, and he recognised

[55] Watt, 29.
[56] *Ibid.*; Davie (1961), 289–90.

that the prospects for a 'Free University' on the Mound had ended. He seemed relieved that year to resign his New College post on being appointed to the University chair of Logic and Metaphysics.[57] Neither MacDougall nor Campbell Fraser was replaced and their chairs lapsed. Following the death of John Fleming in November 1857, no appointment was made for a number of years to his chair of Natural Science, though provision was made for instruction in this subject through part-time lecturers. Eventually, in 1864, John Duns was appointed permanent lecturer in Natural Science and in 1869 the chair was revived, largely because, unlike the other Arts subjects, Natural Science was viewed as an integral part of the theological curriculum.[58]

William Cunningham died in December 1861, at the age of 57, still carrying the wounds of the Colleges controversy and still convinced that the Free Church had made a serious error in not concentrating its resources on the development of New College.[59] His fourteen years as Principal had seen New College narrow its mission to theological education, and move in conservative Calvinist directions. They had been years of controversy and polemic, including much virulent anti-Catholicism. None the less, under Cunningham's leadership, New College was also firmly established and housed in a majestic new building on the Mound. The College was reaping the benefits of its curriculum, with its five core departments. This curriculum provided students with a comprehensive theological education and contributed to a camaraderie among the staff based on a shared sense of mission.[60] The library was growing in its holdings, with a number of valuable acquisitions. New College student numbers had fallen during the later 1850s, in part as a result of the competition from Aberdeen and Glasgow and in part because of the demise of the Arts subjects, yet they remained respectable, averaging well over a hundred per year.

Cunningham's death marked the end of the first phase of the history of New College, overshadowed by the Disruption controversy and dominated by the Disruption fathers. In the years following his death, younger liberal theological voices began to be heard. These younger scholars devoted less effort to confronting threats to conservative Reformed theology and biblical literalism, and showed more concern for movements of Christian unity and for the reconciliation of theology

[57] Fraser, A. C. (1905), 156–64.
[58] Watt, 53–6; *Proceedings . . . Free Church, 1852*, 115.
[59] Rainy and Mackenzie (1871), 374–5.
[60] Knight (1903), 112–13.

and modern thought. Robert Candlish, a Disruption father and minister of Free St George's in Edinburgh, succeeded Cunningham as Principal of New College, but he did not take a teaching post. Heavily burdened with his responsibilities as a city pastor and a leading figure in the Church courts, Candlish left New College to be run by its professors. In 1862, the young liberal clergyman, Robert Rainy, was appointed to Cunningham's vacant chair of Church History. By 1863, he was taking a leading role in a campaign for Church reunion in Scotland, while he worked for a reconciliation of theology and the new ideas of biological evolution.[61] In 1858, recognising that the orthodox and deeply pious John Duncan was nevertheless impossible as a teacher of Hebrew, the New College authorities had appointed the brilliant young Old Testament scholar, A. B. Davidson, as tutor and assistant in Hebrew. In 1862, Davidson had published his *Commentary on Job*, hailed as 'the first really scientific commentary on the Old Testament in the English language', and in 1863 he was appointed Professor of Old Testament Language and Literature.[62] From this position, he introduced advances in higher criticism to his New College students, among them a young William Robertson Smith. In 1868, W. G. Blaikie succeeded Bannerman as Professor of Apologetics and Practical Theology. A moderate liberal in his social views, Blaikie campaigned for improvements in working-class housing and helped prepare students to engage with the new ideas of the 'social gospel'.[63] Under the influence of these younger men, New College increasingly opened up to continental and English scholarship, embracing new theological perspectives while at the same time preserving the distinctively Scottish biblical emphasis and common-sense tradition. The vision of the free university had faded, but a great centre for theological enquiry emerged. A product of religious conflict, New College survived to become a forum for more liberal Christian voices, working for Church union and a reconciliation of religious and secular scholarship. The achievements of these later decades, however, were built on the firm foundations laid down in the 1840s and 1850s.

---

[61] Simpson (1909), I, 148–80, 285–8.
[62] Brown, D. (1872), 355-7, 373–6, 390–2; Innes (1902), 23–4.
[63] Cheyne (1983), 119–22.

PART II

Edinburgh Divinity, from Disruption
to Diversity

Chapter 3

Hebrew and Old Testament

Graeme Auld

1812 OVERTURE

THERE WERE always others involved; but for three-quarters of the period under review the better records concern the holders of two chairs, the courses they taught, and the leadership they offered. It is with Alexander Brunton (1722–1854) that our tale of academic Hebrew in Edinburgh must start. Minister of the city's Tron Kirk from 1809 until his death, he first lost to the 'Shepherd Boy who rose to be the most eminent Linguist and Oriental Scholar of his day' (so the monument in Greyfriars Kirkyard) in the competition for the chair of (Hebrew and) Oriental Languages in 1812. But, on the tragically early death of the brilliant and largely self-taught Alexander Murray (hastened, it appears, by the strain of only six months' lecturing), Brunton became his successor, despite lingering questions over his competence in Oriental Languages. Like many academics, he attempted to dispel these doubts by publishing early in his career: in his case, *Extracts from the Old Testament, with outlines of Hebrew and Chaldee Grammar* (1814) and *Outlines of Persian Grammar* (1822). His other publications were *Sermons and Lectures* (1818), and *Forms for Public Worship in the Church of Scotland* (1848). He served as Upper Librarian of the University from 1822 till his death (one of his Orientalist predecessors was responsible for the first alphabetical catalogue), thereby successfully claiming 'the only private house included in the scheme of the then new University buildings'.[1] And his interests beyond university and parish included concern with Heriot's Hospital (now George Heriot's School), and his

[1] Grant (1884), II, 292.

convenorship over thirteen years of the India Mission Committee of the General Assembly of the Church of Scotland.

The Edinburgh University Almanack of 1833 describes his programme:

Each class meets for five days in the week, one hour a-day: the junior Class at Ten o'clock, and the advanced Class at Twelve o'clock.

The ordinary business of the junior Class is the detail of the Hebrew Grammar; and the translation of parts of the Historical Books of the Old Testament, and of a considerable portion of the Psalms.

The advanced Class read large portions of the Prophetical Books, and all the Chaldee part of the Old Testament. They acquire also the elements of Syriac and Persian. A few lectures are given on Biblical Criticism, and Jewish Antiquities; and many illustrations of both are mingled with the ordinary business.

For most of his career, there were at Edinburgh still only the three Professorships of Theology as established during the seventeenth century – Divinity (1620), Hebrew and Oriental Languages (1642), and Ecclesiastical History (1694). Brunton was joined in this small Faculty of three by Thomas Chalmers (Divinity) in 1825, and by David Welsh (Ecclesiastical History) in 1831. It fell to them jointly to implement in 1835–7 the reform of the B.D., to make the degree 'an instrument for awakening and strengthening in their pupils a desire for professional study . . . a Degree based upon such examination as may make it credible alike to the receiver and to the University which confers it'. The subjects for examination for the revised degree included the following in 1837 under Oriental Languages:

1. Translation and Analysis of the Hebrew Psalter, and of the Septuagint Version of the Psalter, *ad aperturam*.

2. Translation of all the Chaldee passages of Old Testament, and of the Septuagint Version of them, *ad aperturam*.

3. On Hellenistic Greek; and the most prominent examples of it in St Matthew's Gospel.

Brunton was already Dean of Divinity in 1837, when the first available Faculty minute book begins. He notes that 'the Principal [Lee] was received as a member of the Faculty' (3 February 1841). His Faculty minute for Session 1843–4 (not more precisely dated) reads: 'There was no quorum of the Faculty. Drs Chalmers and Welsh had left the Church. The Principal was, during this session doing the work of both. In [blank] he was received by the Senatus as Professor of Theology;

and Dr Robertson as professor of Church History.' There follow a short minute dated December 1844, and a full minute of 9 January 1845. Finally, dated 30 October 1845, there are seven lines in a very bad hand by Brunton – and no further entry for over fifteen years (the next is dated 21 January 1861).

The University Commissioners of 1826–30 had proposed the addition of a chair in Biblical Criticism and Antiquities (we have just seen that Brunton was in the habit of giving some lectures on these subjects). Thomas Chalmers had in fact argued in a submission to them that there should be five Divinity chairs. The government of 1841 finally decided to give effect to the Commissioners' proposal; and Robert Candlish was nominated to the new chair. However, the Disruption intervened before he could be presented to the Senatus; and he too 'left the Church'. It was not until January 1847, shortly before Brunton's resignation, that the first holder of this new chair was installed.

HEBREW IN THE UNIVERSITY
AFTER THE DISRUPTION

Fall-out from the Disruption rendered the succession of the Hebrew chair controversial as well. The Town Council now had a Free Church majority, and by 20 votes to 10 elected Charles McDonall, one of their own, over David Liston. The University Senatus refused to induct him, and successfully defended their position in the Court of Session. The Council then elected Liston by a similar majority over a layman, although the Provost had attempted to please all sides by proposing a second chair of Oriental Languages. Liston, who is variously described as having been a medical missionary or an astronomer in India, had no position in Edinburgh other than the chair and 'was depressed by the extremely low salary attached to the Professorship'.[2] The first *University Calendar* was issued for the year 1858–9, the year in which university government was reformed by the Universities of Scotland Act of 1858. Liston had served for a decade or so; and the business of his classes is described as follows:

> JunHeb at 9: Tregelles's Heads of Grammar; 1st 20 chaps of Genesis and 8 or 10 Psalms.

> SenHeb at 10: The Psalms and a Historical Book on alternate weeks. Syriac and the Chaldee of Daniel.

[2] *Ibid.*

In the following year, in place of 'Syriac and the Chaldee of Daniel', the 'extra study' in the Senior Class was Arabic; and in 1863–4, Hindustani was added. He proved quite willing to teach other languages than Hebrew 'if suitably remunerated', and at once added Hindustani to his repertoire.

Liston's successor was David Laird Adams (1880–92), followed briefly by John Dobie (1892–4) until his untimely death in a train crash in Newtonmore. Liston, Adams and Dobie had all studied Arts and Divinity in Edinburgh, each learning Hebrew from his predecessor. Adams published only his introductory address, 'Our Universities and Theological Study'. Yet the *History of the University of Edinburgh 1883–1933* credits him with raising 'the standard of Semitic scholarship in the University' and, with the appointment of an assistant, beginning courses in Syriac and Arabic.[3] As for Dobie, an unfinished work on Ethiopic was published the year after he was killed. Adams and Dobie must have been well esteemed by their colleagues in Arts: the Oriental Languages chair was included within that Faculty in 1888, and was one of the fifteen chairs listed in Arts as reconstituted in 1893 on the foundation of the Faculty of Science.

The next holder of the Hebrew chair, from 1895, had been born in the same year as the short-lived Dobie. Archibald R. S. Kennedy broke the mould of his Edinburgh predecessors in a number of respects. He had studied outside Edinburgh (Arts in Aberdeen, Divinity in Glasgow), and had already held the chair of Oriental Languages in Aberdeen from 1887. He would demit his Edinburgh chair exactly a half-century later, having witnessed the Union of the Churches in 1929, been admitted to the Senate of New College on the last day of June 1930 and, after due Act of Parliament, seen his New College colleagues become fellow University Professors in 1935. He had in fact long been involved in a number of collaborative ventures with New College colleagues. He represented the Church of Scotland at the public dinner to Principal Rainy which rounded off the celebration of New College's jubilee, on 2 November 1900.[4] During the drawn-out dispute between the new United Free Church (of 1900) and the continuing rump of the Free Church over the ownership of New College, the lectures of the UF College were held first in Old College and then at the nearer end of Chambers Street in Heriot-Watt College. From half-way through the First World War, New College and Divinity Faculty classes were held

[3] Turner (1933), 57–8.
[4] Watt, 87.

together for three sessions. This co-operation led to the establishment in 1919–20 of the Postgraduate School in Divinity in collaboration with New College and the Scottish Episcopal College. Kennedy was its prime mover and its Secretary until his retirement – he used his home address in Fountainhall Road. While still in Aberdeen, he had published translations of German grammars of four Semitic languages – Hebrew, Syriac, Assyrian and Arabic. Once in Edinburgh, however, his output was entirely of commentaries on biblical books: Exodus, Leviticus–Numbers, Joshua–Judges, Samuel, and (in his seventieth year) Ruth. As a tribute to his national standing, he was elected the second President of the Society for Old Testament Study, for the year 1920. His forte was very much Hebrew grammar rather than biblical theology; but he was a careful and much-loved teacher.

HEBREW IN THE NEW COLLEGE

No time was lost after the Disruption in establishing a Theological College in Edinburgh for the new Free Church in a house at 80 George Street, until the completion of the new building on the Mound. John Duncan (1796–1870) was the first Professor of Oriental Literature. He had studied Arts and Divinity in Marischal College, Aberdeen. When minister in the Cowcaddens area of Glasgow, he applied in 1839 for the Hebrew chair in that University. Though he failed to secure it, he had been brought to public notice and was awarded the LL.D. by Aberdeen University. He next served as missionary to the Jewish community in Bupadest (1841–3), until called home after the Disruption to the New College chair.

Chalmers' long-held plans for curricular reform had to be held over, and the advertised programme for the opening session of the New College:

Divinity	Revd Dr Chalmers
Divinity and Church History	Revd Dr Welsh
Hebrew (Junior Class and Senior Class)	Revd Dr Duncan

must have closely resembled the provision within the Divinity Hall of the University in the pre-Disruption session. As in the University, so in the College, it was only in Hebrew that both a junior and a senior class were held in the same year: in the other subjects, topics were handled in rotation over a three- or four-year period. This latter pattern was soon changed in New College. Apart from the place of study, the only overt change was Duncan in place of Brunton. And unlike Brunton and his three University successors, Duncan had neither studied nor previously worked in Edinburgh. In the words of one of his successors, he was 'a man of vast linguistic erudition . . . , conservative orthodoxy, and memorable eccentricity. What he imparted to his students was by way of discursive conversation rather than systematic teaching, and by a hermeneutic which owed nothing to critical method.'[5]

'Rabbi' Duncan's introduction to his subject as Professor of Hebrew and Oriental Languages, delivered at the inauguration of the nearly completed New College building on 7 November 1850, was entitled 'The Theology of the Old Testament'. It opened with a strong plea that all who 'desire the office of bishop' should drink 'the healing waters directly from the inspired fountains':

> Save where an oppressed and impoverished state of the church may preclude, it is disgraceful to profess to be an expositor of a book with whose contents one is not intimately acquainted . . . To be at the mercy of commentators is disgraceful ; nor can any one use them with discretion and to due advantage, but he whose own acquirements entitle him to some place among their number.

His successor, A[ndrew] B[ruce] Davidson, had studied Arts in Aberdeen and Divinity in New College. He taught at New College for forty-four years (1858–1902), as Hebrew tutor, Assistant to Professor Duncan, and as Professor. During Duncan's final seven years, he was responsible for the Junior Class, and for the Senior whenever Duncan was not able. His early *Outline of Hebrew Accentuation* (1861) and *Commentary on the Book of Job* (1862) belong to this period as tutor. *An Introductory Hebrew Grammar* of 1874 went through eighteen editions/printings in his lifetime; and the twenty-seventh (edited by James Martin of St Andrews) was published in 1992. He himself revised his *Hebrew Syntax* of 1894 twice (in 1896 and 1901); and its centenary would be celebrated in a fourth thoroughly revised edition by John Gibson, who also shared Davidson's interest in Job.

Davidson was renowned as a stimulating teacher, one who drew students from overseas to Edinburgh. A large number of these students presented a memorial in support of his nomination for the chair. The *College Calendar for the Free Church of Scotland* contains the same description of Davidson's courses towards the end of his long career in 1899–1900 as a quarter-century earlier:

[5] Anderson, G. W. (1974), xv.

The first Hebrew Class is occupied the greater part of the Session with the Grammar, and in reading Historical portions of the Old Testament. Toward the close of the Session, a number of Psalms and some portions of the prophetical literature are also read. This reading is varied by an occasional lecture chiefly on some subject in Introduction . . .

In the Second Hebrew Class, three days are devoted to reading, chiefly in the more difficult parts of the Hebrew Scriptures, hitherto usually the Prophets, and Messianic Psalms, and two days to lecturing. The lectures refer to the general subject of Old Testament Theology, embracing Prophecy and Typology, and are given so as to bear upon the reading, which itself is always more or less exegetical. Occasional essays on questions suggested by the reading are also prescribed.

Hugh Watt's centenary history reports a student petition in 1885 that the classes in Old Testament should be increased to three, from the two of the standard curriculum.[6] Then in 1896 there was a petition to change the timetable of classes to allow foreign students to hear the senior classes of Professors Davidson and Dods in the same academic year. Both petitions appear to have failed, though they succeed in illustrating the man. His other celebrated books, on *Old Testament Prophecy* and *The Theology of the Old Testament*, were both posthumously edited from his lecture notes. Yet despite his renown, his position was debated within the Free Church Presbytery of Edinburgh, though not in the General Assembly, after the William Robertson Smith case; and pamphlets were written against him and his New Testament colleague, Marcus Dods. He had always voted for Smith, but – to the puzzlement of many – never spoke for him in public.

Shortly before the end of Davidson's career, the Union took place in 1900 of the Free Church with the United Presbyterian (UP) Church. New College became the sole Edinburgh college of the resulting United Free Church; and Davidson was joined on the Mound by James Alexander Paterson (1851–1915). He too was an Arts graduate of Aberdeen; after further study in Oxford he studied Divinity in the UP Hall, then became Professor of Hebrew and Old Testament Exegesis there aged only twenty-five. On Davidson's death in 1902, Paterson became sole Professor of Old Testament, and remained at New College until 1913. Suffering perhaps from his position between the giants Davidson and Welch, he was remembered as 'interested only in grammar and Liberal politics'. Though he edited for publication Davidson's lectures on *Old Testament Prophecy*, he gets little credit for that volume.

[6] Watt, 91.

Paterson's successor in 1913, Adam Cleghorn Welch, had been his student in the UP Synod Hall before spending twenty-six popular years in the ministry, in three charges. With A. B. Davidson and A. R. S. Kennedy, Welch was one of the most assiduous authors in our 150-year story. His earlier interests were in Systematic Theology; and his first book, *Anselm and his Work* (1901), had led to the distinction of an honorary Th.D. from Germany in 1909, when Halle was celebrating the Calvin Quatercentenary. During his convenership of the UF Church's College Committee between 1907 and 1911, he urged both the retention of compulsory Hebrew and proper practical training. This and his studies of *The Religion of Israel under the Kingdom* (1912) and *The Story of Joseph* (1913) must have encouraged the appointment of this long-standing minister to the New College chair.

Despite – or because of – his former teacher's reputation, he set out immediately to reform the Hebrew teaching. 'Short experience has already proved the need for different arrangements, especially for the work of the Junior Class. Some of the men have practically no knowledge of Hebrew at all . . . In these circumstances it is impossible to escape from the need for going through the entire Grammar.' Two entries in the minutes of New College Senate leave this teacher wondering whether Welch was a soft- or a hard-hearted examiner. Of one re-examination in June 1924, it is reported 'that he had passed with 35%'. On the other hand, we learn of two miscreants in March 1930 that, 'on the special work set, both had obtained a pass-mark, but neither, a standard adequate to make up for their previous deficiency. The cases were therefore deferred to the close of the short summer term.'

The page of the *College Calendar* quoted above was to remain unchanged up to 1922–3. It is passionate in the expression of its aims:

> The [Senior] students read in class a section from one of the Prose Books, another from one of the Pre-Exile Prophets, and a third from the Psalter. In this way they are introduced to the most significant period of Hebrew religion, when the great forces and ideals of the faith came to clearest expression. Opportunity is thus taken, both in the running commentary given in the class and in discussion of questions arising from the sections read, to point out where the great lines of division emerge, and where it is important for students to come to clearness in their own views.

By the second half of his career, from 1923, Welch was contributing one of the most succinct outlines in the *Calendar* to his courses, now entitled 'Old Testament Language, Literature and Theology':

During the first term the Hebrew Grammar, for which Dr. MacFadyen's Edition of Davidson's Grammar is used.

During the second term the Grammar and Syntax with reading in the Historical Books of the Old Testament.

During the third term the prophetical books or the Psalter are read, and on two or three days in each week lectures are given on the Course of Hebrew history and the development of the religion.

During the fourth term the development of the religion is continued for three days and lectures on Old Testament Theology proper are given on two days of each week.

He was quite as committed to introducing his students to the contents of the Old Testament as to improving their Hebrew, and they were devoted to him: it was said that 'every lecture by Welch was a religious experience'. His lecture on Saul, in the posthumously edited *Kings and Prophets of Israel*, is particularly commended by the editor. He was apparently the only Old Testament Professor ever to be elected President of the New College Union. Though he retired from his chair in 1934 – the year of his Presidency of the Society for Old Testament Study – he continued to teach for a further session, and to produce new work for longer. His last book, *The Work of the Chronicler* (1939), was the text of his Schweich Lectures in the British Academy the previous year. Typical of his relationships, he sent a copy to D. M. G. Stalker: 'the latest and last production of mine, to one of the last of my students'.

PROFESSORIAL CHAIN RE-LINKED – AND BROKEN

Norman Walker Porteous (1898–) was to occupy the chairs of both his distinguished Edinburgh mentors in Hebrew and Old Testament. He had begun Hebrew with A. R. S. Kennedy while studying Classics in the Faculty of Arts; and was then taught by Welch when a student of Divinity at New College. Welch later sent Porteous to Berlin to study with Hugo Gressmann, as 'the most open-minded of the Germans'; but Gressmann died in Chicago in early 1927 while lecturing in the United States. Berlin remained Porteous's first German port of call, where he worked instead with *Alttestamentler* Sellin, before proceeding to Tübingen and Münster, where he took more interest in Karl Barth. Gressmann had described this new theology as 'not Christian, or at best half-Christian . . . derived from 4th Ezra, and characteristic of a period of collapse and inflation'. Whether, had Welch's choice of

61

mentor survived to teach Porteous, he would have been able to describe himself as the 'first English-speaking student of Karl Barth' is another matter. Suffice it to say that his period in Germany left the young Scot, like Welch before him, with quite as strong an interest in Systematic Theology as in Hebrew and Old Testament.

After two years in the parish of Crossgates in Fife, Norman Porteous' first academic appointment was to the chair of Hebrew in St Andrews in 1931–5. From there he was called to Edinburgh in 1934 to succeed Welch in the chair of Old Testament Literature, Language and Theology. The incorporation of the New College chairs into the Faculty of Divinity was not yet complete. Since he held a regius chair in St Andrews, he did not take up the call till the due Act was passed in the following year. Welch had been lecturing alongside Kennedy in Old College since 1931, and continued two days a week in the year after his official retirement. The *Calendar* from 1931 to 1937 notes that Junior Old Testament was taught by Kennedy at 10 a.m. and the Senior by Welch at 9 a.m. Two Church History classes were taught at the same hours in Old College. Only from 1937–8 was it announced that all classes would meet in New College. Old Testament classes met for the next thirty-five years in the two rooms above the Common Hall – now combined as 'Room 101'. Kennedy transferred with Porteous to New College just before his death. Before the Union, Welch (and presumably his predecessors) had taught in the ground-floor room to the left of the old entrance, the space occupied by the current foyer.

In 1935, Porteous was one of a party of fourteen members of the Society for Old Testament Study who travelled to Göttingen in response to an appeal by their German colleagues for consultations about the growing crisis in their land. On Kennedy's retirement two years later (at the ripe age of 78), Porteous moved to the ancient chair of Hebrew and Semitic Languages, which he occupied until 1968. He was president of the Society for Old Testament Study in 1954. In 1952 he edited for publication Adam Welch's *Kings and Prophets of Israel*; and in 1964 G. S. Gunn's *This Gospel of the Kingdom: Dilemmas in Evangelism*. He seems to have inherited from Welch an interest in the Book of Daniel; and a commentary on that book commissioned by the German series Das Alte Testament Deutsch was published in 1962. It was then issued in English in the Old Testament Library in 1965 (revised and extended editions were to follow in 1978, 1979). A volume of his essays, *Living the Mystery*, appeared in 1967. Not only did he hold first the one and then the other academic chair in his field, but in his final four years as

Professor (1964–8) he was Dean of the Faculty and Principal of New College – uniquely fitted for that role, having acted as Secretary to the Faculty for the previous eighteen years. He was assiduous in promoting the welfare of students of College and Faculty. Yet the writer remembers his brisk response to a protest about the quality of the College lunches: 'Professor Burleigh and I' (surely an example of Hebrew inclusiveness by pairing opposites) 'have been eating them for thirty years – and look at us!' Typical of his wider theological interests, he chose for his inaugural lecture in 1964 the subject 'Theology in Church and University'.

Porteous was succeeded in 1937 in the formerly New College Old Testament chair by Oliver Shaw Rankin. Rankin was thirteen years his senior, and had studied Divinity as well as Arts in the University of Edinburgh (and so had also been a pupil of Kennedy). He came to the chair after twenty-five years in the parish of Sorbie in Galloway, and he was Porteous's very congenial colleague until his death in 1954. While many others of the professors under discussion had been briefly in parish or missionary positions, only Rankin and Welch served so long. Rankin had given the Kerr Lectures in 1933–6; and these were published in the year of his death as *Israel's Wisdom Literature*. His other major publication was a posthumous one in 1956, when Edinburgh University Press brought out his *Jewish Religious Polemic of Early and Later Centuries*.

James Barr (1922–) was to hold the Old Testament chair for only five years (1956–61). A graduate of Edinburgh in both Arts and Divinity, he served the church first – like 'Rabbi' Duncan – in a Jewish environment: in Barr's case in the Church of Scotland centre in Tiberias in the recently independent state of Israel. After two years there, he was Professor of Old Testament for a similar period in Montreal, before returning to Edinburgh. He left Edinburgh in the year his influential *Semantics of Biblical Language* was published, and his work on *Biblical Words for Time* (1962) was in preparation. Barr was the first and only of the Professors in this story ever to move from Edinburgh to a chair in another institution – first in Princeton, then Manchester, Oxford and Vanderbilt. His *alma mater* recognised his distinction with an Honorary D.D. during the 1983 celebration of the University's quatercentenary; and he returned in 1991 to deliver the Gifford Lectures, published in 1993 as *Biblical Faith and Natural Theology*.

Barr's replacement in 1962 was an influential scholar already well-established in an academic career. George Wishart Anderson, a

Methodist minister, was also the first non-Presbyterian to be appointed to any of the Edinburgh Divinity chairs. He had studied Arts in St Andrews and Divinity in Cambridge, gone to Lund in Sweden for his postgraduate studies, lectured in Birmingham and St Andrews, and held a chair in Durham (1958–62), before coming to the Edinburgh Old Testament chair in his fiftieth year. At Leiden in 1950, he had been one of the founder editors of *Vetus Testamentum*. He held several offices in the Society for Old Testament Study: on arrival in Edinburgh, he was in the midst of a ten-year stint as Editor of its *Book List* (1957–66); he was its President in 1963, and its Foreign Secretary for a decade (1964–74). In 1972, he had become the first Edinburgh divine to be elected to a Fellowship of the British Academy, and in 1974, he presided in Edinburgh over the triennial Congress of the International Organisation for the Study of the Old Testament, having been secretary of that organisation during 1953–71. His Presidential Address he devoted to 'Two Scottish Semitists', and to a neat demonstration that the Isaianic motto ('he that believeth shall not be in haste'), adopted by Robertson Smith, was equally appropriate for his teacher, A. B. Davidson. A year before Porteous' retirement, the Faculty voted to combine the two Old Testament chairs into a single chair called Hebrew and Old Testament Studies, which Anderson occupied till his retirement. Whether orally or in writing, he was a master of words. Generations of students in many countries and in several languages were nurtured on two successful handbooks. *A Critical Introduction to the Old Testament* was first published in 1959, with a second and lightly supplemented edition as recently as 1994. And *The History and Religion of Israel* followed in 1966. He was also a very lively lecturer: Tom Bogle was to record appreciatively in *New College Bulletin* that he spent Saturday afternoons 'writing up old notes from GWA and calling them a sermon'.[7] Senior B.D. students and postgraduates particularly appreciated the introduction to deep and wide-ranging scholarship in his Psalms seminars on Saturdays from 10 to 12 at 51 Fountainhall Road. He chose the Psalms when invited to deliver the Speaker's Lectures in Oxford. He chaired the Faculty Research (later Postgraduate Studies) Committee from 1964 to 1969, and served as Curator of New College Library (1971–5) and Convener of the University Library Committee (1972–5).

As we noted at the outset, there have always been other teachers involved in this field, as tutors, assistants and colleagues – and two of

[7] *NCB* 8 (1978), 3.

them, latterly, holders of personal chairs. But, before chronicling them, we should underscore that an ancient line within Edinburgh University came to an end with George Anderson's retirement. He was not – or was not straightforwardly – replaced; and the chair of Hebrew and Old Testament Studies he held, direct successor to the chair established in 1642, has been vacant since 1982.

THEY ALSO TAUGHT

The new chair of Biblical Criticism and Antiquities in the Divinity Faculty, to which Candlish had been called just before the Disruption, promoted to a new specialism one of the responsibilities of the Professor of Hebrew. Its first two holders were Robert Lee (1847–68) and Archibald Hamilton Charteris (1868–98); and each was to serve for a period as Dean (1861–8 and 1875–84). Charteris was also a notable churchman: prominent in the development of the social work of the Church of Scotland, Chaplain to the Queen, Moderator of the General Assembly. In 1858–9, Lee taught Biblical Criticism and Antiquities ('now in curriculum required of Church of Scotland students in Divinity') in two courses in alternate sessions: the Old Testament work included (*a*) Canon of OT; Modern efforts to improve the Hebrew text; Principal Versions, especially Septuagint, Vulgate, Targum; Textual Criticism; History of Printed editions; and (*b*) 'Hermeneutics, or, Principles of Interpretation, as applicable to Sacred Scriptures'. In summary, Charteris described his course as 'Introduction to the Old Testament and Professor Robertson's "Early Religion of Israel"'.

Their remit must have lightened the load of Brunton's successors in the Hebrew chair or, alternatively, freed them for greater attention to Oriental Languages. However, from 1899, John Patrick, the third holder of the chair, was teaching only New Testament. Accordingly, while the description in the *University Calendar* of Kennedy's Senior Class had earlier included the sentence, 'Discussion of Critical and Historical questions associated with the Books read', only from 1900–1 do we read instead: 'A Course of Lectures, extending over two Sessions, on Old Testament Introduction (including History of the Canon, Text and Versions).' Yet a further reduction in load, this time in favour of Kennedy, came in 1912 with the creation of an Arts Lectureship in Arabic. The Revd Richard Bell was to hold this position until 1946, when he was replaced by W. Montgomery Watt who was successively Lecturer, Reader and Professor of the language. Kennedy's other long-term associate was the Revd Dr Duncan Cameron. He had published in 1919 *A First Hebrew Reader*, and demitted his Leith charge in 1920 on appointment as Director of Religious Instruction in the Edinburgh Training College. Norman Porteous's brother remembered him as 'the only decent lecturer in Moray House'. In addition to his position of responsibility there, he was also long-term 'assistant' to the Professor of Hebrew – possibly from 1920 and certainly from 1926, when he is named in the *University Calendar*, right until 1946.

As for New College, Watt's centenary history lists forty-five Hebrew Tutors between the first session in the new building (1851) and 1914.[8] Most served for only one year, their final year of study in the College. And most were to become ministers or missionaries. Some of them followed the example of the first Hebrew Professor ('Rabbi' Duncan) in mission to the Jews (S. H. Semple in Tiberias and Safad, and Robert MacGregor in Constantinople). The first and longest-serving, Theodore Meyer (1851–8), had been born of Jewish parents in Mecklenburg. His successor, A. B. Davidson, was also the next longest-serving. And William Robertson Smith (1869–70) and John Skinner (1878–9) were the only others to become Professors in the subject: Smith in the Free Church College in Aberdeen, and then Cambridge (where he became Professor of Arabic, not Hebrew); Skinner in Westminster College, Cambridge. Skinner would return to New College over forty years later to give the 1920 Cunningham lectures, published as *Prophecy and Religion* (1922). However, James Kennedy was to give long service to the College: tutor in 1867–8, then Assistant Librarian 1873–80, and Librarian for over forty years from 1880 to 1922, he published an *Introduction to Biblical Hebrew* and *Studies in Hebrew Synonyms*. Being Hebrew Tutor was not the only route for a New College student to a chair – the most distinguished student of A. B. Davidson not on the list was George Adam Smith, to be Professor in the Free Church College in Glasgow and Principal of the University of Aberdeen.

David Stalker, already mentioned as one of Welch's last students, returned as assistant in succession to Cameron from 1946 till 1948. In that year, he was appointed to a new Lectureship in Biblical Studies in the Faculty of Arts, where he remained until his retirement in 1979. He put generations of students in his debt by translating two of Gerhard von Rad's works: *Studies in Deuteronomy* (1953), and then the large-scale *Old Testament Theology* (1962, 1965). In 1966, he accepted an

---

[8] Watt, 257–8.

invitation to membership of the Faculty of Divinity. J. G. S. S. Thomson followed him as Assistant from 1950 to 1956, when he went to be Professor of Old Testament in Columbia Seminary in the USA; and the Estonian Arnold A. Anderson in 1956–8, before his move to a lectureship in Manchester.

Ronald E. Clements was appointed to an Assistant Lectureship in Hebrew and Oriental Languages in 1959, and promoted to a full Lectureship in 1964. He was a Baptist, who had studied at Spurgeon's College, then in Cambridge, and finally in Sheffield with F. F. Bruce. His Edinburgh years saw the publication of two influential volumes in the Studies in Biblical Theology series: his *Prophecy and Covenant* (1965) and *Abraham and David* (1967). A further volume prepared in Edinburgh would appear in 1968 – *God's Chosen People*, on the theology of Deuteronomy – together with an essay in *Eucharistic Theology, Then and Now*. In 1967 he moved to a Lectureship in Cambridge, and thence to the Samuel Davidson chair in King's College, London.

EXPANSION AND DIVERSITY

The 1960s were a period of change in the British universities, and this was reflected at New College. John Gibson took up a newly created Lectureship at the same time as Barr's professorial successor was installed. Himself a son of the Scottish manse, Gibson studied Arts and Divinity in Glasgow and took his doctorate in Oxford and then spent three years as parish minister in Aberdeenshire before his Edinburgh appointment. He was to spend the rest of his career in New College, promoted Reader in 1973, and appointed to a Personal Chair in 1987. Only Kennedy, in our story so far, had studied (Divinity) in Glasgow; however, that was no inauspicious precedent. For each of his four main publishing ventures, Gibson inherited the mantle of a well-known predecessor, and wore it with independent flair. His three volumes on Hebrew, Aramaic, and Phoenician inscriptions replaced the *Syrian Semitic Inscriptions* by Cook. *Canaanite Myths and Legends* was a substantial re-edition of the pioneering work of his Oxford teacher, Sir Godfrey Driver. The Daily Study Bible (Old Testament) which he edited, contributing two volumes on Genesis himself and one on his beloved Job, followed the success of William Barclay's New Testament series. And his wholesale rewriting of A. B. Davidson's volume on Hebrew Syntax underscored his affinity with Kennedy as well. He was President of the Society for Old Testament Study for 1994, the year of his retirement.

Throughout most of the period we are reviewing, indeed until the late 1960s, the principal business of the Department was to introduce students of Christian theology to critical study of the Old Testament Scriptures with study of Hebrew fully integral to the business. Lectures on Introduction took up half of the programme of the Junior or First Year class, and on Old Testament Theology of the Senior or Second Level course. For over thirty years from the union of College and Faculty, the Professor of Hebrew taught the Junior class and his Old Testament colleague the Senior; and a large part of their business was to coax minimal Hebrew competence into students who, though demonstrably able in other subjects, would otherwise have had to complete their studies without a B.D. degree.

On Clements' departure for Cambridge in 1967, Robert Davidson had moved to Edinburgh. He was a graduate of St Andrews in both Arts and Divinity and had lectured in Biblical Studies (Arts) in Aberdeen and in Old Testament in St Andrews. Known throughout his career as a popular and effective Hebrew teacher, he did much to keep that language not just alive but a viable option when biblical Hebrew and Greek were made optional for B.D. study soon after his arrival. He was also known in Edinburgh for his sympathetic teaching of Jeremiah. He was at work on a commentary on *Genesis 1–11* (1973) when he was appointed to the chair of Old Testament Language and Literature in Glasgow.

We have already noted that, on Porteous' retirement in 1968, the two chairs had been combined. The number of staff in the Department was maintained at four by the appointment of a third lecturer, Peter Hayman, fresh from study in Durham (B.A. in Theology and Ph.D. in Syriac studies). On Davidson's appointment to the Old Testament chair in Glasgow in 1972, Hayman took over his energetic and popular role as introductory Hebrew teacher, and lavished much care on the development of teaching methods. His doctoral thesis, published in 1973, had translated and introduced the Syriac version of a dialogue between a Christian and a Jew. He then edited Numbers for the authoritative Leiden edition of the (Syriac) Peshitta version of the Old Testament. Peter Hayman was not the first to teach courses in Judaism within the new undergraduate degree in Religious Studies which was inaugurated alongside the B.D. within the Faculty in 1969 – that was Dr Bernard Jackson, an expert in Jewish and also ancient near-eastern

Law, and a lecturer in the Faculty of Law. But Peter Hayman was single-handedly responsible, from Jackson's departure from the University in 1976, for the modern development of Jewish Studies alongside the traditional concerns of the Department in Hebrew and Semitic languages and the study of the Old Testament. He developed popular Honours courses in Judaism in the Graeco–Roman period and Modern Judaism; and promises a substantial edition of the classic Jewish mystical text, *Book of Creation*. Promoted Senior Lecturer in 1984, and elected Head of Department in 1991, he has played a very significant role in the organisation of Department and Faculty.

Graeme Auld was appointed to succeed Davidson. After Arts in Aberdeen and Divinity in Edinburgh he had begun research towards his doctorate with years in Jerusalem and Germany and back in Edinburgh before being appointed Assistant Director of the British School of Archaeology in Jerusalem (1969–72). Awarded a D.Litt. by Aberdeen on the basis of his specialism in relating textual to literary study of the Former Prophets of the Hebrew Bible (what you can learn about Joshua–Kings in Hebrew by reading them in the old Greek Bible), he was appointed to a Personal Chair of Hebrew Bible in 1995. He contributed two volumes to the Daily Study Bible, edited by John Gibson; an undergraduate guide to *Amos*; and he prepared with a Dutch archaeological colleague *Jerusalem to 200 BCE*. Like Anderson before him, he was Editor (1987–92) of the SOTS *Book List*; and was Secretary of the British School of Archaeology in Jerusalem in the same period (1986–93). Within the Faculty he was Associate Dean (1981–5), Postgraduate Associate Dean (1988–92), and Dean (1993–6).

On George Anderson's retirement, an establishment which had stood at four for twenty years was reduced to three, with John Gibson as Head of Department. In the ensuing years, the Department's work was supported by the appointment of John Ashton to a lectureship in both biblical Departments in 1984–5, before his appointment to lecture in New Testament in Oxford, and by a portion of the time of Peter Cameron who was the Meldrum Lecturer with the New Testament Department during 1988–90. Then the transfer in 1988 of the two-man Department of the Principles of Religion in Glasgow University to the Department of Theology and Religious Studies within the Divinity Faculty in Edinburgh brought to New College Nick Wyatt with his wide-ranging interests in Ugaritic and Ancient Canaanite and Egyptian religion, and much else beyond. Under a 1989 scheme to encourage the appointment of younger scholars in the British universities, Iain Provan became a fourth full-time colleague. He had studied Arts in Glasgow and Theology at the London Bible College, and after his Cambridge doctorate had been appointed to a research fellowship in the Department of Biblical Studies in Bangor, North Wales. Energetic publisher on the books of Kings and Lamentations, he was promoted Senior Lecturer in 1995. Finally, shortly before John Gibson's retirement, Timothy Lim (Arts in Vancouver, D.Phil. and post-doctoral fellowships in Oxford) was appointed to a new Lectureship with special responsibility for Dead Sea Scrolls.

INTO THE COMPUTER AGE

One of Hayman's administrative achievements, during his convenorship of the Faculty Equipment Committee, was to secure equipment and develop expertise in computing that made New College the envy of all 'humane' sections of the University. First at postgraduate level, then at undergraduate, the Department took a lead in insisting on student competence in word-processing. And the computer is integral to the recent research projects of Wyatt and Lim. Both are using computer techniques to enhance our ability to read damaged and deteriorating ancient texts; and both are publishing their results in novel ways: Wyatt on the internet (WorldWideWeb), and Lim on CD-ROM.

When the Faculty, towards the end of that noted decade of University revolution, forced optional Hebrew on an unwilling Department, the teaching implications were wide-ranging. Clearly on the credit side, a Department committed to Hebrew had to – and did – develop in a competitive atmosphere a reputation for the quality of its language teaching, at a time when interest in languages, especially in the 'dead' classical tongues, was waning nationally. Competence had also to be developed in the added lecturing on an English text of the Old Testament. The American Revised Standard Version was adopted then and has been retained. From the beginning of the new order, the alternative first-level courses were conceived and taught quite separately. During most of the 1970s and 1980s roughly equal numbers opted for Hebrew 1 and (English) Old Testament 1, though Old Testament 2 was regularly a larger class than Hebrew 2. These second-level courses have always shared the traditional core element of Old Testament Theology. And, more recently, that half-course has introduced students in four-week blocks taught by each of the five teachers to a range of fresh debates: the Nature and Centre of Old Testament Theology

(Provan); Kingship against the background of the Ancient Near East (Wyatt); Feminist Interpretation (Hayman); Jewish debate about Biblical Theology (Auld); Biblical Interpretation in the Dead Sea Scrolls (Lim) – and also recruited them to more extended consideration of such topics in Honours courses.

The Department has drawn its research postgraduates mostly from North America (though one from Brazil) and from East and South-East Asia (Hong Kong, Indonesia, Japan, Korea, Thailand), and also from Australia and New Zealand. While not attracting the large numbers enrolled in Systematic or Practical Theology, its candidates have fared particularly well in competition for University studentships; and a high proportion have returned to their home countries to senior teaching positions in Colleges and Universities. Closer to home, the Department can no longer, as from the mid-1930s to the mid-1960s, claim as its own the Professors of Hebrew in each Scottish University – A. C. Kennedy (Aberdeen), Porteous (Edinburgh), Honeyman (St Andrews) and Mullo Weir (Glasgow) had all studied with A. R. S. Kennedy. And New College may never have helped to produce a rival to Robertson Smith – but what other institution has! But it has taught two Oxford Regius Professors (McHardy and Barr) their Hebrew, not to speak of Calum Carmichael and John Sawyer; and its distinguished doctoral graduates include Robert Carroll (Glasgow) and Andrew Mayes (Dublin).

Chapter 4

New Testament

John O'Neill

'IT MUST be kept in mind that as an independent department of theological study Biblical Criticism is of comparatively recent growth.'[1] In Edinburgh it was not only of recent growth, but of an uncertain start.

The Royal Commissioners into the state of the Scottish Universities in 1827 recommended that a chair of Biblical Criticism and Biblical Antiquities be set up in the University of Edinburgh, but nothing was done until 1840. Then Robert S. Candlish, minister of St George's, Edinburgh, was nominated, but his views on the spiritual independence of the established Church had upset the government and the offer was vetoed in the House of Lords. Eventually Robert Lee (1804–68), the controversial minister of Old Greyfriars, Edinburgh, was appointed in 1846. He insisted on the exception to the Act of the General Assembly of 1817 that forbade a parish minister to continue in his charge while holding a chair *except in the same city*, and he continued in both.

Lee was the eldest son of a boatbuilder in Tweedmouth, who also served as precentor, treasurer and eventually session clerk in the parish church. From thirteen to nineteen he was apprenticed to his father. On the eve of his twentieth birthday he went to St Andrews to study Arts and Divinity. The story that he built a boat and sold it to finance his studies sounds to me like a family joke.[2] In St Andrews he wrote a prize essay for Dr Thomas Chalmers on 'The Origin, the Rights, and the Advantages of Property', and while studying Divinity supported himself as tutor to the son of a landowner. He was a successful minister

---

[1] Patrick (1898), 25.
[2] Story (1870); *FES* I, 42–3, note.

in Arbroath and Campsie; 'You never find Mr Lee *flat*.'[3] He preached
a practical Christianity. Not all were pleased; in the words of a critic,
'The Apostle Paul says with the *heart* man believeth unto righteousness;
Mr Lee says with the *head*.'[4] Quietly, but in the end wittily in
eighty-one questions in the *Glasgow Courier*, he opposed the Non-
Intrusionist clergy who were to walk out of the Assembly of 1843.
For example, 'Whether we should go to church to confess other people's
sins or our own?'; 'Whether the *headship of Christ*, and the headship of
the General Assembly, be exactly the same?'; 'Whether the spiritual
despotism which is driving so many of the clergy into the Free
Church, may not be expected to shake its rod over them when they
are in it?'[5]

Lee did not begin to lecture until 1847. In his first lecture he promised
'to labour with the students, to free them from superstition, fanaticism,
and bigotry; and to instill into their minds . . . principles of true wisdom,
piety, and charity'.[6] He insisted in his inaugural lecture on the need to
ask whether statements in the Bible on physics, astronomy, natural
history or theology were to be understood as 'the dictates of the Spirit
of God, or only as made in accommodation to the popular opinions
prevailing in the times of the writers, whether those opinions were
true or false'.[7] He noticed that textual criticism of the New Testament
had removed two readings in support of the doctrine of the Trinity (in
1 Timothy 3:16; 1 John 5:7–8), and looked for the 'reconcilement' of
Christians when the New Testament should become the text-book
from which all parties were content *immediately* to draw their theology.[8]

Lee, who was ordained the year the first *Tract for the Times* appeared
(1833), directed his energies to reforming the worship of Greyfriars.
He introduced the saying of the Lord's Prayer, read prayers, kneeling
for prayer and standing for praise, stained-glass windows (1855), a
harmonium (1863) and then an organ (1865). The case against him in
the General Assembly was still pending when he fell paralysed from his
horse in Princes Street and died (1868).

According to one student, 'the class-room of Biblical Criticism was
the most lively of them all . . . [Lee's] lectures were clear, instructive,
tolerant, and decided. It was curious to see the volume in which they

[3] A parishioner cited by Story (1870), I, 43.
[4] A Campsie parishioner cited by Story (1870), I, 52.
[5] Lee (1843), Queries 47, 65, 76.
[6] Cited by Story (1870), I, 121.
[7] *Ibid.*, I, 124.
[8] *Ibid.*, I, 126.

were handsomely bound brought in and laid on the desk by his stately servitor, and then read straight on as they had been for many years before.' He was 'a pre-eminent debater, adroit in fence, unerring in aim, cynical and sarcastic'.[9]

In an essay on *Thou art Peter* Lee argued, with an impressive parade of patristic support, that Jesus referred to Peter's confession, not his person; with adroit use of rabbinic parallels he maintained that 'binding' and 'loosing' referred to prohibiting and permitting things, never persons. Mark and Luke omitted the words because those Gospels were written to Gentiles – though whether the evidence of the authors quoted by Eusebius showed that 'they really knew any thing historically regarding the origination and literary history of the different Gospels; or whether we conclude . . . that if they had anything further than their own conjectures drawn from internal evidence, it consisted of little but vague unauthenticated rumours.'[10] Note his scepticism about the very evidence on which he was, for the time being, relying – to my mind, a well-justified scepticism.

The start of the new discipline of Biblical Exegesis in the Free Church College in Edinburgh was also shaky. Alexander Black (1789–1864) had been Professor of Divinity in Marischal College, Aberdeen, since 1832. After the Disruption he taught the Free Church students in Aberdeen. In 1844 he announced his desire to come to Edinburgh and he was accepted as an extra professor at New College, but attendance at his lectures was not at first obligatory, despite the Free Church lament that previous to the Disruption 'there was no distinct provision for initiating Students into the critical study of the Scriptures in the original languages, and conducting them through an accurate examination of some considerable portion of the Scriptures'.[11]

Black insisted on 'the direct plenary inspired divine authority of the very phraseology of the original scriptures';[12] the Masoretic points preserved 'the vocalization, syllabication, and accentuation of the words as they were uttered by the Hebrew organs of speech, while the language was vernacularly spoken' so that 'the very sounds . . . can still be revived and expressed, in which Abraham communed with God, and received the Divine intimations of His will – the very sounds that were addressed to Moses from the burning bush, and the words of the law pronounced

[9] A. H. Charteris's reminiscences, cited by Gordon (1912), 35–6.
[10] Lee (1851), 36.
[11] *College Calendar for the Free Church of Scotland 1874–75*, 5.
[12] Cunningham (1851), 147, cited by Cheyne (1983), 8.

in the hearing of the people amidst the solemnities and terrors of Mount Sinai'.[13]

Textual criticism was necessary – although no case affected doctrine. No cause of variation in ancient manuscripts was more extensive than the practice of writing annotations in the margin of books which subsequent transcribers introduced into the text itself, 'which are known by the appellation of marginal glosses'. But 'all arbitrary alterations of the text, on the ground of mere conjecture, are to be rigorously excluded as inconsistent with fact'.[14] Attention to the relation between the subject and the predicate of logical propositions could demonstrate that such a passage as Philippians 3:9 'presents an irrefragable internal argument in proof of the imputation of the righteousness of Christ, and the personal acceptance and appropriation of that righteousness by all who rest on him alone for salvation'.[15] Attention to the preposition *epi* in 1 Peter 2:24 offered 'a manifest proof of the transference or imputation to Christ of the sins of those who are justified by faith in His blood'. But, though 1 John 5:1 had the same words and logical form as sentences in Acts 9:22, 17:3 and 18:28, the meaning was different, since 'some of the expressions can be accurately understood only by a reference to the heresies of the time'; the words, therefore, did not mean that the Messiah is Jesus.[16] I wonder.

Both Lee and Black were men of high intelligence and wide learning, yet neither was touched by the professionalism of German scholarship. Lee began to learn German in his forty-second year, and drew his inspiration from Origen, Milton, Locke, Mill, Wetstein and Coleridge. Black had blissful confidence that the infant study of the syntax of Hebrew and Greek could solve all exegetical puzzles – and in the direction of Calvinist orthodoxy. Such confidence was good for the students, and each teacher produced students who built on the foundations so laid, but who made it their business to immerse themselves in the professional scholarship of Germany and the Netherlands.

THE SECOND GENERATION

In 1857 George Smeaton (1814–89) succeeded Black at New College, and was Professor of Exegetical Theology for thirty-two years; and in

[13] Black, A. (1856), 57.
[14] *Ibid.*, 13, 15.
[15] *Ibid.*, 32.
[16] *Ibid.*, 61.

1868 A. H. Charteris (1835–1908) succeeded Lee in the University, and was Professor of Biblical Criticism and Biblical Antiquities for thirty years.

George Smeaton was a descendant of Thomas Smeaton, Andrew Melville's successor as Principal of Glasgow University[17] and the grandson of John Smeaton who built the third Eddystone Lighthouse, arched bridges at Perth, Banff and Coldstream, and the Forth and Clyde Canal. He was Thomas Chalmers' favourite student at the University of Edinburgh and later his minister at Morningside. At the Disruption he became minister of Auchterarder and was one of the pioneers in directing attention to German and Dutch theology. He was Professor of Divinity in the Free Church College in Aberdeen (1853) and came to the chair of Exegetical Theology in New College, Edinburgh, at the age of forty-three.

> Not only had he the ordinary acquirements of a teacher of exegesis, exact scholarship, and acquaintance with modern criticism, but he had a quite exceptional theological learning. I do not know [said Marcus Dods] if any man is left among us who is so much at home as he was in Patristic and mediaeval writers. The great Greek Commentators, Origen, Chrysostom, Theophylact, and Theodoret he knew as familiarly as he knew Ellicott or Meyer; but even where the studies proper to his chair had not led him, and in writers such as John of Damascus and Thomas of Aquino, . . . he was quite at home.[18]

His scorn for 'those who break loose from previous conclusions' on the doctrine of the atonement was based on thorough knowledge of what those conclusions were. 'They throw the whole subject into the crucible again, as if it had never taken form before, notwithstanding the arguments employed for centuries by some of the greatest minds that ever acted their part in handling the doctrines of the church.'[19] 'The theory of unconditional pardon, the great untruth of modern theology [a hit at Seeley's *Ecce Homo*, which his pupils were all avidly reading, as we shall see], is opposed to natural as well as revealed theology, and at open war with every correct idea of moral government.'[20] 'Instead of satisfaction to divine justice, we hear of moral redemption, or deliverance from the power of evil, with a tendency to discountenance and throw overboard the judicial side of Christianity

---

[17] Goddard (1953), 1.
[18] Dods (1889A), 5.
[19] Smeaton (1870), 479.
[20] *Ibid.*, 476.

altogether.'[21] 'That which places the Church upon Bible Christianity, and severs her from every phase of rationalism, is the firm belief that the atonement of the incarnate Son is a provision offered by the divine love for the satisfaction of the inflexible claims of divine holiness and justice.'[22]

Smeaton worked on the assumption 'that we can think the very thoughts of Christ and His apostles'.[23] Yet from the very first, Smeaton gave his students a clear and comprehensive picture of modern thought in 'an age of violent intellectual fermentation . . . which thrust mind into violent collision with mind on almost every dogma of importance'.[24] He showed them Rationalism (Semler and Eichhorn who made 'unworthy concessions . . . to the English Deists'),[25] modern Mythicism (Baur, Strauss and the Tübingen School) and the Mediating Theology that took its rise in Schleiermacher. Mediating Theology had the merit of producing a 'realistic taste and turn, which must have everything in connection with the personal Redeemer'.[26] The trouble was that Mediating Theology as represented by Rothe, Tholuck and Auberlen 'allows a Revelation in historic facts, but denies the Book-revelation in any true acceptation of the term. Revelation is by them limited to the divine facts, but disjointed from any accompanying inspiration of the Books or exercised on the minds of those who composed the records'.[27] The representatives of the Mediating Theology went even further and found 'instances of one man personating another – that the book of Deuteronomy, for example, is the fictitious personation of Moses by another man'. 'Even the Mythical School did not impute to the writers conscious fabrication.'[28] An impersonator could not be acting under the guidance of the Holy Spirit. Smeaton thought that the only alternatives were personation or authorship; he plumped for authorship. His students, convinced that Moses did not write Deuteronomy, opted for the Mediating Theology. Mediating Theology became the guiding principle of his pupil Marcus Dods.[29]

[21] *Ibid.*, 480.
[22] Smeaton (1868), 22. See Kinnear (1996), from whom I have learnt much on Smeaton, in particular.
[23] Smeaton (1870), vi.
[24] Smeaton (1853), 3–4.
[25] Smeaton (1889), 408.
[26] Smeaton (1854), 12.
[27] Smeaton (1889), 408.
[28] *Ibid.*, 408–9.
[29] See Dods (1877) and the discussion below.

Charles Archibald Anderson Scott (1858–1941) also attended New College in Smeaton's day, son of a Scottish businessman in Manchester, confirmed Anglican, Head Boy of Uppingham School, who yet, after Cambridge, chose to come to New College to train for the Presbyterian ministry. He was Professor of New Testament Language, Literature and Theology at Westminster College, Cambridge, during 1907–32. It is significant that the New College teacher to whose revered memory his book on *Christianity according to St Paul* (Cambridge, 1932) is dedicated is not Smeaton but Andrew Bruce Davidson; Paul's religion belonged to the prophetic rather than priestly tradition of Israel, and Paul preached not mere acquittal but the restoration of fellowship, the gospel of reconciliation.

Charteris was the son of the schoolmaster at Wamphray, upper Annandale, Dumfriesshire, and of Jean Hamilton, a farmer's daughter and niece of the minister of New Abbey on the Solway, whom her son eventually succeeded. His father taught in the one room some 120 pupils of all ages from six to that of young farmers who had come to repair their early lack of education. He insisted that the girls who were able to do so learnt as though they were going to university too. When Charteris went to the University of Edinburgh just before his fourteenth birthday, he could pass any ordinary examination in Virgil, Livy and Horace in Latin; Homer, Anacreon, and several plays of Euripides in Greek; he could read French easily and German fairly well.[30] He loved being a student. In the Hall he most admired Robert Lee and James Robertson. Lee appointed him tutor to his son. 'I have sometimes wondered what made us all pretty orthodox', he later mused; 'and I have come to think it was especially James Robertson's visible consecration of his life' (a memoir of whom Charteris was later to write [1863]).[31]

After a successful ministry at the Park Church, Glasgow, where he quietly introduced standing to sing and kneeling to pray (1865), an organ (1866) and a Service for the Children, he was nominated by the Crown to succeed Lee, 'with whom', he said, 'my convictions and aspirations were somewhat at variance'.[32] A Free Church Professor later referred to him as 'a raw preacher, thrust for party ends into a Professor's Chair'.[33] He laid on his students the duty to know German

---

[30] Gordon (1912), 9, 12.
[31] *Ibid.*, 37.
[32] *Ibid.*, 172.
[33] McLaren (1914), 14.

theology[34] ('The student must know German or abide in ignorance'),[35] and he took his own medicine, visiting Tübingen in the summer of 1869 and Bonn the summer of 1870. 'The field of criticism was, in my time, in continual flux, and the attempt to make lectures for the present day made new lectures indispensable . . . I have stores of lectures which were only once delivered.'[36] He commended a man at the weekly ten-minute exposition the students had to present with the words, 'Well spoken; a dash of diffidence would improve it', and the words 'a dash of diffidence' apply to Charteris, as is visible in the Lorimer portrait hanging now in the Senate Room, New College. He rejoiced at the end of his life that 'we may stand upon the battlefield and see the forms of the Tübingen critics retreating into the far distance', but he had fought pretty thoroughly over the ground himself.[37] His students thought that he did not take the German views seriously enough.[38]

Charteris' main work as a New Testament scholar was the study of the canon. He published a collection of early testimonies to the canon, based on Kirchhofer's book (*Canonicity*, 1880), and defended the unity of the New Testament, the agreement in theology between Paul and the Gospels, and the proposition that the writers of the New Testament books claimed authority – all still rather unpopular opinions, but akin to those recently defended in an Edinburgh Ph.D. thesis by Dr Peter Balla of Budapest.[39]

Charteris was also the founder of the monthly magazine of the Church of Scotland, *Life and Work*, the founder of the Woman's Guild and the Deaconess Institute and Moderator of the General Assembly (1892–3). He took over the Tolbooth Church and used it for the practical training of theological students. In the New Testament he was most at home in expounding the Pastoral Epistles.[40]

THE THIRD GENERATION

Marcus Dods (1834–1909) was the son of Marcus Dods, minister of the Scottish charge of Belford in England, and author of a book in the Apocrypha Controversy 'to do what he can to prevent England

[34] Gordon (1912), 177.
[35] McLaren (1914), 17.
[36] Gordon (1912), 173.
[37] Charteris (1897), 6.
[38] McLaren (1914), 15, citing Archibald Fleming.
[39] Charteris (1882); Balla (1994).
[40] Gordon (1912), 178.

becoming what Germany, by precisely the same process, has become'.[41] Dods senior died when the future professor was four. The family moved to Edinburgh. After two years in the head office of the National Bank, Dods at sixteen entered the university (M.A. 1854) and then went to New College. As a student he worked as assistant librarian in the Signet Library and laid the foundations of his vast knowledge of books.[42] Smeaton came in his last year at New College. Dods was a prodigious worker. 'I came across a clause in Henry James the other day that will please you', he wrote to Alexander Whyte: '"Effort, effort, always effort, is the only way to succeed."'[43] 'The sacrifice of Christ is of none effect to those who do not sacrifice themselves through it.'[44] Apart from a large number of popular books (on the Lord's Prayer [1866], on the parables [1883, 1886], on Zechariah [1895], on the Bible, its origin and nature [1905]) and meditations and prayers (1881, 1909), he published substantial commentaries for *The Expositor's Bible* (1 Corinthians and Genesis [1889]; John [1891]) and for *The Expositor's Greek Testament* (John [1897]; Hebrews [1910]). He also produced, while still a parish minister, a serviceable *Introduction to the New Testament* (1888) which gives a fair statement of rival theories even if his conclusions were conservative (the Apostle John wrote the Fourth Gospel and can be trusted not to have misrepresented his master;[45] Paul wrote all the Epistles attributed to him, including the Pastorals, but not Hebrews; Acts was written by Luke before Paul's second imprisonment in Rome and martyrdom). He gives an excellent survey of the various solutions to the Synoptic Problem, and rather inclines to Holtzmann's view that there were two lost documents, Ur-Marcus and the Logia, our canonical Mark being an edition of the first, and Matthew and Luke using both.[46]

Dods' significance lies not so much in what he achieved in the way of scholarship as in his open and optimistic acceptance of criticism. His friend Alexander Whyte expressed this mood in the sermon at Dods' induction into the chair.

The historical, exegetical and theological problems connected with New Testament study in our day are not the ephemeral heresies of restless and

[41] Dods, d. 1838 (1828), 30, cited by Cheyne (1983), 6–7.
[42] Nicoll (1921), 240.
[43] Whyte (1909), 54.
[44] Dods (1883), 17.
[45] Dods (1888), 59.
[46] *Ibid.*, 5–15.

irreverent minds; they are the providential result of that great awakening of serious thought, and of scholarly and devout inquiry, which began at the Reformation and has been in steady progress in the best schools of Christendom ever since.[47]

In his inaugural lecture Dods said, 'if criticism err, we cannot appeal from criticism to something else, but only from criticism tentative and immature to criticism mature and final – from Philip drunk to Philip sober'.[48] True to Smeaton, he said no one would want to deny the Westminster Confession on Christ's death as a sacrifice that satisfied the justice of the Father, though they might wish it differently worded, but they would want to say that it lacked words about the love of God to all, and the free gift of Jesus Christ and of salvation to all, not to the elect alone.[49] Although F. C. Baur's conclusions were mostly wrong, his method remained: 'every jot and tittle [of the Apostolic writings must be] shewn to be congruous with the history of the period to which they belong'.[50] 'It might be too much to say that we can now sit with each evangelist at his desk and read along with him the documents he employed and detect the motives which prompted him to omit this incident and give prominence to that, to leave one saying of Jesus where he found it, and shift another to a different connection', but it was only a slight exaggeration of the truth.[51]

Dods defended William Robertson Smith in the General Assembly during the lengthy case (1876–81) which ended in Smith's deposition from his Old Testament chair in Aberdeen. Indeed, Dods had narrowly escaped being tried for heresy for a sermon of 1877 which separated revelation from inspiration and denied the need of the latter.[52]

In 1890, the year after taking up his chair at New College, he was tried in the Free Church General Assembly alongside A. B. Bruce. The case against Dods seems to have rested on his large-hearted tolerance for the positive things said by those with whom he actually disagreed. This is well illustrated by his teaching on the resurrection. He consistently argued for the historicity of the empty tomb. He joined with Rainy and James Orr to give a lecture on the trustworthiness of the Gospels in a series to affirm the supernatural in Christianity in answer

[47] Barbour (1923), 259, cited by Cheyne (1983), 170.
[48] Dods (1889A), 10.
[49] *Ibid.*, 14–15.
[50] *Ibid.*, 33–4.
[51] *Ibid.*, 36.
[52] Dods (1877).

to Otto Pfleiderer's Gifford Lectures concluded a week before; Charteris from the Church of Scotland was prevented by illness from delivering a lecture alongside his Free Church colleagues, but he took the chair.[53] If the resurrection was a delusion, why was it not exposed at the time? Was there no one among the five hundred who could distinguish fact from fancy? Paul believed he saw the Lord in his risen body; 'why mention His *burial*, unless it was His bodily Resurrection he had in view?'[54] But he could still quote at length and with admiration as 'attractive' the words of Harnack, Herrmann and Renan who denied the resurrection while paying unparalleled tribute to Christ's greatness – 'convincing evidence of the justice of His claim to be the life of the world'.[55] Above all, he would not deny the name of *Christian* to someone who believed in Christ's present life and power but could not yet believe in the bodily resurrection.[56]

He was always bold in speech, and his boldness got him into trouble, as when he spoke to the London meeting of the Alliance of Reformed Churches in 1888 of the 'errors and immoralities' of the Old Testament, which brought him into controversy with A. B. Davidson.[57] His portrait by James Guthrie hangs still in the New College Senate Room; under those heavy eyebrows, brooding eyes and firm lips we can see the point of the words of a friend of his: 'He demeaned himself so nobly in the critical and testing occasions of his life, he had such refinements of loyalty, such wonderful secrets of patience and endurance, that one could not fail to be moved and humbled, if nothing more, by intercourse with him.'[58]

In the University, the Regius Chair on Charteris' retiral from ill health in 1898 was filled by his old student, John Patrick (1850–1933). His inaugural lecture breathed a quiet confidence that the dangers from radical criticism were past; what was of interest was *The Conservative Reaction in New Testament Criticism*. By that Patrick meant the earlier dates for most books of the New Testament (save the General Epistles) advocated by Harnack (Mark A.D. 65–70; Matthew 70–75 with later additions; Luke 78–93; John 80–110), the work of the classicists F. W. Blass of Halle and W. M. Ramsay of Aberdeen in reviving trust in the

---

[53] Dods (1894), 71–111.
[54] *Ibid.*, 100–1, 103.
[55] Dods (1904), 86–7.
[56] Dods (1889C), 331; Edwards (1960), 159–60.
[57] Nicoll (1921), 238–9.
[58] *Ibid.*, 241.

historical accuracy of Acts, but above all the work of J. B. Lightfoot, Theodor Zahn and Bernhard Weiss. It was not a clear-cut victory of either party; ' . . . a more liberal attitude on the part of the conservative critics has kept pace with a more reasonable attitude on the part of the adherents of the liberal party'.[59] There is no returning to the old conservative ways; Patrick represents the new conservatism that has reigned in New Testament studies (down to the dates of the Gospels!) since then. 'The substitution of the concept of history for that of inspiration as the determinative norm in questions of Introduction – has been all but universally adopted.'[60] Lightfoot was 'the ideal of the New Testament critic and scholar'.[61]

THE TWENTIETH CENTURY

Patrick was succeeded by his pupil, W. A. Curtis (1876–1935). After taking his B.D. at Edinburgh, Curtis studied at Heidelberg, Leipzig and Oxford. His main scholarly work was *A History of Creeds and Confessions of Faith in Christendom and Beyond*, published in 1911, and he became Regius Professor of Biblical Criticism in 1915. Like Dods, his imagination had been fired by Professor Sir John R. Seeley's book, originally published anonymously, *Ecce Homo* (1865), which painted a picture of Christ's royalty by which he renounced all command of armies or presidency of law courts and simply 'undertook to be the Father of an everlasting state, and the Legislator of a world-wide society' based on philanthropy, edification and mercy.[62] Its distinctive feature was 'the law of unlimited forgiveness'.[63] Curtis summed up his life's work in his book on *Jesus Christ the Teacher*. Jesus started with Old Testament, apocryphal and popular terms familiar to his hearers and stripped ideas like those of 'Messiah' and 'Kingdom of God' of 'every accident and circumstance of the spectacular, the violent, the material'. On 'Kingdom of God',

> the poet in Him would not mock at the symbolism of the clouds of heaven, the angelic hosts, the overwhelming glory of the power from above. The Hebrew in Him made no demur to the rabbinical terms in which the world-wide ingathering could be set forth . . . The kingship which is enthroned 'within', which has no concern with race or nationality, which emerges

[59] Patrick (1898), 17.
[60] *Ibid.*, 18.
[61] *Ibid.*, 30.
[62] Seeley (1865), 36 and *passim*.
[63] *Ibid.*, 288–9.

like the still small voice through tempest, earthquake and conflagration, which evinces its power through the gift of a hallowing Spirit and the restoration of human health and sanity, which ignores statistical adherence, which patiently waits and yearns and grows like a seed and works like leaven, is the conception which we owe to the Son of Man who made it His own and shaped His own filial claims upon its model.[64]

Curtis described his own point of view as both conservative and liberal: 'conservative in its estimate of [the] historicity [of the Gospels] and liberal in its interpretation of the Great Teacher's meaning. He Himself was both conservative and liberal in His attitude to the sacred writing which He handled.'[65]

Curtis was Dean of the Faculty of Divinity in 1928. He played his part in the Union of the United Free Church and the Church of Scotland in 1929 and in 1935 he became both Dean of the Faculty of Divinity and Principal of New College. He wanted his students to dare to believe when preaching that they who listened to them were listening to Jesus. 'One trembles at the thought. Yet on no other footing have we an entry to the pulpit, a licence to open and expound that lonely Book which entered it before us and remains when we have left it, than that we do represent Jesus Christ.'[66]

The two New Testament professors on the United Free Church side who prepared their Church for the union of 1929 were H. A. A. Kennedy (1866–1934) and William Manson.

Kennedy was, like Dods, the son of a minister. He took a first in Classics at the University of Edinburgh (1888) and entered New College to study under Smeaton for his first year and under Dods for the subsequent three years. He also studied at the universities of Halle and Berlin. He was ordained minister of Callander in 1893, married the same year, and two years later, at the age of twenty-nine, he published his first book, *Sources of New Testament Greek*. He started with accepting Edwin Hatch's thesis that the Septuagint was the source of the Greek of the New Testament and ended with a completely new thesis. He argued on a painstaking analysis of the words common to both, peculiar to each, and common in other Greek writings of the time that colloquial Greek was the language of the LXX and the New Testament; 'they are both children of the same parent, namely the colloquial Greek of the time. This is the secret of their striking resemblance.' Only the

[64] Curtis (1943), 120.
[65] *Ibid.*, 5.
[66] Curtis (1940), 7.

Greek of the New Testament was more refined than that of the LXX, because Greek became the common language of Palestine itself and the more gifted and acute of the Jews strove to speak the popular colloquial language in a refined manner.[67] Unfortunately the contemporary Greek of the recently discovered papyri of Egypt was not widely known until the floodgates opened in 1897–9, and Kennedy never returned to this theme. But the debate is still alive and Kennedy's contribution not to be ignored.

In 1904 Kennedy delivered and published his Cunningham Lectures on *St Paul's Conception of the Last Things*, in which he argued that Paul 'grew more and more to distrust the use of earthly imagery and pictures drawn from human experience, to body forth the circumstances of a life belonging to another order . . . The Spirit is the Divine pledge of a future life hid with Christ in God, not the historian of a sequence of outward events framed in the setting of this temporal world.'[68] The book was dedicated to Dods.

The next year he was appointed Professor of New Testament Literature and Exegesis in Knox College, Toronto, returning in 1909 to what was now called (after the fashion of the United Presbyterian Church which had joined the Free Church to become the United Free Church) the chair of New Testament Language, Literature and Theology. In 1913 he produced an interesting book on *St Paul and the Mystery Religions*, and in 1919 two books, one of the Duckworth *Studies in Theology* on *The Theology of the Epistles* and a striking small monograph on *Philo's Contribution to Religion*. All three books are linked by a common theme, that of religion. Despite the points of contact between Paul and the mystery religions, Paul has shaped everything he got from his environment in the fire of his own tremendous crisis, transforming every influence to which his personality is sensitive 'with the freedom born of a triumphant faith'.[69] Similarly, 'the contribution which Philo of Alexandria made to spiritual religion has been largely overlooked, because attention has been focused on the philosophical significance of his thought'.[70]

Kennedy was forced by ill-health to retire at the age of fifty-nine. His last book was on *Vital Forces of the Early Church* (1920). 'The joy of [St Paul's] supreme religious discovery was involved in the abolishing

[67] Kennedy (1895), 146, 151.
[68] Kennedy (1904), 280.
[69] Kennedy (1913), 299.
[70] Kennedy (1919), 1.

of legislation.' 'It is possible for men and women to enter the real presence of the living God, and to find Him not as cold Power or law but as a loving Father; that is the sorest load lifted off human hearts. Here lies the supreme fact of the Forgiveness of Sins.'[71]

WILLIAM MANSON AND J. S. STEWART

In 1925 Kennedy was succeeded by William Manson (1882–1958), who saw in the union and the incorporation of the Church chairs within the University of Edinburgh on 1 January 1935. He retired in 1952.

Manson took a first in Classics in the University of Glasgow (1904) and went straight to Oriel College, Oxford, where he took a double first in Moderations and Greats. He then trained for the ministry of the United Free Church at Trinity College, Glasgow, with James Denney as his professor in New Testament. After nearly four years as minister of Dunollie, Oban, he was called to Pollockshields East in 1914, in which year he married, and delivered the Bruce Lectures on *Christ's View of the Kingdom of God: A Study in Jewish Apocalyptic and in the Mind of Jesus Christ*, published in 1918. Like Kennedy, whom he was to succeed at New College, he spent six years as Professor of New Testament Language, Literature and Theology at Knox College, Toronto (1919–25).

All Manson's teaching centred on the theme of the Bruce Lectures. He rejected both Johannes Weiss's and Albert Schweitzer's purely apocalyptic view of Jesus' teaching and Julius Wellhausen's purely realised view and settled for the view of von Dobschütz (which goes back to Heinrich Ewald) and which von Dobschütz had promulgated in his Oxford lectures at the Third International Congress for the History of Religions of 1908 and the Summer School of Theology of 1909.[72] 'Jesus represents the Kingdom of God as a matter no longer of purely future interest and expectation but of present experience . . . God's Idea for humanity is planted like a seed in the world's life. The Divine spring has begun, and with it comes the assurance that the harvest will not long be delayed.'[73]

In *The Incarnate Glory*, Manson followed C. F. Burney in holding that John's Gospel was composed, or at least thought out, in Aramaic

---

[71] Kennedy (1920), 103, 81.
[72] Dobschütz (1910).
[73] Manson (1918), 155.

by John the Presbyter; behind John the Presbyter stood the authority of the Beloved Disciple. In the Fourth Gospel, 'the translation of eschatological into spiritual values is complete'.[74] But the roots of this translation are to be found in the teaching of Jesus himself. On Luke 17:21–37 Manson argued, 'Jesus is conscious of possessing the secret of salvation, and he and his disciples therefore constitute the present and sufficient "sign" of the nearness of the Reign of God.'[75]

In 1940 Manson gave the Cunningham Lectures published as – and the title should be quoted in full – *Jesus the Messiah: The Synoptic Tradition of the Revelation of God in Christ: With Special Reference to Form-Criticism*. He admitted, with the form critics, that the Gospel tradition was a function of the church's life and faith, but insisted that the church had preserved Jesus' spiritual history and the view he had come to adopt concerning his death. He rejected Wilhelm Bousset's thesis in *Kyrios Christos* that, when the disciples' hope that Jesus would prove the national Messiah perished with his death, they cast the ready-to-hand royal mantle of the Son of Man around the person of their Master and confessed themselves disciples of the one who through suffering and death had entered into glory.

> If Jesus had set no higher interpretation on his calling than that of a teacher of righteousness . . . or a witness to the coming of the Son of Man; if he had said nothing which in any way identified his fortunes with those of the Christ or Son of Man; is it thinkable that the love and devotion of his followers would, after the event on Calvary, have taken the acutely paradoxical form of investing him with the messianic sceptre and glory?[76]

Jesus, he argued, built on Isaiah 53 in expanding the Son of Man doctrine to teach that the Son of Man's exaltation portrayed in Daniel 7 was from a life of suffering on earth. 'Jesus has transmuted the language used by Judaism in its doctrine of the Messiah and the last things.'[77]

In his Baird Lectures on *The Epistle to the Hebrews*, Manson opposed the view that James Moffatt had made prominent in Britain that the Epistle was a late product directed to Gentile Christians. He argued that a straight line ran from the teaching and the apologia of Stephen the proto-martyr to the writer to the Hebrews. Hebrews should be set

---

[74] *Ibid.*, 172.
[75] Manson (1930), 197.
[76] Manson (1943), 5–6.
[77] *Ibid.*, 157.

alongside Paul's Epistle to the Romans 'to obtain a stereoscopic view of the theology of the World Church in the apostolic age', a 'dual witness to the character of Roman Christianity'.[78]

Manson was an intensely shy person.

> Prof. Manson is shyer
> Than you are than I are.
> He'll join that bright choir
> With no hint of disgrace.
> So spotless his way
> That there's nothing to say . . . ,

as a student song at the end of the year put it.[79] There was no selection school in those days, but Manson was known to suggest, 'Mr So-and-so, you should consider whether you have a vocation to the ministry.' Despite his shyness, he played a prominent part in church affairs, being Vice-President of the British Council of Churches (1950–1), and in the affairs of the world-wide guild of New Testament scholars, Studiorum Novi Testamenti Societas, of which he was President (1951–2). His presidential address was entitled, 'Principalities and Powers: The Spiritual Background of the Work of Jesus in the Synoptic Gosepls'.[80] He died on Good Friday, 1958.

In 1946, on the retiral of Principal Curtis, who had held the Regius chair, Manson assumed that chair, to be succeeded in 1947 as professor of New Testament Language, Literature and Theology by James Stuart Stewart (1896–1990).

Before discussing J. S. Stewart, arguably the most widely known of the New Testament professors, we should note that a year before his term as professor began, the era of the Lecturer in New Testament was inaugurated when D. M. G. Stalker was appointed to an assistantship in Biblical Criticism (1946–48). In 1948 a lectureship in Biblical Studies was inaugurated in the Faculty of Arts, which Stalker held from 1948 to 1979, with a seat in the Divinity Faculty from 1966. Stalker was an exceptional teacher, a Hebraist who published a fine commentary on Ezekiel in the Torch series (1968), and a skilled translator from the German.

Michael G. Campbell was the first *Assistant* Lecturer in Biblical Criticism, from 1954 to 1959; the job was to teach Greek, but both

---

[78] Manson (1951), 7, 13.

[79] Written by Ian Fraser, 1940; recalled by William B. Johnston.

[80] Published in *Bulletin* III of the Society, the forerunner of *New Testament Studies*.

Andrew Ross and Alec Cheyne remember his effective lectures on the Parables and the Beatitudes. He was succeeded by Henry A. Shepherd (1959–62), an accomplished Greek linguist like his father. J. R. C. Perkin succeeded Shepherd until 1965, when he became Professor of New Testament Interpretation at McMaster Divinity College, later part of McMaster University, Hamilton, Ontario. He was much concerned with the relation of faith to history. He was succeeded by G. Alistair Weir, Assistant Lecturer 1965–6 and Lecturer from 1966 to 1968, when with his wife Mary he went to the National University of Zaire on the appointment of the Presbyterian Church in the United States (1968–74). He then moved to teach at Huron College, London, Ontario. His Ph.D. dissertation on Tatian's Diatessaron (1969) had been sparked off by a seminar Matthew Black held in the Spring Term 1967, and he was supervised by John Gibson and Ian Moir.

So Stewart had been assisted by these teachers throughout his whole time at New College (as well as by R. A. S. Barbour from 1955 and I. A. Moir from 1961, who will be dealt with below).

Stewart was born in Dundee. His father had given up a career in business to become Y.M.C.A. secretary in Dundee, where he served for fifty years, during thirty of which he conducted a large and thriving Bible Class at which Stewart recalled hearing James Denney speak. Stewart took a first in Classics at St Andrews (1917) and then served with the Royal Engineers on the Western Front (1917–18). He trained for the ministry at New College, taking his B.D. externally from St Andrews. He was awarded the Cunningham Fellowship to study abroad, learnt German in the summer vacation, and spent a blissfully happy year at Bonn sitting at the feet of Wilhelm Heitmüller (1921–2).

Stewart's main scholarly work was done by the time he was thirty, in which year he was called to North Morningside Church in Edinburgh (1935). He had been ordained and inducted to Auchterarder St Andrews (1924) and called from there to Aberdeen Beechgrove (1928). In that year appeared the English translation of Friedrich Schleiermacher's *The Christian Faith*, Stewart having stepped in when Alexander Grieve died in 1927 to assist H. R. Mackintosh in the final editorial work. Two years later came the influential Bible Class Handbook on *The Life and Teaching of Jesus Christ* (1933). Finally his masterpiece, *A Man in Christ: The Vital Elements of St Paul's Religion*, the Cunningham Lectures of 1934, often reprinted and widely translated.

Stewart's life thereafter was devoted to preaching, and his book was a thorough scholarly justification of that move.

> In the days when God let His servant Paul loose upon the earth, with a heart aflame for Christ, the forces which carried the new adventure forward on its amazing career were not precision of doctrine nor skill of definition, but an open vision, a ringing conviction, and a great love. And often when men have succeeded in defining Paul's doctrine most closely, they have lost Paul's Christ most completely.[81]

Paul used inconsistent phraseology about faith, law, spirit, sin, eschatology and ethics – a superb checklist to put alongside the lists in the controversial book of Heikki Räisänan, recipient of an Edinburgh honorary D.D., *Paul and the Law* (1983). But that is only evidence that Paul 'refuses to be tied down to a rigid, petty consistency'; he has a deep *inner* consistency: 'Christ in me – this overmastering experience which was "unquestionably the core of his religion" [Dean Inge], "der eine Brennpunkt" [Johannes Weiss].'[82] 'The heart of Paul's religion is union with Christ.'[83]

Stewart's lectures at New College were preached sermons, and in this he was acting consistently with his deepest conviction about the New Testament. 'And even [Theodor] Häring's bold assertion can be allowed to stand: "God produces Faith. Nothing else? No; for faith is everything."'[84]

Attracted by his preaching, students came from all over the world, particularly from the United States of America, to do research under his guidance. The degree of Ph.D. was first awarded by the University of Edinburgh in 1921. In 1922 three were awarded in New Testament, to J. Logan Ayre for a dissertation on 'The Christology of the Earliest Gospel', to G. R. Johnson on 'The Moral Dynamic of Christian Experience according to St Paul' and to Alex M. MacInnes on 'The Kingdom of God in the Apostolic Writings'. Supervising postgraduate students became an important part of teaching in the Faculty at New College. From 1922 to 1940, twenty-four Ph.D.s were granted in New Testament; from 1941 to 1960, twenty-seven; from 1961 to 1980, forty-nine; and from 1981 to date, fifteen. Stewart's best-known pupil to become a professor in New Testament was Richard Norman

---

[81] Stewart (1935), 15.
[82] *Ibid.*, 27, 28–9.
[83] *Ibid.*, 147.
[84] *Ibid.*, 177.

Longenecker, whose dissertation on *Paul, Apostle of Liberty* was published in 1964.

THE LAST FORTY YEARS

Stewart had refused to assume the Regius chair when Manson retired in 1952, so that Manson was succeeded by Matthew Black (1908–94). Black took honours in Classics and then in Philosophy at the University of Glasgow followed by the B.D. with distinction in Old Testament (1934). He then went to Bonn and did a doctorate with Paul Kahle (1937) on translating and editing a Christian Palestinian euchologion, and so became the first teacher of New Testament in Edinburgh to have done supervised postgraduate research for a doctorate. He was ordained by the Presbytery of Aberdeen on being appointed Lecturer in Biblical Criticism by the University of Aberdeen (a precedent taken up by Dr Iain Provan in Edinburgh in 1992). At the age of thirty-eight he published the first edition of *An Aramaic Approach to the Gospels and Acts* (1946; 2nd edn, 1954; 3rd edn, 1967, with the famous Appendix on 'The Son of Man' by Geza Vermes). He left the chair in Edinburgh in 1954 to become Professor of Divinity and Biblical Criticism and Principal of St Mary's College, St Andrews. John Baillie said, 'The blackbird has fled to another retreat' (William Cowper). So New College lost the nearest to a pure scholar in New Testament studies she had ever had. Two of his Edinburgh Ph.D. students have gone on to make names for themselves as New Testament scholars: E. Earle Ellis whose thesis was on 'The Old Testament in the Pauline Epistles' and Max Wilcox who wrote on 'Semitisms in Acts I–XV'.

With Black's departure the old University chair and the old Free Church and United Free Church chair were in effect combined, and there were never again to be two established chairs in New Testament. R. A. S. Barbour (1921–) was appointed as a lecturer in 1955. He lectured at New College for sixteen years before being appointed to the chair in Aberdeen. He confessed that 'We exist in an uncomfortable twilight about Jesus and his history, not really knowing how much of it to believe.'[85] Robin Barbour was deeply influenced by Ernst Käsemann (1906–). 'What [Jesus] called for turned out to be an act of trust that the whole secret of God's purpose was somehow encapsulated in his own words and actions.' Barbour spoke of 'my enigmatic Jesus'.

[85] Barbour (1973), 19.

Myth and history involve one another.[86] At the end of his time at Edinburgh Barbour became Secretary of the Studiorum Novi Testamenti Societas (1970–7), Matthew Black having been editor of the Journal, *New Testament Studies*, since 1954.

In 1961 Ian Moir (1914–93) joined the Department as Lecturer in Christian Origins. He was a graduate of Aberdeen in Classics (1936) and Divinity (1939) and, after a year in Cambridge and another in Edinburgh, he graduated Ph.D. Cambridge in 1943 for his work on the *Codex Climaci rescriptus* which was published in 1956. He was an erudite and accomplished textual critic, and his long-planned, but only half-executed book for English readers of the New Testament on textual criticism has recently appeared, with J. K. Elliott's name also on the title page. The Faculty's first computer-user, Moir retired in 1981 but continued to give invaluable voluntary service in the Library, indexing and cataloguing masses of papers and collections.

On Stewart's retiral in 1966, the University was fortunate to be able to entice Hugh Anderson (1920–) back from Duke University in North Carolina (Professor of Biblical Theology 1957). He was a graduate of Glasgow University in Classics and Semitic Languages, and took his B.D. with distinction in New Testament, followed by a Ph.D. (1945). After five years as assistant to the Professor of Semitic Languages, he was ordained and inducted to Trinity, Pollockshields (Glasgow) in 1951.

Anderson's *Jesus and Christian Origins* (1964) was an influential early example of the new wave of books on the life of Jesus. It stemmed from the same impulses that had led the young Bultmannians in Germany like Käsemann and Günther Bornkamm to raise again the possibility of cautiously writing the life of Jesus, and gave English readers a judicious and wide-ranging review of their efforts. 'Albert Schweitzer was, I think, right when he declared that no generation of men can really be related to Jesus of Nazareth that is not genuinely concerned for the world's weal and woe.'[87] In 1976 he published an economical but penetrating commentary on Mark's Gospel. He has a long-standing interest and expertise in Jewish literature contemporary with the New Testament, which culminated in outstanding translations and commentary on 3 and 4 Maccabees for his pupil James Charlesworth's *Old Testament Pseudepigrapha*. Charlesworth, another New College student who has made a mark in New Testament scholarship, spent a

---

[86] Barbour (1973), 29–30.
[87] Anderson, H. (1964), 317.

post-doctoral year in Edinburgh under Anderson while working on his edition of the Odes of Solomon (1973 and reprinted).

P. S. Cameron, a former student, recalled the sheer inspiration of Anderson's lecturing to undergraduates, but he was also a great teacher of teachers. The best graduate student he had was probably Makoto Yamauchi, Professor at Tokyo Union Theological Seminary, who has published distinguished commentaries in Japanese. William S. Campbell, Professor at Westhill College, Birmingham, who has written influential articles on Paul's purpose in writing Romans, one of which is reproduced in Karl P. Donfried's *The Romans Debate* (1977, 1991), Lee Martin McDonald, Adjunct Professor at Fuller Theological Seminary, who published an important book on *The Formation of the Christian Biblical Canon* (1988), and Walter Elwell, whose dissertation on William Manson has been useful in preparing this chapter, should also be noted.

In 1968 Douglas A. Templeton (1935–) joined the Faculty as the fourth teacher in New Testament. A graduate in Classics from Cambridge, he took a distinction in New Testament at the University of Glasgow (1962) after two years' National Service with the Black Watch (invaluable experience for organising the SNTS Summer Meeting in Edinburgh in 1994!). He had studied in Jena in East Germany and Göttingen in the West, as well as spending three semesters in Tübingen under Ernst Käsemann. His Ph.D. with Ronald Gregor Smith was on the Kerygma as understood by Bultmann and C. H. Dodd (1967). He published a brilliant collection of aphorisms on Paul, *Re-exploring Paul's Imagination* (1988), and is working on a book, based on the course he taught at Dartmouth College in 1993, about the New Testament as fiction.

A year after Barbour's move to Aberdeen, David L. Mealand (1938–) was appointed to succeed him (1972). He had read Classical Moderations and Theology at Oxford, trained at Lincoln Theological College, and taught at Wells Theological College, at the end of his time united with Salisbury (1966–72). His M.Litt. from Bristol was published as *Poverty and Expectation in the Gospels* (1980). He took an Edinburgh Ph.D. in 1985 for a thesis on *Criteria for Rational Belief*, so giving further evidence of his devotion to clear rigorous thinking as well as scrupulous analysis of historical evidence. About his time lectures began to be supplemented by small seminars or tutorials for first- and second-level courses in New Testament. The era of lectures only had come to an end. Mealand early took to the computer and has written extensively on it as an aid to scholarly research in the humanities, applying it himself, for example, to demonstrate the affinities of the Greek of Acts with contemporary Hellenistic Greek.

John Ashton, who subsequently as Lecturer in the University of Oxford published a widely-acclaimed book on *Understanding the Fourth Gospel* (Oxford, 1991), taught Anderson's courses in 1984–5 and also helped in Old Testament.

John Cochrane O'Neill (1930–) came to Edinburgh in 1985 after twenty-one years at Westminster College, Cambridge, aged fifty-four. He had studied history at the University of Melbourne and trained for the ministry at Ormond College, Melbourne, being taught Old Testament by Hector McLean (who had been student assistant to Adam C. Welch) and New Testament by J. Davis McCaughey, who had himself spent a year at New College (1940–1) and who introduced him to the writings of William Manson and much else. O'Neill unwittingly heard in his Systematic Theology classes on 'God, Man and Sin' by Professor Dudley Hopkirk the very same lectures that W. P. Paterson delivered in Edinburgh about 1920. Very good lectures they were too, if not quite in tune with the Barth he and his fellow-students were reading for themselves. He studied in Göttingen in 1956 (Joachim Jeremias, Ernst Käsemann) and in Cambridge, where he gained a Ph.D. for a thesis in 'The Theology of Acts' with J. A. T. Robinson. He got to know J. Y. Campbell (1887–1978), who had studied at New College under H. A. A. Kennedy and at Marburg under Heitmüller, and was probably the best New Testament scholar Edinburgh ever produced. O'Neill gave the Cunningham Lectures on 'Messiah' (1975–6). He questions current solutions to the Synoptic Problem, the nature of John's Gospel, the date of Acts, the integrity of the Pauline Epistles and the origin of the distinctive theology of Hebrews. His book on *Who Did Jesus Think He Was?* was published in 1995. He began a popularly attended Honours, Postgraduate and Ministers New Testament Seminar, meeting fortnightly in term.

Brian Capper (1956–), who had done research under O'Neill and Ernst Bammel in Cambridge, served as lecturer for two years (1985–7) before moving successively to Cuddesdon, St Andrews and Canterbury. He proved an attractive lecturer and an inspiring teacher of Greek. He was succeeded by Peter S. Cameron, the Faculty's first Meldrum Lecturer (1987–90), who went from Edinburgh to St Andrew's College in the University of Sydney as Principal, a post John McIntyre had held before him. He was an efficient and untiring colleague, at one time every Wednesday writing an article for publication! He has since written of his experiences as a student at New College during 1973–6 (i.e. before the large increase in the proportion of Religious Studies students). His comments bear upon the difficulty of operating a Divinity Faculty when religion comes to be seen as largely a private affair. Cameron was not himself studying for the ministry. He perceived the lecturers as 'understandably reluctant to destroy the deeply held convictions of their students or to offend them gratuitously', 'as apt to collude in the construction of the protective shell [by students between themselves and critical study of the Bible], by holding back at the critical moments'.[88] That is a tribute to the lecturers' great courtesy and consideration, for no longer were all teachers in the Faculty, a Faculty designed to prepare students for the ministerial profession, church members or even believers in God.

When Cameron returned to the Faculty as Meldrum Lecturer, he saw the problem from the other side of the fence. In academic theology, 'everything seemed to be technique with no results, the endless accumulation of intellectual equipment with no discernible goal'. 'We were giving scholarship a bad name because it seemed to be synonymous with a kind of barren cleverness, the endless elaboration of trivia.'[89] Is that, perhaps, where religion as a private affair leads? Clearly no modern university could appoint or dismiss a teacher on a religious test, and of course there has to be room in Religious Studies for teachers of all persuasions. What price, then, the professional school as the Faculty of Divinity, and the state-funded professional training of ministers for the Christian churches? New Testament has always been taught in Edinburgh for potential ministers, and it is now also taught for students of religion. The tension can be fruitful, but Cameron has reminded us of the dangers.

In 1987 J. I. H. McDonald (1933–), a member of the Department of Christian Ethics and Practical Theology, was allowed to give a quarter of his time to the New Testament Department, and the students have benefited from his Greek teaching, his lectures on Introduction and Ethics and his postgraduate supervision. His doctorate had already been published in the SNTS Monograph Series by Cambridge University Press (1980) and during his time in the New Testament Department

---

[88] Cameron (1994), 9–10.
[89] *Ibid.*, 32.

he has published books on *The Resurrection: Narrative and Belief* (1989) and *Biblical Interpretation and Christian Ethics* (1993).

In 1994 the new Lecturer in Dead Sea Scrolls and Christian Origins, Timothy H. Lim (1960–) took up his post in the Department of Hebrew and Old Testament Studies, but with a third of his time devoted to New Testament. He has already made a name for himself as a scholar in his exciting and fast-moving field, and students are responding enthusiastically to his intense interest in the texts of the Bible and Qumran in their original languages.

At a time of renewed financial retrenchment, the University has appointed a successor to John O'Neill, who retires in 1996, Professor Larry Hurtado from the University of Manitoba in Winnipeg, Canada. The double standard of New Testament at New College and New Testament in the University of Edinburgh, which began in 1843, looks set to continue.

In the 150 years of New Testament teaching and learning in Edinburgh two things stand out: the emphasis on close and scrupulous attention to the very words of the text and the constant expectation that the close attention to the words would produce results vital for the life of human beings in the presence of God.

Chapter 5

Ecclesiastical History

Alec Cheyne

THE TEACHERS:
CHURCHMEN AND HISTORIANS

EDINBURGH'S TEACHERS of Church History during the past 150 years or so have been, almost without exception, not only historians of the Church but also *Church* historians: the Church's servants as well as its chroniclers and analysts.

This was certainly the case at New College. From 1843 until the Union of 1929, its professors were all ministers of the Free (after 1900, the United Free) Church, just as the great majority of its students were candidates for the Free Church ministry. The ecclesiastical orientation of the place may be realised by even the briefest scrutiny of the part played by its teachers in contemporary Church life.

WELSH, CUNNINGHAM
AND RAINY

After some ten years of parish ministry, David Welsh became professor of Ecclesiastical History in Edinburgh University in 1831. A protege of Thomas Chalmers, he was deeply involved in the Non-Intrusion movement. As Moderator of the Disruption Assembly, he headed the seceders' procession on 18 May 1843, and from then until his death he was a leading figure in the youthful Free Church. He helped to formulate its schemes for school and university education, and did more than anyone else to raise funds for the erection and endowment of New College, whose first professor of Church History he inevitably became. He crowned his services to the new seminary by supervising the inauguration of its superb theological library.[1]

Welsh's successor, William Cunningham, was also both churchman and scholar. He had been a parish minister before joining the New College professoriate on the morrow of the Disruption – to begin with as second professor of Divinity, and then as professor of Divinity and Church History. Among the Non-Intrusionists before 1843, and the Free Church leaders thereafter, none was fonder of a fight than Cunningham. The tally of his controversies is almost endless: with the 'apostates and perjured' Voluntaries, with McLeod Campbell's 'Rowites', with Moderates like Drs Cook and Inglis, with Free Church favourers of theological colleges in Aberdeen and Glasgow – and, of course, with Arians, Socinians, and 'Papists' of every age including his own. Whether because of his bellicosity or in spite of it, Cunningham was one of Scotland's most prominent ecclesiastics from the 1830s to the 1860s. He became Moderator of the Free Church General Assembly in 1859; and as professor of Church History, and Principal of New College after Chalmers' death, he played a unique part in fashioning – and personifying – the distinctive ethos of his denomination.[2]

When Robert Rainy came to the chair he was already marked out as a coming Church leader. Deflected from a career in medicine by the euphoria of the Disruption, he had joined the first generation of students at New College. After brief ministries in Huntly and Edinburgh, he was called in 1862 to succeed Cunningham in what was looked on as the intellectual and spiritual powerhouse of Scottish Evangelicalism. From that time onwards his exceptional debating and administrative gifts made him master of both the General Assembly (which he attended annually for more than forty years) and the Free Church as a whole. Principal of New College from 1874 until his death in 1906, he pronounced with magisterial authority on nearly all the vital religious issues of the day, evolution, biblical criticism, confessional revision and religious Establishments included, and was the only minister in modern times to be thrice elected Moderator (in 1887, 1900 and 1905). His role in the Free Church could seriously be likened to that of an archbishop in other communions.[3]

[1] Dunlop (1846).
[2] Rainy and Mackenzie (1871).
[3] Simpson (1909).

ROBERTSON, STEVENSON, WALLACE AND TAYLOR

The commitment of New College's Church historians to the Free Kirk was equalled by that of their opposite numbers in the University's Faculty of Divinity to the 'Auld Kirk'. All were ordained ministers of the Church of Scotland, and all had served in parishes for longer or shorter periods.

James Robertson, who ministered at Ellon in Aberdeenshire from 1832 until his presentation in 1844 to the chair vacated by Welsh, had been one of the ablest representatives of the Moderate party throughout the Ten Years' Conflict. After his appointment, he did much to restore the morale and the fortunes of the battered Establishment, and his election to the Moderatorship in 1856 was more than usually well deserved.[4]

Robertson's successor in 1861, William Stevenson, came late to the chair (he was in his middle fifties), after strenuous ministries in Arbroath and South Leith. It is perhaps hardly surprising that he is remembered more for his services to the Church than for his scholarship, considerable though that was.[5]

Robert Wallace was Professor of Ecclesiastical History for only four years, from 1872 to 1876, during which he was also minister of Old Greyfriars. He had a remarkable subsequent career as – successively – editor of the *Scotsman* newspaper, barrister and Liberal M.P.; but his earlier years had been spent in parish ministries, and while a professor he was one of the most vocal leaders of the 'Broad Church' school within the Church of Scotland.[6]

The last nineteenth-century occupant of the Ecclesiastical History chair, Malcolm Campbell Taylor, made a special place for himself in the University administration, serving for some time as secretary of the University Court and (from 1884 to 1899) as Dean of Divinity. But he had previously ministered in the prestigious pastoral charges of Dumfries Greyfriars, Montrose, Crathie and Edinburgh Morningside, and seems to have continued to carry a good deal of weight in ecclesiastical as well as academic circles.[7]

During the present century, the picture has changed much less dramatically than one might expect. Before the great watershed of the

[4] Charteris (1863).
[5] *FES* I, 164; Grant (1884), II, 312–13.
[6] *FES* I, 43–4; Smith and Wallace (1903).
[7] *FES* I, 85; Rice and McIntyre (1957), 200–2.

Union of the Churches in 1929, certainly, the professors' ecclesiastical affiliations were quite as close, and obvious, as ever.

MACEWEN AND WATT

Alexander Robertson MacEwen, an ordained minister of the United Presbyterian and then of the United Free Church, served congregations in Moffat and Glasgow before being called to Rainy's chair in 1901; and his publications were, at least in part, tributes to the religious tradition from which he sprang. Deeply involved in the negotiations that led to the Union of the United Presbyterians and Free Church in 1900 and in the protracted 'Church Case' that followed, he spent a high proportion of his last years in committee work. He helped to plan 'Edinburgh 1910', the celebrated World Missionary Conference, and was one of the United Free Church's chief representatives in Union negotiations with the Church of Scotland. Appropriately enough, he ended his days as Moderator of the General Assembly of the United Free Church.[8]

Hugh Watt (who of course survived – and more than survived – into the post-Union era) was every bit as much of a churchman as his predecessor, holding pastoral charges within the United Free Church before being elected to the chair in 1919. His considerable administrative gifts and his obvious concern for the welfare of New College students and alumni were recognised, and given even fuller scope, by his elevation in 1946 to the Principalship of New College. The year of his retirement, 1950, saw him called to the Moderatorship of the General Assembly.[9]

MACKINNON

The only conceivable exception to the 'churchly' character of Edinburgh's Church historians in the period before the fusion of New College and the University's Faculty of Divinity was James Mackinnon. Though trained in Divinity as well as in Arts, and licensed to preach by the Church of Scotland, he was never ordained and after brief and temporary appointments in Scotland and South Africa he spent the years between 1890 and 1908 lecturing in History – *not* Ecclesiastical History – in Queen Margaret College, Glasgow, and the University of St Andrews. His numerous early publications reveal no particular interest

[8] Cairns (1925).
[9] Cheyne (1986); Small (1967).

102

in or commitment to Church concerns, but after his elevation to the Edinburgh professorship a marked change of direction can be discerned. While he never played a prominent part in Church life, his attention focused increasingly upon the Patristic and Reformation periods. Until his retirement at the beginning of the 1930s, and indeed for more than a decade thereafter, he poured out a stream of substantial works on wellnigh every subject traditionally included in the Church History curriculum at Edinburgh. Devoid of even a touch of zealotry or clericalism, he expressed with erudition and unflagging diligence the distinctive viewpoint of liberal Christian scholarship. Against a background of conflicting ideologies and the descent once again into total war, he could hardly have performed a more valuable service for the Church of his time.[10]

BURLEIGH, TORRANCE, CHEYNE AND BROWN

Mackinnon's pupil, John Henderson Seaforth Burleigh came to the chair in 1931. Soon after, a complete union was effected between the University's Faculty of Divinity and the former United Free Church's New College. The change meant that for a time Church History was taught by *two* professors, one (Burleigh) in the old University chair, the other (Watt, followed briefly by Torrance) in the so-called 'Church' chair. From 1952 onwards, however, no further appointment was made to the latter, and a succession of lecturers filled the gap. It might have been expected that the merging of Faculty and seminary – and the end of New College as an exclusively ecclesiastical institution – would entail a perceptible loosening of the age-old connection between theological teaching and Church life: as a matter of fact, the next half-century provided little evidence (at least so far as Ecclesiastical History was concerned) that this had happened.

Like nearly all his predecessors, Burleigh was an ordained minister. During his occupancy of the chair his services to the Church were many and various, including convenership of its Church and Nation committee and membership of the ecumenical group who produced the controversial 'Bishops Report' in 1957. He was elected Principal of New College in 1956 and Moderator of the General Assembly in 1960.[11]

[10] Rice and McIntyre (1957), 141–2; D. F. Wright in *DSCHT*, 524.
[11] Cheyne (1985).

Thomas Forsyth Torrance who held the 'Church' chair from 1950 to 1952, carried on the tradition of ecclesiastical commitment. He ministered in two parishes before returning to New College, and soon acquired a notable reputation in Church circles both at home and abroad. Moving from Church History to Christian Dogmatics, he played a prominent part in the ecumenical movement, was joint founder and editor of the *Scottish Journal of Theology*, set new standards of scholarly industry and crusading zeal during his convenership of the Kirk's Commission on Baptism, and was called to Moderatorship of the General Assembly in 1976.[12]

All the teachers of Ecclesiastical History at New College since Burleigh's retirement are still alive, most of them continuing to work in Edinburgh: consequently, no lengthy account of them is either necessary or desirable here. After six years as a lecturer in the Department, Alexander Campbell Cheyne succeeded his old teacher in the chair in 1964. Like nearly all his predecessors, he was an ordained minister of the Church of Scotland, though he never served in a parish. The Church appointed him Principal of New College in 1984.[13]

The present occupant of the Chair, Stewart Jay Brown, took up his duties as recently as 1988. He is neither an ordained minister nor a licentiate, but his background in the United States – and his work on Thomas Chalmers – have familiarised him with Church attitudes and practices, and no one can accuse him of indifference to, or lack of sympathy with, the traditional concerns of College and Faculty.[14]

THE LECTURERS

From the 1950s onwards, the teaching at New College was augmented and enriched by the service of a succession of lecturers. James S. McEwen filled the vacancy created in 1952 by Torrance's translation to Christian Dogmatics. A Church of Scotland minister with considerable experience in various parishes, and a fine teacher, he moved to the chair of Church History at Aberdeen in 1958.[15] On Cheyne's promotion to the Edinburgh chair in 1964, David F. Wright succeeded him in the lectureship. The first Englishman to hold

---

[12] McIntyre (1979).
[13] Lewis (1986).
[14] 'Professor Stewart J. Brown', in *NCB* (Autumn, 1982), 2.
[15] *FES*, X, 430.

an appointment in the Department, Wright had no difficulty in transferring from evangelical Anglicanism to Scottish Presbyterianism, and was soon playing a full part in the ecclesiastical life of his adopted city and country; his administrative gifts were demonstrated during a term as Dean of the Faculty. Andrew C. Ross came to the Department in 1966 as its first lecturer with special responsibility for the History of Missions. Ordained by the Church of Scotland, he had spent eight years in Malawi as a minister of the Church of Central Africa (Presbyterian); and the fact that from 1978 to 1984 he was both Principal of New College and Dean of the Faculty indicates the special place he occupied in the esteem of both Church and University. Peter C. Matheson, a licentiate of the Church of Scotland, joined the Department in 1965, and for twenty years it benefited from his exceptional teaching skills; he was called to the chair of Church History and Christian Doctrine at Knox College, Dunedin, New Zealand in 1985.

On Matheson's departure, financial considerations might have made it impossible to fill the vacancy had it not been for the munificent endowment of a Lectureship in the History and Theology of the Reformation by the Kirby Laing Foundation. To this newly-created lectureship in memory of Sir John Laing, a prominent Christian industrialist, there came in quick succession two young scholars who both (as it happened) could be said to represent a Methodist contribution to the predominantly Presbyterian scene at New College: Susan Hardman Moore from the University of Durham, and Jane Dawson from the University of St Andrews. Dr Hardman Moore was not only the Department's first woman teacher but also its first Methodist lay preacher: she did much for both the ecclesiastical and academic life of Edinburgh before moving to King's College, London in 1992. Her successor Dr Dawson, also had a Methodist background, and her special expertise – in the English and Scottish Reformations – placed her in the mainstream of New College's traditional interests.

Although lecturers only made their appearance on the Mound in the 1950s, it is difficult now to think of Church History there without them.

EXTENDING INTERESTS

Church History in its entirety covers a vast field, both in time and space, but its Edinburgh practitioners have always paid special attention to the Early Church, the Protestant Reformation, and Scottish Christianity.

Welsh's full course of teaching spanned three sessions, the period down to Constantine being studied in the first year, that from Constantine to the end of the thirteenth century in the second, and the fourteenth, fifteenth and sixteenth centuries in the third. Cunningham adopted an approach that was more thematic than chronological; but if his *Historical Theology* (2 vols, Edinburgh, 1862) is anything to go by (and we are assured that it represents the substance of his class lectures) the doctrinal controversies of the Early and Reformation periods took up the greater part of his attention.

As for Rainy, the *College Calendar* of 1874–5 provides the following description of the topics which he hoped to cover:

> In the Junior Class the Lectures begin with a brief survey of the History of the Church during the period covered by Canonical Scripture. Afterwards the topics which are chiefly dwelt on are the age of the Apostolic Fathers, that of the Apologists, the controversies regarding the Trinity and the Person of Christ, the history of Sacerdotal and Sacramental tendencies and their results, the Pelagian Controversy; and following upon this, the features and influences which prevailed in the Middle Ages in so far as the time enables the subject to be overtaken. In the Senior Course, a few lectures on the Reformation are followed by a survey of the Popish controversy, and this by a notice of the characteristics of the Lutheran and Reformed Churches respectively. The Socinian and Arminian controversies succeed; and these are followed by a survey of the rise of Rationalism in Europe, and of the effects it produced in Theology, especially in Switzerland and Germany, which leads to notice of the modern German Schools. As an appendix to the Course, in order to supply a fuller view than the textbook presents, the history of the Scottish Church is traced continuously down to the Disruption, and attention is directed to the principles which it illustrates. Special courses on particular topics are occasionally introduced.[16]

With minor emendations, Rainy's programme continued basically unchanged down to his retirement at the beginning of the present century.

Once the difficulties created by the 'Church Case' (1900–5) had been got out of the way, MacEwen settled down on not dissimilar lines. In 1907–8, for example, the Junior Church History Class (attended by third-year theology students) took as its subject the period 'From New Testament times to the close of the fourth century,

---

[16] *College Calendar for the Free Church of Scotland, 1874–75,* 26–7.

including Augustine, and extending to the Christological controversies of the fifth century'; Scottish History was examined during the last month of the session. The syllabus of the Senior Class (attended by students in their fourth and final year) was described as follows: 'During the first month the transition from ancient to modern Church life will be exhibited in connection with the Scottish Church. Thereafter, the Reformation movement will be set forth and scrutinised, and the most important historical developments of Modern Christianity will be traced.'[17]

No major changes were introduced by Watt. Throughout the 1920s, lectures to the Junior Class dealt with the Early Church, both before and after Constantine, together with 'some aspects of the Medieval Church'; the Senior Class studied the Lutheran Reformation (in seminar), the Swiss, French and English Reformations before Christmas, and Post-Reformation history, particularly Scottish, after Christmas.[18]

A very similar pattern was followed by 'Auld Kirk' teachers in the University. Indeed, no really substantial changes took place until the 1960s, when – against a background of rapid academic expansion nation-wide – the B.D. curriculum as a whole was re-shaped and the Church History component within it radically re-structured. For the first time in more than a century, students were not introduced to the subject by a full course on the Early Church. Instead, 'Ecclesiastical History 1' now consisted of a general survey from the beginnings to the present, though special attention was still directed to the traditional priority areas. In the new ordering of things, this introductory class might provide some students' only acquaintance with Church History; but those who wished to take their studies further were offered a course entitled 'Major Themes in the History of the Church', in which such topics as War and Peace, Christians and Jews, Forms of Piety, Controversies and Controversialists, and Grass Roots Christianity (the local mani-festations of movements such as Puritanism and Tractarianism) were examined at a more advanced level. In their third and final B.D. year, specialists were able to select from a wide range of subjects – Augustine, the Crusades, the Fourth Lateran Council, the Urban Reformation, the Church in the Modern World, and so on – and to study these intensively, with much use of original sources.

The result of these changes is that Ecclesiastical History, as now taught at New College, probably ranges more widely than ever before – though

[17] *College Calendar for the United Free Church of Scotland, 1907–8*, 22.
[18] *College Calendar for the United Free Church of Scotland, 1927–8*, 37.

some may wonder whether depth of treatment has (at least for the average student) suffered in the interests of breadth.

FROM HISTORICAL THEOLOGY TO CHURCH HISTORY

Also increasingly evident is a less theological, more distinctively historical, view of the discipline.

The older attitude, now abandoned, may be seen at its most consistent and extreme in the 'prelections' of Cunningham. An address delivered by him at the opening of New College in 1850 contained the following remarks on the title of the Department and the proper content of its teaching: 'This is usually known by the name of Church History, but as I have hitherto treated it, and mean to continue to treat it, it might, with more propriety, be designated Historical and Polemical Theology, as distinguished from, and supplementary to, Systematic Theology.'[19] Never again was the subsidiary role of Ecclesiastical History stated with such assurance and precision.

Rainy's lectures, it is true, were also largely concerned with the history of Christian thought and the great controversies which had engaged so much of his predecessor's attention; but in the younger man we can detect a greater awareness of the context in which the Church's thinking took place, and a greater willingness to consider not just its theology (central as that must always be) but every aspect of its many-faceted life. As he observed in his 1862 inaugural,

> The true religion, being the religion for man, could not but be historical – that is to say, implicated with history, entering into history and coming out of history. It is a religion indeed of principles, truths, laws; but it is and always was a religion of facts, events, historical transactions . . . Revealed religion and historical fact are indivisible.[20]

Rainy's down-to-earth standpoint is also apparent across the denominational divide in his late-Victorian contemporaries, Stevenson and Wallace, though Taylor seems to have reverted to the older view of his subject as a branch of historical theology. But it is in the twentieth century that the understanding of Church History as being related at least as much to History in general as to Theology has come to full expression.

[19] Cunningham (1851), 64.
[20] Simpson (1909), I, 204.

Of the two United Free professors appointed before the 1929 Union, both had undergone an education which almost guaranteed a continuance of the new outlook. MacEwen's years as an undergraduate at Oxford made the admirer of John Cairns (the outstanding divine among the United Presbyterians) a disciple also of Benjamin Jowett and John Ruskin. Watt was the first occupant of the Church History chair to possess an Honours degree in History. On the Auld Kirk/ University side, Mackinnon held 'secular' teaching appointments, and published volumes on a wide range of historical topics, before coming to the Regius Chair of Ecclesiastical History in Edinburgh.

What might be called the Cunningham tradition was even less in evidence from the 1930s onwards. Burleigh's *A Church History of Scotland* was actually criticised by one American reviewer for being 'little concerned' with the development of theology.[21] His successor, Cheyne, was like him a B.D. of Edinburgh; but before studying, and then teaching, at New College he had graduated in History at Edinburgh, undertaken historical research at Oxford (again like Burleigh), and held a lectureship in History at the University of Glasgow. He valued his association with the 'secular' historians of Edinburgh University's History Board, of which he was for a time convener, almost as much as his relationship with the theologians in the Divinity Faculty. The present incumbent of the chair, S. J. Brown, obtained his doctorate in History and Divinity from the University of Chicago; but his first degree (from the University of Illinois) was in History; and he had lectured in History at Northwestern University and the University of Georgia before coming to Edinburgh in 1988. Among the lecturers, Ross, Matheson, Hardman Moore and Dawson were all likewise trained historians.

The older, predominately theological, approach perhaps reappeared during Torrance's brief tenure of the Church History chair. After his departure, however, the attitude discernible in Rainy, Stevenson and Wallace, and even more clearly in Mackinnon and his successors, resumed its almost unquestioned sway. It was strikingly expressed, some time in the 1970s, in a short unpublished paper by Matheson for use in the Department's 'General Survey' course. 'Church History', he argued, 'is, paradoxically, a secular discipline within a Divinity Faculty! Certainly it deals with the Church, and the very concept of the latter implies a theology. Its concern, too, is focused on the Church in all its aspects,

---

[21] Burrell (1961).

the history of its organisation and liturgy, its piety and theology, its creeds and catechisms. Yet it does all this *in a secular way*, arming itself with the techniques and criteria of the secular historian.' And his conclusion was this: 'In a divinity faculty the role of Church history is to bring us down to earth. . . . It is a thoroughly secular discipline with an eminently theological perspective.'

'A secular discipline with a theological perspective': that is a description of the work of their Department with which all, or nearly all, of Edinburgh's twentieth-century ecclesiastical historians would have whole-heartedly agreed.

PUBLICATIONS: EARLY CHURCH

As already noted, the lectures of Edinburgh's Church historians concentrated upon three aspects of their subject; the Early Church, the Protestant Reformation, and Christianity in Scotland. The same concentration is evident in their published work – at least until the second half of the present century.

On the Early Church, the only considerable publications of the Victorian period – apart from Cunningham's two-volume *Historical Theology* (1862), which, as its title reveals, can scarcely be reckoned a work of history – came at its beginning and its end, and both from New College. Neither Welsh's *Elements of Church History,* vol. I: *Comprising the External History of the Church during the first Three Centuries* (Edinburgh, 1844) nor Rainy's *The Ancient Catholic Church* (Edinburgh, 1902) possesses much more than curiosity value today; but both are works of undeniable learning, and need not fear comparison with similar overviews of a textbookish kind by contemporary scholars in England, Germany or North America. Shortly after his appointment to the chair, Welsh spent several months of study in Bonn, Heidelberg and elsewhere, and his acquaintance with the German literature on his subject, as well as the classical sources, is impressive. Moreover, as the thoughtful and wide-ranging introduction to his *Elements* makes plain, ·he had a philosophic cast of mind which armed him against the temptation to utter superficial if 'edifying' judgments and made him a true historian rather than a mere annalist. Rainy for his part possessed a subtle (some would say convoluted) mind which qualified him to deal with the complexities of Patristic thought, while his administrative ability and experience undoubtedly deepened his appreciation of the great ecclesiastics of former days.

In the present century, only Mackinnon has ventured into the area of general surveys. Of his trilogy, *The Historic Jesus* (London, 1931), *The Gospel in the Early Church* (London, 1933) and *From Christ to Constantine* (London, 1936), the two earlier volumes may be said to belong to New Testament studies rather than to Church history. The third, a re-writing of the lectures delivered by him during his twenty-one years' tenure of the chair, is modestly offered 'in the belief that the experience of an old teacher [he was then in his mid-seventies] might be of some service in guiding . . . a new generation of students'.[22] Like all Mackinnon's work, it is based on careful research, meticulously footnoted, and if its theological stance may have seemed a little old-fashioned even in the 1930s, it impresses as the product of an independent, well-stocked and generous mind, and is still a useful work of reference for the non-specialist.

Mackinnon's pupil, Burleigh, was later to become known as one of the leading authorities on the history of the Scottish Church, but he made his early reputation in the Patristic field. His Croall Lectures on Augustine's *City of God* (London, 1949) were a stimulating introduction to some important aspects of the thought of the great North African Father, while his scholarly reputation was further enhanced by his edition (with new translations) of *Augustine: Earlier Writings* in the Library of Christian Classics series (London, 1950). Around the same time, Torrance published his *The Doctrine of Grace in the Apostolic Fathers* (Edinburgh, 1948), a study which – though hardly history – prompts a comparison with Cunningham in the realm of historical theology.

PUBLICATIONS: PROTESTANT REFORMATION

Rather surprisingly, no substantial work on the Reformation period was published by Edinburgh's Church historians during the nineteenth century – unless we include Cunningham's massive *The Reformers and the Theology of the Reformation* (Edinburgh, 1862), which is to all intents and purposes a theological handbook.

Things changed after the First World War. Mackinnon's magnum opus, *Luther and the Reformation* (4 vols, London, 1925–30), mediated the findings of the continental 'Luther renaissance' to English-speaking readers. Britain's foremost Luther scholar of the next generation, Gordon Rupp, rightly observed that this was 'a signal service'. He went on, however, to remark that 'The chief criticism must be that [Mackinnon]

---

[22] Mackinnon (1936B), ix.

commits the one unforgivable sin of Luther study, which is to make Luther dull, and provokes the reflection that his brand of theological and historical liberalism singularly unfits him to interpret Luther's theology':[23] an excessively harsh judgment on a work which is still a valuable, because detailed and well-documented, guide to the reformer's career. Mackinnon's two subsequent volumes, *The Origins of the Reformation* (London, 1939) and *Calvin and the Reformation* (London, 1936), display the distinctive strengths – and weaknesses – of all his work. Modern studies of late-medieval thought, moreover, give a dated appearance to the one, and lack of sympathy perhaps weakens the other; but even today they are not without value as careful and compendious introductions to their subjects.

Since the 1950s, Reformation studies have not ceased to engage the attention of Edinburgh's Church historians. On the borderland between history and theology, with his brother David, T. F. Torrance organised a new translation of *Calvin's New Testament Commentaries* (Edinburgh, 1959–72), and was associated with a re-issue, in three volumes, of *Calvin's Tracts and Treatises* (London, 1958); he also published a number of theological studies on Reformation topics, such as *Calvin's Doctrine of Man* (London, 1952), *Kingdom and Church: a Study in the Theology of the Reformation* (Edinburgh, 1956), and *The Hermeneutics of John Calvin* (London, 1988). Still in the theological field, Wright translated and edited the *Common Places of Martin Bucer* (Appleford, 1972) and edited essays on *Martin Bucer: Reforming Church and Community* (Cambridge, 1994). And that new life could be injected into what the Victorians understood by Reformation history will be seen when some of Matheson's contributions to the subject are presently taken note of.

PUBLICATIONS: SCOTTISH CHRISTIANITY

Throughout our period, Scottish history has attracted a good deal of attention from Edinburgh's Church historians. Admittedly, the occupants of the University chair during the nineteenth century were far from productive. Robertson wrote virtually nothing. Stevenson's scholarly and lively *The Legends and Commemorative Celebrations of St Kentigern, his Friends and Disciples* (Edinburgh, 1874) has been described – perhaps a little dismissively – as 'The best thesaurus of the legends of St Kentigern'.[24] Wallace's *George Buchanan*, in the 'Famous Scots' series

[23] Rupp (1953), 53.
[24] Duke (1932). 186.

(Edinburgh, 1899), slight as it is, was left unfinished. Taylor published only a few semi-popular articles.

The New College men did much better. Welsh's admiring *Account of the Life and Writings of T. Brown M.D.* (Edinburgh, 1825), his old moral philosophy teacher, is of little interest today. But Rainy's brilliant *Three Lectures on the Church of Scotland* (Edinburgh, 1872), though fiercely partisan, should still be required reading for anyone who wishes to understand the central concerns of Scottish Presbyterians over several centuries; while his biographical works, the *Life of William Cunningham* (London, 1871) and *Memorials of Robert Smith Candlish* (Edinburgh, 1880) – the former with James Mackenzie, the latter with William Wilson – are, despite their strongly Victorian flavour, indispensable accounts of the men and their times.

A. R. MacEwen, the first of New College's teachers in the present century, was equally prolific. His boldest venture, the two-volume *History of the Church in Scotland* (London, 1913, 1918), may strike today's readers as somewhat old-fashioned and in need of extensive emendation. Yet as he himself remarked about the histories of John Cunningham (1859) and George Grub (1861), 'All students will acknowledge that narratives written at these dates require to be re-written, and that estimates which then seemed adequate must be reconsidered.'[25] Furthermore, the fact remains that nothing on quite the same scale has appeared since MacEwen's time, and that even our contemporary revisionists concede that cautious use may still be made of his account. In any case, it is probably his biographical works which show him at his best. More than thirty years separate his short memoir of his father (1877) from his *Antoinette Bourignon, Quietist* (London, 1909); in between came the *Life and Letters of John Cairns* (London, 1895) and *The Erskines* ('Famous Scots', Edinburgh, 1900), for which he most deserves to be remembered. If Cairns was the presiding genius of the United Presbyterian Church, it could almost be said that Ebenezer and Ralph Erskine *were* the original Secession: together, MacEwen's volumes bring the men and their tradition attractively – and in the main convincingly – to life.

Between the end of the First World War and the outbreak of the Second, Edinburgh's Church historians published virtually nothing about their own country apart from Mackinnon's two volumes, *The Social and Industrial History of Scotland from the Earliest Times to the Union* (London, 1920) and *The Social and Industrial History of Scotland from the*

---

[25] MacEwen (1913–18), I, vii.

Union to the Present Time (London, 1921) – neither of which was principally concerned with ecclesiastical affairs.

Things have been very different since. Hugh Watt's *Thomas Chalmers and the Disruption* (Edinburgh, 1943), though deeply indebted to the standard Victorian biography by W. Hanna, was a concise and readable contribution to the centenary celebrations; *Recalling the Scottish Covenants* (London, 1946) and *John Knox in Controversy* (London, 1950) reworked familiar material in the author's pleasantly unpretentious way. Of more permanent value were *Published Writings of Thomas Chalmers: A Descriptive List* (Edinburgh, 1943) and *New College, Edinburgh: A Centenary History* (Edinburgh, 1946), the latter a substantial, indeed indispensable work based on an intimate acquaintance with the archival material. Watt, it should also be remembered, was an excellent teacher, and through his supervision of postgraduate students – many of them returning to their religious roots from North America – he promoted much worthwhile research into post-Reformation Scottish history. Indeed, both Torrance's re-translation, with an introduction, of Robert Bruce's sacramental sermons, *The Mystery of the Lord's Supper* (London, 1958) and J. S. McEwen's *The Faith of John Knox* (London, 1961), a perceptive and lucid analysis, can be seen as following the lead of their one-time professor.

The quatercentenary year of the Scottish Reformation saw the publication of Burleigh's *A Church History of Scotland* (London, 1960), the first general survey to appear for over a century. Its comprehensiveness, clarity, balance and broad sympathies won general acclaim, and after nearly forty years it looks like continuing for some time yet as the standard introduction to the subject.

Burleigh's successors, Cheyne and Brown, have both concentrated on relatively modern topics. Much of Cheyne's work is contained in articles on such eminent nineteenth- and twentieth-century ecclesiastics and theologians as Chalmers, Caird, Tulloch, Robertson Smith and the Baillie brothers; but he has also published *The Transforming of the Kirk: Victorian Scotland's Religious Revolution* (Edinburgh, 1983), an edited volume, *The Practical and the Pious: Essays on Thomas Chalmers (1780–1843)* (Edinburgh, 1985), and – a brief re-assessment for the Ter-Jubilee of 1843 – *The Ten Years' Conflict and the Disruption: an Overview* (Edinburgh, 1993). Brown's *Thomas Chalmers and the Godly Commonwealth in Scotland* (Oxford 1982) immediately took its place as the authoritative modern biography and one of the finest pieces of ecclesiastical history published this century. It was followed by a volume of essays co-edited with Michael Fry, *Scotland in the Age of Disruption* (Edinburgh, 1993); and students of the period now await the appearance of his Chalmers Lectures on 'The Crisis of National Religious Establishments: England, Scotland and Ireland, 1833–45'. Nor would the picture be complete without mentioning that the Ecclesiastical History Department may claim a large share in two volumes edited by Wright in collaboration with others: essays on *The Bible in Scottish Life and Literature* (Edinburgh, 1988) and the monumental *Dictionary of Scottish Church History and Theology* (Edinburgh, 1993), many of whose contributors have either taught or studied at New College in recent years.

PUBLICATIONS: A NEW CATHOLICITY

We have seen how the teaching of Church History in Edinburgh gradually extended beyond the traditional areas – Early Church, Protestant Reformation and Scottish Christianity. A similar broadening of interest and sympathy is also evident in the publications of staff members. Mackinnon's massive four-volume *A History of Modern Liberty* (London, 1906–41), and Watt's little sketch, *Representative Churchmen of Twenty Centuries* (London, 1927), may be said to have begun the movement. Matheson certainly gave a wider meaning to Reformation studies with *Cardinal Contarini at Regensburg* (Oxford, 1972) and *Argula von Grumbach: A Woman's Voice in the Reformation* (Edinburgh, 1994), as well as his translation of the *Collected Works of Thomas Müntzer* (Edinburgh, 1988) and his editing of the English version of Goertz, *Thomas Müntzer: Apocalyptic Mystic and Revolutionary* (Edinburgh, 1993). He also illuminated a crucial phase of German history with his documentary compilation and commentary, *The Third Reich and the Christian Churches* (Edinburgh, 1981), and gave a new dimension to an old subject with *The Finger of God in the Disruption: Scottish Principles and New Zealand Realities* (Alexandra, NZ, 1993), an account which might have surprised men like Welsh and Cunningham. Perhaps most startling of all, Ross's *John Philip (1775–1851): Missions, Race and Politics in South Africa* (Aberdeen, 1986) is far more than the conventional missionary biography, while his *A Vision Betrayed: The Jesuits in Japan and China, 1542–1742* (Edinburgh, 1994) breaks fresh ground with its combination of Chinese and Japanese history, religious studies and missiology.

Developments such as these suggest that Church History in Edinburgh has not only a productive and interesting past to look back upon but also a productive and interesting future ahead of it.[26]

[26] For a brief survey from the Disruption onwards, see Wright (1983).

Chapter 6

◦━❦━◦

Divinity and Dogmatics

George Newlands

VARIETIES OF THEOLOGY

THE PURPOSE of this chapter is to trace the development of systematic theology, in the broader history of theology at Edinburgh, roughly from the period after 1843. This is not as easy as it sounds. At different periods, and in different centres of learning, various areas of theology are studied in different sorts of combinations. The mix is often influenced by variations in consideration of method, as well as by the accidents of the particular interests of the personnel involved at given times. For example, within the range of Edinburgh theology over the last hundred years or so, dogmatics may be thought to be especially associated with the chairs occupied by H. R. Mackintosh, G. T. Thomson, T. F. Torrance and J. P. Mackey. But other scholars also taught in the area of dogmatics over long periods, and the dogmatics specialists were inevitably involved in other areas of theology.

The word 'theology' has a long history as a general term embracing all the traditional ecclesiastical disciplines. The older UK universities had faculties of divinity. Dogmatic or systematic theology might be used to distinguish constructive theology from the biblical, historical and practical disciplines. And again divinity could distinguish dogmatic or symbolic theology from philosophical theology or the philosophy of religion, again terms which could have different nuances at different times, notably before and after the deployment of the techniques of Anglo-Saxon analytical philosophy to talk of God. In the views of different scholars, these nuances could be of decisive significance for the understanding of their subject, to the extent of reflecting the infinitely convoluted shades of meaning of the terminology of the classical doctrinal formulations themselves.

Apart from the fluctuating subject divisions within the disciplines there is another central factor for the development of theology to consider, the effect of the Disruption in the Church of Scotland in 1843. From 1843 to the Union of the Churches in 1929 there had to be provision for separate theological education for candidates for the ministry in both the Established Church and on the other hand the Free Church and then the United Free Church, the one continuing over in the Old College of the University of Edinburgh, the other in the new buildings of New College. After the Union teaching was again to be concentrated in New College (though some is done today in the George Square campus). Theological teaching and research continued in the city for other denominations, Free Church, United Free, Congregational, Roman Catholic, Episcopalian and others, and institutions, from St Andrews Drygrange and Coates Hall to the famous United Presbyterian Divinity Hall, came and went.[1] All of these would have to be taken into account in a comprehensive picture of Edinburgh theology over the period.

OLD COLLEGE: THE UNIVERSITY FACULTY

This chapter begins with the faculty in the Old College, where Thomas Chalmers had been the Professor of Systematic Theology since 1828. The contributor of the *DNB* article on Chalmers, W. G. Blaikie, himself a Professor in the Apologetics chair at New College, commented that 'In the theological Chair he was more distinguished for the impulse which he gave to his students than for original contributions to theological science.'[2] After his dramatic departure at the Disruption in 1843 his chair was filled by the Principal of the University himself, the polymath John Lee, till 1859. From 1859 to 1875 the chair was held by Thomas J. Crawford (1812–75), who wrote a number of substantial volumes, including books on *The Fatherhood of God* and *The Doctrine of Holy Scripture Respecting the Atonement*. The most substantial figure of the early part of our period, a scholar highly regarded throughout the country, was Robert Flint (1838–1910), who held the chair of

---

[1] See the chapter in this volume by D. F. Wright.

[2] *DNB* IX, 451. On Chalmers see Brown, S. J. (1982) and Cheyne (1985). *DNB* has a number of useful articles on other figures discussed in this chapter, e.g. Lee, Buchanan and Cunningham.

Systematic Theology in Old College 1876–1903.[3] Flint produced a number of books on the philosophy of religion and apologetics, but he lectured on a much wider range of subjects. For example, the *University Calendar* lists series on 'Ecclesiology and soteriology' for 1893–4, and 'Man, sin and Christology' for 1895–6. Though Flint appears to have been a remarkably quiet, reserved, almost withdrawn figure, almost absent from church affairs, his writings were lucid, rational and well organised. They made their own powerful impact on his students and contemporaries.

In *Theism* (1877) Flint set out an apologetic argument for belief in God, based not on feeling, on Kant's idealism or on Hegel's concept of the absolute (against the currents of much contemporary thought) but on rational grounds. The traditional arguments for the existence of God are rehearsed, not to prove God's existence, but to show the rationality of faith, in the manner of Aquinas. Sell compares him appropriately with Joseph Butler. Flint combines a strong theological sense of the sin of man, in the Calvinist tradition, with a typical nineteenth-century optimism about human progress in society. His may not perhaps have been a theology to fire the imagination, but his learning, especially in his extensive *History of the Philosophy of History* (1893), the acuteness of his philosophical argument and his resistance to prevailing fashions were much respected long after his work in the University had ceased.

Flint's period in office coincided with the revolution in transport which was to make it easier for students to travel around the country by train and to travel abroad to attend other universities. Students from Britain, Germany and America could attend the lectures of the great men in each other's countries. Theology attracted the interest of some of the very best minds in any student generation, and Flint was succeeded in the Old College – the Faculty of the University and the Established Church of Scotland – by another long-serving professor, W. P. Paterson (1860–1939).

W. P. Paterson

Like Flint, Paterson was best known for his work in 'divinity', but lectured also in doctrine – e.g. in 1923–4 he offered a course in Dogmatic Theology. Active in church affairs, he was a prolific author of many books. Perhaps the best known of these was *The Rule of Faith*,

---

[3] For Flint see Sell (1987), 39–63.

a magisterial survey of the origins and substantive content of Christian theology which went through a number of editions from 1912 to 1932. In this work Paterson follows a historical approach to theology, which owes much to the influence of Albrecht Ritschl. Part I of the volume is devoted to 'The Seat of Doctrine'. Here he considers various theories of doctrinal origins, Roman Catholic, Protestant, charismatic, rationalist, and the approaches of what he terms 'The Criterion of Feeling' (Schleiermacher) and 'Biblical Eclecticism' (Ritschl). He concludes that there are important truths in each of the classical theories. He then turns to the substance of doctrine. This starts out from a chapter on 'The Nature of the Christian Religion', summed up in a long definition in a footnote,[4] on the tried pattern of a modification through Ritschl of Schleiermacher's famous definition.

Paterson next considers various confessional and philosophical interpretations of the nature of religion, particular readings of the universal notion, from the orthodox interpretation (the early church) to Roman Catholic, general Protestant, particular Reformed, and rationalist readings. Finally there are chapters on 'The Theology of Schleiermacher', 'The Ritschlian Revision', 'Movements of the Twentieth Century' and an Epilogue. Paterson enters sympathetically into each of these readings. For example, the section on 'The Genius of Roman Catholicism' begins with the affirmation that 'Roman Catholicism attests its greatness by the fact that it is one of the real dividing forces in the modern world. It is easy to take up towards it any attitude save that of indifference.'[5] The section on Schleiermacher's *The Christian Faith*, written long before English speakers had the benefit of the New College translation edited by H. R. Mackintosh and J. S. Stewart, is comprehensive and scholarly. The Epilogue is at pains to distinguish between the centre and the periphery of theology. 'The central content of the Christian revelation, the gospel which forms the soul and power of the Christian religion, is on an altogether different footing from the speculative utterances made by theology in the outlying provinces of religious thought.' But Paterson is much too cautious to attempt the merest hint of where the centre and the provinces begin!

Paterson was as concerned for praxis as he was for theory. In 1915 he edited a volume of academic essays on *German Culture*, in which he sought to give a fair estimate of the virtues and failings of his subject —

[4] Paterson (1912), 199 n. 1.
[5] *Ibid.*, 236.

in marked contrast with the apocalyptic tones already adopted in 1914 by Sir George Adam Smith, the Bishop of London and many others. This becomes clear from his co-editing (with David Watson) in 1918 of the Report for the Church of Scotland Commission on the War, on *Social Evils and Problems*. In the course of a long introduction Paterson surveys the sphere of the family, menaced by drink, poverty and infidelity, the wider circle of friends and acquaintances, the economic sphere, with the dangers of rural depopulation, dubious business ethics, unequal distribution of wealth and political instability. Against this he sets the Christian moral ideal, of duty given through conscience, of Christ as exemplar, of an ethic consisting 'in the main of principles, and not of hard-and-fast legislation'. He suggested the foundation of a special committee, 'a special organ whose business would be to sift and arrange the Church's own knowledge in this field, and to assimilate the important results of the investigations made by the representatives of Social Science'. It was important to have a deliberate discussion of such matters as 'the new and more hopeful methods of dealing with criminals'.

Paterson would perhaps be gratified to know that the Church of Scotland's Church and Nation Committee is actively grappling with these issues (1995), but less happy to learn that there has been nothing remotely like a uniform rate of improvement. The following chapters of *Social Evils and Problems* contain excellent material on such topics as 'The Housing of the People' and 'Industrial Problems', along with essays such as that by Dr Norman Maclean on 'The Decreasing Birth-rate' which make less convincing reading today. The results of contraception are utterly wicked; 'If Australia and New Zealand are not occupied by the British, the yellow man cannot be shut out'; Girls are to be trained 'to be wife and mother, and to reign as a queen in a happy home'. It is indeed difficult to jump out of our cultural skins.

Paterson's successor in the Old College chair, in 1934, bringing us up to living memory, was John Baillie (1886–1960). But by now the Union of the Churches (1929) had enabled the United Free Church Professor of Systematic Theology, the remarkable H. R. Mackintosh, to concentrate on dogmatic theology, and Baillie lectured in divinity or philosophical theology up to 1956. However, Baillie had already published in the field of Christology from America in 1929, and he retained a deep interest in all things theological. He was, of course, aware of the profound contributions to doctrine being made by his brother Donald over in St Andrews.

121

NEW COLLEGE

From 1845 to 1900 there was, of course, an independent Divinity Faculty in the Free Church, meeting during 1843–50 in temporary accommodation and then in New College. From 1900 to 1929, New College was similarly the seat of the United Free Church's Faculty. Thomas Chalmers, late of the Old College, was the first Professor of Divinity, and clearly had numerous other things on his mind. It was intended that he should be succeeded in 1847 by R. S. Candlish, who never took up office, remaining at Free St George's on the death of his chosen successor, and eventually, in 1862, combining the charge with the Principalship of New College. Hugh Watt lists James Buchanan, James MacGregor, John Laidlaw and James Wardrop as early professors of systematic theology.[6] These men built up the reputation of the Edinburgh College, at the time when its Glasgow sister institution in the West, later to be called Trinity College, was at the height of its intellectual powers, in the hands of A. B. Bruce, James Orr, James Denney, James Moffatt, George Adam Smith and Thomas Lindsay, and in Glasgow University on Gilmorehill the Caird brothers, Edward and John, were turning doctrine into magic with the assistance of Hegel.[7] This was a remarkable period when some of the brightest Scots of their generation would turn to theology (some falling by the wayside to become archbishops of Canterbury – Randall Davidson, Cosmo Gordon Lang), when remarkable things were to be done in all four Scottish faculties, an achievement which was all too soon to be confronted with the horrors of global war.

James Buchanan (1804–70) was Professor of Apologetics 1845–7, and then Professor of Systematic Theology from 1847, on the death of Chalmers, to 1868. He wrote books on *Faith in God and Modern Atheism Compared*, on *Analogy* in the tradition of Butler, and on *The Doctrine of Justification*. In his introductory lecture of 1847 he stressed the centrality of the Bible. 'The contents of scripture, however miscellaneous, afford the materials for a complete system of religious truth: and its topics are so related to each other, as to fall naturally and necessarily into the order of a regular scheme.'[8] A. C. Cheyne commented that 'it should

[6] Watt is of course indispensable; cf. too *FES*, *FUFCS* and *DSCHT*. I am grateful to Professor A. C. Cheyne, himself of no small influence on New College theology, for notes on these early figures. On A. C. Fraser, who held the chair of Logic in New College 1846–57, see pp. 38, 48–9, and *DSCHT* 333–4.

[7] See Hazlett (1993).

[8] Cunningham (1851), 88.

be remembered that he and traditionalists like him enjoyed a position of virtual monopoly of all the positions of power and responsibility in the Scottish Churches',[9] while the writer of the *DNB* article observed that 'Although not eminent for his powers of originality, Buchanan had a remarkable faculty of collecting what was valuable in the researches and arguments of others, and presenting it in clear form and lucid language.'[10]

James MacGregor (1830–94) appears to have written little. But he supported strongly Robertson Smith in 1880, disapproved of colleague Robert Rainy's treatment of him, and emigrated to New Zealand. He was succeeded by John Laidlaw (1881–1904), who apparently gave cautious support to Smith, edited Robert Bruce's sermons on the sacrament, had his memoir written by H. R. Mackintosh but was held by at least one acute observer to have 'made a complete and lamentable mess'[11] in New College. James Wardrop (1821–1909) appears to have made little impact, perhaps understandably since he was seventy-nine at the time of his appointment to an additional chair (no ageism here). Mention should be made in this section of William Cunningham, resolutely conservative since as a divinity student he had gone to report the heresies of McLeod Campbell to the presbytery. Cunningham came in 1843 to the Apologetics chair, then moved in 1845 on Dr Welsh's death to the Church History chair. His *Theological Lectures* were not to appear till 1878, at the height of the Robertson Smith controversy.

H. R. Mackintosh

Facile princeps among the systematic theologians at the top of the Mound in this period was Hugh Ross Mackintosh (1870–1936), appointed in 1904, continuing in his chair till well after the Union, and retiring in 1936. Mackintosh established a well-deserved reputation early with *The Doctrine of the Person of Jesus Christ* in 1912. It is worth pausing to take in the full measure of this project, on which essays were to be set for sixty years, and which we may see as a benchmark of the quality which New College would produce. Though a work of systematic theology, it begins quite firmly with Christology in the New Testament. There are six main chapters on what he takes to be six main types of apostolic doctrine – the Synoptic, the primitive (Acts and 1 Peter), the

[9] Cheyne (1983), 68.

[10] *DNB* VII, 194.

[11] W. Robertson Nicoll, in Darlow (1925), 370. And see Laidlaw (1901), and Mackintosh (1907).

Pauline, those represented by the Epistle to the Hebrews and the Apocalypse, and the Johannine. These are distinctive but not contradictory. We begin with the Christ of the synoptic Gospels. Mackintosh makes the point early that the Gospels are not biographies. Their purpose is simply to convey the expression of a great personality, but they make no attempt to cover the entire life.[12] Likewise, Jesus' knowledge is limited.

> It has gradually become clear that to make Jesus responsible for such things as the details of an ethico-political system, valid for all time, or to invest His words with legal authority in matters of Biblical criticism and history, is wholly misleading and irrelevant.[13]

Mackintosh then moves on in Book II to 'The History of Christological Doctrine', indicating in the notes a considerable debt to the classic German historians of doctrine. He covers the whole area from the Apostolic Fathers to Dorner and William Sanday, and then turns in Book III to his 'Reconstructive Statement of the Doctrine', and questions of method. The understanding of the person of Christ is then spelled out in two sections. In the first, 'The Immediate Utterances of Faith', Mackintosh speaks of Christ as the object of faith, as the exalted Lord, and then offers accounts of the perfect humanity and the divinity of Christ.

In the last final section he tackles 'The Transcendent Implicates of Faith', beginning from the Christian idea of the incarnation. He then considers the pre-existence of the Son, the self-limitation of God in Christ (kenosis), the self-realisation of Christ, and finally Christ and the divine Trinity.

There is an appendix on the Virgin Birth, which he regards as a wonderful symbol rather than an essential element of faith (in contrast to the contemporary inclusion among the American *Fundamentals* of the defence of it by Glasgow's James Orr). Mackintosh marshals the evidence, historical and theological, reaches his own judgment, and leaves it to his readers to make up their minds. He is not afraid of deploying contemporary historical criticism of his sources, nor afraid of bringing in philosophical and doctrinal considerations as required. There is an irenic note, a catholicity of spirit which is not dissimilar to the tone of the *Lux Mundi* collection in the revival of Christology south of the border, and which was to be echoed in the Baillie brothers

---

[12] Mackintosh (1912), 7.
[13] *Ibid.*, 13.

and their successors. This openness to genuine theological enquiry without dogmatic censoriousness was to be valued by generations of students who flocked to New College from many parts of the world.

Mackintosh looked back with a firm sense of tradition. He was to speak of McLeod Campbell as 'the greatest of all Scottish theologians, to whom perhaps more than to any other single mind we today owe a spiritual interpretation of the central Christian ideas'.[14] But he was also acutely aware of the social problems of the present – e.g. in his references to international and racial paralysis and to class war in *The Divine Initiative* of 1921.

AFTER THE UNION: JOHN BAILLIE

Mackintosh, translator and editor with J. S. Stewart of Schleiermacher in English, was to be much impressed in later years by Karl Barth, an influence heavily reflected in his *Types of Modern Theology* of 1937, and it was in this tradition that we find his successor, G. T. Thomson (1887–1958), active in beginning the monumental English translation of the *Church Dogmatics*, a task to be completed under the supervision of his successor, T. F. Torrance. Thomson published almost nothing of his own, but also translated Heinrich Heppe's *Reformed Dogmatics* – and lectured directly from it. His earlier militarism left its mark on his language and style; somewhat surprisingly, he was conductor of the College Music Society.

New College theology in the 1940s was to be almost synonymous with the name of John Baillie, active as a philosophical theologian and as a great churchman, chairman of the Baillie Commission which produced 'The Interpretation of God's Will in the Present Crisis', during the War years. The story of the contribution to theology made by John and Donald Baillie has been well documented recently in *Christ, Church and Society*, edited by Professor David Fergusson.[15] Baillie's theology, though not focused on dogmatics, was of course entirely relevant to dogmatic issues, especially in his analyses of revelation. He was an appreciative but sharply perceptive critic of Karl Barth. In his own excellent chapter on 'John Baillie: Orthodox Liberal', David Fergusson discusses Baillie's early Christology, which combines criticism of the Chalcedonian doctrine with stress on the uniqueness and finality

[14] Mackintosh (1929), 157.
[15] Fergusson (1993).

of Christ, anticipating much that was to be developed in D. M. Baillie's *God was in Christ*.

When we turn to John Baillie's last book, the undelivered Gifford Lectures published as *The Sense of the Presence of God*, we find a characteristic combination of an appeal to experience with an exploration of rational grounds for belief in God. 'Our total experience of reality presents itself as a single experience.' But procedures of verification and falsification are required. 'A faith that is consistent with everything possible is not a faith in anything actual.' But faith remains central, as 'an awareness of the divine presence itself, however hidden behind the veils of sense'. Baillie often stresses that the appropriate human response to God is gratitude. 'Gratitude is not only the dominant note of Christian piety but equally the dominant motive of Christian action in the world.' It was no accident that Baillie was as well known for his *Diary of Private Prayer* as for his theology. His combination of openness to liberal scholarship with unapologetic devotion was immensely attractive, and did much for the reputation of New College throughout the world. There was an important social dimension to Baillie's thought, owing much to friendship with Reinhold Niebuhr and clear in the work of the Baillie Commission. This was to bear fruit in the social theology of the post-War period, and might still provide new stimulus to a tradition of socially engaged theology. But for the time being the somewhat hazardous world of the social sciences was to be overshadowed by a new emphasis on transcendental theology in the classical tradition of Reformed thought.

We should not forget here the continuing dialogue with practical theology and Christian ethics in the College (and indeed with the other disciplines; those of us who studied at New College developed our theology from discussion with a wide range of our teachers). There was early in New College a second Divinity chair, later renamed Apologetics, Christian Ethics and Pastoral Theology (and later still, Christian Ethics and Practical Theology), held by William Cunningham, James Bannerman, William Garden Blaikie, Alexander Martin, Daniel Lamont and William S. Tindal. This area is explored elsewhere in this volume.

THE 1950s AND BEYOND: T. F. TORRANCE

With the coming to New College of Thomas Forsyth Torrance, (1913–), first as Professor of Church History (1950–2) and then as

Professor of Christian Dogmatics (1952–79), we reach the period when the influence of Barth in Scotland was to be at its height. This phenomenon has been viewed in very different ways, as a great blessing or as the time of the 'Barthian captivity'. (The writer is glad to recall attending with his wife Barth's last seminars in Basel, the end of a very long line of New College pilgrims to the shrine.) Like Flint, Torrance swiftly made an international reputation through the rapid production of a series of solid books. But if Professor Flint was almost invisible as a man, the same could scarcely be said of Professor Torrance. Coming into the ecumenical movement, newly resurgent with great hopes after 1945, with a strong conviction of the value of Reformed theology and a concern for traditional Christian orthodoxy, Torrance developed international theological contacts, was the chief inspiration behind the new *Scottish Journal of Theology*, helped to found a new Society for the Study of Theology, and influenced deeply generations of candidates for the ministry in Edinburgh. He was greatly concerned for theology in its purest form as a theoretical discipline, for the pastoral ministry, and for the welfare of the church and of all his students. For those who shared his perspectives, he was deeply inspiring. For those who were not persuaded, Tom Torrance was never less than impressive. Unlike most of his contemporaries, Torrance had been born and spent formative years, not in suburban Scotland but in China at a time of great political unrest, in a pious missionary culture, acutely conscious of ancient civilisation, random cruelty, and pagan immorality of biblical dimensions in the closest proximity. This dimension was continued in his experience as a war chaplain. A deep seriousness of purpose is never far from the surface of his work.

Torrance's published work effectively begins with his Basel doctoral thesis, *The Doctrine of Grace in the Apostolic Fathers*. This work exhibits the keen interest in the history of doctrine which characterised much of his later work, and his confidence in reinterpreting conventional wisdom in the light of a distinctive understanding of grace. Its fruits are seen further in *Calvin's Doctrine of Man, Conflict and Agreement, The School of Faith*, and *Theology in Reconstruction*. Some have seen in his controversial but always imaginative work on the history of Christian thought Torrance's most enduring contribution to theology.

Beyond dogmatics, Torrance, following the anti-modern tradition of Barth, came to develop an increasingly sceptical view of the development of the humanities since the Enlightenment, and to focus on the cosmic dimensions of incarnation in a series of studies in theology and science. Here he is generally recognised as a pioneer in an immensely important field, to be developed (albeit often in diverse directions) by Pannenberg, Peacocke and others. On retiral from New College (after winning the Templeton Prize for theology and numerous academic distinctions), he helped to set up the Center of Theological Inquiry at Princeton, through which research on the foundations of theology and the natural sciences was to develop. In later years he continued to publish extensively, combining an appreciation of the most modern cosmological theory with patristic studies and a critique of liberalism in all its forms, maintaining a robust defence of highly traditional positions on doctrine and ethics, notably on the Virgin Birth, conservative biblical interpretation, abortion, fertilisation and embryology, and on sexuality.

Some indication of Professor Torrance's characteristic contribution may be had from the Templeton Prize volume, *Theological Science*. What is required of us here is not a philosophy of religion in which religion is substituted in the place of God, but a philosophy of theology in which we are directly engaged with knowledge of the reality of God. Scientific theology is active engagement in cognitive relation to God in obedience to the demands of his reality. How God can be known is determined from first to last by the way in which he is actually known. God reverses our whole natural relation of knowing, in directing it out beyond all possibility in ourselves to knowledge of God, altering the shape of our minds to receive and recognise the truth. Scientific activity is the rigorous extension of our own basic rationality, as we seek to act towards things in ways appropriate to their own natures, letting them shine in their own light. In theology it is by relation to the incarnation that our statements have their own fundamental ontologic. The human sciences have in large measure lost their way in the distortions created by Enlightenment thought. But there are close analogies between the methods of the natural scientist and of the theologian, properly understood.

John McIntyre

John Baillie's chosen successor was to be John McIntyre (1916–), who like Baillie came to New College after a period abroad, in this case in Australia. Here McIntyre had produced an incisive critique of Anselm's theology, especially of his work on the atonement. *St Anselm and his Critics* reflected close contacts with analytical philosophy in Sydney, and was to be read and cited widely. As with Baillie, philosophical techniques were brought to bear on theological, and often doctrinal topics. Professor McIntyre's careful analytical approach could also be deployed in constructive theology, again with doctrinal interests, in *On the Love of God, The Shape of Christology* and *The Shape of Soteriology*. *On the Love of God* is a profound meditation on the heart of Christian faith. 'The love of God is what the Gospel is about. It is, then, the whole content of our faith, as it is its whole object.' The study then explores various depth dimensions of love, as concern, commitment, communication, community, involvement, identification, response and responsibility. Critical scrutiny of concepts is deployed together with an underlying pastoral motif to produce what amounts to a contemporary restatement of atonement and reconciliation. In some respects we might say that here Anselm is updated and transformed. Perhaps it may be added that the author of this chapter found the study constantly illuminating in writing on the same topic twenty years later.

The Shape of Christology was a more formally structured monograph, which exploited to the full McIntyre's philosophical gifts. It explored the given Christology, methods and models, notably the two-nature model and the revelation model. On a first reading rather skeletal, it becomes clear that it contains numerous clues to fleshing out the skeleton in the relation of the life of Jesus to the life of God. The book provided an exacting paradigm of an approach to Christology which eschewed the rather overblown rhetoric of revelation then in fashion, and called for faithful but critical discernment. The search for a more adequate and more accurate approach to God, through faith without fideism and reason without rationalism, was to issue in the 1987 volume, *Faith, Theology and Imagination*. Here 'the Parabolic Imagination' is exegeted in relation to ethical discourse, metaphysics, methodology and epistemology. We are offered no less than thirteen roles for the use of images in theology, the last being appropriately the recreative character of images, renewing and revitalising significant experience of God and of Christian community. McIntyre seeks a proper balance between the human dimensions of faith and the divine initiative, while laying characteristic stress on the links between theology and worship. *The Shape of Soteriology* continued this strand, arguing for example for the importance of the reading 'This is my body which is *broken* for you' in the eucharistic liturgy. Examination of the logic of the various biblical models of salvation shows that they complement each other, and each has a role to play in pastoral counselling. As often, a cool sense of humour is just about allowed to emerge, in the entitling of a chapter, 'Universalisers, Relaters and Contemporanisers', and the work ends with a focus on forgiveness.

McIntyre followed John Baillie in combining appreciation of the constructive content of Barth's theology with scepticism about the doctrine of revelation which was integral to his theological programme. He reinforced the influence of the liberal evangelical tradition, and though not especially liberal by contemporary standards was widely held to represent the best of the broad church inheritance in Scotland. New College, situated in the city of Edinburgh, where the Church of Scotland office is also located, has always had close links with the Church. John Baillie, Tom Torrance and John McIntyre were all Moderators of the General Assembly and all played an active role in the affairs of the Church of Scotland. Those who had the privilege of sitting under Torrance and McIntyre had the benefit of a uniquely valuable double perspective in systematic theology.

INFLUENTIAL LECTURERS

In addition to the professors there were lecturers in these areas from the 1950s on, many of whom were later professors in other places. Though Victorian notions of professorial hierarchy still linger on in the universities, each one of the lecturers has had an increasingly deep influence on developments in theology and made important contributions to the churches.[16] D. W. D. Shaw, later to be Principal and Dean both in Edinburgh and St Andrews, introduced process thought to Scots divinity, along with squash and most other essential aspects of civilisation. James Torrance reminded students tirelessly, and in view of increasing fundamentalism perhaps prophetically, of the absolute priority of grace. John Zizioulas, later a Metropolitan Archbishop, introduced Orthodoxy to an astounded Northern world. Alasdair Heron, now Professor in Erlangen, imaginatively recreated the living tradition of Reformed theology for those who knew it not. Ruth Page, theologian of 'ambiguity' and of the animal kingdom, has become prominent in ecumenical theological circles as a representative of the Reformed tradition. Alan Lewis was to write most profoundly about Christ and suffering before himself dying tragically at an early age, with immense courage and faith. At one level, if the history of New College

---

[16] See the titles of representative publications listed under the names of each of the following in the Bibliography.

dogmatics means anything, *si monumentum quaeris*, we may remember Alan Lewis. David Fergusson demonstrated that you could utter the dreaded word Bultmann, play football, and still believe in the resurrection and do serious theology. Elizabeth Maclaren (later Templeton) was to found a lay theological institute in Edinburgh, and to make an impressive contribution as a freelance but highly professional theologian to ecumenical and doctrinal dialogue. Fr Noel O'Donoghue, O.D.C., was the first Catholic priest on the Faculty, and Canon Roland Walls the first Anglican, important signs of the times and tangible avenues to alternative rich spiritual perspectives. Beyond the traditional roles of administration, teaching, postgraduate supervision and research, the wider membership of the Departments (the two Departments of Divinity and Dogmatics were later amalgamated with the title Systematic Theology) made important contributions to the pastoral care of students, and to the rich and varied social life of the college.

It is not possible to convey the substance of the reality of New College theology by indirect description. Here is a paragraph from Alan Lewis:

> Christendom's God of causal power is dead: and so too is the pagan illusion of immortality. Death terminates human life, and history is no unstopping process with its own dynamic to resist and survive the invasions of non-being. Rather, we lurch through time, impeded by a syncopated series of catastrophes: Egyptian captivity, Babylonian exile, Roman crucifixion, disasters natural and man-made, genocides particular and global. To all of this Christian theology has no principle it can synthesise about survival, only a story to tell about grace. That speaks of a triune God who does indeed create new beginnings beyond death and cataclysm. But the spirit creates such possibilities only by raising from the dead the Father's own son, in whom God allows death to work its rupturing effect, unreduced, upon himself. Only as the victim of sin's increase is he victor over the magnitude of evil, and the giver of life to his fellow-dead. Yet through this love, whose substance is weakness and surrender, he exceeds humanity's ample memory and fear of termination with an even greater promise for the future, and quietly seeks recognition as the saviour of the world.[17]

THE PRESENT AND THE FUTURE

After T. F. Torrance retired, the chair of Christian Dogmatics was redesignated the Thomas Chalmers chair of Theology, after another Edinburgh professor. The new incumbent was, for the first time since

[17] Lewis (1987), 362.

the Reformation, a Roman Catholic scholar, a married priest and a fairly radical theologian. The appointment was a remarkable instance of the flexibility of which an established tradition can be capable, though it was not without its critics, both in the Kirk and in more traditional Catholic circles. James Mackey came to New College with a solid reputation based on a number of studies, notably on *Tradition,* and on a newly published Christology, *Jesus the Man and the Myth.* This volume presented a theological assessment of the consequences for doctrine of the most recent historical scholarship, in an eminently lucid and persuasive form. There shortly followed *The Christian Experience of God as Trinity,* a radical reappraisal of traditional Trinitarian theory, characterised by imaginative historical interpretation (somewhat in the tradition of his predecessor but reaching different conclusions) and by a lively interest in the positive consequences of contemporary theology for a contemporary spirituality. This concern for faith in the present continued in essays on theological imagination, in a series of projects in Celtic Christianity, in a study of modern theology, and in a timely and perceptive study of *Power and Christian Ethics.* These may provide pointers to escaping the theological dichotomies which constrain much in theology and church today.

It is perhaps appropriate at the end of this chapter to look a little more closely at Mackey's *Power and Christian Ethics,* an interesting example of the ways in which the concerns of dogmatics reach out and interact with other disciplines in theological construction in ways which might have astonished William Cunningham, though we have to concede that his own grasp of the exercise of power might leave mere moderns looking like helpless amateurs.[18] Mackey sounds notes that we have not heard much in earlier sections of this survey – the importance of the social sciences and cultural anthropology for Christian theology, the discovery of a hermeneutic of suspicion, typified by the work of Foucault, the need for an even more self-critical theology in the future, the centrality of Christ as sacrament. Perhaps a sure sign of the health of a tradition is its continuing innovation, reappraisal and search for better paradigms for the human experience of the divine mystery. Mackey considers the anatomy of power, power as authority and power as coercive, the anatomy of morals, powers secular and powers sacred, the Christian experience of power and the anatomy of church, and draws conclusions about the uses of power in churches and secular states. The centre of Christianity is the eucharist. 'In other

[18] For a more favourable estimate of Cunningham see Macleod, J. (1943).

words, an adequate and adequately perceptive account of a dramatic, communal action with a piece of bread – taken, thanked for, broken, given – could provide a complete Christian theology.'[19] Here is a paradigm for the development of a communitarian structure of morality, which neither takes refuge in romantic individualism nor indulges in institutional violence. There is here too a refreshing directness which is often all too lacking in theology and church. 'In addition the very last thing we need in the Roman Catholic Church is an influx of failed Anglican opponents of women priests. Rome is only too capable on its own of inflicting the kind of communitarian damage which one can only illustrate here.' Those of us who are Protestants may ask ourselves how good we are at identifying and minimising the sources of communitarian damage through denial of justice in the sight of God.

Systematic Theology has been enriched by a series of scholars with overseas experience – Ruth Page, Bruce McCormack, Chris Kaiser, Kevin Vanhoozer, Gary Badcock, each with a distinctive contribution to make. Recent expansion of the Department into a Department of Theology and Religious Studies – with Frank Whaling, Alistair Kee and Nicolas Wyatt – has opened new horizons, from which we confidently expect fresh and once again surprising initiatives in the future. In recent years there has been a change in the balance in student numbers from a majority of candidates for the ministry, especially of the Church of Scotland, to a majority of students with other career aims. This too is reflected in the composition and work of the Department, and coincides with considerable expansion.

Looking back over the period we see a remarkable variety, both in the approach to theology and in the constructive proposals which have emerged. At some points it may have seemed that a particular perspective would prevail and would become established as *the* New College theological style. But this has not happened. Instead a succession of scholars have each made distinctive and imaginative contributions to a continuing quest for a deeper understanding of the nature of Christian faith. We may reflect that it is on the basis of a solid tradition from the past that the confidence and capacity to develop, to take risks and to seek to enlarge the bounds of the theological imagination are made possible, and we may be grateful to those who have laid these foundations so securely. For a Faculty which is only 400 years old, in systematic theology as elsewhere, New College may be said to be coming along rather nicely.

[19] Mackey (1994), 178.

Chapter 7

❧

Christian Ethics and Practical Theology

David Lyall

PRIOR TO the Disruption in the Church of Scotland in 1843, neither Christian Ethics nor Practical Theology appears to have found an explicit place within the curricula of the Divinity Faculties of the Scottish universities. The subjects taught at Edinburgh were Divinity, Ecclesiastical History and Hebrew and Semitic Languages. The chair of Biblical Criticism was first filled in 1847. An examination of the subjects taught in New College in 1851, as set out in Principal Hugh Watt's history of the College, suggests that they too were of a similarly academic nature.[1] Looking solely at these curricula from a present-day perspective, one might be tempted to ask how men (and of course there were only men at that time) were trained for the practical work of the ministry. How did they learn to conduct public worship and to preach? How did they hone their pastoral skills, equipping themselves to visit the sick and comfort the bereaved? Perhaps, however, these are modern questions which would have hardly been understood by the founding fathers of the Free Kirk. If pressed, they might have replied that these were the on-going tasks of all teachers in the divinity halls for all of them had been pastors and preachers. Indeed some professors held pastoral charges concurrently with their academic posts.

PRACTICAL THEOLOGY WITHIN NEW COLLEGE

There were those who, at an early date in the history of the College, felt that there was a gap in the curriculum. The Countess of Effingham,

[1] Watt, 30.

one of the earliest benefactors of the Free Church, offered an endowment of £3,000 for a combined pastorate of the students and Professorship of Practical Theology, an offer which was gratefully but provisionally accepted by the General Assembly of the Free Church in 1849. Before negotiations could be completed, however, doubts were being expressed in the Church. Principal Watt summarises them as follows:

> Who was the minister the noble lady had in mind when she refused to relinquish entirely her right to nominate the first occupant of the post? Would he be an adequate Professor of Theology? And even if he were, would not this new chair or semi-chair be favouring Edinburgh at the expense of Aberdeen and Glasgow? Was not this practical endowment calculated to entail expense for the Church in days to come? Were not the present professors adequate supervisors?[2]

The issue eventually became a matter of public debate and was taken up in the national press, with criticism mainly taking the line that the proposed new post was not the most urgent educational need at the time, and that a chair of Sacred Oratory or of Gaelic or of Ecclesiastical Finance (!) ought to have precedence. The proposal was then sent down (somewhat irregularly) under the Barrier Act to presbyteries who voted overwhelmingly against it. In view of this the General Assembly of 1853 felt themselves constrained to decline the offer while expressing their warm admiration of the high intentions and unstinted liberality of the donor. Thus ended the first attempt to have Practical Theology established as a separate and independent department within New College.

The story of the evolution of the present chair of Christian Ethics and Practical Theology is complex. In his Inaugural Lecture in 1978, Duncan Forrester argued that the chair is a successor to the chair of Evangelistic Theology first held from 1867 to 1878 by Alexander Duff, the missionary strategist and statesman.[3] The present chair, however, seems to have evolved mainly from the second Divinity chair in the College. W. Garden Blaikie, who held this chair from 1868 to 1897, tells how this came about:

> Dr Chalmers, as professor of Systematic Theology, had no fewer than four courses of lectures, which he delivered in four successive sessions. But this entailed on students the disadvantage of having to begin their studies at

---

[2] Watt, 49.
[3] Forrester (1980).

such part of their course as at the time of their entering the professor might happen to be at. In order to remedy this, the Free Church instituted an additional chair, and by appointing each professor to have two classes daily, was able to arrange the course of study so that each student should take it in the natural order. In this way the subject of apologetics was detached from Dr Chalmers at the beginning of his course, and the subject of Church government and practical theology at the end, and a new chair was instituted for these subjects.[4]

We see therefore how a chair of Apologetical and Pastoral Theology came into being, not apparently because of any supposed theoretical coherence between these two branches of theological study but for more mundane and pragmatic reasons connected with the construction of the College timetable. Blaikie felt it to be a great disadvantage to have to deal with two subjects so diverse. Indeed he saw himself as responsible for three separate subjects, since the government of the Church and pastoral theology were not, he believed, homogeneous. James Bannerman, who was professor from 1848 to 1868, had devoted his energies mainly to the study of church government. Blaikie describes the state of pastoral theology when he assumed office:

> [A]t that time pastoral theology was rather in disrepute. It was considered to belong to an inferior department of things. Students came from the class of logic and metaphysics permeated by the conviction that 'there is nothing greater in the world than man, and there is nothing greater in man but mind'. . . . The impression was general that the objective of the divinity hall was to cultivate the theological intellect, and that if that were done, nature would supply all the rest. It was necessary, therefore, in dealing with pastoral theology, to create, in the first instance, a sense of its value.[5]

Blaikie's affirmation of the value of pastoral theology is enshrined in his book *For the Work of the Ministry*.[6] While this volume has a major emphasis upon homiletics, there is an appendix dealing with other aspects of ministry, such as visitation of the sick. Quoting with somewhat guarded approval the *Tractatus de Visitatione Infirmorum* by a certain Dr Stearne, Blaikie writes as follows:

> The visitation of the sick is of all duties that for which the spirit of formality is most unsuitable, and where the speaking must be thoroughly from the heart to the heart. Yet a rubric like that to which we have referred [Stearne

[4] Blaikie (1901), 197.
[5] Blaikie (1901), 199.
[6] Blaikie (1873).

had given quite precise instructions for every pastoral eventuality, including that of criminals sentenced to be hanged!] might not be without its use in the way of suggestion – it might show the minister how great a variety of cases he is called to deal with, and of what value it is for him to be provided with manifold Scripture texts and references, sayings and anecdotes of suffering Christians, counsels and encouragements of well-tried value, in order that to every sick and suffering person he may be able to give his portion of meat in due season.[7]

Blaikie then goes on to quote with approval many helpful hints listed by Stearne regarding the manner of visiting the sick, the timing and length of visits and appropriate Scripture texts and other literary references which have been found helpful in sick visiting. Thus we see in the last quarter of the nineteenth century an approach to the training of ministers in which, certainly in the classroom, the imparting of 'helpful hints and tips' plays an important role.

NEW COLLEGE MISSIONARY SOCIETY AS AN ARENA OF PRACTICAL TRAINING

Whatever went on in the classroom, the nineteenth-century divinity student did not lack opportunity to practise the craft of ministry. A prominent feature of the life of New College from the beginning has been the Missionary Society. The Edinburgh University Missionary Society had been founded in 1835 with a primary concern for the diffusion of Christian knowledge in the foreign field. Unfortunately, the Disruption led not only to the establishment of separate divinity halls but also to a split in the Missionary Society. With a similar initial purpose of promoting interest in foreign mission, there soon developed a parallel concern for work in the poorer areas of the city. From 1847 the New College Missionary Society was actively supporting Home Mission work begun in the West Port area of the city under the College's first Principal, Dr Chalmers. Moreover, Principal Watt tells us that by 1853 'Groups were at work in the Infirmary [surely one of the earliest recorded hospital placements], in the Cowgate and elsewhere.'[8] In 1875, interest was transferred to the Pleasance and in 1893 a Residence or Settlement was built to accommodate a student warden and a number of other students, in the belief that more good would be done if the students most actively involved were to stay in the district.

[7] *Ibid.*, 259.
[8] Watt, 116.

In 1904, the Revd T. Struthers Symington, who had just completed a year as student warden, became the Society's more permanent missionary.

The Senate of New College had always taken an active and benevolent interest in the work of the Missionary Society. Certain developments during the tenure of office of Mr Symington's successor formalised the position of the Settlement as a sphere of practical training. Appointed Warden in 1908, the Revd J. Harry Miller became aware of its relevance as an arena of theological education. In the Annual Report of the Missionary Society for 1908–9, he wrote:

> I saw last year that there were great possibilities in the Settlement work for the training for the ministry, but I am more convinced than ever that there is an unequalled opportunity for practical training.

At the time when these words were written forty-five out of fifty-seven ministerial students in the College were in close contact with the work. In March 1911, Miller was appointed by the Senate to be Director of Practical Training for the term of his office, and hours were arranged for him within the first-year course for a seminar on home mission problems. The Missionary Society made an appeal to the Church for funds and in 1913 did so not only because of the importance of the work in its own right but also on the grounds that 'it gives the students an opportunity to study actual social conditions and prepare themselves for ministry under the direction of the warden'.[9] By this time Professor Alexander Martin occupied the chair of Apologetics and Pastoral Theology, a position which he held, after succeeding Professor Blaikie in 1897, until 1927. Professor (later Principal) Martin left little in writing on the work of the ministry but his legacy to the teaching of practical theology was otherwise of great importance, as we shall see from the developments which took place while he was professor.

'CHRISTIAN SOCIOLOGY' – AND CHRISTIAN PSYCHOLOGY?

The year 1900 saw the Union of the Free Church and the United Presbyterian Church with New College as one of the three divinity halls of the new United Free Church. An early hope of the United Free Church was to strengthen the theological curriculum particularly

[9] *New College Missionary Society Annual Report 1912–13.*

in the areas relating to practical theology. One of these was 'Christian Sociology'. In 1909 the Assembly approved its inclusion in the curriculum, a move which meant little more than that those responsible for the teaching of Christian Ethics would devote some time to the subject. It was not until after the First World War that further developments took place. In 1921 a course in Sociology became part of the regular College curriculum, as the Senate agreed

(1) that the teaching of Sociology should belong to the Department of Apologetics, Christian Ethics and Practical Theology;

(2) that the field should be covered by an extension of the [Pleasance Settlement] Warden's present work;

(3) that the teaching of Sociology should be kept in as close touch as possible with the work of the Settlement.[10]

These developments involving Harry Miller are highly significant because they demonstrate an early awareness of the need (i) to provide *supervised* fieldwork experience for divinity students, (ii) to initiate a dialogue between the nascent social sciences and the practice of ministry, and (iii) to make the supervision and the dialogue part of the on-going process of theological education. The contribution of the New College Settlement to this process cannot be overestimated.

Alexander Martin was succeeded in 1927 by Daniel Lamont, with the chair now re-titled Apologetics, Christian Ethics and Practical Theology. One of Professor Lamont's interests was the relationship between Christianity and contemporary scientific culture, the subject of his book *Christ and the World of Thought*.[11] Curiously, this book demonstrates little awareness of the significance of one aspect of modern thought which was to have a profound influence upon human consciousness for the rest of the century. While there are one or two rather slighting references to the Behaviourist school of psychology, the work of Sigmund Freud and his followers is totally ignored. However, in a little pamphlet written some years later, *The Restoration of the Soul*, Lamont managed to incorporate a great deal of Freudian jargon without actually mentioning the name of the founder of psychoanalysis.[12] Lamont took seriously his responsibility for apologetics, which after the Union was covered in Divinity.

[10] Watt, 103–4.
[11] Lamont (1934).
[12] Lamont (1943).

PRACTICAL THEOLOGY IN THE AULD KIRK AND THE UNIVERSITY

After the Disruption, we find remarkable similarities in the way the two churches – the Church of Scotland and the Free Church – set about training men for ministry. At the same time as the New College Missionary Society was at work in the West Port and in the Pleasance, the University Missionary Society was developing work in the Lawnmarket based in the Tolbooth Church (the building immediately behind the New College). This involvement in the enterprise of home mission owed its inspiration to Professor A. H. Charteris, who in 1869, after eleven years in the parish ministry, came to the University as Professor of Biblical Criticism and Biblical Antiquities. Because of a dispute over ecclesiastical rates, the ancient charge of the Tolbooth had been suppressed by the Ecclesiastical Commissioners, who in 1860 sanctioned no more provision for its ministry than temporary arrangements for its supply by licentiates. Thus although the Tolbooth was the building in which the General Assembly met, this district according to Charteris' biographer was a 'lapsed parish, an ecclesiastical "No Man's Land"'.[13] This situation was seen by the new professor as both a scandal and an opportunity. His biographer writes:

> He now seized his opportunity, and laid before the University Missionary Society the needs of the desolate Tolbooth, dwelling also on the reflex benefits which would accrue to the students themselves. He had not much faith in mere lectures on Pastoral Theology, though in their own way quite good, apart from practical training and personal tackling of the problems which present themselves to every serious minister. He did not appeal in vain; for an earnest band of young men, a large proportion of his class, accompanied him to the meeting of Presbytery in December 1870, and made the joint offer that if the court would entrust to their leader and themselves the fabric of the church, the entire work of the district would be fully undertaken.[14]

With the support of presbytery, a licentiate of Charteris' own choosing was appointed as parish missionary, and under the professor's vigorous leadership, new life was breathed into the dry bones of the nearly defunct Tolbooth parish. Districts within the parish were allocated to each student who was expected to visit fortnightly the families placed under his pastoral care, keeping a careful record of his visits so that an

[13] Gordon, A. (1912), 155
[14] *Ibid.*, 156–7.

accurate and up-to-date account was built up of every family in the district despite frequent changes in personnel. Charteris made himself responsible for the initiation of new visitors into the techniques of pastoral visiting, supervising their continued involvement in the work: 'Once a fortnight the Professor presided at a gathering of all the "Tolbooth workers", at which every case of difficulty was considered and decided on and helpful counsels given.'[15]

What is fascinating about Charteris' method is that, as long ago as 1870, it involved a supervisory model of training for ministry with a distinctly modern ring to it. Furthermore Charteris himself referred to the whole enterprise as 'Clinical Divinity', again anticipating by a hundred years a movement with a very similar name. As a result of the efforts of the professor and his students, the Tolbooth was subsequently re-endowed and restored to full status. The University Missionary Society transferred its activities to other needy parishes in the city, eventually landing upon the parish of St Margaret's, where, as we shall see, other developments in the training of ministers took place in the 1920s.

THE PASTORAL INSTITUTE

After the First World War, the General Assembly of the Church of Scotland set up a Commission on the Life and Efficiency of the Church. Consequent upon the Report of that Committee in 1919 the matter of Training for the Ministry was remitted to the Church and Nation Committee, which reported in 1921. It examined the whole spectrum of theological education from the pre-Divinity course to post-ordination training.[16] Academic, devotional and practical training were each the subject of scrutiny and new proposals. An appendix to the 1921 Report, headed 'Institutes of Practical Training', shows that from 1871 successive General Assemblies had been concerned about the spiritual life of the students. In 1893 the Assembly had approved a deliverance regarding a chair of Pastoral Theology, with a pious aspiration for the generosity which might found such a chair.[17] Nothing happened, however, and in 1896 the Assembly resurrected a proposal which had been discussed frequently in previous years, that in each university centre a 'Pastoral Institute' be set up.

[15] *Ibid.*, 162.
[16] *Reports to the General Assembly of the Church of Scotland 1921*, 563–601.
[17] *Ibid.*, 597.

The idea of the Institute, it may be inferred, was not so much that of a building or a place, as *personnel* consisting of (*a*) a Head with such staff as might prove to be needful and (*b*) of the body of 'regular' students of Divinity at any university where the Institute should be set up. It was in no sense to interfere with the university relations or with professorial authority or responsibility; it would incorporate not all matriculated students in the Faculty of Divinity as such, but only such as are in a recognised relation to the Church as proceeding to the Ministry; it would be the Church's provision for the specialised and non-academic training for such students and for the development of their spiritual life; but if it were to be useful, would necessarily be very closely correlated and co-ordinated with the Faculty.[18]

Again nothing seems to have happened for a long time. Indeed, it was not until a vacancy occurred in the Edinburgh parish of St Margaret's (in the Dumbiedykes area between the Pleasance and Holyrood Palace) that the presbytery appointed a committee to confer with the congregation and others concerned, with a view to a minister being appointed who might be qualified to give guidance and help to divinity students along the lines indicated in the above Report. This proposal received a cordial welcome from the Divinity professors and students and financial assistance was provided by the Home Mission Committee and the Baird Trust. The minister appointed and called to the parish was the Revd D. Bruce Nicol (who, so it happened, had been born in the manse of the restored Tolbooth parish in 1880). The 1921 Report noted this development with approval and commended it to the other university centres. With this began the first systematic attempt at the teaching of Practical Theology in the University, the course being listed in the *University Calendar* for the first time in 1924, with Bruce Nicol as lecturer and Warden of the Pastoral Institute based at St Margaret's.

In a short biography of her late husband Helen Nicol presents us with a vivid account of his work with students as he sought to acquaint them with every branch of congregational life, through both involvement in the life of the parish and the organisation of special courses in the University.[19] When other Institutes were established in Glasgow and Aberdeen, they followed the guidelines laid down by Bruce Nicol. He also had an important influence upon the teaching of Practical Theology in the re-united Church of Scotland after 1929.

[18] *Ibid.*, 599.
[19] Nicol (1930).

Before he moved to Dundee in 1925, he drew up a memorandum which was accepted by the Board of Pastoral Institutes, laying down the scope of Practical Theology. His proposals were accepted by the relevant committee which made arrangements for the training of Divinity students after the Union. These were that lectures in Practical Theology should cover the following:

1. Preaching.
2. Public worship and the administration of the sacraments.
3. Pastoral theology.
4. Religious instruction of the young.
5. Church constitution, organisation and law.
6. Theory and practice of missions at home and abroad.

A personal communication from the Revd C. W. G. Taylor, minister of St George's Edinburgh, to Mrs Nicol reveals an awareness that there were other matters of importance in the teaching of Practical Theology besides the content of the lecture course: 'From the outset, the promoters of the Pastoral Institute realised the importance of the personal or pastoral relation which might exist between the warden and the students.'[20] In this statement we see an awareness of the cruciality of the supervisory relationship, and the establishment of a model of ministry with which the students could identify. What is unfortunate is that this exciting and visionary project never seems to have realised its full potential within the united Church. After Bruce Nicol moved to Dundee, his place was taken by the Revd Cecil Thornton, whose name appears in the *University Calendar* as Lecturer in Practical Theology until 1930–1. From then on Practical Theology was clearly seen to be the responsibility of Professor Lamont, while the Christian Sociology was taught by the Revd Harry Miller.

Complete constitutional union of the two academic establishments did not take place until 1935, and it was not until the end of the decade that a chair of Christian Ethics and Practical Theology was established in the University with Professor Lamont as the first occupant. During the 1930s, while his status in the Senate of New College was that of Professor, his University status was that of Reader. The University Court had agreed in 1934 to erect a chair of Christian Ethics and Practical Theology should the Church of Scotland so desire, but the matter was delayed because of a wish to keep in step with Trinity

[20] *Ibid.*, 92.

College, Glasgow, where a similar proposal was less certain of a favourable reception. In fact it was only in Edinburgh and St Andrews that university chairs were established linking the two disciplines.

THE POST-WAR YEARS

In 1945 William S. Tindal became professor, having previously succeeded Harry Miller as Warden of the New College Settlement and as Lecturer in Sociology. Except for the last two years of his incumbency, Professor Tindal was the only full-time member of his department, certain specialist courses being taught by outside lecturers. Thus the Revd John (Ian) Gray came from Moray House to teach Christian Education and, latterly, first Dr Ian Fraser and then the Revd Ian Reid, Minister at the Old Kirk (and later Leader of the Iona Community), gave the lectures on Sociology. In the final year of the course, instruction was given to candidates for the ministry (and until the late 1960s apart from postgraduate students there were few others) in the conduct of worship, the administration of the sacraments and in pastoral visiting. Significantly, it was not possible at that time to offer Practical Theology as a subject for the B.D., though Christian Ethics was an optional paper for those specialising in Systematic Theology (Troeltsch's *Social Teaching of the Christian Churches*[21] was invariably the prescribed text). In one important innovation of Professor Tindal's time, which was a forerunner of things to come, final-year students were able to spend an hour per week in the Department of Psychological Medicine at the Royal Infirmary observing patients being interviewed by a consultant psychiatrist and exploring the implications of this for the practice of ministry. Actual practical experience of ministry was gained by means of paid student assistantships in the second and third years of the course. In this ministerial apprenticeship a student worked in a parish under the direction of the minister for several hours per week and was introduced to the work and Sunday worship of the congregation. (Later, student assistantships were replaced by a system of unpaid attachments in which the students were participant-observers in a wide range of congregational activity and ministerial practice.)

In 1964 James C. Blackie was appointed Lecturer. After a ministry in the parish of Carnock, Blackie had been appointed University Chaplain in 1957 (in succession to David H. C. Read). He was one of the founders of the Scottish Pastoral Association and the first editor of

[21] Troeltsch (1931).

Contact, which now flourishes as an interdisciplinary journal of pastoral studies based in New College and supported by all of the principal British organisations in the field. Professor Blackie brought to practical theology a vision of interdisciplinarity which he was able to make concrete by virtue of the network of relationships he had established throughout the University during his years as Chaplain. Appointed to the chair on the death of Professor Tindal in 1966, his tenure of office coincided with the post-Robbins expansion of higher education in Britain. Soon the number of established posts rose to four. Ian Gray moved permanently from Moray House to teach Christian Education and Homiletics, a full-time lectureship in Sociology of Religion was established, to be held first by Peter Sissons and then by Robin Gill, and Alastair Campbell, a recent graduate of New College with a doctorate from San Francisco Theological Seminary, was appointed to develop new courses in Pastoral Care and in Medical Ethics. The late 1960s saw the beginning of courses in Pastoral Studies in certain universities, pioneering work being done in Birmingham, Manchester, Cardiff, St Andrews and Edinburgh. Blackie and Campbell were together instrumental in ensuring a significant Edinburgh contribution to this development. During an eighteen-month period in 1970 and 1971 the three full-time chaplaincies in the major Edinburgh teaching hospitals became vacant and the Department became associated with the Lothian Health Board and the Church of Scotland Home Board in filling the vacancies. The three chaplains appointed, Stewart McGregor at the Royal Infirmary, Murray Leishman at the Royal Edinburgh Hospital and David Lyall at the Western General Hospital, were also given part-time posts within the Department, with responsibilities for developing hospital-based courses and supervised placements.

This period also saw important changes in New College, both in its courses and in the composition of the student body. The B.D. degree was re-structured and for the first time Practical Theology became an examinable subject; a four-year 'first' B.D. was introduced open to students entering the Faculty straight from school; women were admitted to the ordained ministry of the Church of Scotland; and the Religious Studies programme was inaugurated, bringing into the Faculty an even greater diversity of religious belief and commitment. No longer was New College a predominantly male, presbyterian enclave!

James Blackie died suddenly and unexpectedly in 1976, leaving a Department very different from the one which he entered twelve years previously; but he had also laid the foundations for even greater changes to come. He was succeeded as professor in 1978 by Duncan B. Forrester, another graduate of New College who brought to the post experience both as a Church of Scotland missionary at Madras Christian College, where he was Professor of Politics, and latterly as Chaplain to the University of Sussex.

CHRISTIAN ETHICS AND PRACTICAL THEOLOGY TODAY

The past twenty years have seen changes in personnel as well as developments in the programme of the Department. In 1980 Ian Gray was succeeded by Ian McDonald, who also came from Moray House and brought with him a reputation for New Testament scholarship as well as skills in education and in ethics. Robin Gill left the University, appointed first of all to the Leech Professorship of Applied Theology in the University of Newcastle and then to the Michael Ramsey chair in Modern Theology at Canterbury. He was succeeded by Michael Northcott, another Anglican who came to the Department from teaching Practical Theology at an Anglican theological college in Kuala Lumpur. A pioneer in the academic study of medical ethics, and the first editor of the *Journal of Medical Ethics*, Alastair Campbell was appointed to a chair of Bioethics in the Medical Faculty at the University of Otago in New Zealand. He was succeeded by David Lyall, who returned to New College after teaching Practical Theology for three years in St Andrews. Two further posts, in Theology and Development and in the Theology and Ethics of Communication (of which more will be said later), bring the present full-time complement of the Department to six.

The work of the Department is characterised by both continuity and change. Preparation for ministry, the original *raison d'être* of the discipline, remains a high priority though in a very different context from 150 (or even thirty) years ago. Of the Faculty's present under-graduate complement of around 300 (split about equally between the B.D. and the B.A./M.A. in Religious Studies), normally around fifty are candidates for the ministry of the Church of Scotland. The positive aspect of this is that candidates cannot prepare themselves for ministry without having fundamental theological assumptions challenged by their peers. Yet considerable care is given to equipping women and men for the ordained ministry. The first-year course, Christian Ethics and Practical Theology 1, has modules on worship, communication and preaching, mission in contemporary society, pastoral care and Christian education. There is a large field-education component in this course, with visits to churches, social service agencies and a week-long Easter-vacation hospitals conference. In addition, candidates have to undertake two attachments in local congregations, organised by a part-time Director of Field Education.

The Department is equally committed to teaching and research in Christian Ethics. Edinburgh is one of the few British universities having Christian Ethics and Practical Theology located within one department. The second-year course focuses upon the theological dimensions of a wide range of contemporary ethical issues, and opportunity for advanced study is offered in a range of Honours options. Duncan Forrester teaches a module on Political and Social Justice, an area in which he has several publications.[22] Ian McDonald's expertise is in Theological and New Testament Ethics.[23] A noteworthy feature of his most recent book in the field, *Christian Values*,[24] lies in the contribution made to it by recent students in the Department. Michael Northcott has special interest in Environmental Ethics,[25] while David Lyall teaches in the area of Bioethics and Family and Sexual Ethics.

A further contemporary issue is the transformation of Practical Theology as an academic discipline. While in the nineteenth century Schleiermacher had described practical theology as 'the crown of theological study', in the twentieth the discipline had degenerated largely into a compendium of hints and tips for budding pastors. Within the past fifteen years, however, the discipline has been rediscovered as critical theological reflection upon the life of the church in the world. There is a new concern for relating theology and practice, not simply the application of theology to practice (we are not a department of Applied Theology!) but a concern for what David Tracy has called the 'mutually critical correlations'[26] between theology and practice. There has also been an emphasis upon the close relationship between Practical Theology and Christian Ethics (our forefathers in establishing the chair of Christian Ethics and Practical Theology in Edinburgh had greater foresight than they knew). This new interest in Practical Theology was formalised in the establishment at Princeton in 1993 of the

---

[22] Forrester (1985), and (1988).

[23] McDonald (1993).

[24] McDonald (1995).

[25] A major study entitled *The Environment and Christian Ethics* is nearing completion.

[26] Tracy (1983), 62.

International Academy of Practical Theology, a conference in which the staff of the Department were heavily involved. The international interests of the Department were also evident in 1979 when the First International Congress on Pastoral Care and Counselling was held in Edinburgh, a development which grew out of Alastair Campbell's involvement in new European and international movements.

A marked feature of recent years has been an increasing number of postgraduate students in the Department both as doctoral candidates and in taught (as the University calls them) M.Th. courses. It is in the latter group that growth has been most marked. Certain recent developments may be noted. A postgraduate Diploma in Ministry course was establishment in 1979, but it was obvious by 1990 that it was in need of radical overhaul. There was also concern to provide an in-service Masters degree for parish ministers which could be taken on a part-time basis. Both of these issues were addressed in 1992 when the first students enrolled for the M.Th./Diploma in Ministry. In this course ministers and students study together in a Theology and Practice course taught by members of all Departments in the Faculty using a case study approach. Serving ministers are enabled to reflect upon their current parish work and the students upon specially arranged placements in a variety of settings. It is anticipated that more serving ministers will be enabled to participate in this and other kinds of postgraduate study through the release by New College Senate of monies dedicated to providing postgraduate scholarships for Church of Scotland ministers.

Two further developments in the Department contribute to the number of students taking M.Th. degrees. In 1986 the Media and Theological Education project was established in response to an initiative from the Jerusalem Trustees, who were concerned to incorporate media issues into theological education. Since then an M.Th. in the Theology and Ethics of Communication has been initiated which aspires to both academic integrity and practical relevance. It has already attracted a considerable number of postgraduate students from around the world. It may be taken either full-time or in one of two part-time modes, making it accessible to ministers and media professionals from a wide variety of work situations. A lectureship has been held successively by Chris Arthur, Derek Weber and Jolyon Mitchell, each contributing to the range of options offered by the Department, not least in homiletics.

In 1990 Christian Aid, the leading Christian relief agency in the UK, sponsored a new M.Th. course in Theology and Development. Each year since then 10–15 students from around the world have participated in this interdisciplinary course which brings another dimension to New College's traditional and distinctive international ethos. Administered in the first year by M. P. Joseph, an Indian graduate of Union Theological Seminary, New York, the course was consolidated by Romy Tiongco from the Philippines. The current holder of the post is Marcella Althaus-Reid, an Argentinian with a doctorate from St Andrews.

All these developments, together with the Centre for Theology and Public Issues discussed in Duncan Forrester's chapter in this volume, are further witnesses to the concern of the Department to be active on the interface between theology and practice. It seeks not only to be part of the on-going dialogue between church and university but to make a relevant theological contribution within the maelstrom of public debate. The dialogue with the churches will undoubtedly continue, particularly as new approaches are sought to prepare women and men for the diversity of ministries within the churches in Scotland and beyond. And there will be a continued attempt to exercise that wider function of a Department of Christian Ethics and Practical Theology, to provide a forum for continuing debate and theological reflection upon the relationship between theology, church and world.

Chapter 8

❧

Religious Studies

Frank Whaling

IN ONE SENSE, the study of religion in Edinburgh has a long history – one much longer than the history of our Religious Studies degree. Christianity itself, most obviously, and to a lesser extent Judaism, have always been on the agenda. Certain of the theoretical problems associated with the study of religion also have a place in the older Edinburgh tradition. One of the early pioneers of the phenomenology of religion, for example, the nineteenth-century theologian Schleiermacher, has long had a place in the Edinburgh curriculum. In fact, Schleiermacher's description of religious experience as a fundamental dimension of human life, and of empirical religion as an expression in differing contexts of that basic experience, is still a theme in the study of religion today.

For much of the present century, moreover, John Baillie's own treatment of the nature of religion, as developed in particular in his monumental study *The Interpretation of Religion* (1929), constituted part of the staple diet of New College classes in Divinity. Although nothing like a full course in comparative religion was offered before recent times, Baillie provided his students with a sustained and sensitive analysis of the problem of the classification of religion alongside his more conventional teaching concerning faith and reason and the like in his philosophical theology. Baillie argued that a proper understanding of human religion requires that it be seen historically, like all other cultural phenomenon. It appears in particular human societies and cultures, and so develops across time 'horizontally', as he puts it. Our understanding of religion must correspond to this, and in particular, we must avoid what he calls the 'vertical' accounts of supposedly 'lower' and 'higher' forms of religion. Although this was, in the end, only one theme in his theology, it is important to note that an enlightened view such as Baillie's was found in the Edinburgh context before the present day.

Such treatments of religion were, however, explicitly subsidiary to the study of Christian theology. It was only round about 1970 that discussion began about the possible introduction of a full Religious Studies degree at Edinburgh University. The idea was first mooted in October 1968 by the Professor of Arabic in the Arts Faculty, W. M. Watt. Before proceeding to analyse the details of how this was eventually accomplished, it is helpful first to consider the three main reasons why this new departure was seriously considered.

FORCES FOR CHANGE

The first reason lay within universities themselves. Course offerings were expanding within both the older universities and the new universities that were springing up around Great Britain. Newer universities, such as Stirling in Scotland and Lancaster in England, were, opting for Religious Studies degrees or courses *rather than* Theology. The supposition was that Theology, if it were to be offered, should find its place within Religious Studies. Older universities, outside Oxford and Cambridge which at first resisted the temptation, moved in the direction of including Religious Studies within Theology or of adding a Religious Studies degree to a B.D., or other Theology degree, that already existed. Edinburgh University moved in the latter direction and took steps to bring into being a Religious Studies degree alongside the traditional B.D. for which it was famous.

The second reason lay within developments within Religious Education. The Education Act of 1944 had fashioned Religious Education along Christian lines on the implicit assumption that day schools were allies of the Christian churches in nurturing children into and within the Christian tradition. By 1970 this had begun to be questioned, not least because Religious Education had been designated the only compulsory subject in schools and yet was seen to be often badly taught or not taught at all, thus raising discussion about its role, meaning and end. In both Scotland and England professional bodies were emphasising the need for professional teachers of RE to emerge with their own career structure, their own examination structures, their own curricula, and their own advisers. Although in practice many RE teachers were Christians, they began to see their task in educational terms rather than as an extension of the work of the churches. It was necessary for universities to take account of this demand for a more comprehensive and sophisticated kind of Religious Education.

The third reason lay within society itself. It was becoming clear, both within Britain and globally, that 'religion' could not be confined to the Christian or the Judaeo–Christian tradition. The Second World War itself had taken many Britons into the bosom of different cultures; the horrors of the Holocaust had become known and Israel had emerged as a state; a number of European empires had disappeared and independent nations had seen a renaissance of their own religious tradition with the coming of independence – Hinduism in India, Buddhism in South-East Asia and Islam in the Middle East. Furthermore Marxism had emerged as a seemingly potent force opposed to *all* religion, and the force of nationalism and new models of economic development and modernisation were raising questions for *all* religions. The accelerating process of industrialisation and technological development had prompted by 1970 the Club of Rome study, *The Limits to Growth*, with its premonitions of ecological crisis applicable to *all* religions. More importantly, from the viewpoint of ordinary people, an awareness was arising of other religious perspectives: from television where the oil crisis in the Islamic Middle East dominated the early 1970s, from increasing opportunities for travel becoming available to young folk, and from the immigration into the West of Tibetan Buddhists who had fled from Tibet with the Dalai Lama, of Ugandan and other African Asians (Hindi, Muslim and Sikh) seeking refuge from another kind of tyranny, of refugees from Palestine or Vietnam, and of ordinary Pakistani Muslims and others seeking a better life in the heartland of the Commonwealth.

FIRST BEGINNINGS: THE STRUCTURES

In the light of the new situation developing by 1970 in universities, in Religious Education and in society generally, serious consideration was given in the early 1970s by Edinburgh University to the academic emergence of Religious Studies as an intellectual concern within its wider life. Again three matters were paramount in the discussions that took place: should there be a separate Religious Studies degree? Should Religious Studies be in Divinity or in Arts? and what should be the form of the Religious Studies that was to emerge?

One option was to keep the B.D. degree as the only degree within the religious field but to include elements of Religious Studies within the B.D. degree. It would have been possible to add on another department of Religious Studies or History of Religions to the existing Departments of Christian Dogmatics, Divinity, Ecclesiastical History, Old Testament, New Testament, and Christian Ethics and Practical Theology. There was the possibility of integrating Religious Studies elements into the already existing B.D. It was decided not to pursue this path, and to this day there is little about other religious traditions in the Edinburgh B.D.

Once the decision had been made to bring into being a new Religious Studies degree, it was then necessary to reflect upon the question of where that degree should be situated in terms of Edinburgh Faculties. The Arts Faculty was clearly a possible option containing as it did prestigious professors such as William Montgomery Watt, a world authority in Islam, and Ronald Hepburn, a well-known philosopher of religion, whose home was in the Department of Philosophy. Other departments, such as Chinese, Sanskrit, Islamic Studies and History had a potential stake in the new degree, as did the Faculty of Social Sciences with its relevant departments of Social Anthropology, Sociology and Psychology. A further consideration was that there was already a one-man department in the Arts Faculty offering two Biblical Studies courses enabling teachers to supplement their existing skills in order to gain a basic qualification to teach Religious Education as a further subject.

In the end it was agreed that the Religious Studies degree should have its base in the Faculty of Divinity at New College but that it should make use of the expertise present in other faculties, including the Faculty of Law where a knowledgeable Jewish lawyer, Dr Bernard Jackson, was available to teach Judaism. Thus the headquarters for the new enterprise and its direction would be centred at New College but it would make use of colleagues from other parts of the University. This *modus operandi* reflected fundamental principle. The project would depend on experts not in 'Religion' (Religionswissenschaft) but in specific religions and disciplines.

Factors germane to this decision included the strength in reputation and staff numbers of the Divinity Faculty (whereas the Arts departments teaching other religions were small), the concentration upon 'religious' matters at New College (whereas the Social Science departments' primary motivation lay elsewhere), and the involvement of the Divinity

Faculty already in the wider affairs of the University through people such as John McIntyre, who was soon to be Acting Principal of the University.

The strengths of the wider University were fed into the new B.A. degree, first offered in 1971–2, using only existing courses in the three Faculties. In addition to the twenty scholars at New College with expertise in the Christian tradition there were present elsewhere experts in the Hindu, Jewish, Muslim and Chinese religious traditions. Thus the major religions could be taught. Furthermore other scholars could bring to bear expertise in different approaches to the study of religion. It became possible to teach the sociology of religion, the psychology of religion, the anthropology of religion, the history of religion, and the philosophy of religion, as well as the theology of religion. And so, after a couple of years, in 1973–4 two new courses were created in these two different areas. These courses offered in the first year an overview of the main religious traditions of the world – the Christian, Jewish, Muslim, Buddhist, Hindu and Chinese – and in the second year of the main methods, theories and approaches in the study of religion – through anthropology, sociology, psychology, history, phenomenology, philosophy and theology.

These two basic courses – called Comparative Religion and Religious Studies – were set up under the general oversight of John McIntyre, Professor of Divinity, who took a close interest in the enterprise from the first. Co-ordinating the details fell to Elizabeth Maclaren (later Templeton, on her marriage to Douglas in New Testament), who had been appointed to a lectureship in Divinity in 1970. Her main concentration lay in the philosophy of religion. There was no intention on the part of the Faculty, which as a whole consciously owned the new developments, to recruit a corps of specialists in Religious Studies. Nor was a need felt to create a new institutional structure to contain the new courses – for they were essentially inter-departmental and inter-disciplinary and were the responsibility of the Faculty at large.

Nevertheless, both the two foundation courses and the larger programme that grew out of them presented a special challenge of academic logistics. Over the quarter of a century under review, various attempts have been made to meet this challenge. None of them can lay claim to conspicuous success, and at the time of writing the organisational framework is again undergoing fresh scrutiny.

The Department of Divinity (later, on its merger with Christian Dogmatics, the Department of Systematic Theology, and later still by quick metamorphosis, the Department of Theology and Religious Studies) exercised from the outset a keen interest in these curricular developments. Consistent with this was the decision to make an appointment of a lecturer in Divinity with expertise to co-ordinate the developing work of Religious Studies spanning various departments of the University. In 1973 the Revd Dr Frank Whaling, a Methodist minister with missionary experience in India, and with a Cambridge theology degree and a Harvard Th.D. in Comparative Religion, was invited to take up this role in the Divinity Department at New College.

In the first year (1971–2) four students enrolled for the new B.A. degree. Over twenty years later, in 1995, there are over 100 students in the first-year course, and around forty students enrolling annually for the two degrees. The story of how this happened unfolded in two main stages, 1971–88 and 1988 onwards. This story will be elaborated on during the remainder of this chapter.

THE SHAPE OF THE NEW DEGREES

The first need was to secure the structure of the new degree and this was done by basing it upon a B.A./M.A. model. The B.A. was a three-year non-honours degree, and the M.A. (which came on stream in 1973–4) a four-year honours degree. The B.A. served two functions. On the one hand it served as a fall-back possibility in case students were not able to gain the standard necessary for entry into honours; on the other hand it also offered wider possibilities to students without high academic pretensions who wanted to teach in schools. It allowed them to take a double course in a non-religious subject (such as History, Geography, English, a language, etc.) that would give them a teaching qualification in that subject as well as in Religious Studies, so that they could teach RE and something else within the school situation.

However, all things being equal, encouragement was given to students to opt for the M.A. degree which lasted for four years. Within this structure the first two years were seen as being a preparation for honours, and the last two years were devoted to more specialised study of honours courses. Thus in the first two years all students took the two overview courses in the content of the main religious traditions and in the main theories, methods and approaches to the study of religion. In addition to these basic courses students could go in three directions. It was possible to specialise in one religion by taking courses in it, including the language central to that religion – Greek for Christianity, Arabic for Islam, Sanskrit for Hinduism and Buddhism, Hebrew for Judaism; it was possible to specialise in two religious traditions *without* necessarily doing the languages concerned, so that one could combine Christianity with the Jewish, Hindu, or Muslim traditions – and other combinations were also possible; or it was possible to combine a religious tradition with a particular method of studying religion, so that one could take courses in a religion together with courses in sociology, psychology, anthropology, history, or philosophy. At honours level more specialised in-depth courses would then be taken in the religion (including language), in the two religions, or in the religion plus method of studying religion so that the end-result gave a degree with an overview of all the main religions and methods of studying religion together with a specialised knowledge of part of the wider field taken to great depth.

By comparison with the B.D. it offered the possibility of studying Christianity within a much wider religious context, and it also offered much wider potentialities that gave Edinburgh right from the beginning possibly the widest Religious Studies programme in Great Britain. It was able to achieve this by using the combined specialised resources of different faculties of the University.

In accordance with this principle, teachers from various departments outside New College became involved in the new enterprise, including Professor W. Montgomery Watt (and later Dr Ian Howard and Dr Carole Hillenbrand) from Islamics, Dr John Brockington (and later Mr Paul Dundas) from Sanskrit, Professor Ronald Hepburn (and later Dr John Jenkins, Dr Geoffrey Madell and Mr George Morice) from Philosophy, Dr Tony Jackson from Social Anthropology, Dr John Chinnery from Chinese – so that, in one way or another, something like twenty teachers were involved in the total endeavour.

THE STUDENT EXPERIENCE

As far as students were concerned, Religious Studies grew in appeal so that by 1988 there were around fifty students in the first-year course and around twenty students enrolling for the degree annually. Part of the appeal was the width of choice opened up. It was possible to do honours in courses involving Christianity, Judaism, Hinduism, Buddhism, Chinese Religion, Philosophy of Religion, Sociology of Religion, Anthropology of Religion, Psychology of Religion, History and Phenomenology of Religion in the M.A., and in other combinations in the B.A.

Student motivation and involvement was varied. A number used the degree as a means of getting a flying start towards a committed teaching career in Religious Education in Scotland or England or occasionally further afield. Some passed on to do a B.D. degree and to become ministers in different churches. Others gained First-Class Honours in Religious Studies and a Ph.D. and went on to teach the subject in universities and colleges at home and abroad. One student in the first cohort completed the three-year B.A. and went off to help build boats on Tyneside. Ten years later he came back and finished the M.A. with First-Class Honours and then a Ph.D. and is now teaching in Higher Education in the United States. Others read Religious Studies out of interest and then passed on into other careers including law, social work, the armed forces, the media, business, writing, service to the Third World, and lay service in the church. A common factor in the comments of returning students, whatever their career, is a continuing fascination and concern for the subject.

Students involved in Religious Studies were often Christians who were seeking a grounding in religion wider than that offered by the Edinburgh B.D. A small but continuing number of students were Jews, Muslims and Buddhists who offered to the New College community contact with people outside the Christian tradition. Others had an academic and often existential interest in religion that was not necessarily linked to an identifiable institution. Teaching and student visits to various churches (including the awe-inspiring Easter service at the Ukraine Catholic Church), to the synagogue, the mosque, the Hindu temple, the Sikh gurdwara, and to wider venues such as the iconography at the Royal Scottish Museum, the Glasgow mosque, the St Mungo's Museum, and the Tibetan Buddhist monastery at Eskdalemuir further heightened interest in the subject.

WIDER DEVELOPMENTS

Outside factors supervened to create a growing awareness of and interest in religious matters that would make it more likely that students would want to become involved in Religious Studies. On the one hand religion became more publicity-worthy for negative reasons. The oil crisis beginning in 1973, followed by the revolution in Iran associated with the name of Ayatollah Khomeini, brought militant Islam more to the fore of public and political attention. Although often unfair, the media's highlighting of Islamic Fundamentalism (so-called) made it clear that religion was an important force in the wider world. The media also focused upon the theme of religious conflict in Northern Ireland, the Middle East, the Lebanon, Sri Lanka, the Punjab, and parts of Africa, thus emphasising the more aggressive side of religion. On the other hand religion became more publicity-worthy for positive reasons.

Inter-faith dialogue grew in importance and esteem locally and around the world. In 1986 Pope John Paul II called together a gathering of religious leaders at Assisi to discuss peace, and later there were similar meetings to discuss ecology and other matters of global concern. It was becoming clear that the world was moving into a newer, more global, phase of its history and that all religions were 'in it together' in a way that had never been true before. Students were drawn academically into discussion of these wider topics by the Edinburgh University Religious Studies Centre which hosted a variety of meetings including a Muslim academic opening up in a helpful way the implications of Salman Rushdie's *Satanic Verses*, the Professor of Computer Sciences talking about Buddhist meditation, and world figures such as Professor Jacques Waardenburg of Holland sharing their thoughts about basic matters.

In the meantime Religious Education was developing in professionalism in Scotland and in England to the extent of becoming examinable like any other subject, having its own Advisers, and revising its curricula to take account of the growing multi-faith nature of British society. A lively debate ensued about the nature of Religious Education, but the bottom line was that the subject began to be taken more seriously throughout Great Britain and was no longer regarded as a cinderella. Edinburgh University played its part in the debate itself and in providing a new generation of RE teachers professionally equipped to lead in the field.

CURRICULUM: THE EDINBURGH APPROACH

During the period 1973–88 the Religious Studies course at Edinburgh continued to develop. The original course on content was expanded to two year-long courses, Religion 1 and 2, which over two years gave an overview of the main religious or quasi-religious traditions of the world. In addition to the major religions of Christianity, Islam, Judaism, Buddhism and Hinduism, the other options taught were Jainism, Baha'ism, Chinese Religions, Sikhism, Primal Religions, New Religious Movements and Secular Worldviews that could be regarded as quasi-religious in nature. The former course on methods of studying religion was adapted and became Religion 3. Included in it were elements of the Philosophy of Religion, including a consideration of scholars such as Kant, Kierkegaard, Hegel and Hick, as well as an analysis of basic issues in the History and Phenomenology of Religion and other approaches to the study of religion. Religion 4 took up comparative issues considered in depth across four religious traditions: the Christian, Buddhist, Hindu and Muslim. The three main areas tackled were ethics, spirituality and war and peace. Thus Religion 1 to 4 gave an overall insight into the total religious field in regard to content, methodology and comparative issues.

It is probably true to say that along with the development of the programme there was also the development during this era of an 'Edinburgh approach'. This was influenced by the contiguity between Christian Theology and Religious Studies at Edinburgh. It is a truism that ideas are influenced by environment. Elsewhere in Eastern Bloc countries Religious Studies arose within a social scientific milieu, in the United States (with its constitutional insistence on freedom of religion) Religious Studies often developed in a liberal arts milieu, at places like Stirling or Lancaster within a humanities setting. At Edinburgh Religious Studies emerged with its base in the Divinity Faculty at New College but with a presence elsewhere in the University.

Within this context Religious Studies at Edinburgh pioneered an approach combining a concern with the content of different religious traditions with a concern for taking seriously the various methods of studying religion. Along with this there arose at Edinburgh a sense of the complementarity between Christian Theology and Religious Studies. Neither was dominant; both were inter-related; each could learn from the other. Thus various theologians, from different disciplines, contributed to Religious Studies and attention began to be given to the nature of courses in Christianity on the understanding that they could become relevant both to the B.D. and to Religious Studies. There was avoidance at one end of the sense that Religious Studies is nothing more than a scientific and historical discipline, concerned only with the data of religion devoid of philosophical or transcendent implications; at the other end there was avoidance of Christian imperialism in relation to Religious Studies: transcendence, empathy and faith were part of the data of religion in a non-exclusive sense.

Yet the impression must not be given that the endeavour to domicile Religious Studies within a world-famous home of Christian divinity –

dominated traditionally by the requirements of the professional formation of ministers – has all been sweetness and light. One stubborn question – perhaps only now, in the later 1990s, being tackled with full seriousness – was this: should the only teaching of Christianity (which a goodly proportion of RS students have opted for) available in the RS programme be the hallowed range of specialised B.D. offerings? Could it never be presented in the round, like, say, a year-long introduction to Hinduism? The failure of a short-lived Christianity first-year course lay partly, if not largely, at the door of Departments whose energies were spent in defending their specialist stalls in the B.D. market. Some colleagues, with dogmatic scepticism, judged it impossible – certainly unprofessional – to dare to teach 'Christianity', or even 'the Bible', rather than, for example, New Testament.

At a more elusive level have lurked issues of commitment and presupposition. Is it still tolerable, as we near the end of the second (and last) Christian millennium, for some lectures to be opened with prayer – given the rich mix of the typical student auditory? Why should it be assumed that a tutor's lack of explicit Christian faith makes him or her any more (likely to be) critically objective? Neutrality is surely a chimaera, a secular outlook is not absence of commitment (unless it is, *per impossibile*, entirely empty-headed) – and in any case, when did the University of Edinburgh declare itself secular or non-Christian? The batting of such arguments to and fro is the very stuff of staff common-room engagement in a modern Divinity Faculty. Among undergraduates they more easily descend to the personal and the emotional, to despite of vocation and excess of proselytising zeal. The New College community of the mid-1990s has not been a stranger to such frictions and tensions. There has probably been more smoke than fire, yet some real fire none the less. At stake is the viability of the distinctive New College venture into Religious Studies – the grafting of the new academic programme on to the vigorous stock of a church-related Divinity Faculty. Given the nature of this operation – undertaken with eyes wide open to its rare, perhaps unique, character – growth stresses were inevitable. We must be confident that they will be outgrown.

FRESH RESOURCES AND GREATER BREADTH

Towards the end of the 1980s a further evolution occurred within the programme at Edinburgh. Two new sets of people arrived to add their weight to Religious Studies; the programme itself increased in range;

and student numbers rose dramatically so that the Religious Studies intake virtually caught up with the B.D. intake and Religious Studies courses surpassed B.D. courses in class size.

The first significant addition to New College and to all programmes was the transfer of the Centre for the Study of Christianity in the Non-Western World from Aberdeen University. Headed by Professor Andrew Walls, a Methodist layman who was shortly to be created O.B.E., it offered research and archival resources in Christianity in the wider world and also in Primal Religions. In addition to this the small Principles of Religion department at Glasgow University was transferred to Edinburgh in the persons of Dr Alistair Kee (soon to be Professor Kee) and Dr Nick Wyatt. Dr Kee brought expertise in secular Christianity and secular worldviews, and Dr Wyatt in Ancient Near Eastern Religions, in iconography, and in mythology. All these elements were added to the curriculum, so that it was now possible to take honours courses in Christianity, Judaism (Dr Peter Hayman), Islam, Hinduism (Dr John Brockington and Dr Frank Whaling), Buddhism (Mr Paul Dundas), Chinese Religion (Dr Whaling), Primal Religions (Dr John Parratt, who had joined the Centre), and Ancient Near Eastern Religions (Dr Wyatt).

Furthermore Dr Kee took the initiative in absorbing into the operation various honours options within Arts and Social Sciences. In effect this took into the M.A. degree possibilities that had been there in the old B.A. degree and made them available within the M.A. Thus in addition to being able to take honours in a religion plus a method as had been the case before, it was now possible to take honours in a religion and in one of a broad range of options in Arts or Social Sciences. It was still feasible to specialise in one religion in great depth, including immersion in the language of that religion; it was still possible to study two religions without the need for a knowledge of language; it now became admissible to study a religion along with any one of the following fifteen options: Ancient History, Archaeology, Art, Classics, English and Scottish Literature, History, Music, Philosophy, Politics, Psychology, Scottish History, Social Anthropology, Social Ethics, Social Policy and Sociology.

Edinburgh now had the widest course in Religious Studies in the United Kingdom and, together with the rise in students that was happening anyway due to the growth of higher education in Britain, numbers grew dramatically. The first-year class in Religious Studies, Religion 1, went up to 120 students. It had already been located away from New College in George Square (the Arts and Social Sciences campus) anyway to make it available to students in the wider University but it was now necessary to move it into the Psychology Building into a large lecture theatre. Teaching Religion 1 became an exercise in public oratory! The demand for the Religious Studies degree also took its intake to fifty during one year and this put its numbers, at any rate temporarily, above those for the B.D. This was good for New College, as the numbers of students flocking into the non-B.D. programme greatly improved the situation as far as student recruitment was concerned.

The composition of the student body was also interesting. The B.D. was attracting a larger number of mature students who were either offering for the Christian ministry in later years or coming to the B.D. late for other reasons. The Religious Studies students were mainly straight from school or alternatively they tended to come to university after a year or two out of education. They were therefore predominantly young. Those who were more mature often brought with them a rich experience of life in many different backgrounds. For example a middle-aged lighthouse keeper who had spent years in his career on the far headlands of Scotland felt the sudden urge to go in a new direction. He came to university and discovered that he had an aptitude for Islamic Studies and his career became launched along completely new lines. Many stories could be told to illustrate the compelling power of a new affection triggered by an often haphazard selection of Religious Studies as a subject to be studied. In the nature of things, Religious Studies students often found themselves spending a lot of time in other faculties. But there was the opportunity for them to mix with B.D. students and with students from Africa, India, China, South America, Korea, Japan, and elsewhere who were congregating in Edinburgh to study in the Centre for the Study of Christianity in the Non-Western World or to take the new Masters course in Theology and Development. The possibilities for mixing across the disciplines and cultures were vastly enhanced.

COPING WITH GROWTH

The rapid increase in numbers had consequences, and will have consequences, for the logistics of Religious Studies. In addition to lectures and visits to religious ceremonies and occasional audio-visual presentations, another feature of undergraduate teaching had become the use of seminar groups. Small gatherings of ten or so people met together weekly to study a text or a project on the basis of discussion and academic sharing. In spite of significant student input into these seminars leadership of the groups remained vital. The new challenge was to provide something over twenty seminar leaders a week to service 110 students in Religion 1, sixty students in Religion 2, forty students in Religion 3, and thirty students in Religion 4. In practice graduate students were drafted in to help (a development still relatively new in British universities, as least in humanities), and some members of staff had to double up in order to meet the demand. The need for larger rooms and for more books, the requirement to mark many more essays and exam papers all fitted into the new logistical challenge. The increased demand fed into specialised honours classes as well. Honours courses that had formerly had three or four takers now had twelve. The numbers of students climbed rapidly, the numbers of staff did not. Nevertheless, in spite of the drawbacks as well as the blessings of expanding numbers, Religious Studies at New College remains a success story. The small coterie of pioneering students of 1973 have become the vast hordes of 1995.

WIDER IMPLICATIONS AND INFLUENCES

Throughout this chapter the point has been made, implicitly or explicitly, that the introduction of Religious Studies into New College was a new departure in the College's history. From being a College providing a B.D. course for training for the ministry of the Christian church (primarily the Church of Scotland) it had expanded into one offering the B.D. to a wider constituency, and now it had expanded further to take a radically wider religious remit into its orbit. There had perhaps always been those in the College who were not necessarily committed Christians. However they had been western agnostic uncommitted Christians! Now there was the possibility, indeed the actuality, of a minority of people of other religions being part of the community, and of there being people present in the building who were committed to the study of other religions and other methods of studying religion outside the remit of Christianity and Christian theology. The whole operation involved the embracing of diversity.

Through the coming of Religious Studies to New College there were also implications for wider society. The influence upon Religious Education in Scotland and elsewhere has already been touched upon.

Through the Religious Studies Centre's input into bodies such as the Edinburgh Inter-Faith Association there has also been an influence upon the relationships between religious communities in Scotland. It has been remarked in informed quarters that these relations, although susceptible to improvement, are strong in Scotland. At key times interventions were made that were crucial. For example at the time of the furore over Salman Rushdie's *Satanic Verses* Frank Whaling was invited to speak to a joint meeting of the Edinburgh mosques, and the eventual outcome was that Edinburgh was the only place in Great Britain where the *Satanic Verses* affair was treated on an inter-faith rather than on a purely Islamic basis. At the time of the anniversary of the murder of a young Somali Muslim for what were suspected to be but never proved to be racial reasons, an inter-faith service was held to heal the wound and bring peace. When the synagogue suffered a distressing incident solace and friendship were offered. When feelings were running high in India and in England over the destruction of the Ayodhya mosque by right-wing Hindus in North India, in Edinburgh the Muslim and Hindu leaders were brought together and they gladly agreed that, whatever was happening elsewhere, in Scotland the usual friendly relations would remain. In these and in other ways the rise of Religious Studies at Edinburgh University has had consequences not only for the academic life but also for the wider life of the city of Edinburgh.

PART III

College in Context: Books, Neighbours and New Horizons

Chapter 9

꜔⸜⸝⸺⸝⸜꜔

Dual Identity: Church College and University Faculty

Bill Shaw

INTRODUCTION

O N 3 JUNE 1846, on the occasion of the laying of the foundation
stone of New College, Dr Thomas Chalmers in his famous speech
was able to say:

> There is no substantial difference between the theology taught at a College,
> and the theology taught in a Church. Only in the preparation of ministers
> . . . it is necessary that it should be taught in the form of a science, and
> receive an academic treatment in the hands of academic men . . . The great
> object, then, of an education here, is that our pupils may learn to understand
> the Bible, and to handle it aright in plying the hearts and the consciences of
> men.[1]

In November 1966, the solicitor Mr David Bogle, then Secretary to
the New College Financial Board, was not in jest when he asked the
Board, 'Does New College still exist? And is the Senate still a legal
entity?'

In May 1994, when the Faculty was considering the wording of a
suitable plaque to commemorate New College's 150th anniversary,
one member saw fit to query the suggested wording on the
grounds that the 'wording suggested that the College was a theological
college for a Christian Church', the clear inference being that this was
untrue.

---

[1] Watt, 2–3.

ORIGINS OF A CHURCH COLLEGE[2]

New College was a creature of the Disruption of 1843 and the Free Church of Scotland which was founded then. Even before the decisive split with the Church of Scotland, preparations were made. The Education Committee appointed by the Disruption Assembly rapidly set about establishing a college in George Street, and named Thomas Chalmers as Principal and three others as Professors. That the highest standard of theological education was intended from the very start is movingly vouched for in the Education Committee's Reports. One of the nominated Professors, Dr William Cunningham, because he would not be needed immediately, was deputed 'to proceed to the United States of America, partly with the view of pleading our church, and partly that he might have the opportunity of witnessing the manner in which education, and particularly theological education, is conducted in the seminaries of the New World'.[3] When one considers the rigours and duration of a trip across the Atlantic – and of travel on land once the ocean was crossed – the founders of New College could not be accused of taking their task lightly, or in a narrow, partisan spirit.

So on the second day of the Disruption Assembly in 1843, it was agreed that 'three, or if found desirable four Professors of Divinity must be appointed . . . that a hall or classroom must be procured . . . that a library must be founded', it being 'of the utmost importance that the whole system of education should be under an effective religious control . . . that piety should animate it in all its branches'. It was taken for granted that the College was to be under the control of and responsible to the General Assembly of the Free Church. An important College Committee was set up to supervise the work of the College and to report annually to the General Assembly, whose consent was required for every aspect of life in the College. Such was the importance the Church attached to the education of its future ministers that not only the General Assembly was involved. In 1849, while classes were still being held in 80 George Street, a draft constitution was sent down by the Assembly for the approval of Presbyteries. Under this constitution, the leading objects included:

1. To secure the connection with the Free Church of Scotland in all times coming;

[2] For a full account, see Watt, 1–52.

[3] Report of Education Committee, in *Proceedings of the General Assembly of the Free Church . . . October 1843*, 62.

2. To insure as far as possible that the Professors and teachers should be men not only of the highest attainment in their respective departments, but thoroughly imbued with the spirit of evangelical religion.

Also included, interestingly, and perhaps surprisingly to those who might have suspected a narrow denominationalism, the following objects were also included:

3. That the constitution should be framed on principles admitting of the development of the institution as the circumstances of the church and country might require, and providing against the evils incident to such institutions, of not keeping pace with the intelligence of the age and the progress of knowledge;

4. [Providing] inducements to continue the connection with the College ... so as to raise the standard of literature and theological education as high as possible ... and to afford means of a more thorough and efficient training of students.

Other points to be noted in this 1849 constitution were the vesting of College property in trustees appointed by the Church; the election of professors nominated by a Board of Electors; a Senatus Academicus consisting of the principal and professors; and a College Court, which, together with a Board of Visitors, was to report to the General Assembly annually.

Perhaps one ought to remember at this stage that the construction and maintenance of the College, the financing of the academic and other staff as well as the library were entirely dependent on the generosity of the members of the Free Church. There was initially little difficulty in raising the necessary sums. Indeed, at the start it was deemed not necessary, and not wise, to launch a public appeal: the money could be raised by personal approach to known benefactors. Incidentally, the sum estimated for the building of New College on 'the piece of ground at the head of the Earthen Mound' was £39,700, though the actual cost proved to be a good deal more.[4]

One of the first matters to be decided was whether the new College should be a seminary for training of ministers only, or whether it should be an even more ambitious project – what would now be called a liberal arts college, offering not only theological education but higher education in all subjects (except law and medicine, which were presumably sufficiently catered for in the University of Edinburgh). This latter project was eventually abandoned and it was decided to

[4] See Watt, 22, 23.

stick to such subjects as were essential for a well-educated ministry. These included, in addition to the theological disciplines, not only moral philosophy, logic and metaphysics, but natural science as well.

THE RUNNING OF A CHURCH COLLEGE

It was clear that the Church intended to take a very close interest in the education of its ministers and the running of the College and for many years this intention was diligently fulfilled. Administration was generally left to the Senatus Academicus, but all important (and some not so important) questions had to be transmitted to the General Assembly through, first, the College Committee, and then through Quinquennial and Triennial Visitation Committees. Such questions obviously included: (1) who should do the teaching? and (2) what should be taught?

The first professors, as has been noted, were appointed by the General Assembly on the recommendation of the College Committee. Thereafter, a Board of Electors or, later, a Committee on the Election of Professors had the responsibility of nominating, but the election and appointment was made by the General Assembly after consultation with all the Presbyteries. This was a lengthy and cumbersome procedure but one which secured the interest and guaranteed the authority of the Church. As for the curriculum, this too had to be approved by the General Assembly. The first curriculum, approved as early as 1843, looked as much like an advanced course in the Greek and Latin classics as a theological curriculum. However this was revised in 1848. The curriculum concentrated on the various branches of theology ('systematic', 'exegetical for the Greek New Testament and the Hebrew Bible', 'historical and polemical') with one course in 'Natural Science'.

This scrupulous and detailed oversight by the Church through its committees, presbyteries and General Assembly was readily acquiesced in by the principal and professors, and was certainly not considered a disincentive by students. On the contrary, the courses proved popular, not only with 'theological students' (i.e. candidates for the ministry) but with the general public as well. In the session 1843–4 there were 168 'theological students' and this figure rose to 258 in 1851–2, with between 300 and 400 altogether attending Free Church courses each year in the first ten years.

Thus, in addition to 'theological students', there were from the start others attending New College, seeking to take advantage of the high quality of education being offered. Over the years, these 'others' were to play a very significant part in the evolution of the College, as Andrew Ross's contribution to this volume makes clear.

DEVELOPMENTS TO THE END OF THE CENTURY

Relations between the College and the Free Church remained largely unaltered during the second half of the nineteenth century. One principal (from 1862 to 1873) was even a minister of an Edinburgh church – Robert Candlish of Free St George's. (Later when St George's was a United Free congregation, Alexander Whyte continued to serve as its minister for most of his years as Principal of New College, 1909–18.) Perhaps supervision by the General Assembly became a little less rigorous, but Visitations were taken very seriously and the General Assembly continued to take a close interest in appointments – at one time refusing to institute a chair of Pastoral Theology even though the money to fund it had been privately provided! – and in the curriculum and finances of the College. There is no evidence of the kind of financial crisis one might have expected, members of the Free Church being more than willing to provide for the education of its ministers. It is not without significance that although a New College Financial Board was instituted in 1869, it did not need to meet between 1875 and 1913! Suffice it to say that the College prospered, and given the quality of scholarship and teaching it provided the Free Church had good reason to be proud of it.

One might have suspected that the union of the Free Church with the United Presbyterian Church in 1900 would have created real problems for the College. That this was not the case was a tribute to the skill and foresight of those preparing the details of the union, particularly the transfer of teaching from the Theological Hall of the United Presbyterian Church in Castle Terrace to New College. The transfer and the augmentation of the Senatus seem to have gone so smoothly that New College was ill-prepared for the crisis that was shortly to overtake it.

CRISIS

The crisis was that precipitated by the famous 'Property Case'[5] of 1904, when the House of Lords finally decided that the continuing Free

---

[5] *Bannatyne v Overtoun* (see *DSCHT* 336–7).

Church, not the United Free Church of Scotland, were the lawful successors to all the property formerly belonging to the Free Church of Scotland prior to the Union of 1900. Included in this property was, of course, New College. It is astonishing that the first mention of the impending crisis in the Minutes of the New College Senate is in 19 October 1904, only some ten days before teachers and students were required to vacate the premises. The non-uniting Free Church did suggest that certain rooms might be temporarily retained but the Senate turned this down as derisory. At this point, the Faculty of Divinity of the University came to the rescue with an offer to provide teaching accommodation and the use of its Library. Obviously, there had been a remarkable change in relations between New College and the University since the days of open antagonism in the 1840s. It was not until January, 1907 that the College was able to return to its building on top of the Mound, but thanks to the co-operation of the University and of Heriot-Watt College, the availability of church premises in the Pleasance and elsewhere, and the continued generosity of the members of the United Free Church, neither the teaching nor the reputation of the College seems to have suffered. It is perhaps not too fanciful to speculate that it was this period of close proximity between College and University Faculty that paved the way for a smooth amalgamation three decades later. Certainly, when the Mound buildings were re-possessed the University's hospitality to its ancient rebel was not forgotten.

In the Senate's own minutes there is a curious lack of reference to the difficulties which must have been encountered during the First World War. There was obviously severe reduction in the number of students attending but there do not seem to have been any appeals for help to the Church, nor any chronicling of hardships endured. What is clear is that the College was keen to 'do its bit', and this took the form as early as March, 1917 of proposing to the General Assembly appropriate academic concessions to returning ex-serviceman. After the War, it was New College's turn to offer hospitality – this time to American and New Zealand servicemen training for the ministry of their own churches. Ever since its foundation, the eminence of its teachers had drawn to New College visiting students from the continent and North America, but this influx of ex-service students must have done much to establish the College as an international centre of theological study. It is worth noting, though, that the Assembly's permission was still necessary for any adjustments in curriculum, just as such permission had been necessary in 1917 for teachers at New College to accept lectureships in the University, and to take part along with the University Faculty in a scheme for postgraduate study.

UNION WITH THE CHURCH OF SCOTLAND

A radically new stage in the life of the College in its relation to the Church was reached in 1929 with the Union of the United Free Church with the established Church of Scotland. It must be recalled that up to that point the two Churches had been pursuing parallel courses for the preparation of candidates for the ministry, with Church of Scotland students at the University and taking degrees there. New College, on the other hand, was not a degree-awarding body, though of course most of the New College students were already graduates of one or other of the Scottish Universities. The Union, however, meant a change both in the relation with the united Church and with the University Faculty of Divinity.

It has been noted already how the Faculty had offered hospitality to the College during the time of the expulsion from New College buildings in 1904–6. Co-operation between the two had been furthered by the setting up of the School of Postgraduate Study involving teachers from both bodies. Students in New College as well as in the University were eligible for the new degree of Doctor of Philosophy, but the College had already been a draw for overseas students (more, apparently, than all other theological colleges in Britain together!). At the time of the Union of 1929, it was clear to all involved in negotiations that arrangements for the training of the future ministers of the uniting churches would have to be worked out.

The solution was to merge the four-professor Faculty of the University (the degree-awarding body) with the six-professor Senate of New College. Although this appears a simple enough objective, it proved extremely complicated, but the details need not be gone into here. It should be noted, however, that it involved the consent not only of Faculty and Senate, of University Court and General Assembly and Presbyteries, but also the obtaining of Ordinances through Privy Council and Acts of Parliament. It is perhaps not surprising then that it was not until 1935 that the union of Faculty and College was fully consummated. One could sum up the arrangement that was made as follows:

1. The College Senate and the University Faculty of Divinity to merge (i.e. function as a single unit, without losing their distinct constitutional identities).

2. Faculty to provide the curriculum for the B.D. or other degrees and 'also the normal curriculum prescribed by the Church for the training of students for its ministry'.

3. Four New College professors to become professors of the University (holding 'Church Chairs').

4. Church Professors' salaries to be paid by the Church, but the University to reimburse a proportion of fees paid to the University in respect of Church candidates.

5. A Board of Nomination (six Church and six University nominees) to be responsible for selecting future professors and for proposing to University Court and General Assembly the person to be both Principal and Dean.

6. The Church to provide accommodation at New College for teaching, for which the University would pay rent.

New College now became a Faculty of the University, with its students eligible for the degree of B.D. (assuming they had a previous degree) and subject to all the regulations of the University. There must have been those who felt that the Church (i.e. the United Free Church) had sold the pass and surrendered its educational rights and theological heritage to the University. This was certainly not the case. Negotiators on the United Free Church and New College side achieved some remarkable concessions from the University – the uniting of the offices of Principal and Dean to be held by the professor concerned (a minister of the Church of Scotland) until retirement (no other faculty dean enjoyed a similar privilege), the institution of a joint Church–University body to recommend appointments, and the advantageous financial provisions made. Moreover, as far as Church of Scotland candidates for the ministry were concerned, the new Faculty was certainly treated as a church college, with annual and triennial 'visitations' taking place as previously. The Education of the Ministry Committee of the Church reported each year to the General Assembly, which was free to make recommendations as to the spiritual and material welfare of the Church of Scotland students, as well as to additions to the curriculum and improvements in practical training.

In retrospect one can only say that however the merging of Faculty and College must have seemed at the time to the students from both traditions, and however complex the machinery which brought it about, the merger was accomplished remarkably smoothly. It is significant that although, in the original agreement, provision was made for amendment after a period of ten years, this provision was never appealed to. But then before the ten-year period elapsed, the Second World War had broken out.

AFTER THE UNION

Once the Senate of New College merged with the University Faculty it was clear that the College could no longer be called strictly a church college. But did it continue to be a church college in *any* sense? It is true that all students there were students of the University, that the professors (and later lecturers) were members of the staff of the University, and that degree curricula were fixed, examinations conducted and degrees awarded in accordance with University regulations. Yet, as already implied, the Church's interest was by no means surrendered. Quite apart from its rights through the Board of Nomination to have a say in the appointment of professors, quite apart from the powers of oversight of the Financial Board, the Church still owned the buildings of New College and still had the right of visitation to ensure that candidates for its ministry were being adequately educated for the ministry and pastorally cared for. This right of visitation was exercised for many years, both through the New College Visitation Sub-Committee of the Education for the Ministry Committee and through a special triennial visitation. Through such visitation, the General Assembly was informed about the adequacy or inadequacy of all branches of education for its candidates, and although the actual visitations seemed good-natured, non-controversial affairs on the whole, their reports, often reflecting students' feelings, sometimes led to heated debates in the Assembly and the demand for the strengthening of one or other aspect of the curriculum. (They never seemed to ask for the weakening of any aspect!)

During the Second World War, student numbers were considerably reduced,[6] firewatching took place from the roof, and teaching continued uninterrupted. A request to use the basement of the Library as a public air-raid shelter was refused on the grounds that it was needed by students. (The vaults of the Assembly Hall were offered instead!) Visitations continued. In 1943, a scheme proposed by the Church Committee for

---

[6] From 169 in the session 1938–9 to 74 in the session 1944–5.

accelerating training for the ministry was disapproved by the Senate but by 1944 proposals were being discussed for implementing a five-term curriculum for War Service candidates for the ministry. In the summer of 1945, in a repetition of arrangements that had been made at the end of the First World War, New College provided a School for American Chaplains, and in 1946 and 1947, a number of German chaplains, former prisoners of war, spent a week studying at the College.

In the aftermath of the War, there was no diminution in Church interest or influence. Indeed, the Education for the Ministry Committee provided funds for secretarial help for practical training. Moreover, the property adjoining New College, which belonged to the Church, was made over as a students' residence to be an integral part of the College, and financial assistance was given to the Library.

In 1961, with the concurrence of the Financial Board and on the recommendation of the Education for the Ministry Committee, the General Assembly agreed to the transfer of the buildings of New College to the University. To some in the Church, this was further evidence of the surrender of the Church to the University. In fact, it was far more of a relief than a defeat, for the upkeep of the buildings and their badly needed renovation far exceeded available New College or Church funds. Without this transfer, the gradual upgrading of the College, including the major alterations of 1975, would have been impossible. Furthermore, the funds previously required for the upkeep of the building now became available for educational purposes, such as scholarships or upgrading the Library or the supplementing or funding of academic posts. Yet the terms of the transfer decreed that, if the University failed 'to provide a course of theological training for candidates for the ministry of the Church of Scotland', the buildings shall revert to the ownership of the Church of Scotland – and without compensation to the University for any alterations or improvements!

Although the Church no longer owned the property or laid down the degree syllabus, it by no means resiled from its interest in both the welfare and education of the students. There were always those on the Education for the Ministry Committee who felt that the courses required at New College (and at the other colleges, all now firmly within their respective universities), were too academic, with not enough concentration on practical subjects. There was scope for disagreement here (e.g. over the Committee's 'Divinity Curriculum' Report in 1963), but usually, sometimes after some frank speaking, the parties involved reached amicable agreement. Thus when, in 1963, the Faculty introduced its four-year B.D. as a first degree the Church was consulted both about this and about new Diplomas (in Pastoral Studies, Christian Education, Mission Studies and, eventually, Ministry) which would meet Church requirements for its candidates.

By the 1960s, Church visitations had become something of a formality, although they did provide an occasion where Church men and women could meet staff and students. While the latter usually found something to complain about (regularly the compulsory Bible exam, or the quality of lunch!), the comment of the Visitors in 1964 was not untypical: 'There seemed to be no specific complaint this year on matters for which the senate and faculty were responsible.' After the visitation of 1969, however, the Faculty asked the church committee to consider a looser, freer and less formal association but closer co-operation through the Faculty/Church Liaison Committee. This was agreed to, and did indeed lead to closer co-operation between Church and College on matters pertaining to Church of Scotland students. It was succeeded by a Liaison Committee of the Church's Committee on Education for the Ministry, which included the Principal and other members of the Faculty.

With the merging of Senate and Faculty and with the same person holding the offices of Principal and Dean, the respective areas of concern and authority of Senate and Faculty were always clear. The question of the precise possible application of the Craigfoodie endowment necessitated in 1966 a Memorial to Counsel, and this provided the opportunity for the clarification of the role of the Senate. Here it was confirmed that the Senate consisted of the principal and professors and that its distinctive functions were 'oversight of the academic activities of Church of Scotland students, the organisation of fieldwork for these students, the discipline of such students, the financial administration of the several funds owned by the senate and designed for the furthering of the purposes of theological training'. The separate identity of the Senate was thus again confirmed, but it did not meet separately from the Faculty except on rare occasions when it was necessary to make nominations for principal or acting principal, or to make specific recommendation to the Financial Board as to the application of funds at the disposal of the Senate.

This last matter – the making of recommendations for the use of Senate money – became in the last two decades a matter of considerable importance, necessitating more frequent meetings of Senate, at times when the University and with it the Faculty were facing severe cutbacks. At such times, the Senate was able to recommend to the Financial Board that not inconsiderable sums be applied to supply, for example, the Meldrum Lectureship (named after the original donor of Easter Craigfoodie) in New Testament (later Dogmatic Theology) and to enable the computerisation of the Library.

The Senate became more active still after 1984 when Professor J. P. Mackey was elected Dean and Professor A. C. Cheyne nominated Principal, both offices, in accordance with principles previously laid down in 1968, to be for a term of four years (although technically, in accordance with University practice, the Dean had to be elected annually). It is worth noting that although the Board of Nomination to Church Chairs continued to report to the General Assembly, New College Senate itself did not do so. A report concerning New College was – and still is – made annually by the Education for the Ministry Committee.

OTHER CHURCHES

Up to this point we have been concerned with relations between New College and the Free Church, the United Free Church and the Church of Scotland. It would be an error of the greatest magnitude to imply thereby that other churches were not interested in New College, nor New College interested in other churches. It has been indicated that from the first days students came to study at New College from all over the world, mainly from Reformed or Presbyterian churches. The academic reputation of New College (as well as its competence after the Union to award degrees) began to be recognised in non-Reformed Christian circles. In 1964 the first students from the Edinburgh Theological College of the Scottish Episcopal Church (then in Coates Hall) matriculated at New College, and thereafter a full complement of Episcopalian students took the complete B.D. degree course, or certificate or diploma courses as part of their theological training. There can be no doubt that the fact of would-be ministers from the two traditions studying alongside each other has greatly helped the ecumenical situation in Scotland, quite apart from increasing the range of understanding and, no less important, friendship of the students themselves.

Another breakthrough came with the arrival in 1976 of two Dominican students to take the full B.D. degree as part of their theological training for priesthood and membership of the Order. New College had had a Roman Catholic, Noel O'Donoghue, on its staff since 1971, and there had been several Roman Catholics among lay students of theology at the college. Also, relations between New College and St Andrews College, Drygrange, the Roman Catholic seminary, were such that occasional exchanges of members of staff and visits by students had been taking place for some time. Nevertheless, the fact that the Edinburgh B.D. degree was being recognised as in part at least suitable preparation for the priesthood was surely significant.

However, Church/College relations were somewhat strained in 1979 on the occasion of the appointment of Professor James P. Mackey, a Roman Catholic and laicised priest, to the Thomas Chalmers chair of Theology. Immediately prior to the joint Church/University Nomination Board's recommendation to the University Court, the General Assembly accepted a motion requesting the Court 'in the event of a Roman Catholic priest or ex-priest being nominated . . . not to ratify the appointment, if that course be open to them . . .' The Court, however, was satisfied that the appropriate procedures had been followed and that there was no statutory barrier, and accordingly appointed Professor Mackey to the chair. This attracted a good deal of publicity and generated in some quarters real concern lest the Reformed traditions of the College were being threatened. The heat was taken out of the situation on the one hand by the Court's issuing a statement in which it assured the Church of Scotland concerning the acknowledged obligation on the part of the University to provide academic training for the Church's students for the ministry; and on the other hand by the Church Committee's acknowledgment of 'consultation at the invitation of the Faculty . . . which had resulted in the restructuring of the Edinburgh B.D. degree to the greater advantage of intending ministers'. A lengthy report to the 1980 General Assembly expressed the Church's satisfaction with the situation (see n. 7 below), and harmonious relations between Church and College were once again restored.

A further advance in the relation between College and churches was the institution in New College in 1986–7 of the Centre for the Study of Christianity in the Non-Western World. This interesting development, though novel, seems natural enough when one remembers the number of missionaries who over the years have received their theological education at New College and when one recalls the many students from the younger churches overseas who have looked to New College for furthering their theological studies.

STUDENT CONSTITUENCY

Quite apart from the constitutional and legal position, the greatest single factor affecting the relation between New College and the Church, or even the several churches, has been the change in the make-up of the student body. This had never consisted entirely of candidates for the ministry. Reference has already been made to the presence of students from abroad and the growth of the Postgraduate School, although most of the students in these categories were either ministers themselves or candidates for the ministry of other churches. Nevertheless, the majority of students were candidates for the ministry of the Church in Scotland. This continued to be the case long after the integration of the College in the University. Even as late as 1961, of 113 matriculated undergraduates, sixty-three (i.e. 56%) were candidates for the ministry. However, with the introduction in 1964 of the B.D. as a four-year first degree (i.e., no longer open only to graduates), and even more with the introduction in 1972 of the B.A. (Religious Studies), the situation rapidly changed. The number of students increased dramatically, but so did the number taking courses out of general interest, often without specific religious affiliation, far less with any intention of proceeding to the ministry. In the session 1994–5, of the total student body of 538 only forty-five or 8% were candidates for the ministry of the Church of Scotland. Given such statistics, it would not be surprising if there were not a change in the ethos and atmosphere of the College.

IS NEW COLLEGE STILL A CHURCH COLLEGE?

Has the current situation so changed the original *raison d'être* of the College that what was initiated as a church college can no longer be said to be such in any sense, and so has become a place no longer suitable for the education of ministers of the Church? Certainly there are those both within and without the Church who would take this view, some (though not many) suggesting that the Church of Scotland should establish a separate college, a seminary, specifically for the training of ministers. The General Assembly, guided by its Committee on Education for the Ministry, do not take this view,[7] but it is a view which surfaces from time to time. So can New College still in any sense be considered a church college?

A number of factors might seem to suggest a negative answer. As a university faculty, the vast majority of its students are not candidates for the ministry of any church, and subscription to the Christian faith or any religious belief is no longer required for entry. Moreover, the majority of the staff, not now being appointed through the Board of Nomination procedure which applies to professors and successors of professors only, are appointed only on the basis of academic excellence and without regard to personal belief. Anyway, should a university faculty be in any sense a church college? Is it right that the state, as supporters of the University, should provide the means for the education for the ministry of one or more churches? Should not candidates for the ministry be educated separately from those who have only a general and often uncommitted interest in the faith or the Church? Why should the Church still retain its rights through the Board of Nomination to Church Chairs? Why should the Principal of New College still have to be a minister? Does not this smack too much of a kind of patronage from which the British universities have by and large struggled free?

These are all substantial questions, yet neither the Church nor the University seems to find them so embarrassing as to be unanswerable. On the contrary, there are good reasons why New College retains a dual function as both a university faculty and a college for the education for the ministry, working, far from the detriment, to the very great advantage of both, in a symbiotic relationship. From the University side, just as it is natural that doctors and lawyers should gain their professional education at the University, there is no reason why the professional training for ministry should be done elsewhere. At Edinburgh, there is of course the advantage of inheriting the remarkable tradition in scholarship and churchmanship which New College enjoyed before the merger. More than that, the Faculty as a whole, not just the Church candidates, have benefited very substantially over the years from subventions from New College endowments. Those who are inclined to regret the Church connection would do well to speculate what the Library would be like without the aid it has received over the

[7] The advantages and dangers of candidates for the ministry being educated theologically in a University context are carefully considered in *Reports to the General Assembly of the Church of Scotland 1980*, 372–6 (Committee on Education for the Ministry). See also Shaw, D. W. D. (1988), and *Reports . . . 1995*, 579–87 (from the same Committee).

years; or what the make-up of the Faculty would be like without the support it has received from the generosity of generation after generation of church people through Senate funds; or what postgraduate numbers would look like without the strong Church connection which attracts so many students from overseas. Certainly, without the Church connection, the Faculty would be a different, and one must say poorer place.

What, then, from the Church side has been gained through integration with the University, given that compared with its original powers, so much control has been surrendered by the General Assembly of the Church of Scotland? First, it is simply not the case that the Church has surrendered control of the education of its candidates. It still controls the selection of candidates. Through regular consultation it can comment on courses being offered, and, more than that, approve the particular courses being taken by its candidates. More positively, the status and backing of the University has been added to that already enjoyed by New College: degrees awarded, research furthered, the ability of students and staff alike playing a full part in the wider affairs of the University. Second, because Church candidates are studying side by side both with others from different church traditions and with others who have no similar vocation or intention, they are protected from the 'ghetto' atmosphere which is always a danger with a seminary type of formation. They have the opportunity to be better acquainted with the world in which ministry is to take place, and so be able to guard against 'the evils incident to such institutions, of not keeping pace with the intelligence of the age and the progress of knowledge', as it was put at the very start of New College's history. Similarly, the fact that so many students are choosing to study theology in a university context with no intention toward the ministry is surely in its own way to be welcomed by the churches. The spread of genuine theological education among the public can only be applauded. The reason why the resources of modern theology take so long to percolate through the pulpit to the pew is surely because of a theological aversion or at least lack of theological sensitivity among church people. Anything which increases this sensitivity and interest must be welcomed.

Often, the complaint from those who would prefer a Church college entirely separate from the Faculty and entirely under control of the Church is that, while academically standards are well maintained, spiritually and on practical matters, the education offered in an integrated Faculty setting is defective. It is true that spiritual direction after a seminary pattern is not imposed. This does not mean, however, that spiritual discipline is not available: it is, through daily prayers, frequent services and communions and annual and other retreats or 'week-ends away'. As for training in the practical work of ministry, the Faculty has over the years shown itself ready to introduce courses and lectures as suggested by the Education for the Ministry Committee or General Assembly, as often as not following Faculty/Church discussion. An account of the expansion of the teaching of Practical Theology is given elsewhere. Suffice it to say here that the development of Practical Theology in its various branches, its offerings at first degree as well as at postgraduate level, have greatly enriched the quality of initial and continuing theological education for ministry, an enrichment which would not have been possible in a seminary or non-university setting. New College has long had a tradition of offering what are now called in-service courses for ministers and continuing education classes for the public, and with the development of extramural teaching these activities fit very well with current educational thinking.

Elsewhere in this volume accounts are given of the work of distinguished teachers at New College in the various disciplines. Their influence in forging and strengthening relations between the Church on the one hand and the College and Faculty on the other has been of paramount significance. Small wonder that so many of them were looked to for leadership as Moderators of the General Assembly[8] and conveners of major Assembly committees. Yet in the longer term, no less significant and decisive in bearing influence and office in the Church have been those ministers and missionaries, men and women who have gained their theological education at New College and who over the years, and still, look to it for the expansion and dissemination of theological knowledge in its widest and most open sense. The conclusion must be that New College is not merely (in the words quoted at the start of this article) 'a theological college for a Christian Church'; as a Faculty of the University it is much more than that. Equally, there can be no doubt that as an institution it not only has been and is a powerful influence in the Church but one which can continue to be confidently looked to for the education and training of its servants.

[8] Ten Principals of New College have been Moderators of the General Assembly of their respective churches, as have a number of professors.

Chapter 10

❧❧❧

New College Library

John Howard

N EW COLLEGE LIBRARY is the largest separate theological library in
the United Kingdom, and one of the premier libraries in its field
in the world. This survey of a century and a half of the history of the
Library is arranged in four main divisions: the collections (printed books;
growth by amalgamation; and manuscripts); catalogues and subject
arrangement; the building; management and finance; with selected
statistics and a list of Librarians.

THE COLLECTIONS: PRINTED BOOKS

Books were required for the students of the Free Church of Scotland's
new College as soon as courses began to be organised for the autumn
of 1843. Dr David Welsh, the Professor of Divinity, played the leading
part in collecting for this purpose, stipulating only that ministers who
had newly left the established Church of Scotland should not contribute.[1] (It was important that they preserved their libraries, if necessary
in storage until proper manses could be erected.) Contributions did
arrive at his house in great quantities, were stamped and listed by student
'curators', and by the time they were transferred to the new building
on the Mound in 1850, numbered about 13,000.

The early Donations Ledgers survive, and show repeated and
remarkable series of gifts from many people, notably Major-General
McDoual of Stranraer, George Waddell of Rashiehill and Frederick
Sargent of London. Many of these listed donations are in fact rare or
valuable books, and have become the core of the Library's historical

---

[1] On Welsh see *DSCHT* 860.

collections. There must have been many more ordinary books which were not recorded in this way. Publishers such as Thomas Nelson gave copies of their titles, and one donor paid for 500 volumes to be bound. Purchases were also made, a large one being the library of the late Andrew Thomson, minister of St George's Church, Charlotte Square, Edinburgh.[2] Another collection, the library of the Revd W. C. Burns,[3] was lent by its owner for the use of the students, provided that it was kept separately from the other books.

No library can continue indefinitely to rely on the goodwill of donors, and there is no substitute for a regular purchase fund and a systematic selection policy. The students' matriculation fee of ten shillings a year was assigned to the Library, and the same sum was the subscription fee for ministers of the Free Church who wished to use it. There was also some income from fines for late return of books. The College Committee assigned ten pounds a year to the Library. But the Librarian's salary of fifty pounds a year also had to be paid out of these funds. The minutes of the curators show that they did systematically consider titles proposed for purchase, and that they were very hard-headed in their dealings with the booksellers. The successful bidder had to offer them over 20% discount to secure their orders.

Hand in hand with selection for acquisition in an efficiently managed library goes disposal of unwanted books. The nature of donors is often to give regardless of the suitability of the material for the purpose. After a few years, disposals of duplicates and other unwanted items were frequent, partly to save shelf space and partly to raise funds. It is recorded that 2,000 volumes were sold by public roup in 1852 for about £100.

In 1862 the stock had reached 25,000 volumes. The annual report deplores 'the shameful inadequacy of the funds hitherto available', but goes on to record the bequest of £500 from Dr Binny Webster, who had given much in his lifetime, and the gift from Mr John Maitland of a house for the Librarian. The admirable Mr Maitland, who was curator of the Court of Session in Edinburgh, also gave 450 books, and the Library of the late Principal William Cunningham was purchased by friends of the Library – a further 2,534 volumes. In 1863 Mr Maitland gave the sum of £1,000, and in 1872 a further £3,300.

---

[2] Andrew Thomson (1779–1831) was one of the leading evangelical ministers of his day; see *DSCHT* 819–20.

[3] William Chalmers Burns (1815–68), missionary to China; *DSCHT* 114–15.

The book stock would have reflected the Protestant and Reformed teaching in the College. It at first included Arts subjects (Classics, Mathematics, Moral Philosophy and Logic) in addition to Divinity. These courses were discontinued early on, but another extension of the teaching range was towards Natural Science. The mid-nineteenth-century controversies over evolution and natural selection ensured that geology was particularly well represented. James Hutton, Lyell, Darwin and Huxley were all purchased and presumably argued over, but the great name for Free Churchmen was Hugh Miller, former stonemason and editor of *The Witness*.[4] There was a Hugh Miller Memorial Library of geological and related books, associated with a substantial collection of geological specimens in the College Museum.

One early donation for the 'Class of Natural Science' was of books in full calf bindings, together with minerals, shells, etc. and books for the general Library, from a lady who would allow herself to be identified only as Mrs ΦΦ. But a letter from Professor John Fleming on 10 May 1852 speaks of 'Madame La Harp's donation' as 'magnificent'. She has not been otherwise identified. The chair of Natural Science was occupied until 1934, and books were added in these subjects by the Librarian of that period, Adam Mitchell Hunter, who was personally interested in astronomy and other sciences. But this part of the collections became less used and was largely disposed of after 1980 by transfer to the main University Library special collections, or by sale.

The breadth of the interests of the early professors, if not of the students, is reflected in the quantity of theological literature of other Christian traditions acquired for the Library. Many volumes of Roman Catholic doctrinal works, mainly in Latin, are present, as well as all the classic Anglican writers of the sixteenth and seventeenth centuries. There is, naturally, all the Presbyterian Secession literature. Incunabula (books printed before 1500) number about 100, many of these given at an early stage by Frederick Sargent. There is a substantial collection of original editions of the sixteenth-century German and Latin tracts by Luther, Melanchthon, and other Reformers.

One of the entertaining stories in Dr Mitchell Hunter's chapters on the Library in Hugh Watt's centenary history of 1946[5] is about the acquisition of the 53-volume set of the *Acta Sanctorum* in massive blind-stamped calf bindings over wooden boards with brass clasps. Compiled in the Low Countries between 1643 and 1794 it was the ultimate work

[4] Hugh Miller (1802–56), brilliant but brittle geologist and editor; *DSCHT* 564.
[5] Watt 152–212; on the *Acta Sanctorum*, 194–6.

of hagiographical scholarship for Western Christendom. Robert Southey bought this set in 1818 when the continental monasteries were being suppressed, and it came on the market again at his death in 1843. John Henry Newman, who resigned from St Mary's, Littlemore, in September of that year, apparently saw these volumes advertised for sale, and had in hand an appropriate donation from a well-wisher. But he agonised too long about the purchase, which was made by Dr Cunningham for the Free Church College.

Although many editions of the early Fathers of the Church had been acquired, it was not till a century later that a serious attempt was made to build up a set of the texts published by the Abbé Migne. This was begun using a donation by Mrs A. M. Findlay. But the Senate Minutes for November 1950 record the fact that some members were in favour of using the gift to renew the College telephone system. The *Patrologia Latina* and *Patrologia Graeca* (the latter being in neither the University Library nor the National Library of Scotland) fortunately won the day, and were completed some twenty-five years later, after the purchase of many second-hand or reprinted volumes.

Liturgy is another subject area in which the Library is particularly strong, in the Catholic, Orthodox and Anglican traditions, as well as in the publications of the Church Service Society. Dr John Lamb, Librarian in the 1950s (and liturgical scholar and editor of the United Free Church *Fasti*), was responsible for adding considerably to this section. It was one of the regrets of his successor (the present writer) that the George Hay Forbes liturgical library was deposited by the Scottish Episcopal Church College (Coates Hall) in St Andrews University Library rather than in New College. The renewal of interest in forms of worship in Presbyterianism is connected with the practice of the Catholic Apostolic Church. A notable collection of the publications of this Church was bequeathed in 1947 by Professor Plato E. Shaw, whose doctoral dissertation at New College was on this subject. It complemented a collection of the writings of Edward Irving in the Library. Additions to those 'Irvingite' collections have been made subsequently.

The James Thin Hymnology Collection originated with the gift in the 1880s of 2,000 hymnbooks from the founder of Thin's famous bookshop in South Bridge. This has had substantial additions by gift and purchase, so that it now totals well over 7,000 volumes. Its main strength is in books and pamphlets published in English, with representative selections of books in other European languages, and from America and the former British colonies. It is probably the largest collection in the United Kingdom. There are also manuscript collections on the revision of the *United Presbyterian Hymnal*, 1877–82, and the revision of the *Church Hymnary*, 1927.

In the early years of the College the matriculation roll shows that a high proportion of students were Gaelic speakers. Texts of commentaries, devotional works, dictionaries and other Scottish Gaelic works were provided. This collection was assigned to the Free Church of Scotland in 1909 as a result of the law suits following the creation of the United Free Church in 1900. A new collection was begun, founded on the bequest of the Revd Donald Campbell of Greenock and later of Boat of Garten.[6] It includes most of the early editions of the Psalter and the Bible in both Scots and Irish Gaelic.

Church history is of course very well covered in the Library's collections. All the expected areas of Scottish, English, Irish and Welsh church history are included, with European Protestant traditions and the history of Christian missions in all parts of the world. But useful collections of the publications of English Quakers, of the Plymouth Brethren, and of the Primitive Methodists have also been added in recent times.

The ecumenical collection contains both printed and manuscript material. The English-language publications of the World Council of Churches are regularly subscribed to, as well as those of the Council of Churches for Britain and Ireland (formerly the British Council of Churches). There are deposits of working papers of various church re-union negotiations, successful or otherwise, including both Presbyterian and Episcopalian sides of the talks which led to the ill-fated so-called Bishops Report of 1957.

The pamphlet collection extends to about 30,000 volumes or boxes. A decision to acquire pamphlets on current controversies was made in 1867, and this policy is still followed, though contemporary ephemera seem to be less contentious – mainly parish histories and church guidebooks, experimental hymnbooks and liturgies. The bulk of the collection has come from libraries of individuals, put together in one lifetime, either chronologically, or by topic. They cover all periods of Scottish and British church history and affairs, and much non-ecclesiastical matter, from the sixteenth to the twentieth century.

In 1852 the students began subscriptions to 'theological and popular periodicals' for display in their Common Room, and established rules

---

[6] On Campbell, see *FUFCS* 157, *FES* IX, 231, 633.

for borrowing them, with fines for late return. The theological periodicals subsequently became part of the regular Library stock, and long, and in many cases complete, runs of these have become an essential source for research. From 1956 the Library began to receive forty further titles (reduced to twenty-one by 1995), many from Europe and the USA, in exchange for the *Scottish Journal of Theology*, which had built up a high reputation since its foundation in 1948. Church newspapers have not usually been kept permanently, but two titles of special interest are exceptions: these are *The Witness* (1840–64) and *The British Weekly* (1886–1954), 145 bound volumes of the latter having been presented by the editor, the Revd Dennis Duncan,[7] in 1974, together with volumes for 1900–1 and 1936–48, annotated to show the advertisers' payments.

THE COLLECTIONS:
GROWTH BY AMALGAMATION

As with industrial conglomerates, New College Library has grown by taking over others that were going out of business. This happened with the 1900 Union of the Free Church and the United Presbyterian Church, and in 1936 it happened with the Edinburgh Theological Library, as a consequence of the 1929 reunion of the United Free Church and the Church of Scotland. The Edinburgh Theological Library was the library of the University Divinity School, founded by the students themselves in 1698 and located till 1936 in the Old College. Its 10,000 volumes were one of the reasons which compelled the Senate of New College to find new premises for its Library at that time. This collection included many historical volumes, some of which had come to the University under the right of legal deposit (granted to the Scottish Universities in 1709 after the Act of Union of 1707), and with it came detailed borrowing ledgers covering the eighteenth and early nineteenth century, which show what books were borrowed by divinity students later to become famous, such as Thomas Carlyle and Sir David Brewster.

The next major take-over was that of the Library of the General Assembly, housed till 1958 in Tolbooth St John's Church, where the General Assembly of the Church of Scotland had met until 1929. Its theological collections had been transferred to New College at the time of the Union, and the Tolbooth Church Library had become the

---

[7] On Duncan, see *FES* IX, 18, 310, X, 182.

repository for the Kirk Session, Presbytery and Synod Records of the united Church. In 1958 the Scottish church historical collection, including the Dumfries Presbytery Library, was transferred to New College, and the manuscript church records were deposited in the Scottish Record Office.

In 1962 the Longforgan Free Church Minister's Library arrived from Dundee. The necessary proceedings in the Court of Session to transfer ownership to the Senate of New College had been set in motion by the Revd James Torrance (who had been minister at Longforgan) and Professor T. F. Torrance (who was then Curator of New College Library). This collection of 1,300 handsomely bound volumes of useful patristic and other texts, originally provided in 1875 by David Matthew Watson, papermaker, of Bullionfield, Dundee, came complete with its own fine glazed bookcases. It was lodged at first in the Mackintosh Library of the Department of Christian Dogmatics. Although it was later transferred to the College Library, the Mackintosh Library remains the most substantial of the class libraries, which are no longer retained by all Departments.

About 2,000 volumes from the Church of Scotland Lending Library also came in 1971, on its closure at the offices of the Church at 121 George Street. This brought a substantial increase in the printed histories of Christian missions, biographies and popular Bible commentaries.

The latest of these large acquisitions was the Paterson Bible Collection from the National Bible Society of Scotland in 1991, consisting of about 250 Bibles collected by John Paterson (1776–1855), missionary in Russia and Scandinavia.[8]

THE COLLECTIONS: MANUSCRIPTS

The very few medieval manuscripts are described in Mitchell Hunter's chapter on the contents of the Library, and in more detail by Neil R. Ker in his *Medieval Manuscripts in British Libraries*, vol. II, *Abbotsford–Keele*, Oxford, 1977. These remain in New College, but other small collections of Arabic, Persian, Hindi, and Turkish MSS have been transferred to the special collections of the University Library, along with some South-East Asian MSS on palm leaves.

The Scottish MSS begin with the sermons of Robert Bruce, Minister of St Giles, in 1590–4, and include the histories of Robert Baillie, David Calderwood and Robert Wodrow. A well-known collection is

---

[8] On John Paterson, see *DSCHT* 647–8.

James Kirkwood's 'MSS anent Highland Bibles and libraries, 1676–1709'. Writings of the Covenanters such as James Renwick, and Secession leaders such as Adam Gib and Ralph and Ebenezer Erskine are also on these shelves. James King Hewison's collection on the Covenanters is very extensive. The Dundee parish visitation diaries of Robert Murray McCheyne (1813–43), who was also the first Presbyterian missionary to the Holy Land, and William McCulloch's detailed accounts of individual experiences in the Cambuslang Revival of 1742, are quarries for historians of the activity of the Holy Spirit.

The most notable nineteenth-century collection of MSS is that of Thomas Chalmers, founding father (perhaps unwillingly) of the Free Church of Scotland, and first Principal of New College. It was given by two branches of his family, part in 1939 and part in 1963. There are 15,000 letters and many other papers. Their scope is far wider than the church life of Scotland, and many researchers in history, economics and social affairs have made use of them since an inventory and author index were made in 1971–82.

The papers of Alexander Thomson of Banchory are also an important source from this period. Thomson was a wealthy supporter of the Free Church who wrote much on social questions, and whose correspondence reveals his wide interests, including also some of his family's eighteenth-century correspondence with members in the American colonies. Dr Thomas Brown's materials for his *Annals of the Disruption* (1884), are a well-used historical source, supplemented by the Thomas Brown family papers (acquired 1987). Charles Watson, Minister of Burntisland, left twenty-one volumes of diaries (1817–66) and other papers.[9]

Large collections of miscellaneous correspondence of Scottish churchmen and others are indexed in the autograph collections of James Cunningham and William Dickson. The extensive archive of the Scottish Ecclesiological Society was deposited by its last secretary.

The papers of Alexander Whyte, and those of other notable Principals of the College, William Cunningham, Marcus Dods, Robert Rainy, and Alexander Martin, are in these collections. From the twentieth century the papers of John White, architect of the 1929 Union, of John Baillie (Professor of Divinity, Principal, and opponent of White's Tory politics), and of James S. Stewart (Professor of New Testament and a celebrated preacher) are included. In 1987 the papers of Archibald

[9] On Watson, see *FES* V, 83–4.

C. Craig, Glasgow University chaplain and lecturer, secretary to the British Council of Churches and ecumenical pioneer, were deposited and studied for a biography published in 1991.[10] The papers of J. H. Oldham, missionary and Christian statesman, were deposited in 1989, and have also been subsequently arranged for research.

CATALOGUES AND SUBJECT ARRANGEMENT

The rapid accumulation of books at the beginning of the Library's history required systems of arrangement and indexing so that readers could find what they needed. Nothing is known of the earliest shelf order. But a 192-page printed catalogue arranged alphabetically by authors was published in 1846, largely the work of Charles Watson, secretary of the student curators (and subsequently Minister of Burntisland, see above).

In 1868 was published *Catalogue of the Printed Books and Manuscripts in the Library of the New College, Edinburgh*, a 939-page volume. The curators' minutes on 6 December 1862 record that the Librarian, John Laing, was then 'able to spend the greater part of his time on it'. In his preface he disclaims completeness or exhaustiveness or systematic arrangement. But it has very full entries, again in an alphabetical author sequence, with systematic groups of titles under the headings Bible, Catechisms, Confessions and Liturgies. There is a short section for manuscript items, and a supplement listing the 'Library in connection with the chair of Natural Science'. The value of this catalogue has remained for at least a century, partly for its comprehensiveness for the stock up to that time, and partly for its accuracy and reliability.

The multiplication of copies of a printed catalogue allows many potential readers to see what the Library has, but it is not an up-to-date record of a growing collection. Mitchell Hunter says that 'For many years the catalogue of books consisted of written slips kept in packages accessible only to the Librarians.'[11] These could have been the original slips from which the 1868 Catalogue was printed, with fresh slips for new acquisitions interfiled. In any case, the students naturally objected to this paternalistic regime, and a team of 'six picked students' supervised by the Librarian Dr James Kennedy and Mrs Kennedy compiled a new catalogue which was published in 1893 as *Abridged Catalogue of Books in New College Library, Edinburgh*. It ran to

[10] Templeton (1991).
[11] Watt, 163.

223 pages and was arranged in two parts, the first alphabetically by authors, and the second by subjects, also A–Z. Entries were usually confined to one line. About 110 periodical titles were listed at the end.

The last printed catalogue was *Supplementary Catalogue of Books Added to New College Library, Edinburgh from 1893 to 1906*. It had fifty-two pages of author entries arranged A–Z, and was in the same format as the 1893 volume. One peculiarity was an occasional dagger warning the reader that the book listed was by a Roman Catholic author. The other peculiarity it shared with all the previous printed catalogues was that no location marks for any of the books were given.

In 1922 Dr Mitchell Hunter compiled a new card index (or probably arranged for the typing of the entries from the previous printed catalogues on cards). The card index itself was superseded after a decision in March 1935 to provide a sheaf catalogue with fresh typed slips in Moore's Modern Methods looseleaf binders. In addition to an author catalogue of books, there were separate catalogues of hymnology and of the pamphlet collection. These were gradually filed into one sequence, involving much editing and recataloguing, during 1970–84. The combined sheaf catalogue still survives, though not added to since 1986, gradually being superseded by the on-line electronic database common to the whole University Library.

There have been three periods in the subject arrangement of the Library, not counting the wilderness period before 1850. In the new building they occupied what is now the Martin Hall, and, eventually, all the smaller rooms above it on the second floor. Each room appears to have been devoted to one broad subject, e.g. New Testament, and printed bookplates survive, saying 'Department of New Testament', etc. Within each room the books do not seem to have had any fixed order: at least, no location marks appear in books before the rearrangement of 1936.

In 1936, the Library was moved into the present building, formerly the Free High Church, and in the next two years two young women graduates, who also had the Diploma of the London University School of Librarianship, sorted the books into subject order and put the shelfmarks on the books and on the catalogue entries. (There are still catalogue slips without shelfmarks: the deduction is that the book was not found in 1936–8.) Gaps were left for further additions, but basically it was a fixed-location arrangement, and it was inevitable that it would one day break down.

Most libraries of any size had, since about 1900, adopted a relative location system such as that of Melvil Dewey. In 1967, after comparing the various systems available, the subject arrangement of Union Theological Seminary, New York, was chosen. It was a similarly large library with wide-ranging stock, and a new edition of its detailed schedules had just been published. A printed edition of its catalogue, both in author and in subject arrangements, was also available. Finally, its combined letter and number notation – the actual shelfmarks – were usually brief and memorable. Along with this relative location system, which allowed for detailed subdivision of subjects and infinite expansion, a shelf list and a subject index were begun.

Most of the books shelved on open access in the Library, except the runs of periodicals, or about 40%, were eventually arranged by the Union Theological Seminary classification scheme. Then, from 1986, came computerised cataloguing, and the invasion of a team of temporary Manpower Service Commission assistants for retrospective conversion of the catalogue. These disappeared again with the waning of MSC itself, but the conversion was continued slowly with support from the New College Appeal. By the end of 1994 approximately 33% of the open access books (those available for lending) were included in the University's on-line database.

Cataloguing of manuscripts was neglected for far too long. Reference has been made to the inclusion of some in the 1868 catalogue, and to the new beginning a century later when the Thomas Chalmers archive was indexed. Since 1986, the literary and historical manuscripts, and the New College archives, have been rearranged systematically, with most of the major and minor collections now having inventories and indexes available. Some of this work has been done by the Librarian, but a large proportion has been done by the voluntary work of retired library and academic staff. They have made collections which were virtually unknown before accessible to resident or visiting researchers.

THE BUILDINGS

The books which were to form the Library were collected first at 59 Melville Street in the New Town, the house of Dr David Welsh. Then, on his death in 1845, they were transferred to the first 'New College' at 80 George Street, and then to the present building on the Mound. Here, from 1850 to 1936, they occupied high locked presses in the first floor hall in the north-west front of W. H. Playfair's gothic college.[12] There was also a gallery along the south wall of the hall, connected by an internal stair. The presses remained till the redecoration about 1966, though the gallery was removed much earlier. In the north-east corner of the hall, hiding behind a normal panelled door, is the steel door of the strong room. This strong room is probably unique in also having a back door which leads on to a turret stair connecting the Senate Room with the attics.

As already mentioned, the books gradually spread through the second-floor rooms above the Library Hall, until the imminent arrival of the 10,000 volumes of the Edinburgh Theological Library from the Old College as a result of the 1929 Union compelled drastic action. The first proposal was a new building to house the whole of the expanded Library on the site of the hostel now called the Patrick Geddes Hall (to the west of the College, formerly New College Residence). The pseudo-Playfair design by Sir George Washington Browne (1930) is preserved in the Library. But the College could not afford to build anew in a period of recession. The solution which eventually emerged was the acquisition and conversion of the Free High Church building on the east of the quadrangle. Its congregation removed to the new, and empty, Reid Memorial Church on the slopes of the Blackford Hill.

The conversion, by the architect A. Lorne Campbell,[13] inserted four floors into a building which had only had one (at ground level) and a gallery. The gallery entrance at first floor level became the main entrance into the Library Hall, the new reading room. Below this were three stackrooms, the lowest about 12 feet below ground level, built of steel and reinforced concrete, with modern adjustable steel shelving. The total capacity was estimated at 200,000 volumes. The Librarian's office was the former session room at the north end, on a higher level. A bay window into the Library Hall was inserted so that readers below could be observed.

The open timber roof of the Library Hall and the stained glass windows commissioned by Grace Warrack and executed by Douglas Strachan from 1911 to 1934 were kept unaltered.[14] The island bookcases

[12] On Playfair see *DNB* XLV, 415–16, Gow (1984) and Colvin (1978), 645–8; on New College, Watt 16–18, Gifford *et al*. (1984), 184–5 and Youngson (1966), 280–1.

[13] On A. Lorne Campbell (1871–1944), see Watt 170–6, and obituary in *Builder* 167 (July 1944), 57.

[14] On Strachan and his windows, Watt 176–8 and *DSCHT* 800.

and radiators were cased in oak with a series of individual carvings on the gable ends.

About 1960, when library staff had increased, the former teaching staff common room next to the Librarian's office, was transferred to Library use. In 1992 the eastern section of the Martin Hall was transferred to the Library as a postgraduate reading room under the title of the Thomas Chalmers Reading Room.

The original eight tables in the spaces between the bookcases in 1936 each seated eight readers. In 1995, with tables in the centre of the Hall and elsewhere, about 130 reader places were available. These included some for consultation of the on-line catalogue and some for using CD–ROMs and other electronic databases.

The problem of places for readers paled beside the problem of accommodating the books. The length of shelving available in 1971 was 7,610 metres, or about four and a half miles. At that time 6,041 metres were occupied, and only a year later the figure was 6,220 metres. In 1978 it was estimated that at the current rate of acquisition, about 1,500 volumes a year, there would be no empty shelves at all in 1988. It was also ascertained, in 1981, that the introduction of movable 'compact shelving' was not possible because of the spacing of load-bearing uprights in the lowest stackroom. The solution has been for successive Librarians to continue the policy of transferring to the main University Library sections of the stock which were less relevant to the Faculty's subject interests, and withdrawing or selling unwanted duplicate books. This rationalisation provided the needed shelf space, and gave the collections more coherence, but left the Library in 1995 with the unresolved problem of space for normal annual expansion or for accommodating any major purchase or donation.

By the standards of the 1990s the Library fails to provide the ideal environment either for readers or for books. Each move has been an improvement, but heating, lighting, ventilation, cleanliness and security have only advanced slowly. Better heating of the Library Hall and control of the stackroom temperature was achieved in 1969, but the ceiling fan for ventilation on summer days is inadequate. Landmarks in the history of the Library Hall were its redecoration in 1964 and again in 1994. Repeated flooding of the lowest stackroom was controlled after excavation of the courtyard in 1974, but extensive waterproofing was again necessary in 1994, and constant dehumidification was still required. (The major moves of stock to allow this work were very disruptive for regular service.) John Knox's statue may still have to be temporarily moved if his writings are going to be preserved for posterity!

MANAGEMENT AND FINANCE

The early management of the Library by elected student curators was not an experiment in radical democracy, because some of them were already men of experience, and 'mature students'. In any case they had the austere William Rowan as Librarian at their elbow, and it was not long before their meetings were presided over by Principal Cunningham. Their financial dealings with booksellers have already been mentioned, and they succeeded in getting Mr Rowan's salary raised from £40 to £50 a year. Systematic accounts have not survived, though their minutes record with pious gratitude the gifts which they received from time to time to supplement the meagre income from matriculation fees and fines.

Real authority seems to have been in the hands of the College Senate, who appointed the Librarian, and who used the Agnes Nairne Bursary to pay students to re-shelve books and do the routine work. In the 1930s there was also a Books Sub-Committee responsible for selection. At what stage the periodicals subscribed for by the Common Room became the responsibility of the Library is not clear.

In 1934 Mitchell Hunter tried to get his salary increased on the grounds that the founding of the Postgraduate School had brought more readers and more work. He also tried, and failed, to be appointed Professor. He got his increased salary, but he also got extra duties as a supervisor of postgraduates, and had to be content with a place 'in attendance' at the Senate. He was however confirmed in his post in the newly constituted University and College organisation in 1935.

For nearly thirty years after this the endowments of New College continued to finance the 'church' chairs and the upkeep of its buildings and the Library. But by the late 1950s it became clear that these funds were no longer adequate. An agreement was reached in May 1961, and ratified by the General Assembly of the Church of Scotland in May 1962, by which the buildings of New College and Mylne's Court were transferred, and by which the Library and other moveable properties were given on loan to the University 'for the purpose of the Faculty of Divinity'.

The Senate asked the University Librarian, E. R. S. Fifoot (later, Bodley's Librarian in Oxford), for a professional survey of the Library's needs under twelve heads, including cleaning, cataloguing, security, withdrawal of non-theological books, and an estimate of the cost of 'bringing the Library up to date and to full working standard'. This was done, and agreement was reached that the Library would become a 'sectional library' within the University Library system like the Medical Library or the Law Library, as a semi-independent administrative unit under the University Librarian and the University Library Committee. The Curator of New College Library would have a seat on the latter. A New College Library Committee was established, not for book selection as before, but as a consultative body of users, concerned also with policy for the endowment funds remaining.

The endowment funds were subsequently strengthened by the investment of sums derived from sales of duplicates and non-theological books, enough to support the payment of the salaries of some members of staff beyond the allocation of University Funding Council funds. Tribute should also be paid to several retired members of library and academic staff who have done voluntary cataloguing work over long periods. A substantial sum was also contributed in 1992–3 by the Senate of New College for retrospective cataloguing on-line. During 1991–5 Dr Murray Simpson, the New College Librarian, also had extensive responsibilities in other areas of the University Library. In 1995 he followed his predecessor at New College, John Howard (the Library's first professional Librarian), round to George Square to take charge of rare books and manuscripts in the University Library. To succeed him New College has welcomed its first female Librarian, Mrs Pamela Gilchrist, whose wide experience has included library service in Addis Ababa and Yale.

SELECTED STATISTICS

Stock

1847	*c.*9,000 volumes
1850	*c.*13,000 volumes
1936	*c.*100,000 volumes
1946	*c.*150,000 volumes
1966	211,750 volumes
1976	225,330 volumes
1986	237,376 volumes + 2,159 MSS
1995	*c.*232,000 volumes + *c.*3,000 MSS

Borrowing

1966	7,251
1976	20,300
1986	25,478
1995	52,583

Photocopies

1968	376
1976	c.15,000
1986	51,203
1995	215,014

Expenditure

	[University funds]	[Endowment funds]
1967/8	£3,489	£2,423
1975/6	£8,730	£810
1985/6	£28,272	£4,930
1994/5	£46,674	c.£6,900

LIBRARIANS: NEW COLLEGE

The Revd William Rowan	1843–53	[Watt 158–60, 179]
The Revd John Laing	1854–80	[*DSCHT* 468]
The Revd James Kennedy, D.D.	1880–1922	[*FUFCS* 585]
The Revd Adam Mitchell Hunter, D.D.	1922–46	[*DSCHT* 417]
The Revd J. B. Primrose	1946–51	[*FUFCS* 540; *FES* IX, 118, 785, X 67–8]
The Revd John Lamb, D.D.	1951–65	[*FUFCS* 152; *FES* IX, 785, X, 440; *NCB* 2:1 (Easter, 1965), 5–6]
John V. Howard, M.A., F.L.A.	1965–86	
Murray C. T. Simpson, M.A., Ph.D., L.R.A.M., A.L.A.	1987–95	
Pamela M. Gilchrist, B.A., F.L.A.	1995–	

LIBRARIANS: GENERAL ASSEMBLY LIBRARY

The Revd John Morrison, D. D.	1913–32	[*FES* VII, 703; *Reports to Gen. Ass. . . . 1932*, 20–21]
The Revd John Campbell, D.D.	1932–59	[*FES* III, 204, VIII, 24, IX, 43, X, 26]

Chapter 11

❧ ⟅≈⟆ ❧

Student Kaleidoscope

Andrew Ross

WHAT CAN one say in one brief chapter about the students who have attended New College during a period of 150 years? One thing that can be said immediately is that they have come from every quarter of the globe. They have come from Argentina, Brazil, Colombia and Mexico as well as the USA and Canada. They have come from Ghana, Nigeria, Cameroon, Kenya, Uganda, Rwanda, Malawi, Zambia, Zimbabwe and South Africa. They have come from Korea, Japan, Hong Kong, China, Taiwan, Singapore, Malaysia, the Philippines and Indonesia as well as New Zealand and Australia. Almost from the very beginning of the New College students came from France, Switzerland, the Netherlands, Germany, the Czech Republic and the Magyar churches, whether in Rumania, Slovakia or their native Hungary. The last overseas connection to be mentioned is one of the most important connections that New College has had, yet one that has received almost none of the academic attention it deserves – the steady stream of Irish students that have studied in New College, during its Free Church, United Free Church and post-1929 periods. Indeed no history of the Presbyterian Church in Ireland would be complete without an analysis of the part this connection has played in the history of that Church over the years, not least the last twenty years when certain groups in Ireland have mounted strong pressure to stop students coming to New College.

EARLY WOMEN STUDENTS

A second point to be made at the very beginning concerns women students. It has long been a commonly accepted notion that women students are a recent addition to the student mix in the College. When they are supposed first to have appeared in any numbers varies depending on the age of the group of gossips one listens to, but, despite the variety among them, opinions tend to point to some time after the Second World War, focusing more especially on the late 1950s. However, the reality is that there has been a small but steady stream of able women students taking classes in New College since the end of the First World War. That same session, 1924–5, that saw Norman Porteous begin his course also saw Ms (later Professor) Elizabeth Hewat, M.A., Dr Jean Mackey, M.B., Ch.B. and Ms Catherine Reid also begin their study. These three were committed to overseas missionary work, Ms Hewat going on to be Professor of Modern History at the University of Bombay. They were typical of the women students of the inter-War years who were either intending missionaries, missionaries on furlough taking classes for a year or women students from abroad, some of them ordained, like Ms Yi Chi from Manchuria. Whether it was her presence along with three other women students in session 1932–3 which led to the Theological Society making the topic of its annual debate 'Women in the Ministry', is difficult to decide from the scant records. It is, however, equally likely that it was because of the presence on the very committee of the Theological Society of Ms J. Tweedie-Stoddart. For three years she took a very active part in the society, leading in the debates with other student societies in the University, as well as with the other theological colleges, and also regularly reading papers to the Theological Society. But 1932–3 was not an unusual year. In session 1929–30, fourteen women students attended classes regularly; nine were the wives of American students and five were missionaries in training or on furlough, Mlle Marieleine Teutseh, B.D., Ms Isabella Drennan, M.A., B.Sc., Ms Effie Young, M.A., Ms K. B. Gardner, B.A. and Ms A. M. Nicolson, B.A.

Certainly it is not until after the Second World War that there were enough women students around – some full-time students, some, as ever, missionaries preparing for service abroad or on furlough, and others North American wives taking classes – that they were encouraged to form their own organisation. This was the US-inspired society, 'The Divinity Dames'. However, it seems that it was not until the arrival of women students who were training for the ministry of the Church of Scotland, the United Free (continuing) or the Presbyterian Church in Ireland that the consciousness of women as a major element in the make up of the New College community finally penetrated the popular image of the place. As the self-understanding of women changed and a new confidence emerged, so a separate organisation like 'The Divinity Dames' seemed inappropriate and disappeared. The appointment of Elizabeth Templeton (then Maclaren), the outstanding New College student of her year, as a lecturer in the Divinity Department in 1970 can be taken as the final public recognition of what had been a real presence in the life of the College since 1920.

The third general point to be made is that the student body at New College was, almost from the beginning, an international body, a community which spread its influence widely abroad through the return home of overseas students who had come to New College and through its own Scots students going abroad to serve. One of the most notable examples of this international interaction, and the very first chronologically, is that between New College and the Nederduitse Gereformeerde Kerke van Suid Afrika (NGK).

THE SOUTH AFRICAN CONNECTION

This relationship had its roots in pre-Disruption days when Dr G. Thom was sent to Scotland in 1820 to recruit ministers and schoolteachers for the then almost moribund NGK. He had a very successful visit and brought to South Africa a group of outstanding men from the Popular party within the Church of Scotland. The most notable among them was Andrew Murray Snr, founder of a dynasty which played a major role in the shaping of the Afrikaner people and their beloved 'boer kerke'. Their very success in acculturating themselves among their people can be measured by the number of their sons and grandsons who served as officers in the transversal or Free State armies in both of the so-called Boer wars.

In 1860, one of Andrew Murray's fellow 'Scots Afrikaners', Dr. W. Robertson, was sent to Switzerland, the Netherlands and Scotland to recruit young evangelical ministers willing to come to South Africa and commit themselves to the NGK and its people. Robertson obtained one volunteer from Switzerland and two from the Netherlands but in Scotland he struck it rich. Eight young ministers or licentiates of the Free Church of Scotland volunteered, seven of whom had done their theological study at New College. These seven were: Alexander McKidd (1844–9); John McCarter (1856–9) who wrote, both in Nederduitse and English, the first history of the NGK; Andrew McGregor (1854–8), medallist in Moral Philosophy in his Arts course at Edinburgh, after whom the town of MacGregor in Cape Province would be named; Dugald Macmillan (1855–9); Thomas M. Gray (1856–60), the winner of two major competitive scholarships while at New College; Thomas McCarter (1850–4), and David Ross (1858–62), who sailed later than the others. Ross was undoubtedly the outstanding student produced by New College in this period, having won the class prize in almost every class he took both in his Arts course in Edinburgh University and at New College.

In addition James Turnbull (New College, 1855–9), was sent to South Africa by the Colonial Committee of the Free Kirk to minister to an English-speaking Presbyterian Church in the Cape. However, after seven years he joined the NGK and worked hard at building new congregations in Natal where he was seven times the moderator of the Natal Synod.

These eight and the famous group recruited by Thom in 1820, dominated by three generations of the Murray family, shaped the spirituality of the NGK. The nature of this spirituality can be characterised as a warm evangelical piety, emotional and biblicist and yet with great respect for academic work and academic standards. In 1829 the Synod totally dominated by Scots had declared there must be no race distinction made at communion services. Then in 1857 a Synod still dominated by Scots ministers, the Synod which recruited the New College men, decided

> according to the Scriptures that our members from heathendom should be taken in and incorporated into our existing congregations, everywhere, where it can be done; but where this measure, owing to the weakness of some, will stand in the way of the furtherance of the cause of Christ amongst the heathen, the congregations formed or still to be formed of heathen shall enjoy their Christian privileges in a separate building or institution.

Nothing then must be allowed to stand in the way of the Christian community growing in numbers.

The connection between the NGK and New College continued to be very strong. Between 1865 and what in Britain is called the 'Boer War', forty-four young Afrikaner candidates for the ministry of the NG Kerke did their training (some completely, none for less than a year) as New College. The consensus among modern South African church historians is that this Scottish connection provided the dynamism and the evangelical piety that transformed the NGK from a formal institution to which Afrikaners gave only nominal allegiance into a dynamic spiritual institution which was at the centre of Afrikaner life and played a major part in shaping it. This 'Scots piety', as David Bosch named it, was indifferent on the whole to socio–political circumstance, flourishing in the Cape (which was legally non-racial from 1850 to 1910) as well as in the rigidly racially divided and authoritarianly ruled Transvaal and Free State, without passing any kind of judgment on either social system. As long as social and political structures did not inhibit preaching and formal church growth it was not a matter for Christian concern.

It was the pre–Disruption Popular party in the Church of Scotland and then the Free Church's New College which provided a majority of the clergy of this church up to the tragic events of 1899 which changed so much in South Africa. Indeed, New College was the single most important academic institution shaping the NGK ministry in this period. One has to conclude that this particular pattern of Christian spirituality, more akin to continental Pietism than to Calvinism, represented a very strong presence, to say the least, among the students of New College throughout the nineteenth century.

AN OUTSTANDING GENERATION

The opening decade of the twentieth century saw a generation of students pass through New College (which was by now the college of the United Free Church) who have rarely, if ever, been surpassed in terms of intellectual ability, and certainly never yet surpassed in terms of their impact upon the Christian church throughout the world.

What is particularly noticeable about this extraordinary generation is that their Christian piety and theology was not at all that of those who had such an impact on the NGK. Their Christianity with its concern for the impact of the Christian gospel on society and politics was in stark contrast to continental Pietism. It cannot however be categorised or neatly pigeon-holed as a form of the Social Gospel. John and Donald Baillie, Joe Oldham and Archie Craig belonged to, perhaps we should say shaped, a tradition that Alec Cheyne has called very aptly, 'Liberal Evangelicalism'. Joseph Houldsworth Oldham, after service as a lay missionary in India, where he had been born, came back to enter New College in 1901. In 1905 he became a licentiate of the United Free Church. Before he could embark on a career he was in 1908 dramatically and extraordinarily recruited to be the Organising Secretary of the World Missionary Conference to be held in the Assembly Hall in Edinburgh in 1910. This meeting was the most representative held until then and the first where leaders of the so-called 'younger churches' attended. It has been hailed as the beginning of the modern ecumenical movement, and it marked a new beginning in so many ways for Protestant Christianity. Oldham, whom the organisers almost certainly chose simply to be an efficient and hard-working bureaucrat, became a driving force from the beginning of the Conference and on the world stage for the next thirty years. He became secretary of the Continuing Committee which, held back by the First World War, eventually formed the International Missionary Council in 1921, and he was also the founding editor of the *International Review of Missions* begun in 1912 and still running. He went on to be throughout the 1920s and 1930s as secretary of the British Conference of Missionary Societies an extraordinarily effective one-man pressure group, lobbying the British government over its colonial policies. He played a crucial role in the bringing about the Devonshire Declaration of 1923 which declared that the interests of the indigenous people should come first in British policy in her colonies in African north of the Zambezi, and helped write the report of the Hilton Young Commission Report of 1931 which in effect prevented a white settler take-over of the East and Central African colonies. Later, along with Archbishop William Temple, he was the driving force behind the 1937 Oxford Conference of the Life and Work Movement, another movement contributing to the later World Council of Churches.

The two Baillies and Archie Craig and many of their fellow students were recruited by Oldham to be stewards at Edinburgh 1910. John Baillie, whose life story needs no rehearsing here, went on to be one of the first Presidents of the World Council of Churches and helped lay the foundations of that organisation in Amsterdam in 1948. In 1934 he returned from a very successful career in the United States to take up the old University chair of Divinity at Edinburgh, in a Faculty which from 1935 was housed in New College, following the Union of the Churches in 1929. That same year, 1934, his brother Donald, who had been the year behind John, first in Arts at Edinburgh and then at New College, became holder of the chair of Systematic Theology at St Andrews. How much more, but for the terrible slaughter of the First World War, that generation of New College students might have influenced the church and the world, we can only speculate. German, French and Hungarian members of the New College community all died in that awful conflict. (The Hungarian link was one of the oldest and most continuous overseas connections with New College.) It was the Baillie generation of Scots that was particularly outstanding and particularly badly hit.

John Baillie, in a biographical preface to his brother Donald's *The Theology of the Sacraments*, insisted that he and his brother were equalled, if not surpassed, intellectually by two of their Scottish contemporaries at New College. These extraordinary young men were Cecil Simpson and Ross Husband. Their story gives us an insight into the experience of New College students of that generation. Both Husband and Simpson had been ordained and inducted into parishes by the time the War began. However, as the first-hand accounts of men on leave corrected the propaganda picture of what the fighting on the Western Front was like, both these young ministers, intellectually brilliant and deeply spiritual (John Baillie and his brother attributed near saint-like qualities to Simpson), became deeply troubled. Both felt that they had nothing to say in the pulpit in the face of the pointless slaughter and the appalling lies being told about it. All they could do as Christians was share the anguish and the pain. They were in no way like the clergyman pilloried in *Oh What a Lovely War*, the type who preached the gospel of the Christian hero fighting the beastly Hun. They felt they had no other Christian choice but to identify with the poor infantrymen who died in the mud in one or other of the generals' great 'victories'. Both demitted status and were killed as infantry subalterns on the Western Front, Simpson with the Seaforths, Husband with the Black Watch.

One who survived the slaughter on the Western Front – extraordinarily since he was also an infantry officer – was Archie Craig. He started his course at New College in 1912 just after the Baillies, but did not finish till after the War. He did his last two years, in 1918 to 1920, as a war veteran with a Military Cross but now a convinced pacifist, exactly like George MacLeod, decorated veteran and pacifist, who was studying in the University Faculty at the same time. They would later come together as Leader and deputy Leader of the Iona Community. For the next sixty years Archie Craig was to be a leading influence on young people across Scotland and the rest of the United Kingdom, as well as playing a major role in the development of the ecumenical movement.

'REGULAR STUDENTS' . . . AND OTHERS

It was immediately after the First World War that postgraduate study began to make up a large part of what was and is New College. The

Faculty of Divinity of Edinburgh University awarded the degrees but the New College staff and certain teachers from the Congregational and Episcopal Colleges were also recognised as lecturers in the new Postgraduate School of Theology, which predated the uniting of the Faculty and College by nine years. Perhaps it was the presence of a large number of soldiers from the United States awaiting discharge who were permitted by their authorities to do some study at New College in the years 1918 and 1919 that helps explain the extraordinary popularity of New College for American students in the succeeding years. This popularity was expressed either at the level of doing one of their B.D. years at New College or doing postgraduate work at Edinburgh. This tendency reached extraordinary lengths in the two decades 1950 to 1970, when American students in New College in every year outnumbered the students in any one 'year' of the B.D. programme, more often than not outnumbering the total number of students in the whole regular B.D. programme. The academic session 1958–9 was not unusual for this period when there were sixty-two students studying for the ministry of the Church of Scotland while seventy-two American students were doing B.D. classes or postgraduate work. When one takes into account that there were also nine Irish, three African, one Swiss, one Chinese and one Korean student doing B.D. work, the usual situation for this period clearly was one where the students studying for the Church of Scotland ministry were a minority in New College.

This situation in which those students who, until the early 1960s, were called the 'regular students' were very often a minority in the College is not at all reflected in Professor Watt's centenary history published in 1946. When he is writing about the student community he writes as though the 'regular students' were the student community. This without doubt reflects the self-consciousness of the students at New College during that first 100 years. It is also a result of his use, of necessity, of the records of the student societies as his primary source material. What is significant for us today about these records is both that they appear to reflect accurately the life and concerns of these same 'regular students' and that they do not reflect the actual make-up of the student body of New College during the 100 years he was considering.

A careful reading of these records for the period, indeed up to the early 1960s, makes clear that both the Missionary Society and the Theological Society, whether going through a low period or a period of popularity, were channels of activity primarily for the 'regular students'. Not only were the 'other students' almost never senior office-bearers in the societies, but nor was their presence reflected in the names of those reading papers or leading the formal debates so popular with both Theological Societies in their pre-Union days. (Prior to the 1929 Union, New College and the University Faculty each had its own Theological Society and Missionary Society.) The Missionary Societies had somewhat more room for the 'other students' but not significant enough to change the 'regular student' character of those societies either. Indeed, as can be learned from David Lyall's essay in this volume, the activities of the New College Missionary Society until the Second World War were inextricably involved with what was effectively the practical training for the ministry, first of the Free Church, then of the United Free and latterly of the Church of Scotland.

The old University Missionary Society with its primary concern for the mission of Christianity overseas does not appear to have had much impact on the shape of the new society created by the union of the two missionary societies in 1929. The new society of the 1930s did however, produce Bill Stewart, a missionary to India who went on to be Principal of Serampore, the oldest university in India.

This anomaly of the official student life reflecting only that of the 'regular students' while they are quite often outnumbered by the 'other students taking classes', is revealed only once but very dramatically in Hugh Watt's chapter on the students. Apart for a reference to the creation of the graduate school immediately after the First World War and the overseas students who attended then, there is almost no reference to others in the narrative. Then suddenly almost out of the blue, reference is made to a pre-First World War novel, written by a French Calvinist pastor, a New College alumnus. The hero of the novel is also a French Reformed pastor, who, during the Franco–Prussian War, gets into trouble with the occupying authorities. As a result he is to be executed by firing squad. The pastor is then saved by the Lutheran chaplain of the German regiment who recognised him as having been a fellow student years before in New College. Professor Watt then goes on, and rightly so, to praise the international nature of the student body of New College during its 100-years existence and how it has linked people over international and denominational differences. Yet apart from this story, international and ecumenical are not the characteristics of the student body portrayed in the chapter nor in the student society records. Professor Watt's brief assertion of these features of the student body reflects the actual composition of the student body over the years and not the records of the societies. It is to be doubted, however, that he would have dreamed that by the 1970s New College students would bridge the Protestant–Roman Catholic divide that has been so bitter in some lands but no more so than Ireland and Scotland.

It is perhaps appropriate to explain at this point that the terms 'regular students' and 'other students taking classes' come from the New College Handbooks issued each year containing staff and students names and addresses. It was by these categories that all students who were not studying as postgraduates were listed until the session 1964–5. Since then students have been listed by the degree (a little later also by certificates and diplomas when they were introduced) for which they were studying irrespective of nationality or denomination. Postgraduate students were listed as such and then those students from other universities and seminaries who were studying at Edinburgh to gain credit towards degrees taken in their home institutions were listed as non-graduating students.

This new pattern was not simply a formal change but represents a new self-understanding of the student body. Had it been pursued earlier, the young shy Taiwanese student, Choan-Seng Song, now perhaps the leading East Asian theologian, and Ian Thomson, the South African leading light of the Missionary Society's new St James Mission which replaced the old one in the Pleasance, would have been listed with their fellow candidates for the B.D. These included their friend Duncan Forrester, leader of the St James Mission, later Professor in Madras Christian College and Principal of New College, and Alastair Campbell, now Professor of Medical Ethics at Otago. Instead, Song and Thomson are lost among the long list of 'other students taking classes'.

STUDENT SOCIETIES AND CONTEMPORARY ISSUES

Despite their grave limitations, it has to be said that the records of the Missionary and Theological Societies do give a very enlightening and informative picture of the concerns and perceptions of the 'regular students' down these 150 years. Unhappiness with the curriculum turns up again and again, not only in the 1850s and 1860s but very notably in the years between the two World Wars. Immediately after the end of the First World War demands for radical restructuring of the curriculum were made through well-received papers delivered to both the University and New College Theological Societies. The two societies had been united during the War but were again separate, though still united on this issue. The University Society even went so far as to set up a special committee headed by George MacLeod to draft a new curriculum to be presented to the Faculty. I could not find out whether it was ever presented or what form it took. There is no mention anywhere in the minute book of the Society of any response from the Faculty. Again, in 1936 while replying to the valedictory address given as retiring president of the now united Theological Society by Ian Henderson (later Professor of Theology at Glasgow University) Stuart Louden remarked that he was completely puzzled as to how 'such a flower flourished on the arid soil of the New College curriculum'. This was far from being the only hit at the curriculum by a generation of 'regular students' who produced more than their fair share of future professors.

In this period the curriculum may have been arid but the Missionary and Theological Societies brought to Edinburgh a galaxy of speakers who were at the forefront of theology and of politics (in the widest sense) at that time. In the two years before the outbreak of the Second World War, the student societies brought to New College, Karl Barth (Ian Henderson translating), Reinhold Niebuhr, Donald Baillie, Joe Oldham and Archie Craig. Reinhold Niebuhr was to return in 1946 to give the Honorary Presidential Address of the Theological Society. That three of these genuinely giant figures were themselves New College men must not be allowed to go to our heads!

The records of the societies' meetings in the 1930s, quite apart from the visiting luminaries, show an openness and awareness of the intellectual and political trends of the times that is striking. The German Church Struggle, Dialectic Theology, the importance of Karl Barth, the challenge of Bultmann's Formgeschichte, and the International Missionary Council conference at Tambaram were all among the topics of discussion. This lively period compares well with the very early days of the New College Theological Society. Its first meeting, on 5 January 1844, was in the building in George Street that housed the College before the buildings on the Mound were built. The records make clear that this meeting was of the old University Theological Society founded in 1776, that auspicious year, under a new name. The members of the Society, to which one had to be elected in those days, had adhered to the new Free Church along with all the other students of the University Faculty. Their first debates discussed issues such as

'Should females have a vote in the election of church office-bearers?', 'That the Covenanters were justifiable in armed resistance to the Civil Power', and 'That the Evangelical Churches were justifiable in holding communion with Churches countenancing slavery'. This latter motion, carried by a large majority in a full house, chimes in very neatly with the theological style of the New College connection with the South Africa NGK to which we have already referred.

These two periods of student debate and discussion are in direct contrast with that at the turn of the nineteenth and twentieth centuries. At that time the discussions of the student societies in both New and Old College show an astonishingly introverted and narrow perspective. They manage to go through the bitterly controversial South African War of 1899–1902 without any reference to it. Again in the intellectual world, the impact of Social Darwinism in the English–speaking world was immense, yet it provokes only one indirect discussion. It was a meeting at which two papers were presented on the topic of 'Heredity'. The titles of the two papers were 'Heredity, its scientific truth' and 'Heredity, its value for religion and morality'. It is impossible now to know how the discussion went, since, unlike in time past, there were no detailed minutes of what transpired. However the shape of both titles could be taken to imply an acceptance of Social Darwinist ideas as a scientific 'given'.

THE COMING OF THE AMERICANS

The end of the Second World War saw the beginning of a new and very dynamic period in the student life in the College. Just as in 1918 and 1919, the US military authorities in Europe allowed large numbers of GIs to undertake academic study while waiting for demobilisation. A large number who hoped to go to 'Div School' back in the States came to study at New College. This was an enormous reinforcement of the New College–US connection which had existed for some time. It still goes on in the late 1990s but not in the numbers that flocked here in the twenty years after 1945. In those two decades the total of US students was never below eighty and more usually well over 100. Canada was also especially well represented during this period with a high of eighteen during 1955–8. It is worth noting that these American students came from all over the US and were not simply 'Old School' Southern Presbyterians, as I have heard asserted in the US. Their quality was as distinguished as that of the smaller contingents of the 1930s that had included Eugene Carson Blake. This post-War period saw distinguished future academics like Professors Harold Nebelsick, Ira Zepp and Bob Voelkel study at New College as well as a host of men and women who would go on to fill with distinction pulpits across the country from Hollywood to New York City.

Two students of this period stand out in particular. The first is Bill Moyers who became deputy head of the Peace Corps under President Kennedy and then became an adviser to President Johnson, who was known to refer to Bill as 'ma Baptist preacher'. After leaving the service of the President because of a disagreement about policy on Vietnam, he went on to have a career in serious TV journalism of the highest order. He is now, in the judgment of many, the outstanding contributor, as producer and interviewer, to the serious discussion of religion on television in the United States. In the last few years some of his shows have been shown on BBC2 and Channel 4 in Britain. The second is James Deotis Roberts, the first African-American to graduate with an Edinburgh Ph.D., and later the D.D. Back in the United States he became one of the first Black Christian intellectuals to challenge traditional theology from the perspective of the injustice suffered by the Black community. His *A Black Political Theology* (1974) was the first substantial work of that genre to appear in America. It was a privilege for the College to welcome him back for some months of study on his retirement in 1994.

AFRICANS, EAST ASIANS, EUROPEANS

This post-War period was also the time when African Christianity, which was entering an era of astonishing expansion which still goes on, first began to change the face of the New College student body. Initially the students were from West African countries, Ghana, Nigeria and also Cameroon, where a church rooted in both the French Reformed and Scottish tradition is very strong. Since then students from many African countries have come, women as well as men. They have been not only Presbyterians from countries with strong Scottish connections like Malawi and Kenya, but Anglicans from Sierra Leone and Uganda and Methodists from South Africa and Zimbabwe. The first Black Presbyterian woman minister in South Africa, the Reverend Charity Majiza, studied at New College, as did one of the first Black Presidents of the Methodist Church of Southern Africa, which covers all the nations south of the Zambezi.

It was in the 1950s that the first Korean student appeared on the rolls of New College, the first sign we had seen of the astonishing growth of Korean Christianity which has characterised the second half of the twentieth century and has sent many Koreans to study in Europe and America. So in New College a steady, if small, stream of Korean, Indian, Japanese and Chinese (both from the diaspora and the People's Republic) have come to balance the rapid growth of the African presence which has become so strong in the 1990s. It should be noted however that of all the overseas connections outside Europe and North America, the Japanese connection is the oldest, dating from before the First World War.

The 1970s in Britain produced a political development that looked for a time as if it might cut off the international element of the New College community. This was the government's imposition of so-called real-cost fees on overseas students. Initially this had a bad effect on the flow of overseas students from every country in the world. Gradually, through changes in the world economy, the situation has altered for students from more prosperous countries. However, for students from the poorer countries of the world the fees are still a problem which we struggle, with a little success, to overcome. Our little success is measured by the fact that today New College has a large contingent of students from Africa and Asia as well as Europe and North America.

Students from the European Union have for some time now been treated as 'home' students (as are British students in any other EU country). This has resulted in German students being the single largest contingent among the 'foreign' undergraduate students in the College, building upon our long-standing student exchange with the Stift in Tübingen. Among postgraduate students no one country dominates today as students from the United States did from the 1920s to the end of the 1960s. Now the continents of Africa, Asia, Europe and North America are evenly balanced in numbers with the occasional and very welcome student from South America and Oceania.

A number of fundamental academic changes as well as changes in the general ecumenical climate in the 1960s brought about shifts in the composition of the New College student community. The first of these was the creation of the so-called 'first' B.D. degree, a four-year degree that could be entered upon straight from school, similar in that way to the traditional Oxbridge B.A. in Theology. This meant the arrival in New College of students younger than any of their predecessors had ever been. Until 1990 the number taking the old B.D. requiring a previous degree for entrance had remained a majority of B.D. students, but this has changed in the 1990s.

Another major change was the arrival of a significant number of Scottish Episcopal and Anglican students in New College to take the B.D. as an integral part of their training for the priesthood. This brought another bright new colour to the 'Jacob's coat' that has always been the student community of the College. This development began in 1967. The students lived in Coates Hall where they received their spiritual formation but did their academic study on the Mound. For twenty years the Coates Hall contingent were a significant presence in the College. It has become more marginal only recently, because of major changes in the training for the priesthood in both the Scottish Episcopal and Anglican Churches.

CATHOLICS AND RELIGIOUS STUDIES

Two other changes have taken place in this period that have been more surprising, indeed disturbing, for those with the 'regular student' image of New College in their minds. These are first the arrival of Roman Catholic students training for the priesthood and doing the B.D. as part of that training, together with Roman Catholic women also doing the B.D. The second was the creation of the B.A. and M.A. in Religious Studies which brought into the New College student community those with faiths other than the Christian or with no particular religious conviction at all.

The first significant Roman Catholic presence came in the session 1967–8, when a young candidate for the priesthood was permitted by the bishop to take the B.D. and two Jesuit postgraduate students from Louvain came to do a year's study with us. Since then some secular priests and a few from a variety of Orders have studied at New College, but the regular Roman Catholic presence has been made up of students from the Dominican novitiate. They live in the Dominican House in George Square and study for the B.D. in New College. Two pictures produced by their presence stand out in my memory. The first is of two friends, both outstanding students who were always at the centre of student discussions and student events. One was a Dominican, his partner in all this activity, an Irish Presbyterian from the Orange heartland of County Antrim. The other memory is of the ordination of one of our Dominican students to the priesthood. At the service, other than the bishop, all other five priests concelebrating mass with him were what would have been referred to in the Centenary History as 'New College men'.

The Religious Studies students, whose programme first began in the year 1971–2, were initially few, but the numbers have steadily grown since then. Now in 1995 they more or less equal the number of undergraduates on the Divinity side. There are 156 students taking the B.D., L.Th. and Certificates, while there are 148 students taking the B.A. or M.A. in Religious Studies, commonly abbreviated as RS.

For many people this situation causes real concern over the lack of integration. Some RS students feel ill at ease in New College while others find the RS presence disturbing. Some people appear to see this as a new problem. However, it is one new element in a continuing problem of integrating the many different groups who study in New College. The old 'regular students' / 'others taking classes' situation simply ignored the problems of integration, it never solved them. Another new and related difficulty in the last twenty years is that the 'first' B.D. students and the RS students tend to be young, coming straight from school. These students often have problems when in discussion, whether informal or in class, they are faced with a majority of fellow students who are mature and with a lot of life experience, ranging from the thirties to the unambiguously middle-aged. It is difficult for an eighteen-years-old fresher to take on another student who only the year before was an Advocate or a senior civil servant or a university lecturer. Again since around 1970 more and more women students have come to New College so that they now make up 50% of the undergraduate student body. This also raises a number of thorny problems for some men at many different levels, as well as problems for the women students. These tensions and difficulties cut across each other in different directions. For example, women candidates for the ministry may be united with women RS students of no particular religious belief against the attitudes of certain men. However, it would be wrong to see this situation as one only of problems and tension. Many see it rather as an opportunity for learning and personal growth. I see it as an enriching of the coat of many colours that has always been the student body at New College.

However, it should be noted that the postgraduate students in New College, while from many nations and many traditions, are still over 90% on the Divinity side of the College's activities. The postgraduates today outnumber either of the two main undergraduate groups. In

1995 there are 192 matriculated postgraduate students in New College, a significant number of them from the churches outside Europe and North America where the majority of the world's Christians now live. This large number of postgrads means that Divinity is now one of the strongest postgraduate research units in the University. Major contributions have been made to this development by the coming to Edinburgh of the Centre for the Study of Christianity in the Non-Western World and new M.Th. programmes in Theology and Development and in Media Studies.

The coat of many colours that is the student body of New College today has received some new colours to add to the variety, but it has been always so. The difference is that the enormous variety of the student body is now recognised at every level. From the beginning of New College, the student body was not just 'regular students'. In many periods of our past they were only about 50% of the student body and already in the 1950s they were a minority. The way the College community saw itself, as reflected in the Handbook and the way the societies operated, did not recognise that until recently. Perhaps it is possible to sum up by saying that New College has never been able to cope satisfactorily with the enormous wealth and variety of its students, but we go on trying.

Chapter 12

The Free Church College 1900–1970

Donald MacLeod

THE TINY handful of Free Church ministers who refused to enter the Union of 1900 looked a forlorn crew. There were only twenty-six of them, they were mostly Highlanders, and among them, according to Lord Balfour of Burleigh, there was not a single man 'of large ideas or of knowledge of affairs'.[1] Everyone who was anyone had entered the Union; and everything that was anything had gone with them.

At the General Assembly of 1901 the decision was taken to appoint a Training of the Ministry Committee. To begin with, the Committee had to rely on outside help, the early tuition being given by Professor Robert Morton and Dr Hay Fleming of the Secession Church and Dr James Kerr of the United Presbyterians. Dr William Menzies Alexander, who joined the Free Church in 1903, was appointed to give lectures in Church History and Apologetics that same year. In 1904, Robert Moore, a minister of the Irish Presbyterian Church, became tutor in Hebrew.

The first decisive step toward re-establishing a Free Church College came in 1904 when the General Assembly appointed Dr Alexander Professor of Divinity 'to the Church'.[2] In October that same year, as a result of the House of Lords decision in the case of *Bannatyne v Overtoun*, the Free Church re-occupied New College. The following year, the Revd James Duff MacCulloch, Minister of Hope Street Free Church, Glasgow, was appointed Principal of the College; the Revd Colin Bannatyne, who had played a key role in co-ordinating both opposition to the Union and the conduct of the Church's law-case, became

---

[1] Stewart and Cameron (1910), 285.
[2] *Proceedings of the General Assembly of the Free Church of Scotland, 26 May, 1904.*

Professor of Church History; and Robert Moore became Professor of Hebrew and Old Testament. The two remaining appointments were made in 1906: John Kennedy Cameron to the chair of Systematic Theology, and John Macleod (newly admitted from the Free Presbyterian Church) to the chair of New Testament.

These arrangements (with Dr Alexander as Professor of Apologetics) gave the College a full complement of staff. Sadly, New College was not to be the scene of their labours. The Royal Commission re-allocated the building to the United Free Church, and the Free Church College had to move to its present accommodation in the adjacent Free Church offices on the Mound.[3] Classes met there for the first time on 8 January 1907.

WILLIAM MENZIES ALEXANDER

The Union of 1900 took place in an intensely charged theological atmosphere. Controversy had focused particularly on the authority of Scripture. It was through the Free Church that the Graf-Wellhausen approach to Old Testament criticism had been introduced to Scotland, quietly by A. B. Davidson of New College and explosively by William Robertson Smith of Aberdeen. Smith was removed from his chair in May, 1881, but he cast a long shadow. His case left the Free Church with an endemic reluctance to appoint young men to College chairs (Smith was only twenty-three when he went to Aberdeen). It also bequeathed a persistent attitude of mistrust between the College and the Church as a whole.

This became apparent immediately after Dr Alexander's appointment in 1904. Principal John Macleod once described Alexander as 'a polymath whose erudition was as rare as it was extensive'.[4] This was no hyperbole. Alexander was a graduate in Arts, Science, Divinity and Medicine. He also held the degrees of M.D., D.Sc. and D.D. Ordained as a missionary by the Free Church Presbytery of Glasgow in 1889, he served for a time as a Professor of Biology and Chemistry in Bombay. Subsequently, he lectured in both New Testament Exegesis and Church History at the Free Church College in Glasgow. During his first year as Professor in the Free Church he conducted four classes four days a week, teaching most subjects in the curriculum, including Hebrew.

[3] Watt, 98; Anderson, W. S. (1994). The Free Church had occupied the purpose-built offices since 1862.

[4] *Monthly Record* (November, 1929), 276.

But storm-clouds were gathering. In 1902, Alexander had published a book entitled *Demonic Possession in the New Testament: Its Relations Historical, Medical and Theological*. The book itself is not particularly exciting. Its central thesis, reflecting Alexander's interest in medicine, is that demonic possession in the New Testament consisted of two elements, one natural, the other supernatural. The natural element was mental illness. The supernatural was the recognition and confession of Jesus as Messiah: 'Where this classical criterion is found, there we postulate without hesitation, the activity of an evil spirit' (157).

Among other items of interest the book contains a useful appendix on witchcraft and some perceptive comments on Jesus' attitude to the demonology of his own day. It concludes by asserting that genuine demonic possession was 'a unique phenomenon in the history of the world; being confined indeed to the earlier portion of the ministry of our Lord' (247). There was a clear explanation for this: the outbreak of demonic possession was a counter-movement by the powers of darkness against the establishment of the kingdom of God in the incarnation (249).

When it first appeared the book attracted little attention. The Free Church's *Monthly Record* contented itself with saying, 'It discusses the whole subject with an abundant assurance of scholarship, and in a fashion more than ordinarily exhaustive.'[5] In November, 1904, however, a mischievous article by Principal Sir James Donaldson of St Andrews appeared in the *Highland Witness* (a United Free Church publication) under the headline, 'A Free Church Professor Among the Higher Critics'.[6] The clear intention was to embarrass the Free Church in view of the recent House of Lords decision (announced in August 1904). The argument was subtle enough: Dr Alexander does not believe in inspiration; therefore the Free Church's profession of unqualified submission to the Westminster Confession is hypocritical; therefore the Free Church has secured the property on false pretences and the lawyers should re-open the case.

The Royal Commission took no notice of Donaldson's article, but the Free Presbyterian Church did. Its magazine, which had originally ignored Alexander's book, now devoted no fewer than nine pages to a

[5] *Monthly Record* (April, 1902), 66.

[6] I am grateful to the Revd Dr Donald Boyd, Minister of the Free Presbyterian Church, Inverness, for furnishing me with a copy of this article. Dr Boyd also provided copies of the relevant articles in the *Free Presbyterian Magazine* for 1905.

critical review.[7] 'We procured a copy of the book and read it for ourselves,' wrote the Editor. 'The result was the amazing and painful discovery that here was actually the work of a higher critic, and that Dr Alexander's views of the composition of the Holy Scriptures were very much the same as those of Professor Marcus Dods and George Adam Smith.'[8]

As a result of the publicity generated by the unholy alliance of Principal Donaldson and the Free Presbyterians, the Free Church Assembly of 1905 received two overtures (one from the Presbytery of Lochcarron and the other from the Synod of Glenelg), craving action to allay anxiety about Dr Alexander's book. The Assembly had already been informed, however, that Dr Alexander had withdrawn his book, the overtures were departed from 'and the matter took end'.[9]

But 'take end' it did not; and it has still not taken end. It has remained a major influence on Free Presbyterian separatism down to the present day. It was the basis for their decision in November 1905 not to enter into discussions with the Free Church; and for a similar decision in 1917. Even those Free Presbyterians who did enter the Free Church felt bound to refer to the matter. When, for example, the Revd John R. Mackay and two other ministers joined the Free Church in November 1918, they included among their reasons for doing so that 'not only has the work entitled "Demonic Possession" been by its author withdrawn from circulation, but that it was and is regretfully acknowledged by the Church, and not least by its author, to have given expression to views that are not in keeping with this fundamental principle of the inerrancy of Holy Scripture'.[10] And the most recent edition of the *History of the Free Presbyterian Church of Scotland* (carrying the story down to 1970) treats the matter in exactly the same terms as the earlier edition of 1933.[11]

It seems to me that the case against *Demonic Possession* was never proven and that, for one reason or another, Alexander never said in his

---

[7] *Free Presbyterian Magazine*, vol. IX, nos. 10 and 11, 361–4, 401–6. The *Magazine* devoted a further five pages (435–9) to *Remarks* on Dr Alexander's reply to his critics.

[8] *Ibid.*, 362.

[9] *Proceedings of the General Assembly of the Free Church of Scotland, 25 May, 1905.*

[10] *Free Presbyterian Magazine*, vol. XXIII, no. 9, 273f. It does not seem to me that either of the two major claims in this statement is true. Neither the Free Church nor Alexander acknowledged that the book was heretical. The Free Presbyterians, of course, rejected Mackay's claim that the matter had been satisfactorily dealt with (see *Free Presbyterian Magazine*, vol. XXIII, no. 10, 307.).

[11] McPherson (1974), 110–13, 121–31.

own defence all that might have been said. Principal Donaldson's argument that the book is anti-Confessional rests on absurd views of the Confession's teaching. If plenary inspiration means, as the Principal thought it did, that the human authors were mere automata writing at God's dictation, that the Septuagint is an inerrant translation and that the Hebrew and Greek manuscripts have been totally free of error, then all the stalwarts of Reformed orthodoxy, from Thomas Chalmers and William Cunningham to B. B. Warfield and James I. Packer, would have to be arraigned in heresy. What Alexander's book does show is a welcome awareness of current trends in biblical studies and an honest acceptance that in some instances inerrancists have no answers.[12] Besides, while the book does contain a few statements on which it is possible to put a construction inconsistent with the Westminster doctrine, it contains many others which explicitly assert the veracity of the biblical accounts and the miraculousness of Jesus' action.[13] It is a pity that those who were so expert in harmonising the statements of Scripture did not bestow some of their skill on harmonising those of Dr Alexander.

In the Commission of Assembly in December, 1905, Alexander made a moving statement as to his own personal faith:

> Some men have entered into their faith without a struggle; others have had to wrestle with intellectual doubt. I am of the number of the latter. I was once plunged into that sunless gulf. I, here, testify to the long night vigils: to the prayer that was but a despairing cry. By the grace of God I emerged from that deep distress: but how? It was by grasping, in the strength of God, that fundamental doctrine of our holy religion – namely, the utter infallibility of the Word of God. To some that doctrine has become as an idle tale; to me it is the profoundest, the most vital, of all convictions.[14]

Dr Alexander never wrote again. According to anecdote, his colleague, Dr John R. Mackay, once asked him, 'Why, Dr Alexander,

[12] For example, in the story of the Gadarene demoniacs, where Matthew refers to two demoniacs while Mark and Luke refer to only one. See Alexander (1902), 197f. Curiously, Alexander cites the wrong references for all three Synoptists (Matt. 20:30, Mark 10:46 and Luke 18:35). He was not taken to task for this!

[13] See, for example, the statement on page 143: 'He did what no other has been able to accomplish; for we freely challenge the records of medicine to produce (three) similar cases of epileptic insanity, acute mania and epileptic idiocy, where the cure was effected "by a word" and "instantly".' Alexander's work has, of course, been overtaken by modern psychiatry.

[14] *Monthly Record* (January, 1906), 27. It is to the credit of the Free Presbyterians that they published a longer extract from this statement in their *History* (McPherson, 1974, 112), even though they were not satisfied with it.

do you never write? Who's to blame?' 'You are to blame,' came the quiet reply. The words of the Free Presbyterian Church, with which Mackay had once fully identified, had left wounds which never healed.

The effect may not have been confined to Alexander, however. It looks very much as if other Free Church professors took stock of what happened and decided it was safer to keep their opinions to themselves. Certainly, the literary output of the College has been disappointing, although Alexander's experience was probably not the only reason. Many of the Professors were so heavily involved in the wider work of the Church that they had no time for specialist research. Five of them (Kennedy Cameron, William J. Cameron, Clement Graham, John L. Mackay and Hugh Cartwright) have served as Principal Clerks to the General Assembly. Three (R. A. Finlayson, G. N. M. Collins and J. W. Fraser) gave long years of service as editors of the Church's magazines. Two (Clement Graham and A. C. Boyd) had additional responsibilities as Secretary to the Foreign Missions Board.

But there may have been a deeper reason still. In the early days of the Free Church its leading theologians were giants of sufficient stature to wear their orthodoxy confidently. Men like Chalmers, Cunningham, Smeaton and Candlish may seem like dinosaurs to modern academic theologians, but by the standards of their own day they were frequently innovative in method and sometimes bold in their conclusions. With the Union controversy (1863 onwards) the mood changed. As those who were pro-Union became looser and looser in their attachment to the Confession, those who were opposed became more and more rigid. Calvinist orthodoxy developed a siege mentality, isolating itself from ideas which threatened it and offering little welcome to those which might have enriched it. The creativity of the early days had gone, and men were lauded for conserving the past, not for building on it.

JOHN R. MACKAY

One from whom great things might have been expected was John Robertson Mackay, who became Professor of New Testament in 1919. There is no doubt that Mackay was a scholar of considerable potential. The Principal of New College, Dr Robert Rainy, even went so far as to say that he had not had his like for twenty-five years.[15] He was a close friend of some of the best known theologians at Old Princeton

---

[15] From the obituary to Mackay in the *Monthly Record*. The writer, Principal John Macleod, probably could not bring himself to mention Rainy by name.

(particularly Robert Dick Wilson and B. B. Warfield), wrote occasionally for the *Princeton Theological Review*[16] and was once approached by that Seminary with a view to accepting a chair.

Yet Mackay's literary output can be described only as meagre. He was a specialist in Old Testament studies, yet produced nothing in that field, apart from a very thin analysis of Isaiah 53 which appeared in the *Evangelical Quarterly*.[17] In 1914, while still Free Presbyterian minister in Inverness, he published *Armageddon: Two Discourses on the Great European War* (Inverness), where he argued that, 'Christendom has now come to that solemn pass which in Scripture is known as Armageddon.' History has judged it as it judges all such apocalypticism. His other main surviving work, *The Inquisition, The Reformation, the Counter-Reformation*, was also written while he was still in Inverness and consisted of lectures delivered in 1911 under the auspices of the Protestant Institute of Scotland. It is lucid, interesting and charitable, but not a work of original research.

Mackay made his one lasting contribution to evangelical scholarship by taking the initiative in founding the *Evangelical Quarterly* in 1929. He and his colleague, Professor Donald Maclean, were joint-editors (John Macleod joined them soon afterwards as consulting editor). The early numbers contain substantial reviews which give tantalising glimpses of what Mackay was capable of, but there are few substantial contributions from his pen. The most substantial is an article entitled 'Positive Reasons for Believing that the Bible is the Word of God'.[18] Significantly, it is the text of a lecture delivered under the auspices of the Newcastle and Gateshead Bible Witness League. Mackay's arguments show clear traces of the influence of B. B. Warfield, but although there are allusions to a large number of scholars (including Baur, Pfleiderer, Harnack, Orr, Bigg and Sir William Ramsay) there are no references.

The most fascinating feature of the article is its optimism: the tide has turned in favour of the conservative doctrine of Scripture. Referring, for example, to the Tübingen reconstruction of New Testament history, Mackay declares: 'But a tide in an opposite direction is set in. The genuineness of the New Testament as a whole is today received with more intelligence than was the case before Baur's assault came forth.' Luke–Acts has been rehabilitated as a serious historical work. The date

[16] See Mackay (1910) and (1913).
[17] Mackay (1931B).
[18] Mackay (1931A).

of the Johannine writings has been pushed back into the first century and although the Johannine authorship is not yet widely accepted Mackay can announce with undisguised relish, 'I am reliably informed that at this moment the occupant of F. C. Baur's Chair in Tübingen actually maintains the Johannine authorship of the Fourth Gospel.' There was even good news for the *International Critical Commentary* ('a series where, if anywhere, criticism is supposed to be abreast of the times'): 'Is it not a striking thing that what is probably the ablest vindication of 2 Peter in the English language . . . should appear over the name of the learned Dr Bigg?'[19]

Like many since, Mackay was too ready to believe that one favourable thesis betokens a revolution in evangelical fortunes. Had he not heard that in 1926 Bultmann had made his memorable comment that 'we can know nothing of the life and personality of Jesus, since the early Christian sources show no interest in either, are moreover fragmentary and often legendary'?

The first two numbers of the *Evangelical Quarterly* involved Professor Mackay in a new controversy with his former Free Presbyterian friends. The *casus belli* on this occasion was a series of articles by his ill-fated colleague, Dr Alexander, on 'The Resurrection of our Lord' (three were planned, but only two appeared, due presumably to Alexander's death on 30 August 1929). In the second of these articles[20] Alexander referred repeatedly to 'the Appendix to Mark', clearly implying that he regarded Mark 16:9–20 as unauthentic. His old foes were quick to pounce.[21]

This serves to put in perspective the earlier accusations against Alexander. They came from men who believed (quite sincerely) that it was fatal to the authority of Scripture to question the authenticity of the longer ending of Mark and the Johannine Comma. Such obscurantism betrays the extent to which Alexander's critics had lost touch with the original theologians of the Free Church, particularly William Cunningham.[22] It also indicates the emergence in Scotland of a hyper-orthodoxy which regarded even Old Princeton as 'liberal'.[23]

[19] Bigg (1901).

[20] Alexander (1929).

[21] McPherson (1974), 379; cf. 153, referring to yet another Free Church (1931) approach for closer co-operation: 'grave and serious reflections have been cast on the genuineness of certain passages of Scripture by some of the Free Church Professors'.

[22] See Cunningham (1878), 525–50. For a wider survey, see Needham (1991), 11–32.

[23] For the Princeton attitude to textual criticism see Warfield (1893).

JOHN MACLEOD

John Macleod, like J. R. Mackay, came into the Free Church from the
Free Presbyterians, becoming Professor of New Testament in 1906,
accepting a call to the Free North Church, Inverness, in 1913, appointed
Principal of the College in 1927 (while remaining in Inverness) and
finally occupying the chair of Apologetics from 1930 to 1942.

Macleod set out his vision for the College in his inaugural address as
Principal.[24] The governing consideration was that the College was
vocational. Academic it might be, but it was 'academic with a definite
bias. The Schools of the Prophets are meant to equip for the work of
the Christian ministry.' Years later, in a lecture at Westminster
Theological Seminary, in Philadelphia, he would make the same point
more sharply: 'If the rising ministry comes out from the schools of the
prophets bled white of Christian convictions after a starvation regimen
of empty negations, it is not fitted to awaken wonder that they should
prove barren and unfruitful in the service to which they have devoted
their lives.'[25]

It followed from this that the College had to be confessional. There
should be 'no haze of suspicion or cloud of doubt' as to the personal
faith of those entrusted with the instruction of the rising ministry. The
same criterion applied even to students, since in Macleod's mind
admission to College was linked with a vocation to the ministry: 'It is
clear that a man who does not cordially accept the Truth of the Gospel
is out of his place altogether when he embarks on a Theological course.'

As far as the College curriculum was concerned, Macleod naturally
insisted that it had to be shaped by the needs of the Church. But he
also assumed that before students came to College they had gone
through the discipline of a degree in Arts; and he argued strongly that
the Arts course and the Divinity course should be an integrated whole.
Indeed, he looked back with nostalgia to the time when 'the course of
study in the University Faculty of Arts was largely one that was specially
fitted to prepare the student for a Theological course as its crown'.
Philosophy, he regretted, was no longer compulsory. Neither was
Greek, leaving the poor student woefully deficient: 'Acquaintance with
History, or with British History, or with Scottish History, or with
Economics, or with Geography makes for general information; but
the substitution of any of these as Degree subjects will not compensate

[24] *Monthly Record* (November, 1927), 266–71.
[25] See Collins (1951), 152.

for the lack of knowledge of Greek in the equipment of the Divinity student.' (The counterpoint to this was the typical student's lament: 'irritation at Prof. Moore's senseless and slave-driving policy'.)[26]

Macleod's vision is a far cry from what happens in the Religious Studies Department of a modern university. But each type of institution has to assess itself in light of the other. The modern Scottish university has to ask itself whether it provides the churches with the kind of training their ministers require. And the modern evangelical seminary has to ask itself whether it gives its students a real higher education.

Macleod's *magnum opus, Scottish Theology*, was published in 1943.[27] It consists of ten lectures originally given in Philadelphia, USA, to mark the tenth anniversary of Westminster Theological Seminary, founded in 1929 to continue the tradition of Old Princeton. Macleod regarded the founders of Westminster (particularly Dr Robert Dick Wilson and Dr J. Gresham Machen, both of whom had died by 1939) as his personal friends; he had a genuine interest in the future of the Seminary; and he donated many of the most valuable books in his collection to its Library (I still turn pale at the thought of it!). Only after repeated requests did he agree to publish the lectures.

This is the most significant publication to emerge from the Free Church College since 1900. G. T. Thomson of New College reviewed it enthusiastically in the *Evangelical Quarterly*,[28] concluding:

> It makes one tremble to think that, being so familiar with all that he relates, Dr Macleod might *not* have considered recording it for posterity. The rich contents of these lectures, delivered in Philadelphia in 1939 and reproduced as delivered, read so easily and are so full of knowledge not readily accessible, as to stimulate our curiosity as to the profundities of information which underlies the volume before us. How much has been inevitably omitted of that store! How we wish that the author's study had been furnished with unobtrusive dictaphones, taking verbatim note of the treasure assembled, co-ordinated and expressed in one great theological brain! The much that we receive here makes us greedy to have had the whole.

Scottish Theology inevitably invites comparison with James Walker's Cunningham Lectures *The Theology and Theologians of Scotland* (1872).[29] But Macleod's approach is completely different. Whereas Walker's

---

[26] Murray (1980), 45. Robert Moore taught Hebrew.

[27] A second edition appeared in 1946 and this was reprinted in 1974 with an improved index.

[28] 16 (1944), 74f.

[29] The second edition of 1888 was reprinted with additional notes in 1982.

treatment is topical, Macleod's is chronological, telling the story of Scottish theology from John Knox to John Kennedy, and relating it all the while to the ecclesiastical drama which produced it.

Yet Macleod and Walker have one thing in common: both books lack documentation. In Macleod's case the problem is somewhat mitigated in that he sometimes cites authors and titles in his text. But it is still tantalising to read that, 'There had been, of course, such a type of Sacramental teaching as goes by the name of historical Zwinglianism' (23). Of course! But where? And where can I find Henderson's comment on presbyterianism: 'Here, then, is a superiority without tyranny . . . Here is a parity without confusion and disorder . . . And, lastly, there is a subjection without slavery' (67)? And why does the reader have to suffer fascinating glimpses of James Morison, Andrew Marshall and John Brown (Tertius) without a single reference to their published works?

The only merit of such a policy is that it stimulates a game of 'trace the allusion'. The 'friendly hands' (329) which sketched the lives of the great evangelists and divines of the Highlands were those of Macleod's Free Presbyterian friend, Donald Beaton.[30] And James MacGregor's pamphlet on the Scottish Amyraldian debate was entitled *The Question of Principle Now Raised in the Free Church Regarding the Atonement* (Edinburgh, 1870).

Amid the wealth of detail there are many lighter moments. We are reminded, for example, that Robert Murray McCheyne and the Bonar brothers were dismissed as 'The ELI' (The Evangelical Light Infantry) by their heavyweight counterparts. And we hear some delightful anecdotes.

One relates to Thomas Boston, who died in 1732. 150 years later, a gentleman from the American West wrote Boston a letter, c/o The Presbyterian Board of Philadelphia, informing him that he had greatly enjoyed *Human Nature in its Four-Fold State*; and would Mr Boston please let him know of any further works that he might write.[31]

Another relates to a divine so obscure that only Macleod would have heard of him: Neil MacMichael, a mid-nineteenth-century minister of the Relief Church. 'He may not,' says Macleod, 'have been perhaps a great theologian; but he had a tart way of putting things.' He once preached on 1 Corinthians 10:1f. ('all our fathers were under the cloud, and all passed through the sea, and were all baptised into Moses

[30] Beaton (1929).
[31] Macleod, J. (1943), 146.

in the cloud and in the sea') and could not resist the temptation to strike a blow at Baptists. His conclusion was as follows:

1. The Israelites were baptised, both adults and infants; for the Apostle declares it.

2. They were not immersed, a fact which Moses and other inspired writers testify.

3. The Egyptians who pursued them were immersed.

4. The Israelites had baptism without immersion and the Egyptians immersion without baptism.[32]

John Macleod was himself the kind of man around whom legends grow. There were legends, for example, about his microscopic handwriting. One exasperated reporter complained that he had crammed almost 3,000 words into a page measuring only 8 × 5 inches. And there were legends about his prodigious memory. Once, when visiting the Nicolson Institute in Stornoway, where he had taught as a young man, he found the class studying Euripides' *Hecuba*. He asked what point they were at and then proceeded to rattle off the next twenty lines straight from memory.[33]

Behind the legends there was, beyond doubt, a very competent academic. John Macleod graduated from Aberdeen University in 1890 with First Class Honours in Classics and a formidable collection of prizes. One of his professors was Sir William Ramsay, who not only urged him to take up a Classical scholarship at Oxford but asked him to serve as his assistant in his archaeological researches in Asia Minor.[34] It is clear, too, that Macleod was a bibliomaniac and, as a result, gleaned an encyclopedic knowledge of the movements of orthodox Christian thought. The range of reference and allusion in *Scottish Theology* makes plain that he could have lectured just as readily on American Presbyterianism, the Puritans or the great dogmaticians of the seventeenth century.

Yet in the end the output is disappointing; and much of what there is is merely antiquarian. This may have been because he felt he had nothing new to say. He was conservative by temperament and by conviction and probably thought that the last word had been spoken (at least for his generation) by Cunningham, Kennedy and the great doctors of Princeton. Besides, he was a cult figure in the Free Church;

[32] *Ibid.*, 254.
[33] Collins (1951), 45.
[34] *Ibid.*, 28.

and he was such because he adhered so reassuringly to a past which both he and his admirers venerated. The Church, particularly the laity, trusted him implicitly, and the last thing they wanted from him was the expression of new ideas. One searches John Macleod's writings in vain for a single risky opinion.

It could be said, too, that for most of his time in the Free Church College Macleod was in the wrong chair. G. N. M. Collins hints at this with his guarded tribute to his class lectures.[35] But Collins did not tell all that he knew. He knew, for example, that Macleod, embarrassed by the questions put to him by Cornelius Van Til, his counterpart at Westminster Seminary, had confessed that in a chair of Apologetics he was a square peg in a round hole.

But is this the whole truth? John Murray, Professor of Systematic Theology at Westminster, knew Macleod well and admired him greatly.[36] He once remarked to me that John Macleod committed intellectual suicide. Here was a brilliant Classics student who could have done some outstanding work in New Testament studies. But that would have meant immersing himself in the world of Wrede and Schweitzer, Bultmann and Dodd, and Macleod had no stomach for that. If he ever read 'unsound' literature, he never let the fact slip. Instead, he immersed himself in the anecdotal history of Highland Evangelicalism. The paradox is that he so much admired the work of such scholars as Warfield and Machen: men whose effectiveness depended precisely on their exhaustive acquaintance with the current literature.

DONALD MACLEAN

It is interesting to compare Macleod's output with that of his colleague, Dr Donald Maclean, Professor of Church History in the Free Church College from 1920 to 1943. Maclean was not Macleod's equal intellectually, although he should not be underestimated. Apart from Church History, he was a distinguished Gaelic scholar, was once a serious candidate for the chair of Celtic at Edinburgh University and produced an impressive list of publications in this field, including *The Literature of the Scottish Gael* (Edinburgh, 1912).

Maclean took this productivity with him to the Department of Church History: the list of his publications fills fifteen pages of his

[35] *Ibid.*, 151.
[36] *Ibid.*, 198f.

biography.[37] These included three substantial works: *The Law of the Lord's Day in the Celtic Church* (Edinburgh, 1926); *Aspects of Scottish History* (Edinburgh, 1927; lectures delivered on the Calvin Foundation in the Free University of Amsterdam); and *The Counter-Reformation in Scotland, 1560–1930*.[38] The vigorous Protestantism of this last volume will be too strong for the modern palate, and its animus against Irish immigrants may be too much even for vigorous Protestants. But the book as a whole is an effective foray into a neglected field. It highlights the ineptitude of the Presbyterian churches, paralysed by their own divisions: and it raises interesting questions as to the nature and limits of toleration. Maclean may have been wrong in his view that Roman Catholicism was an essentially intolerant system, taking 'undue liberties with Scottish tolerance'.[39] But he was surely correct to write (in 1931, remember!) that to tolerate a system that will not tolerate is to invite ruin.[40] What Maclean dreaded, of course, was that Protestantism would cease to be the formative principle of Scottish culture. History has proved that he was no alarmist. He would have been bemused, however, to discover that it was ousted not by Catholicism but by a pluralistic humanism.

R. A. FINLAYSON

In the forty years following Donald Maclean the pattern of theological training at the Free Church College continued as before: orthodoxy, competent tuition and sterling contributions to the wider work of the Church, but little by way of research or publication. Dr P. W. Miller, Professor of Old Testament from 1936 to 1966, was a recluse of legendary erudition, legendary devoutness and legendary hypochondria. Dr Alexander Ross (New Testament, 1937–52) wrote a stylish commentary on *The Epistles of James and John* (London, 1954). Dr A. M. Renwick, a former missionary of intrepid spirit and charismatic presence who became Professor of Church History in 1943, produced two popular works: *The Story of the Church* (London, 1958) and *The Story of the Scottish Reformation* (London, 1960). Dr G. N. M. Collins, who succeeded him, produced a large number of popular biographies and histories, the most important being *Heritage Of Our Fathers*

[37] Collins (1944), 149–63.
[38] Maclean (1931).
[39] *Ibid.*, 276.
[40] *Ibid.*, 278.

(Edinburgh, 1974), dealing mainly with the 'origin and testimony' of the Free Church. David McKenzie, who succeeded John Macleod in Apologetics and Pastoral Theology, was a paragon of order, protocol and elocution. W. J. Cameron, an intensely shy man with whom nobody ever took liberties, was memorable for his class-room prayers, the work he expected students to cover and his determination to introduce them to the wide world of New Testament scholarship. For good or ill, he gave his main strength to the Clerkship of the General Assembly and wrote virtually nothing, apart from two articles in the *New Bible Commentary* of 1953, 'The Prophetical Literature of the Old Testament' and 'The Song of Solomon'.[41]

Far the most significant post-War contribution came from Roderick Alexander Finlayson. For twenty-one years (1937–58), Finlayson was Editor of the *Monthly Record* and his writing in that connection alone represents a considerable intellectual achievement. He had a reputation for merciless wit. I well remember his approaching me after one of my own more passionate pulpit performances and remarking, 'There's a lady over there asking if it was Gaelic or English you were preaching!' But it was equally well known that he was a superb pastor. No-one ever excelled him in his care of the sick and dying, a skill which owed much to his experience as both soldier and chaplain.

Finlayson divided his course into two. The first year consisted of Lectures on Christian Doctrine, following the lines of Louis Berkhof's *Manual of Reformed Doctrine* (1933). The second year was devoted to Historical Theology, adhering closely to James Orr's *Progress of Dogma* (1901). This latter course is reflected in *The Story of Theology*, published by the Tyndale Press, London, in 1963. The readership aimed at, however, is the intelligent laity, not academics. The same is true of *God's Light on Man's Destiny* (Edinburgh, n.d.), a series of popular lectures on individual eschatology. In 1954, Finlayson gave the Bible Readings at Llandrindod Wells Convention. These addresses were subsequently published under the title, *The Cross in the Experience of our Lord*,[42] and although they were put to the press without his being consulted they represent not only homiletical skill of the highest order but acute spiritual and theological insight.

To see Finlayson at his best, however, we have to turn to an essay he contributed to *Revelation and the Bible*.[43] This international symposium

[41] Davidson, F. (1954), 45–51, 547–55.
[42] Finlayson (1955). Reprinted with biographical introduction, Fearn, 1993.
[43] Finlayson (1959).

set a new benchmark for evangelical scholarship and although it has been overtaken by later symposia[44] and by new developments such as deconstructionism and narrative criticism, it is still a useful window into the evangelical mind. There were twenty-four contributors, but Finlayson was the only Scot (apart from F. F. Bruce, who was then teaching at Manchester).

The topic assigned to him was 'Contemporary Ideas of Inspiration' which allowed him to relate his own position to the ideas of such scholars as John Baillie, J. K. S. Reid and Emil Brunner. He rejected the alleged connection between inerrancy and what was referred to as 'bare literalism', arguing that the science of hermeneutics developed freely within the premises of verbal inspiration, and even insisting that the evangelical doctrine 'actually makes imperative an acceptance of the Bible as authoritative *in whatever form it has pleased God to communicate it*'.[45]

The major part of the essay deals with three antitheses derived from Existentialism, which, Finlayson alleged, was basic to both neo-Liberalism and neo-Orthodoxy (he did not consider the possibility that it was also basic to much modern Evangelicalism). These antitheses were, first, the antithesis between revelation on the one hand and Scripture as the record of revelation on the other; secondly, the antithesis between revelation as encounter and revelation as (propositional) communication; thirdly, the antithesis between the Word of God and the text of Scripture. In this last connection, Finlayson dissociated himself from the idea that divine inspiration extended to the transmission of the text. But he dismissed as 'singular perverseness' the practice of setting the living Word and the written Word in sharp antithesis: 'Since we are completely dependent upon the text, in the first instance, to understand the message, it follows that text and message stand or fall together.'[46] The only result of setting them against each other had been to drive neo-Liberalism and neo-Orthodoxy into mysticism and even agnosticism: 'We are left in the impossible position of having to accept as true as a matter of religious experience what we must reject as false as a matter of objective reality.'[47]

---

[44] See, for example, *New Testament Interpretation*, ed. I. Howard Marshall (Exeter, 1979); *The Authoritative Word*, ed. D. K. McKim (Grand Rapids, 1983); *Scripture and Truth*, ed. D. A. Carson and J. D. Woodbridge (Grand Rapids, 1983); and *Hermeneutics, Authority and Canon*, ed. Carson and Woodbridge (Leicester, 1986).

[45] Finlayson (1959), 223 – italics mine.

[46] *Ibid.*, 231.

[47] *Ibid.*, 230.

Finlayson retired in 1966 but lived for a further twenty-two years. He never again produced anything of the quality of this essay. Why? It may have had something to do with the fact that he was always distrusted by a section of the Free Church. When Kenneth Macrae published his pamphlet, *The Resurgence of Arminianism* (1954), Finlayson saw it as an attack on himself; and although he was made of sterner stuff than Professor Alexander there is no doubt that he was deeply wounded.

FACING THE FUTURE

Today, the Free Church College, like all similar institutions, is having to face radical self-appraisal. In September, 1995, the traditional three terms gave way to two semesters. In 1996, oversight passes from the Church's Training of the Ministry Committee to a specialist College Board. And with a view to possible accreditation all courses are being modularised.

Such a process is particularly painful for the Free Church College. As the seminary of the Free Church it has to defer to the sensibilities of the most vociferous conservative elements in the denomination. As an institution seeking academic accreditation it has to conform to criteria laid down by the liberal–humanist establishment.

It is difficult to see how we can accommodate both sets of prejudices.

Chapter 13

Elsewhere in Edinburgh: Colleges Newer and Older

David Wright

ONLY A CIRCLE OR TWO OR AN ELLIPSE?

THIS COLLECTION of essays, which purports to present *Edinburgh Divinity* over the last century and a half, could easily convey the impression that serious theological activity in the city during this period has orbited around one, or two, pivotal points, like a circle or two circles or an ellipse. At the outset, prior to the Disruption, it had the shape of a circle, around the single centre in the University's Divinity Faculty in Old College, in essence as old as the University itself. The vigorous child of the Disruption, the Free Church of Scotland (although its self-understanding refused any upstart identity; it was no more, and no less, than the Church of Scotland Free, Free of necessity and only *pro tem*, in order to maintain the true identity of the Scottish Kirk) – this Church almost immediately planted a second centre – a moveable one until it took up fixed abode in New College on the Mound in 1850. Two circles of theological endeavour around two separate centres – barely half-a mile apart – or a single ellipse extended around two foci?

The chapters in this book on the theological disciplines powerfully suggest the two-circles configuration, at least for most of the era from 1843 to the Union of 1929. The story shifts from one to the other – and it is well told only if the reader is left in no doubt which of the two centres is in view at any one point. The two tales barely intersect with each other, certainly during the nineteenth century. Rather than forming an ellipse, the circles hardly overlapped.

The geometry had begun to change well before the constitutional union of the two centres into one, which was finalised at the beginning of 1935.[1] Amid the exigencies of the First World War the two circles increasingly interacted with each other.[2] The experience of co-operation in teaching between the College and University Faculties during the War prepared the ground for the Postgraduate School of Theology inaugurated in 1919.[3] From the earliest planning stages this was a joint enterprise between College and University. For another decade or more, two centres persisted, but they began to look increasingly like the twin foci of an ellipse. Then after 1929 the ellipse was rounded into a single circle as the two centres met in one. The Senate of New College and the University Faculty met as a single body until the 1960s (when several lecturers joined the Faculty who were not members of the Senate of professors), and the same person was both College Principal and Faculty Dean until 1984. (See appended note, on pages 257–8.)

TWO OR ONE? TWO IN ONE

The geometric analogy may bear yet further extension. For the post-Union institution has a dual identity as both the University Faculty of Divinity and a Church of Scotland College. This two-fold reality is more clearly grasped in the constitutionalese of ordinances and schedules[4] than visibly apprehended in the common experience of staff and students. How are the two entities related to each other? To talk of co-existence would be to pitch it too low, while symbiosis – defined as 'a permanent union between organisms each of which depends for its existence on the other' – may aim too high. If at all, symbiosis may be applicable to the decades from the Union to the 1960s.

In any case, why resort to biology when classical Christology or Trinitarianism might provide highly suggestive models? If one opts for Chalcedon's hypostatic union, it is certainly a simple matter to recognise the equivalent, in the one 'person' of the College-Faculty, of the Apollinarian and Monophysite distortions – reductionism of one kind

[1] Even then, life in the combined College-and-Faculty retained an elliptical shape for a while. Classes were held in both Old and New College, with students orbiting between the two. Cf. Watt, 146.

[2] Watt, 107–8.

[3] Watt, 109–13.

[4] See the chapter in this book by D. W. D. Shaw, and Watt, 130–48.

or another of its inescapable duality. And the present writer can remember a phase when Nestorian tendencies threatened. I will spare the reader further speculation along this trajectory – however seductive I might find it to apply the esoterica of anhypostasia and enhypostasia to the dyophysite character of post-Union New College. And by the way: no New College graduate worth his or her salt will by now have failed to rumble my unspoken assumption – that the Church College represents the divine nature, and the Faculty the human, in the hypostatically united New College. How could it be otherwise?

From a Trinitarian angle, the subtleties are if anything even more taxing. The mutual interpretation or co-inherence of the three-in-one posited by the Cappadocians (later to be known as *perichoresis*, or in Latin *circumincessio*) might with no greater difficulty be conceptualised of two than of three realities – and the *peri/circum* compounds conveniently bring us back to our circle or ellipse. Perhaps the New College of the post-1929 era – or rather of the post-1960s – is best envisaged as two concentric circles, with the smaller, presumably the Church College, contained within the larger, the Faculty of the University. Or is it better still visualised as an ellipse extended around two foci – which might be understood as the Senate of New College and the Faculty (in the more restricted sense of the ruling body within the community)? Each focus exercises its own gravitational pull, as it were, and it is critical for the contours of the ellipse that these twin forces remain in balance, or in tension. At least it bears thinking about. One thing is certain: New College is no simple reality – in the philosophical meaning of 'simple'. It is a compound of two histories, the coalescing of two theological orbits. Those who fail to recognise this are sure to lose their bearings.

JUST OUTSIDE THE CIRCLE:
THE FREE CHURCH COLLEGE

We may seem ourselves to have wandered far from the point – our original intention in musing about the circle and ellipse. For our aim in this essay is to consider to what extent there has been theology in Edinburgh this past century and a half outside the University and New College Faculties – at least theology worthy of occupying space in such a volume as this. Donald MacLeod's tasty account of theology in the College of the continuing Free Church – deriving from the remnant who declined to enter the United Free Church in 1900 – is evidence enough that there certainly was theology outside the Old College/ New College nexus. His chapter brings the story of his College down only to 1970. Of his own theological stature none should be in doubt. No living Scottish theologian knows his country's theological traditions better than he, and no College's rostrum or Church's pulpit can offer a more eloquently preached and preachable theology than his. Conservative it might be (though some of his Free Church colleagues seem to find it inadequately so), yet it is not without surprises to those who never get past the stereotypical caricatures of the Wee Frees.

Donald MacLeod's essay exempts me from the need to say anything more about the Free Church College. Yet readers who know not Edinburgh should be apprised that it stands, and has done so for nearly a century, scarcely 100 metres to the east of New College, sharing the same northern outlook over Princes Street Gardens and the New Town and away to Fife across the Forth.[5] It shares its building with the Free Church offices, which occupied it long before 1900. A particularly fine postcard, photographed from somewhere down in Princes Street, captures the two-College skyline of what it calls 'Presbyterian Ridge'. The fact that New College has for some time become less specifically Presbyterian does not alone explain why between two Colleges so closely contiguous (albeit so disparate in size) so little theological traffic passes. Students come and go more frequently than staff – although Donald MacLeod has more than once taught Scottish theology in New College.

Few Free Church College students have of late availed themselves of the special provision made by the regulations of the University for graduates of a Scottish university (formerly, only of Edinburgh) to take courses in their College and be examined in the Faculty for the B.D. degree. The two institutions' curricula are now widely divergent, and continuous assessment schemes have complicated the examination process. More recently a trickle of students apprenticed in the Free Church College have moved west for their postgraduate training. Books are now the main medium of our inter-communal commerce; Free Church professors and students use New College Library, and the Free Church Bookroom has, by the quality and range of its service, decisively overtaken longer-established rivals in the competition to satisfy our book-buying needs.

[5] There is an excellent guidebook to the Free Church College, Anderson, W. S. (1994).

Recollection of the Disruption and all that followed from it in Scottish church life and theology necessarily evokes widely divergent sentiments. The cause of Crown and aristocratic patronage in church appointments rallies no support today, but judgments divide over whether the disputes of the Ten Years' Conflict (1833–43) justified the trauma of the Disruption. Yet if national Church and Free Church can scarcely be expected to mark the anniversary of the Disruption together,[6] the sesqui-centennial of the New College building in 1996 will witness the two Colleges jointly recognising, in common worship and commemoration, each other's stake in what the original Free Church so expansively built. It can only foster hopes of more substantial theological encounter.

THE CONGREGATIONAL – UNITED FREE CHURCH COLLEGE

The Union of 1929 between the Church of Scotland and the United Free Church also left an unreconciled rump in its wake. The leader of the UF minority was the colourful James Barr, a Labour M.P. for almost twenty years (and twice UF Moderator at the same time) and grandfather of his namesake who occupied the Old Testament chair in New College 1956–61.[7] The continuing United Free Church needed a college to train its ministers, just as the continuing Free Church did in 1900. As on that earlier occasion, none of the professors in the three United Free Church colleges – New, Edinburgh; Trinity, Glasgow; Christ's, Aberdeen - stayed out of the Union.

The way forward for the small UF community lay in co-operation with another independent cause, that of Scottish Congregationalism. When, a decade before the 1929 Union, New and Old Colleges combined to establish the Postgraduate School of Theology, the University Senatus extended the status of lecturer for this purpose not only to the New College professors but also to the principals of 'the Theological Hall of the Scottish congregational Churches' – then Alexander J. Grieve, already a D.D. of the University – and 'the Theological College of the Episcopal Church in Scotland' – then Canon W. Perry.[8] To return to our earlier image, just as the two circles of Old and New College were blending into an ellipse it was also becoming

---

[6] But note Donald MacLeod's essay (MacLeod, 1993) in the symposium on the Disruption edited by Brown and Fry.

[7] On James Barr grandfather, see briefly *DSCHT* 63.

[8] Watt, 111; Escott (1960), 216.

increasingly clear that theological teaching in Edinburgh was by no means confined to their twin orbits. The Congregational, and in some sense also the Episcopal, college, in fact, had a longer history than New College. It was with the former, located in Hope Terrace in the Grange suburb of southern Edinburgh, that the new United Free Church College joined forces in 1930. To it came as the UF Professor to teach New Testament Allan Barr (son of James and father of James), and Barr also soon enjoyed lecturer status in the Postgraduate School. He produced a widely used diagram-synopsis of the first three Gospels (re-issued in 1995 with a new introduction by his son), and taught in the combined College for almost four decades. He died in 1988.

Mount Grange, 29 Hope Terrace (recently demolished for re-development), housed a lively if small theological community for over sixty years. The Congregational Theological Hall had moved from Glasgow to Edinburgh in two stages, as it were, during the nineteenth century.[9] In the aftermath of the confusion sown among Scottish Congregationalists by the conversion of the dynamic Haldane brothers, James and Robert, to Baptist views in 1808, an initiative by Greville Ewing, in company with Ralph Wardlaw, led to the founding of the Glasgow Theological Academy (1811). (The Congregational Union itself was organised the following year.) The new Academy, in which Ewing and Wardlaw tutored while retaining their pastoral charges, promoted practical evangelism – reflecting the Haldane lineage – alongside Arts (partly in Glasgow University) and Theology. In 1855, when William Lindsay Alexander (1808–84) and Anthony Gowan were appointed its 'professors', the Academy was translated to Edinburgh where the two professors continued in their ministerial duties – Gowan in Dalkeith 1843–72 and Alexander in various buildings in Edinburgh until he was settled in Augustine Church on George IV Bridge – almost equidistant between Old and New College – in 1861.

W. L. ALEXANDER (1808–84)

The transplanted institution was now designated 'the Theological Hall of the Scottish Congregational Churches'. For premises it was dependent

[9] For the next paragraphs see Escott (1960), 91–3, 126–32, 145–50 and 216–21, the articles in *DSCHT* on Greville Ewing (309), Ralph Wardlaw (854), Evangelical Union (305–6), Congregational Union of Scotland (206), W. L. Alexander (9–10), Education, Theological (284–5), and James Morison (607–8), and the prosopographical detail in McNaughton (1993).

to start with on churches, latterly in Augustine's basement, until in 1884 it was gifted a spacious house at 30 George Square (long before the University colonised the Square, later to clear this and adjacent houses to make space for the new Library). From there it moved to Hope Terrace in 1921. W. L. Alexander taught Systematic Theology and Church History until 1881 (and on being appointed the first principal in 1877, he became full-time), while Gowan covered the two Testaments and their languages.

Alexander was 'a scholar, preacher and theologian with a European reputation', 'Scotland's best known minister outside Presbyterianism', even if he espoused a 'rather aristocratic species of Congregationalism'.[10] He failed in his bid for the Edinburgh chair of Moral Philosophy, but both Edinburgh and St Andrews gave him honorary doctorates. He contributed to the Revised Version of the Old Testament,[11] produced *A System of Biblical Theology*, completed the revision of John Kitto's *Cyclopaedia of Biblical Literature*, translated I. A. Dorner's *Entwicklungsgeschichte der Lehre von der Person Christi* and wrote part of the *Encyclopaedia Britannia*'s article on Calvin. He also published a tribute to Thomas Chalmers, who had significantly influenced him as a student in St Andrews.

The tally of Alexander's gifts and achievements is not briefly told – he was, for example, a major creator of Congregational hymnody, both as a composer and translator – but his preaching prowess must not go unmentioned. He 'turned his pulpit into a throne and, in a city of preachers, held sway over the minds and hearts of multitudes'.[12] Nor was his theological learning discarded, it seems, when he ascended the pulpit steps, as we learn from a story repeated by Mr Sloan, his 'minister's man' for many years.

> Ae Sabbath, when I took in the Doctor's lunch, we were hawin' a crack, and he telt me that they couldna hit on a richt name for the new kirk. I said, Doctor, there's a man ye spoke o' in your sermon the day, and ye often quote him, and ye aye approve o' him, Augustine. Would his name dae? The Doctor lookit at me, and then he lifted up his haund, and when he brocht it doon a' the dishes dirled, and says he, Mr Sloan, Augustine it will be.[13]

---

[10] Escott (1960), 284; *DSCHT* 9–10.
[11] Cf. *EB* I, 565: 'by his thorough biblical scholarship [he] rendered exceptional service to the board'.
[12] Escott (1960), 135.
[13] *Ibid.*, 284–5.

In 1896 the merger of the Evangelical Union and the Congregational Union entailed also the uniting of their two colleges. James Morison had been both the principal architect of the Evangelical Union and the genius of its Theological Academy, at first in Kilmarnock and then in Glasgow. In 1897 two of his successors travelled east to join the teaching staff of the now united Scottish Congregational College in George Square, Edinburgh. It was with this College, after its removal to Hope Terrace, that the new United Free Church College made common cause in 1930. At least from the formation of the Postgraduate School in 1919, there was considerable movement between Hope Terrace, South Bridge (Old College) and the Mound. The College course enjoyed recognition as qualifying students to sit the B.D. examinations in all the Scottish Divinity faculties. Allan Barr, Charles Duthie and James Wood all offered courses under the aegis of the School, and with others such as Morton Price were regular participants in the Edinburgh Theological Club which met in New College.[14]

Charles Duthie (1911–81) became Congregational College Principal at the age of thirty-three in 1944. Ten years later student numbers reached a post-War high of twenty-four. Duthie was the most outstanding scholar in Scottish Congregationalism during the twentieth century, the author of a perceptive *Outline of Christian Belief*, and earlier of *God in His World*. He was prominent in international Congregational councils and in the Scottish Union's Forward Movement, and was responsible for sharpening both the academic and the evangelistic cutting edge of the College. His leadership of student mission teams in many places in Scotland (of the kind that once enlisted New College energies) recalled the roots of Congregational witness in the Haldane era. In 1947 a second professor was added to the teaching strength in the person of James Wood (1906–91) a lively biblical scholar and author of a valuable introduction to the history of the interpretation of the Bible, as well as reflections on Job and the Sermon on the Mount. Wood succeeded Duthie as Principal in 1964 (Duthie went south to head New College, London) and served until 1977. Morton Price, professor from 1964, was Principal 1977–83.[15]

To the Congregational College belongs the distinction of having trained the first woman to be ordained to a pastoral charge in a

[14] See p. xxiii.
[15] On Price see McNaughton 250; and 283–5 for a complete list of professors and principals.

mainstream Scottish denomination – Vera Findlay in 1928–9.[16] Other students of note included two who entered College together in 1924. Peter Marshall emigrated in 1927 to the USA, where he earned renown and respect as minister of Washington's New York Avenue Presbyterian Church and chaplain to the US Senate (an office held from 1995 by a New College alumnus, Dr Lloyd Ogilvie). Eric Liddell won his spurs in very different theatres – at the Paris Olympics of 1924 and serving with the London Missionary Society in China for almost twenty years, dying there in a Japanese prison camp in 1943. His athletic exploits, and something of his courageous Christian faith, were celebrated in the highly successful film *Chariots of Fire*, which was shot partly in New College. Ian Charleson, playing Liddell, was seen doffing his cap to John Knox in the quad. The producer was wiser than he knew.

As a footnote to the story of the Edinburgh Congregational College, note should be taken of the Congregational ordinands sent to study in Edinburgh from the Yorkshire United Independent College in Bradford between the end of the First World War and the late 1950s. They lived together under a warden (for long Henry Parnaby) in a house in Regent Terrace. Some studied in Arts as well as Divinity; some completed the B.D., while others took only one or two years of Divinity.

THE EPISCOPAL COLLEGE AND COATES HALL

The other Edinburgh theological teacher accorded University status in the Postgraduate School in 1919 was the principal of the college serving the Scottish Episcopal Church.[17] The beginning of formalised instruction of Episcopal ordinands over a century earlier had adhered to a pattern widely followed in Scotland in times past (and still today in the Free Presbyterian Church) – the students travelled to where the tutor exercised his normal ministry. And so when a Miss Panton made provision for a 'Seminary of Learning or Theological Institution' for

---

[16] See *DSCHT* 320–1. She was not, however, the first woman to be ordained in Scotland – Olive Winchester in 1912 (*DSCHT* 876), nor the first woman to receive theological training for ministry (Winchester was the first woman to take Glasgow's B.D., two years after Frances Melville graduated B.D. in Edinburgh; *DSCHT* 557–8), nor the first Scot to be ordained – Jane Sharpe in 1917 (*DSCHT* 770; Winchester was American).

[17] For this section see Goldie (1976), Crosfield (1992), and Luscombe (1994). *DSCHT* provides introductions to Walker (850), Terrot (817), Dowden (255–6), Jolly (448), Hay Forbes (327), Maclean (528) and Mitchell (594).

the Episcopal Church, her first nominated (Pantonian) Professor, James Walker (1824), taught ordinands at his home when he became Bishop of Edinburgh in 1830. His successor as both Bishop and Professor, Charles Terrot (1841–63), used other *ad hoc* premises in the city.

Trinity College, Glenalmond, Perthshire, was founded with William Gladstone's patronage in 1847 as both a public school and a theological seminary, but the latter fluorished only for a decade or so.[18] John Dowden (1840–1910), appointed Pantonian Professor there in 1874, was induced by both paucity of students and a fire to remove the seminary to Edinburgh (1876). His teaching had no fixed abode until 9 Rosebery Crescent in the Roseburn area of west Edinburgh was purchased to house twelve students in 1880. Dowden demitted his chair when made Bishop of Edinburgh in 1886, a shift which did nothing to stem his considerable liturgical and historical researches, of which the most fruitful outcome were posthumous publications on the Scottish Communion office of 1764 and the bishops of Scotland down to the Reformation. His historical passion found voice in his remark: 'To make *certain* of one fact in history gives more satisfaction to me now than all the metaphysical problems in the world.'[19]

In 1892 the College began life in Coates Hall, nearby in Rosebery Crescent. In 1923 the adjacent house (21 Grosvenor Crescent) was acquired for extra space and to accommodate the rich libraries of Bishops Alexander Jolly (1756–1838) and George Hay Forbes (1821–75) (both subsequently removed, to the National Library and St Andrews University respectively). Presiding over the College have been a series of principals of mostly short duration. Among those more distinguished for scholarship were A. J. Maclean (1903–5), Syriac linguist and liturgist, chief architect of the Scottish Church's 1929 Prayer Book and author of major articles in Hastings' *Dictionary of the Bible* and of studies on early service-books.[20] His successor, Anthony Mitchell (1905–12), was more a historian, and compiled an account of the Episcopal Church – entitled *A Short History of the Church in Scotland*!

But for most holders of the office the principalship has proved a step on the *cursus honorum* towards the episcopate, sometimes furth of

---

[18] On the 'Theological Department' at Glenalmond see Saint Quintin (1956), 3, 38, 64–7, 76, 99–100. In 1851, with thirteen students, the Department was full; by 1853 twenty ministers serving in the Episcopal Church has been trained there. Yet its isolation, even from the school community, seems to have attracted or fostered eccentrics – not unknown later in Coates Hall.

[19] Cited by H. R. Sefton in *DSCHT* 256.

[20] *DSCHT* 528.

Scotland, and towards wider responsibility in the Anglican Communion. More recently it became difficult for a College of the size of Coates Hall to avoid being influenced, for good or ill, by patterns of ordination training in the Church of England. In 1967, under the forward-looking principalship of Kenneth Woollcombe (followed by the dynamism of Alastair Haggart), the College began sending its qualified students to take the B.D. in New College, alongside their spiritual formation and specifically denominational instruction in Coates Hall. English ordinands found this arrangement attractive, and for two decades or so New College benefited both in ecumenical diversity and in the intellectual quality of several outstanding students. At the same time, several Coates Hall staff members contributed to courses in the Faculty, chiefly in Christian Ethics and Practical Theology. Of these the most enduring was Gian Tellini, who imparted liturgical expertise for many years until 1995.

FAREWELL TO COATES HALL

But as recruitment of ordinands in Scotland and more so in England tailed off, so Coates Hall suffered. It was not alone. In 1984 the United Free–Congregational College closed through lack of numbers, and the Congregational College found lodging in Coates Hall. (Henceforth the United Free Church has had no collegiate facilities of its own, and its few candidates generally have taken the B.D. in one of the Divinity Faculties.) Further change was to come. More comprehensive visions of training for ministry turned Coates Hall in 1989 into the base for the Episcopal Church's Theological Institute, responsible for laity also. Finally, in 1994, financial pressures combined with other forces – familial, social, theological, ecclesiastical – to convert the Episcopal Church to a largely non-residential regime for ministerial formation. Coates Hall was sold, and the core of the College's operations, with full-time staff reduced to two, was given house-room in St Colm's (of which more anon). The small Congregational College accompanied it.

The Faculty still welcomes Episcopal – and, especially since 1984, Congregational – students, but in greatly reduced numbers. The absence of a significant cohort of Episcopal or Anglican ordinands has impoverished New College at several levels. Yet the Episcopal Church's venture into more dispersed, on-the-job, non-residential training may well be the sign of the things to come, against which the happy providence of government subsidy may cushion the Church of Scotland's theological colleges longer than most. Those observing the Episcopal Church from the outside must sympathise with the inevitable sense of bereavement occasioned by the loss of its college – the more precious because the only one – while at the same time appreciating the freedom of movement which the Episcopal Church won by laying down a burden that had become no longer tolerable.

OTHER PRESBYTERIAN COLLEGES

At this point we must back-track to note how Edinburgh featured in the schemes for theological education mounted by other bodies that dissented from the Presbyterian establishment. Without exception they upheld the principle of a highly educated ministry, and most assumed a preparatory or concurrent university Arts course. Many required students to travel to wherever the designate professor of Divinity fulfilled his pastoral charge, there to receive intensive teaching for several weeks each year. As the period lengthened, so it became increasingly necessary to release professors from their ministerial responsibilities.

Among the church professors appointed by the Reformed Presbyterians, heirs to the faith of the Covenanters, was William Goold (1854–76), minister of the Edinburgh congregation, assigned to teach Biblical Criticism and Church History.[21] A pioneer of the National Bible Society and editor of John Owen's shelf-long *Works*, Goold maintained the distinguished RP theological succession. As Moderator he led an impressive procession of Reformed Presbyterians from Martyrs' Church in George IV Bridge (now host to an Elim congregation) to the Free Church Assembly Hall behind New College, to enact the union of 1876. (Not all such processions were centrifugal.)

Among the divines of the eighteenth-century Presbyterian Secession church (the esoterics of whose branches need not detain us here), George Paxton of the General Associate Synod was the first to be released from his charge (in Ayrshire) and established in a settled Divinity hall, in Edinburgh (1807–20).[22] This arrangement took cognisance not only of his uncertain health but also of the burdens falling on minister-professors. It enabled Paxton to introduce a supplementary winter session, for Hebrew in particular (optional, it seems), and to prepare students better for attendance at the hall. But it did not outlive Paxton's

[21] *DSCHT* 369, 281.
[22] *DSCHT* 281, 650.

resignation on his declining to move with his Synod into the United Secession Church.

The United Secession appointed serving ministers to act as professors, and before mid-century had no fewer than four in office, with appropriate division of curricular responsibility (Biblical Literature and Criticism, Systematic Theology, Pastoral Theology, Exegetical Theology).[23] Some concentration on Edinburgh developed (Robert Balmer, minister in Berwick-on-Tweed, taught first Pastoral and then Systematic Theology in the capital), although students still shuttled between Glasgow and Edinburgh in the junior class. But as soon as the United Secession joined with the Relief Church (which had fixed its Divinity hall in Glasgow) to form the United Presbyterian Church in 1847, it brought together five theological professors (soon reduced by death to four) in the Synod Hall at 5 Queen Street (now the BBC's base in Edinburgh). They still combined two-month teaching sessions for each of five years with their congregational ministry, but now all taught in the same building.

THE UP SYNOD HALL

Ambitious reform followed in 1875–6, and the purchase was made of a new theatre built that year by the architect Sir James Gowans in Castle Terrace. (R. H. Wyndham's theatre company had gone bankrupt.) It was one of the largest halls in Europe and its columned façade presented a gigantic arcade to the view from Princes Street. By 1880 it had been adapted as the UP Synod Hall, accommodating five full-time professors teaching six-month sessions each year.[24] Those occupying chairs in 1900, when the UP Church united with the Free Church (without remainder on the UP side) to form the United Free Church, transferred to one or other of the former Free, now United Free, Church colleges. The noble Synod Hall descended to other uses, latterly as Poole's cinema, until in the 1960s it was demolished to make way for an opera house that never got built. After years as Edinburgh's most embarrassing hole in the ground, a not ignoble commercial centre filled the gap in the 1990s. Known as the Saltire Court, its massive columns surely recall the Synod Hall. *Sic transit gloria ecclesiae.*

The most reputable of the UP divines between 1880 and 1900 was James Orr (1844–1913), in the Church History chair from 1891. He

---

[23] For details, see conveniently *DSCHT* 282.
[24] On the Synod Hall, see Gifford (1984), 263–4, *DSCHT* 809.

assumed the mantle of John Cairns (1819–92), professor since 1867 (full-time since the reorganisation of 1875–6) and principal from 1879 until shortly before his death. Cairns' energies as a writer were expended on pamphlets, church reports and serial articles rather than weighty monographs (although his Cunningham Lectures were published as *Unbelief in the Eighteenth Century*). Yet his theological leadership was immensely influential. He 'prized evangelical catholicity more than Reformed confessionalism',[25] and steered the UP Church's approval of the Declaratory Act of 1879, which authorised qualified subscription to the Westminster Confession, allowing liberty of opinion on points that did not touch on the substance of the faith. For Cairns himself the latitude envisaged was limited, but a watershed had been crossed. The force of currents as diverse as German idealism and Moody and Sankey's evangelism presaged in Cairns the shift to the liberal Evangelicalism of the next century.

Orr too promoted the Declaratory Act of 1879, but his published works betokened a stiffer apologetic stance in favour of a thoughtful and learned but essentially conservative orthodoxy. His contribution to *The Fundamentals* (1910–15) would bear this out. During his Edinburgh years he issued *The Christian View of God and the World* and *The Ritschlian Theology and the Evangelical Faith*, and followed them in Glasgow with a succession of volumes, some of which are still consulted with profit today.[26]

FROM THE 1890s TO THE 1990s

Where else but Edinburgh could one find in the last decades of the nineteenth century no less than three theological schools of the calibre of Old College, New College and the UP Synod Hall – four, if one includes the Congregational Hall under W. L. Alexander – not to mention Coates Hall with its fine library? The church Unions of 1900 and 1929 combined the three into one, and the Congregational College is now but an echo of its earlier distinction. The 1980s and 1990s have witnessed a rather bewildering variety of institutional changes and other developments, which on the one hand have left the Divinity Faculty in New College looking once again more like the single hub of Edinburgh's theological universe, but on the other hand have spawned

[25] N. R. Needham in *DSCHT* 117–18. See also Cheyne (1983), 65–6, 72, 83–5 on Cairns' role in the 'confessional revolution' in nineteenth-century Scotland.

[26] On Orr see Scorgie (1989), and his summary account in *DSCHT* 638–9.

other, potentially competitive, forms and centres of theological education.

Although 1984 was the end of the line for the UF College, as the Congregationalists (under Hamish Smith, former Chaplain of Edinburgh University, Principal 1983–8) began to co-habit with the Episcopalians at Coates Hall, it was during the 1980s that co-operation between Coates Hall and the Faculty flourished, and also a small but highly significant Roman Catholic presence in the New College community developed. In 1986 the major seminary for the Archdiocese of St Andrews and Edinburgh, which had opened at St Andrew's College, Drygrange, near Melrose in 1953, transferred to Edinburgh. It occupied the capacious premises of the former St Margaret's Convent and school, in Whitehouse Loan just south of the Meadows, and took the name of Gillis College, after James Gillis, the energetic priest who helped to found St Margaret's in the 1830s.[27] A few students were sent from Gillis to New College to take the B.D. course, until the hierarchy's policy changed (one or two Gillis students had ceased to be candidates for the priesthood, but for reasons unconnected with their studying at New College), and the College sought qualifications from Louvain. But numbers at Gillis were never high, and in 1993 it was closed, with Chesters College, Bearsden, outside Glasgow, becoming the major seminary for all the Scottish dioceses.

Antedating the link with Gillis College, and continuing still is an initiative of the Dominican houses in Oxford and in George Square, Edinburgh (where the Dominicans run the Catholic chaplaincy to the University). From the 1970s a slender but sparkling stream of Dominican candidates have shone in the B.D. prize lists and in some cases gone on to take postgraduate degrees in the Faculty. The George Square house has been designated a House of Study by the Order, and its senior members have included scholars of the calibre of Anthony Ross (who served also as Rector of the University), Marcus Lefébure and Fergus Kerr, who has given several years of assistance in teaching theology to undergraduates and postgraduates in the Faculty.

EXPANDING HIGHER EDUCATION

By the end of the millennium the monopoly enjoyed by the Divinity Faculty in the awarding of degrees in theology in Edinburgh (which

---

[27] See *DSCHT* 195, 362.

has lasted in effect since the University's foundation over four centuries ago) will most probably be a thing of the past. The government has multiplied universities in Britain, and competition between them has intensified at the same time as small colleges of all kinds are finding it imperative to offer degree qualifications. The Free Church College, for example, having somewhat desultorily debated closer liaison with New College (too near and big, and perhaps too bad, a neighbour for comfort, one guesses), seems set to seek validation of its degrees from another Scottish university.

The potentially most far-reaching innovations of this kind have been taking shape outside Edinburgh (in Glasgow Bible College, the most mature non-university theological centre in Scotland, and in the lusty infant Highland Theological Institute in Moray College, Elgin), but even the Bible College of the Faith Mission, recently relocated in the ample rooms of one of Dr Thomas Guthrie's 'Ragged Schools' in Gilmerton village in south-east Edinburgh, has aspirations to become degree-awarding. Like Glasgow Bible College (under its earlier name, the Bible Training Institute), the Faith Mission was a fruit of D. L. Moody's Scottish campaigns. For decades its training school occupied a villa in Ravelston beyond Edinburgh's West End. Its quest of higher educational credentials in part reflects a heightened intellectual self-consciousness within Evangelicalism (seen also, for example, in the much younger but already influential study centre in Rutherford House, Edinburgh), but will no doubt not be allowed to compromise the deeply conservative and heavily practical ethos of its training programme.

Such minor advances must be plotted against extensive re-drafting of the map of the church's place in British society. The galloping secularisation which rapid church decline indicates must call for a more mission-orientated role for the ministry of the church than inherited educational patterns – assuming an essentially pastoral function and appealing when challenged to legal and medical professional models – have provided. Faculties and departments of theology, decreasingly resistant to the secularised and pluralist culture of their universities, already seem to perceptive observers south of the border, such as Lesslie Newbigin and Robert Runcie, increasingly unpromising places to teach ordinands theology. The English churches can compensate through their own colleges, but the Church of Scotland's only colleges are the university faculties. Will they in future be allowed to train ministers in the skills needed to re-evangelise Scotland?

ST COLM'S: DEGREES FROM ELSEWHERE

This is the broader context in which independent colleges enjoy greater freedom of movement to frame degree programmes more directly geared to the home mission task of the churches. Other examples could easily be cited from England. Instead we must note the very recent history of a hallowed Edinburgh institution known to most people simply as St Colm's.[28] It began life in 1894 in 31 George Square (next door to the Congregational College at no. 30, and like its neighbour demolished for University expansion in the 1960s). It was then the Free Church Women's Missionary Training Institute, presided over by the remarkable Annie Small. Students attended some lectures at New College. After a sojourn in Atholl Crescent at the West End, the Institute (now United Free) moved in 1910 to new premises at 23 Inverleith Terrace, overlooking Edinburgh's world-famous Royal Botanic Gardens. After the 1929 Union, the Church of Scotland's women's training programme, hitherto in 27 George Square (happily still standing, as part of the School of Scottish Studies), combined with the UF Institute. Together they were renamed the Church of Scotland Women's Missionary College (St Colm's).

The College's role has steadily diversified, not least as overseas missionary personnel have diminished, providing training for Christian service and citizenship on a wide canvas, and latterly promoting schemes of study in various formats and at various levels, leading even to university validated certificates, diplomas and degrees.[29] For these St Colm's Education Centre and College, in one or other of its bewildering array of units and programmes, has turned to Westminster College, Oxford (for an M.Th. in Applied Theology, fully operational from 1996) and to Napier University, Edinburgh's youngest and least theologically literate university. When we recall that the Episcopal Church's Theological Institute, with the Congregational College in tow, moved to the enlarged St Colm's in 1994 (in 1988 it bought the redundant Christian Science building next door, and transformed it into the Annie Small Centre), we cannot miss the emergence of a significant new centre of theological activity – in the broad sense – in northern Edinburgh.

[28] See Small (1944); Wyon (1953), 57–83; *DSCHT* 741, 779 (Small).
[29] See *Reports to the General Assembly of the Church of Scotland 1994*, 614–15, 622–5, and *Reports to the General Assembly of the Church of Scotland 1995*, 591, 594–8.

Distinguished teachers at St Colm's have included Elizabeth Hewat, missionary historian and the first woman made an honorary D.D. by Edinburgh University (1966), Mary Lusk (later Levison), pioneer of women's ordained ministry in the Church of Scotland, and Kenneth McKenzie, brilliant and godly missionary and champion of Africa, who began his theology in the Free Church College.[30]

A FREE MARKET IN THEOLOGY?

For some years in the 1970s the Faculty in New College offered a Diploma in Mission Studies, co-ordinated by Dr Andrew Ross of the Department of Ecclesiastical History, which chiefly served students in training at St Colm's. But in those days, as was explained earlier, the Faculty still possessed a monopoly in theological degrees in Edinburgh. Why the different agencies now based in St Colm's are not to have their graduating programmes validated by the one local university which has a Divinity Faculty – heir to diverse traditions and versatile host of new centres and curricula – is perhaps too sensitive a question to be yet explored in public. Edinburgh University may be big enough already, but it is open to degree-validating relationships with institutions long associated with it in teaching and research and sharing its distinctive commitment to a research-led educational mission. After 1919 it was a Postgraduate School that incorporated Congregational, Episcopal and later United Free college teachers into the New College Faculty's work. If these and similar colleges in Edinburgh today are looking elsewhere for degree accreditation, that may clarify the special, even unique, function of the Faculty in the foreseeable future as the research-based centre of theological excellence – in Edinburgh but playing a world role.

One thing is clear: whatever the impression given for earlier decades by the organisation of this book, the Edinburgh market in theology is ever more open and free. The grounds for thinking of Edinburgh divinity as a circle (or two concentric circles, or even an ellipse) with New College at its centre are diminishing all the time. And if St Colm's seems set to become a second focal point, at least at first degree level, there is inadequate co-ordination with New College to suggest a newly reshaped ellipse around these twin foci. More germane is this question: which of the theological institutions that will flourish in Edinburgh in coming decades will faithfully embody for their own time the distinctive Edinburgh divinity of the past 150 years?

[30] *DSCHT* 402, 481, 521–2.

NOTE: THE SENATE OF NEW COLLEGE

The Senate of New College did not cease to exist in 1935, although it ceased to meet separately. Its minute books stop at the end of 1934, and from the beginning of 1935 the minutes record that 'The Senate and Faculty met' (or some such combined wording). 'The Principal' presided and signed the minutes. This continued until early 1967; on 28 February 'The Faculty and Senate' met . . .', but from 16 March on 'The Faculty met . . .' The minutes fail otherwise to notice or explain the change. Even thereafter, 'Principal McIntyre' continued to 'preside', until October 1969, when he becomes 'Professor McIntyre'. Yet still the minutes continued to be signed over the name of the 'Principal and Dean' until June 1970, and only thereafter of the Dean alone. The two offices were not held by separate persons until 1984.

When did the Senate of New College first begin meeting again after the Union? Minutes to hand go back only to 9 October 1974, when no earlier minute was approved and 'It was agreed that the Senate should meet regularly before meetings of the Financial Board of New College'. It was not obvious from this record that an earlier minute book is missing, but Professor Alec Cheyne was appointed on this occasion Secretary of the Senate in succession to the Revd Bill Shaw. After 1935 it was the Financial Board of New College (which initially included members appointed by the General Assembly in addition to the principal and professors who comprised the Senate) which most clearly embodied the separate constitutional identity of the Church of Scotland's New College. (Minutes held by the present Secretary of the Board, John M. Hodge, W.S., of Messrs Balfour & Manson, Nightingale & Bell, go back to 12 February 1942, but an earlier book has obviously been missing for some time.) Yet although the Board's minutes depict it as exercising responsibilities that today would belong to the Senate (e.g. planning centenary celebrations of New College in 1946, and meeting with the General Assembly's Quinquennial Visitors), they also attest the separate identity of 'the Senate', for example, as consulted by the Board (1949), receiving remits from it (1958) and submitting proposals and schemes to it (1963, 1965).

The minutes of the combined 'Faculty and Senate' similarly bear out the continued distinctness of the Senate, without implying that it formally met on its own. Thus on 31 January 1967 the minute records that 'The Financial Board meeting was fixed. . . . Only the Senate to attend.'

By early 1967, then, the two bodies that had been meeting together for over three decades were no longer co-terminous in membership. As noted above, it was only two months later that meetings of 'The Faculty' ceased to be also meetings of the Senate. By 1967 the Faculty included a dozen lecturers, who were not members of New College Senate. But as sundry chapters in this volume make clear, lecturers had been around for several years (and some of them had been members of the Financial Board of New College!). Nevertheless, it seems likely that it was the considerable expansion of the teaching complement in the golden post-Robbins era, by the addition of lecturers appointed, in most cases, without any Church of Scotland involvement, which chiefly lay behind the separating out in the late 1960s of the distinctive entities and roles of the Faculty and the Senate.

The working membership of the Senate of New College has itself been broadened more recently – to include, for example, a non-professorial Dean and non-professorial Heads of Departments. Nevertheless, it has been suggested that, in the context of the growing diversity of the Faculty and its teaching and research agenda, the Senate of New College may well develop a more significant role in 'the fulfilment of [the Church of Scotland's] responsibilities towards the students in training for its ministry', as the post-Union agreement between the University and the Church expressed it (Watt, 136).

Chapter 14

❧❦❧

New Wine in Old Bottles

Duncan Forrester

NEW WINE, the Good Book tells us, bursts old bottles. But not invariably, or so it seems. 'I think the British have the distinction above all other nations of being able to put new wine into old bottles without bursting them,' said Clement Attlee. And in a strange way the history of New College demonstrates this, for time and again new initiatives have taken up old projects and brought them to a new flowering. The new wine, to mix my biblical metaphor, has shown that it can fulfil the promise of the old. In this chapter I shall examine two of the liveliest recent developments in the College, and show how in each case they build upon foundations laid long ago on the ridge above the Mound. They are the new wine of the Centre for Theology and Public Issues and of the Centre for the Study of Christianity in the Non-Western World.

THOMAS CHALMERS' SOCIAL VISION

On 3 June 1846 the first Principal of New College, Thomas Chalmers, laid the foundation stone of our present buildings, and thereafter delivered a memorable oration. It was a time of great suffering for many working people in Scotland, and there was much hunger in the Highlands. The young Free Church of Scotland was suspected by many of being a dissenting body dangerously subversive of the established order of things. Perhaps Chalmers had this accusation in mind when, after expressing his delight that 'so many of the working classes in our city now stand within the reach of my voice', so that those whose hands would raise the walls of the College would hear him expound what would today, rather quaintly, be called the 'mission statement' of the new institution, he went on:

> We leave to others the passions and politics of this world; and nothing will ever be taught, I trust, in any of our halls, which shall have the remotest tendency to disturb the existing order of things, or to confound the ranks and distinctions which now obtain in society. But there is one equality between man and man which will strenuously be taught – the essential equality of human souls; and in the high count and reckoning of eternity, the souls of the poorest of nature's children – the raggedest boy who runs along the pavement, is of like estimation in the eyes of heaven with that of the greatest and noblest in the land . . . Let kings retain their sceptres and nobles their coronets – what we want is a more elevated ground floor for our general population, and this without derangement to the upper stories of the social and political edifice – where may our beloved Queen, God bless her, long retain upon its summit the place of gracefulness and glory which she now occupies.[1]

These famous words may not be understood in a pietistic manner, as if Chalmers were announcing that his College would concern itself with the individual's soul and disregard the issues of society. Such would have been totally incompatible with his overall position and theology. He was, I think, assuming that the social question would be a continuing concern of the College, but that his own High Tory view of society and his distinctive understanding of political economy were understood to be integral to the theology and the ecclesial stance of the Free Church, and should be reflected in the teaching of its College. Any other interpretation of Chalmers' speech would suggest that he was either devious or radically inconsistent. For Chalmers was as significant in his day in political economy as in theology; he was one of the leaders in what Boyd Hilton calls 'the baptism of political economy',[2] and he even received the accolade of being denounced by Marx as 'the arch-Parson Thomas Chalmers' who was a disciple of Malthus and who had his suspicions of Adam Smith for 'having invented the category of "unproductive labourers" solely for the Protestant pastors, in spite of their blessed work in the vineyard of the Lord'.[3] Chalmers' significance as a political economist has been explored recently by Hilton and A. M. C. Waterman, among others.[4] It is now obvious that

[1] Watt, 3–4.
[2] Hilton (1988), 56.
[3] Marx (1965), I, 617–18.
[4] Hilton (1988) and Waterman (1991).

R. H. Tawney was wrong in asserting that Christian social thinkers ceased to matter in the eighteenth and nineteenth centuries because they could not cope with the complexities of modern society; Chalmers and Malthus and others were taken seriously in their day, and deserve to be taken with equal seriousness in ours.

This is, of course, a complex area into which I cannot go at any depth at present. But one or two points are relevant. Chalmers saw his political economy as arising directly out of his endeavours to grapple with what he called 'pauperism' through the parish system of an established church. There is a sense in which his move from St John's in Glasgow to the Moral Philosophy chair in St Andrews made him a *practical* theologian. Certainly much of his teaching and publication while at St Andrews was in a real way a sustained reflection on the lessons he had learned in St John's. In St Andrews he taught political economy as part of moral philosophy; and when he moved to the Edinburgh chair of Divinity he continued to teach political economy, now significantly as part of natural theology. And in all this he sustained a vital practical concern with the problem of poverty, the search for a community which might be a 'godly commonwealth', and the central role of the church in dealing with social problems. He may have been somewhat trapped into regarding the social and economic systems as part of the divine ordering of things, and his social thought is pervasively paternalist and conservative, but despite the surface meaning of his foundation-stone speech, he certainly never thought that theology can or should be taught in abstraction from social and economic questions.

AFTER CHALMERS

It is not easy to detect a steady line of social concern in the history of New College. The Disruption itself had made it hard to sustain the Chalmers vision of a restoration of a godly commonwealth in Scotland, with the established Church at the heart of things. Increasingly attention was concentrated on the inner life of the churches, and competition between churches absorbed energy that ought to have been directed towards responding to the gigantic social problems of the day, as Smout and Donald Smith have so depressingly demonstrated.[5] An increasing nervousness about the dangers of political and social radicalism encouraged even the Free Church to distance itself from any kind of

[5] Smith (1987); Smout (1986).

identification with the working class and to be very nervous about movements for reform. By claiming to confine itself to its 'proper spiritual tasks', the church and theology lent largely tacit support to the existing order of things. There is little evidence that social questions featured to any great extent in the teaching of New College after Chalmers.

Nor did members of staff continue the Chalmers tradition of publishing works which from a theological angle addressed the issues of the day. The one exception I have noted is the work of Professor W. Gordon Blaikie of the second Divinity chair, devoted to Apologetics, Christian Ethics and Pastoral Theology. Blaikie was minister of Pilrig Free Church in Edinburgh, where he had followed in the Chalmers tradition by concerning himself with the spiritual and material conditions of the poor. The social order, he wrote, is God-given:

> [A]ll cannot be ladies and gentlemen; all cannot attain to a refined and easy mode of life; the vast majority must continue to be hard workers, content with mere food and raiment, hewers of wood and drawers of water. This is the inexorable law of Providence, and it were about as wise to change the law of gravitation as to interfere with this.[6]

Accordingly the poor should find their fulfilment in doing the duties of their station and protecting themselves against the degradation of pauperism by cultivating virtues of frugality, industry and the fear of God. Like a cross between Samuel Smiles and F. D. Maurice, Blaikie tirelessly delivered lectures to working men, and produced a series of popular books on how the labouring classes could improve their lot, larded with biblical references, a rather sanctimonious piety, and practical advice on diet and hygiene. He gave advice to employers, too, but he obviously assumed a simple harmony of interests between capital and labour, and was at his hottest when inveighing against what he believed to be the characteristic vices of the working classes – drink, and a tendency to strike. Hugh Miller appears again and again as the examplar *par excellence* of the self-made man of devout Free Church piety. Self-respect, self-reliance and self-control were the three levers for personal uplift.

Blaikie had nothing like the intellectual power of Chalmers. He had little interest in the causes of deprivation and social problems, and does not appear to have had a vision of how the church and the state might

[6] Blaikie (1867A), 85.

respond. Compared with Chalmers' robust intellectual Evangelicalism, Blaikie was a pietist who believed that responsibility and remedy lay in the hands of the individual.[7] But for all that, Blaikie stands as a reminder that social issues, and particularly poverty and the lot of working people continued to be addressed, in however cautious and inadequate a fashion, in the teaching that went on in New College. Chalmers would have found nothing to take exception to in Blaikie's writings, although he might have been disappointed at his lack of economic and theological depth. No one could say that Blaikie's teaching and writing had 'the remotest tendency to disturb the existing order of things'!

But another type of engagement with social issues which for long was a central aspect of the life of New College certainly deeply influenced generations of students, shaping their understanding of ministry, and giving them a disturbing contact with the realities of poverty and degradation in the overcrowded slums of the Old Town. Students from the Missionary Society were active from the early days in work in the West Port area, in the Cowgate, and in the Royal Infirmary. On Chalmers' death, the Missionary Society saw its role as carrying on his vision of sustaining 'territorial churches' in the needier parts of the city. The Society worked in various parts of the Old Town, before in 1876 establishing in the Pleasance a mission which was shortly to become the New College Settlement, with a Warden and some students in residence, and many others involved in the various activities of the Settlement. The impact of the settlement movement in England in generating social concern and radicalising young people from privileged and protected backgrounds has been well documented. The equivalent Scottish initiatives have not as yet to my knowledge been properly studied. Among them New College Settlement was prominent, and generations of eminent Scottish churchmen and missionaries acknowledged that their experience in the Settlement had been formative – in many cases, far more so than the teaching they had received in the lecture room.[8] The charismatic Warden of the Settlement, Dr J. Harry Miller, became in 1923 the first Lecturer in Sociology, and this post (which continued into the 1960s) represented an endeavour to earth the discussion of social problems and the proper

---

[7] Blaikie was a prolific writer. His main works relevant to this discussion are: *Six Lectures Addressed to the Working Classes on the Improvement of their Temporal Condition* (1849), *Heads and Hands in the World of Labour* (1865), *Counsel and Cheer for the Battle of Life* (1867), *Better Days for Working People* (1867).

[8] A case in point is Archie Craig; see Templeton (1991), 29–30.

Christian response to them in the work of the Settlement, which became a kind of laboratory of what used to be known as 'Christian sociology'. Other contexts too fed into the teaching of sociology. In the 1950s the Revd Ian Fraser, former industrial chaplain and then minister of Rosyth, and the Revd Ian Reid of the Old Kirk in Pilton, in Edinburgh, later to become Leader of the Iona Community, presented a radical vision as lecturers in sociology under Professor William Tindal, who had himself been Warden of the Settlement. Two World Wars also contributed to increasing social concern in New College. Students returning from war were both alarmed at the tenuous link to the Christian church of so many they had encountered in the forces, and determined that the church and they in their vocations should make a major contribution to post-war reconstruction.

Professor S. J. Brown has shown the serious limitations of the Church of Scotland's response to social problems in the 1930s, and in particular its reluctance to challenge the government or call for statutory action in response to the sufferings of the Depression. The Church and Nation Committee's report on unemployment in 1932 suggested that the government could do more, and called for a greater level of state intervention in the economy. But the main recommendations of the report were rejected by the Assembly, no criticisms of the government were approved, and the Assembly simply encouraged parishes to provide clubs and emergency assistance for the unemployed. Clearly, many commissioners to the Assembly saw a major cause of unemployment to be the moral failings of the working class, and several Church leaders made it clear that they believed that the Church did not have the technical competence or knowledge to pronounce on such matters. All it could properly do was to give solace and assistance to the victims.[9]

THE BAILLIE COMMISSION

When John Baillie returned from the United States to the chair of Divinity in Edinburgh he was very unhappy with the 'quietism' and caution of the Church's social teaching, with hesitations about a broader ecumenism in the aftermath of the Union of 1929, and with the tendency of some senior figures to see the German Christians' response to Nazism as similar to the endeavour built into the Declaratory Articles to have a reunited Church of Scotland as the sole representative of the

[9] S. J. Brown in Morton (1994), 17–18.

Christian faith of the Scottish people, a kind of folk church. Baillie's opportunity came when he was invited to convene the Commission for the Interpretation of God's Will in the Present Crisis, which was set up in 1940, and later became known as the Baillie Commission.[10] The Commission's remit was remarkably wide: on the conviction that 'God is speaking to mankind in the solemnizing and chastening events and experiences of our time', it was charged 'to seek reverently to guide the Church in the interpretation of the Holy Will and Purpose of God in present-day events, and to examine how the testimony of the Church to the Gospel may become more effective in our land, overseas, and in the international order'. The task was therefore seen as both an ethical and an evangelical one: how to understand and proclaim the gospel in current circumstances. The Commission accordingly saw theology as at the heart of its endeavours. Its theological position was close to that of Reinhold Niebuhr, who was a friend and colleague of John Baillie, and whose remarkable Gifford Lectures, *The Nature and Destiny of Man*, were given in New College as the Commission started its work.

The Commission argued that the major values of Western society were derived from Christianity, but have been increasingly secularised, and were now free-floating, without anchorage in faith. This had led to distortion and instability: values needed to be 'fortified and purified by return to that source from which they drew their first life'; without this they 'are in danger of losing their power of conviction and their hold over men's minds'. Thus 'all our ideals and standards must once again be related to a true conception of man's chief end. Christian faith must repossess and renew its social ideals.'

Thus the Commission argues that the gospel cannot be separated from Christian values, nor can either be separated from the problems of the world. As John Baillie put it in presenting the Commission's Report to the 1942 Assembly:

'How', we ask, 'can man be drawn to a Gospel whose one practical expression is serving Christ by serving the least of His needy brethren, if we preach it in abstraction from the crying needs of the poor and oppressed of our society?'

Although the Commission recognised that public life involved numerous technical matters in which the Church had no special

---

[10] My treatment here of the Baillie Commission draws on Morton (1994), and Forrester (1993A) and (1993B).

competence, it also suggested that there was a spiritual and ethical dimension in every problem, so that no issue could be left to the experts alone. Using a version of the middle axiom method, the Commission then proceeded to enunciate principles and suggest how they might be put into practice. Thus in relation to the economy the Commission insists that 'economic power must be made objectively responsible to the community as a whole. The possessors of economic power must be answerable for the use of that power, not only to their own consciences, but to appropriate social organs'; extreme inequalities of wealth must be controlled and a living wage provided for every active adult citizen. This could be implemented by 'a far greater measure of public control of capital resources and means of production than our tradition has in the past envisaged'.

The Baillie Commission reports aroused great interest and not a little controversy. They had considerable influence on public opinion both within and without the Church, and provided the general backing of a major denomination for the broad thrust of the reforms introduced by the Labour government in the aftermath of the Second World War. In the work of the Baillie Commission we see a high point in the social awareness of the Church of Scotland, and its reports remain something of a classic in Christian social ethics.

THE CENTRE FOR THEOLOGY AND PUBLIC ISSUES[11]

For a number of years from the mid-1970s various Scottish academics and church leaders had felt the need, not so much for another Baillie Commission as for a think-tank which could give sustained attention to the churches' responsibilities in the public arena, draw together academics and churchpeople, and stimulate more informed and constructive research and debate which would give proper attention to the issues of value, principle and theology which underlie public policy decisions. More mobilising of academic resources, particularly in theology and the social sciences, might help to undergird church contributions to public debate.

It was with such needs in mind, and after a period of gestation and consultation that in 1984 an ecumenical Centre for Theology and Public Issues was established in New College. It was located in the Department

---

[11] In this section I draw on my articles, Forrester (1991) and (1993B).

of Christian Ethics and Practical Theology, and supported by an interesting variety of people from other departments and universities, from the churches, and from Scottish public life. The Centre embarked on a programme of conferences, seminars and lectures; publications; and the development of a resource collection and library available to researchers and students. Quickly the main focus of the Centre's work became a small number of study projects typically carried out over a two- to three-year period by a working group, and producing a substantial report, usually in the form of a book, at the end of that time. The Centre has completed studies on dependency in social welfare, on the distribution of wealth, income and benefits (for the Church and Nation Committee of the Church of Scotland), on finance and ethics, on the principles and assumptions of penal policy, on security and peacemaking, and on Christian responses to the AIDS crisis.

The Centre has four particular emphases in its work. There is, first, a stress on *interdisciplinarity* in the belief that no one form of analysis is capable of providing adequate understanding of complex problems. This has resulted in the Centre providing a rather unusual kind of forum, in which social scientists, philosophers, theologians and people with a wide range of practical experience wrestle together with a specific problem and learn from each other's insights and perplexities. But it is not just interdisciplinarity as such that is unusual; rather it is the particular mix in the Centre's activities which opens special possibilities. The sharp distinction between fact and value which was for long dominant in the social sciences still makes it difficult for some to treat moral issues as belonging in the academic scene. And in an increasingly fragmented society such as ours, professional practice and professional ethics have become increasingly problematic. In the Centre a rare mix of people together face questions which are too often dodged elsewhere in society.

Secondly, within this context the Centre has a special concern for the *integrity of the theological contribution*. This is, of course, a problematic matter today. Theology and the problems of the world have tended to drift apart, as theology has sometimes seen the academic world as a refuge from relevance. Nor is it any longer possible to expect a magisterial theology which descends from above to interpret and resolve the world's problems, more or less on its own. We clearly need to develop a theology which is neither deductive nor inductive, but which grows out of a dialectic between the tradition and the praxis of those who are involved in endeavouring to transform the situation.

The third emphasis is on the need to *attend to the powerless*, to the people whose lives are dominated by other people's decisions, who are more the recipients of policy than policymakers. The Centre tries to avoid élitism, and talking about people behind their backs. Thus in discussing poverty it is important to have poor people taking a full part in the proceedings, in investigating housing the voice of the homeless and the poorly housed must be heard. This is not easy. The anger and frustration that is often expressed seems to many academics, including some theologians, to be disruptive and lacking in a proper objectivity, and so they back off. But without the contribution of the powerless discussions about policy lack a vital dimension which is particularly harmful to its Christian integrity.

Finally, the Centre tries to take *experience* very seriously as an object and source of theological reflection. Facts and statistics do not convey the reality of poverty, for example; only shared experience and shared feeling can do this. The reality that we experience and of which theology must take account, is always more confusing, fragmentary and incoherent than neat academic theories would suggest. But thinking which does not accommodate the diversity of the real world simply adds to the confusion and frustration.

Two examples may show something of the way of working which the Centre is developing. The first is the working party on Distribution. The Church of Scotland General Assembly of 1984, 'recognising the fundamental importance of a system of distribution of wealth, income and benefits which incorporates Christian values', called for a study on distribution. The Church and Nation Committee in association with the Centre established an interdisciplinary working group chaired by Duncan Forrester, the Director of the Centre. The first task was to face the facts, and discover something of what these facts mean in human terms for individuals, for families, for communities and for the nation. We discovered that poverty is not simply shortage of money. It is about exclusion and powerlessness, it is about loss of self-respect and limitation of freedom. We learned from poor people about the 'feel' of poverty, and about the solidarity and joy and dignity which are still often to be found in poor communities. We then moved on to reflection and interpretation, seeking clues, insights, signals and challenges in the Christian tradition and in the Bible. We found that the facts made us variously angry, frightened or threatened, because our own interests and possessions are inevitably involved and our own faith or lack of it is deeply implicated in the situation. Several members of the group had had their understanding of the faith and of their own calling deeply influenced by involvement in Britain or overseas in situations of extreme maldistribution – a reminder that our own thoughts, prejudices and attitudes should be shaped by our committments and by the facts. We found in the Christian tradition deep and challenging insights. Finally, we discussed how we should respond to what we had found, in three areas – our personal lifestyle, the way the church orders its life and its resources and its priorities, and public policy.

A brief report was made to the General Assembly of 1987, which was commended for discussion throughout the church. In the spring of 1988 the full report was published as *Just Sharing – A Christian Approach to the Distribution of Wealth, Income and Benefits*, edited by the present writer and Danus Skene (Epworth, London, 1988). This book was widely discussed and got considerable coverage in the press, along with several mentions in parliament. Two useful conferences in Urban Priority Areas carried the discussion further, and after her 'Sermon on the Mound' at the 1988 Assembly the Moderator, Professor James Whyte, presented a copy to the then Prime Minister, Margaret Thatcher, as a doubtless rather unwelcome example of the church's thinking on social issues.

Just Sharing in its basic structure reflects clearly the approach of the Centre. First comes a serious engagement with experience, followed by an analysis of the situation with the help of social science. Only then comes a sustained theological reflection in which a serious attempt is made to translate the material out of technical academic jargon into language which is generally accessible. And the book concludes with some examples of the kind of recommendations which seem to follow from the argument, assuming that only individuals and churches that take these matters seriously in their own life are entitled to call on government to take action.

A second example of the work of the Centre was the study project on the Principles and Assumptions of Penal Policy. This grew out of a conference on law and order which we held in 1986 to address the mounting crisis in the penal system, which seemed to relate to a kind of moral vacuum, a pervasive uncertainty about what the system was for and how it could be justified. It became clear that those with responsibilities within the system were often confused and perplexed by the varied and contradictory expectations of the public and of politicians. This in turn reflected deeper uncertainties about values and goals, and differing beliefs about human beings and society.

The working group we established included a long-term prisoner, chaplains, prison governors, a forensic psychiatrist, the director of a youth treatment centre, a social worker, two advocates, one with much experience as a sheriff, a criminologist, a lecturer in law, and four theologians. We started by examining the major theories of punishment, and found that when they were put together with current experience, none of the theories, or even all the theories together, explained much of what actually happens in the penal system. As we went more deeply into experience – the experience of being a prisoner and trying to survive, the experience of trying to work with integrity within the system, the experience of confusion and uncertainty about values and aims, the experience of struggling to be faithful and human in one's vocation within a system in disarray – theological themes began to emerge. We tried to take account of guilt and forgiveness, of the necessity of hope and the need to take risks if anything were to be achieved. As we probed these and other themes we found that we were dealing not so much with a coherent theology of punishment as with a set of insights and questions which were at one and the same time probing, challenging, suggestive, and supportive to people striving to be innovative and humane and to act with insight and integrity. The group produced two sets of conference papers, on *Justice, Guilt and Forgiveness in the Penal System* (1990) and *Penal Policy: The Way Forward* (1992), and its work was written up in Chris Wood's book, *The End of Punishment: Christian Perspectives on the Crisis in Criminal Justice* (1991). And this work is commonly regarded as having made some useful contribution to the debate about penal policy in Scotland.

The Centre celebrated its tenth birthday in November, 1994, with a crowded audience for a lecture on 'The Common Good Today' by Dr David Jenkins, the former Bishop of Durham, followed by a reception in the University's Playfair Library Hall in Old College. This confirmed that the Centre now had a recognised place not only in New College and the University of Edinburgh, but in Scottish and British public life. It is the lively heir to a tradition of social concern going back through John Baillie, William Blaikie and Thomas Chalmers to the radical interest in social justice found in the Scottish Reformation and expressed in varying ways in the theologising in New College and the University of Edinburgh. That tradition might well be symbolised by the figure of poor John the Commonweal who, in Sir David Lindsay's play *Ane Satyre of the Thrie Estaitis* (1540), appears at the turning point of the action to denounce the exactions and oppressions of the nobility, the burgesses and the church, supported by Divine Correction and Gude Counsel, grasping the Gospels.

ALEXANDER DUFF'S MISSIONARY VISION

The second story in this chapter starts with Alexander Duff and his great project of establishing in New College a chair of missions, an institute for the training of missionaries, and a journal, a project which found only partial fulfilment in his own day but has come to a remarkable flowering in the 1990s. Duff was not an Edinburgh man. Born and raised in Moulin in Perthshire, at a time when the mother tongue was still Gaelic, Duff went to St Andrews, where he fell under the spell of Thomas Chalmers, was intellectually shaped by the Enlightenment Calvinism which could happily co-exist with a lively evangelical faith, and felt a compelling call to become a missionary. In 1829 he was sent as the first official missionary of the Church of Scotland, to establish a mission in Bengal. He was not the first Scottish missionary; various missionary societies in Scotland and England had already sent a number of Scots overseas as missionaries. But his appointment meant that the Church of Scotland was officially and practically affirming that it had a world-wide evangelistic task, and repossessing and putting into practice for the first time the hints in the Scots Confession and the documents of the Westminster Assembly that such a responsibility might exist.

Duff's missionary career in Bengal was spectacular. He found Calcutta in a ferment of intellectual excitement. The younger generation were demanding English-medium education as the key to the possibility of good employment in the public service or with European businesses. But there was also a strong protest movement against the tradition. Young high-caste Bengalees ostentatiously ate beef, drank alcohol and in general behaved in ways which outraged their elders. At the Hindu College, under the influence of a remarkable Anglo-Indian teacher, Henry Derozio, the sceptical thought of David Hume and Tom Paine became immensely popular. Duff discovered that a whole generation of able young Hindus were being entranced by the very debates of the Scottish Enlightenment out of which his own theology and strategy of mission had emerged – but only one side of the discussion had been adequately presented to them. As a result he reported in the year of his arrival in Bengal, 'The more advanced of the young men have in reality,

271

although not openly and avowedly, shaken off Hindooism, and plunged into the opposite extreme of unbounded scepticism.'[12] This situation, he believed, was full of possibilities for good or ill. Duff saw his task as to claim for Christianity 'these wanderers, whose education and worldly circumstances invest them with such mighty influence among their fellow countrymen'; this effort, if successful, would, 'in some degree affect and modify the future destinies of India'.[13]

Derozio had opened up a discussion in which Duff and his Scots colleagues felt very much at home; his teaching was not to be undone, but corrected and built upon. Duff established a school and college close to the Hindu College, and in addition to the work of the school he established a series of lectures and debates on 'the Evidences of Natural and Revealed Religion', which attracted 'a number of heathen youth, whose minds were previously opened by an acquaintance with European literature and science'.[14] Duff's missionary strategy involved the direct confrontation and refutation of basic Derozian ideas, the conversion of key individuals, and the gradual percolation of Christian truth through these converts to society as a whole. Ultimately he sought a 'decided permanent change of the *national intellect*'.[15]

To begin with, Duff was strikingly successful. Among the most notable of his early converts were Lal Behari Day, K. M. Banerjea, Michael Madhusudhan Dutt, Kali Charan Chatterjee, Gopinath Nandi and Mohesh Chunder Ghose. Such converts were, Duff and his colleagues believed, to be the real leaders of the process of renaissance and reformation on which the future of India depended. The rest of this story cannot be told here. But it is relevant to mention that in Scotland Duff quickly became a living legend, promoted foreign missions to the top of the churches' agenda, and raised large sums for the advancement of the work in India and elsewhere.

From 1844 Duff promoted a project to strengthen the 'home base': the establishment of a theological chair of missions, or 'evangelistic theology'; the setting up of an institute in which missionaries could be trained and prepared for their work; and the publication of a journal of mission. The chair was 'to infuse the missionary spirit into the minds of our students and young ministers, and through them into the minds of the people, and to secure a larger supply alike of men and pecuniary

---

[12] Letter of 15 October 1830: National Library of Scotland, MS 7530.
[13] *Ibid.*
[14] *Ibid.*
[15] Duff (1840), 317.

means'. The institute was to be a kind of Protestant equivalent to Propaganda in Rome, or to Iona, ecumenically sponsored and intended to equip missionaries with the local knowledge that they required and to help them develop strategies of mission. A scholarly review of missions would involve a wider readership in the discussions and insights arising from the chair and the institute. For a variety of reasons, neither the institute nor the journal got off the ground, but when Duff finally retired from India a chair of Evangelistic Theology was established, and he was named as the first occupant. The chair was based in New College, but the professor was expected also to deliver lectures at the other two Free Church Colleges, in Glasgow and Aberdeen.[16]

'Evangelistic Theology', Duff proclaimed in his inaugural lecture as professor, 'is only another name for the vast and comprehensive subject of Christian missions, considered in all their varied and multiplied bearings, in relation alike to God and man, time and eternity'![17] Duff was concerned to demonstrate that mission was a core subject in the theological curriculum, and to show the relationship of mission to everything else. But he was now an old man and by the standards of Scotland of the 1860s an intellectual reactionary, whose lectures were immensely prolix and tedious. Those who expected him to have an impact on the youth of Scotland like that which he had exerted in Calcutta in the 1830s were sorely disappointed; the best students in the divinity halls scorned his lectures; he for his part declared most new movements in theology and in biblical criticism to be examples of infidelity.

When Duff died in 1878, the chair was held for a time by his friend Thomas Smith. It was then suppressed. But as Olav Guttorm Myklebust argues in his two-volume examination of the study of missions in theological education, Alexander Duff is the real pioneer of the academic study of missions.[18] The tripartite project that he proposed, despite the fact that only one part got off the ground, and that did not last for long, is still an attractive and academically serious vision.

AFTER DUFF

For many decades after the suppression of the chair of Evangelistic Theology many New College men went overseas as missionaries, and

[16] Myklebust (1955–7), I, 190–3.
[17] Cited *ibid.*, I, 188.
[18] *Ibid.*, I, 19–24, 164ff.

gradually a reciprocal flow of students from the 'mission fields' was to be noted. But missions did not feature in the curriculum to a noticeable extent. Every few years the Alexander Duff Missionary Lectureship brought a distinguished missionary or overseas church leader to give a short course of lectures. The most notable of this series were perhaps those by A. G. Hogg (*The Christian Message to the Hindu*, 1947) and M. M. Thomas (*The Christian Response to the Asian Revolution*, 1966). The great landmark, the World Missionary Conference of 1910, although held in the Assembly Hall, and involving a number of New College people, had no discernible impact on the New College curriculum. And when the present writer (who spent eight years as a missionary in Madras) studied in New College in the late 1950s, the only reference to missions that he can remember is one of his lecturers suggesting to a class that some of us might care to read some Hendrik Kraemer!

THE CENTRE FOR THE STUDY OF CHRISTIANITY IN THE NON-WESTERN WORLD

One of the nice ironies of recent New College history is that the original venture into the study of mission in Edinburgh, which was conceived in St Andrews and matured in Calcutta, had to wait for a fulfilment conceived in Nigeria and born in Aberdeen, to reach maturity in Edinburgh! Andrew Walls came in 1970 from heading the Department of Religious Studies at the University of Nigeria (Nsukka) to establish a new Department of Religious Studies in the University of Aberdeen, 'to study religion in its own terms, and in its historical, social and phenomenological aspects'. The Department expanded, with the appointment of Harold Turner, who developed a Centre for the Study of New Religious Movements, Adrian Hastings, the historian of African – and English – Christianity, James Thrower, and others. A major concern of the Department from the start was with non-Western Christianity, and in 1982 Andrew Walls established within it a Centre for the Study of Christianity in the Non-Western World. The Department flourished exceedingly, attracting a large number of research students from around the world and gaining a world-wide reputation. Meanwhile, however, the University of Aberdeen was experiencing a severe financial crisis. Two members of the Department moved to chairs elsewhere, one retired, and Andrew Walls himself suffered a severe heart attack, and had to seek early retirement as head of the Department, although he hoped to remain as Director of the Centre. In a fit of collective madness (no other interpretation seems possible) the University closed the Department in 1984, and in 1985 suggested to Andrew Walls that he might find another home for the Centre. In 1986–7 the Centre moved to Edinburgh, bringing with it its invaluable collections of materials on third-world Christianity, a goodly number of research students, and, most valuable of all, Andrew Walls himself, who in the aftermath of heart surgery and as an honorary professor, put in more hours of imaginative effort than many a younger and healthier colleague!

The Centre exists to further the study and understanding of Christian history, thought and life in Africa, Asia, Latin and Caribbean Americas and the Pacific, and the collection and preservation of resources for such study. It is also concerned with issues of Christianity and culture, and Christian mission. It has an extensive and growing collection of mission archives, periodicals and pamphlets which, together with the resources of other libraries in Edinburgh, makes the city one of the best places in Britain for research in this area of study. But it is the human resources that are the most important of all. Andrew Walls brought down with him from Aberdeen Dr Christopher Smith, who worked on the completion of the index and the cumulative bibliography of the *International Review of Mission(s)* before leaving to take up a post with the Pew Foundation in Philadelphia. Dr Kwame Bediako, the Director of the Akrofi-Christaller Memorial Centre for Applied Theology and Mission Research in Ghana, has taught for a term each year, initially as Duff Lecturer. In 1991 the University funded the post of Assistant Director, and Dr John Parratt was appointed. Dr Parratt had been Professor of Theology and Religious Studies in Botswana, and before that in Malawi, and also has teaching and research experience in India and Papua New Guinea. A major grant from the Pew Charitable Trusts to establish the African Christianity Project enabled the appointment of Dr James Cox, formerly of Alaska Pacific University and the University of Zimbabwe, and the Overseas Board of the Presbyterian Church in Ireland has seconded Dr Jack Thompson, who was formerly in the Department of Mission at Selly Oak Colleges and Director there of the Centre for the Study of New Religious Movements, and previously served in Malawi.

But most importantly the Centre attracts researchers and students from around the world, who enrich the community life of New College and enliven the theological debate. With a constant succession of academic visitors from around the world, with well-attended weekly seminars and regular conferences, with close collaboration with institutions in Africa and Asia and with Yale, with the academic globe-trotting of Andrew Walls and the other staff, it can truly be said that the Centre is 'a network of co-operation and goodwill across the world'.

This is surely the fulfilment in a most exciting way of one part of Alexander Duff's dream: a major academic centre for mission studies. And the other two parts are being fulfilled as well. In 1994 the University decided to establish a chair in Christianity in the Non-Western World. Among British universities, only Birmingham has a similar chair; and this was the first new theological chair to be established in a Scottish university for many years. Professor David Kerr has been appointed to it, with effect from January 1996.[19] The second part of Duff's dream has been realised. And in April 1995 the first issue appeared of *Studies in World Christianity: The Edinburgh Review of Theology and Religion*, under the editorship of Professor James Mackey. This can fairly be seen as the fulfilment of the third part of Duff's dream.

Space does not allow me to mention a number of other new initiatives, although some of them are mentioned elsewhere in this book. The student body is larger, more diverse, and richer than ever before. There is an increasing stress on interdisciplinarity, which brings theology into lively interaction with other disciplines. We have never had so many research students. We have promising initiatives in in-service education for clergy and others, particularly in the M.Th. in Ministry and the M.Th. in Communication. The Centre for Theology and Public Issues brings people from all sectors of society into college for conferences, seminars and study groups. And the traditional theological disciplines continue to flourish. It would be hard to imagine a more stimulating and relevant context for the study of theology and religion today and tomorrow.

There is a lot of new wine about. The old bottles show no sign of bursting. But we urgently need more of them if we are to accommodate adequately all the good wine that is around!

---

[19] David Kerr comes immediately from the Macdonald Center for the Study of Islam and Christian–Muslim Relations in Hartford Seminary, Hartford, CN, and more distantly from service in Lebanon, teaching in Selly Oak Colleges, Birmingham, and the United Reformed Church.

Chapter 15

New College and the Reformed Tradition: The Promise of the Past

Gary Badcock

WHEREAS ONCE the identity of Edinburgh Divinity within the Reformed tradition was secure, the picture now seems by no means so simple. Previous chapters have detailed developments past and present which can be, and often are, seen as threats to the historical status of New College as one of the great citadels of Reformed theology in the English-speaking world. Among these developments are new degrees in Religious Studies, rapid demographic changes in the make-up of our undergraduate population, increasing theological pluralism among staff members, and the sometimes uncertain or confusing relationship between New College as a Church of Scotland entity and as the University Faculty of Divinity.

Some concluding assessment is needed, and needed especially, I wish to suggest, in order to correct possible misunderstanding. That we stand historically within the Reformed tradition can hardly be doubted; many of the great names of nineteenth- and twentieth-century Reformed thought are our own predecessors, or have strong links with us. That we still stand within that tradition, and that we are likely to do so for the foreseeable future, may be a somewhat more controversial thesis. It is one, however, that I propose to defend, for I am convinced that New College retains and will retain a clear Reformed identity. In fact, I wish to go farther, and to suggest that the truth is that the milieu of faith, and specifically faith as conceived in the Scottish Reformed tradition, is what has made and makes New College what it is.

This is not in any way an attempt to denigrate the significance of the University connection. The larger story of Edinburgh Divinity is, in the main, located in a University context, while New College too has for almost half of its history been immensely strengthened by the University as well as by the Church. The scholarly environment of the former, its ideals of free enquiry and open debate and the physical resources it provides are of crucial significance to our subject, just as are the values and traditions of the latter. Nevertheless, the University connection is itself, in the end, something that needs to be understood as a function and feature of the Scottish Reformed tradition, which has always deliberately chosen, and still chooses, to commit its academic theology to the universities.

LEARNING AND THE REFORMED TRADITION

To begin at the beginning, we may say that the foundation of New College was the product of more than the bare fact of the Disruption of 1843. That it came into being was due also to a certain vision on the part of its founders of the central importance of higher learning for the life of the Christian church and for society generally. It was a product also of their awareness of the responsibility laid upon them to do good in the world. Such values derived, however, from their Christian faith, anchored in the Reformed theological tradition, though allied with and perhaps also tempered by a certain Christian humanism. As other contributors to the present volume have pointed out, the original plan was for a great new university, and not just for a theological college, which reveals how far from a narrowly sectarian ambition the foundation of New College was. To a man such as Thomas Chalmers, New College rather represented the ideals of spiritual and intellectual independence working together to promote evangelical religion, yes, but also with it the highest standards of scholarship in the Church, economic progress, a modern democratic intellect for the nation, and the general physical and spiritual welfare of the common people. The intention was that the theology taught at New College should have its home in such a context, and not in a religious ghetto.

The ideal of learning is, of course, central to the special genius of Reformed Christianity. In fact, we may say that it is nothing less than its high theology of the Word that makes a commitment to learning – learning secular as well as sacred – so appropriate and so necessary. If the primary mode of God's presence in the world is through the Word, and if that Word is intelligible, then intelligibility as such is implicitly dignified as the gift of God and the *locus* of practically everything in the human encounter with God. It is interesting in this light to compare the vision of men such as Knox and Chalmers – of education as basic to Christian vocation and life – with the outlook of many of the early Greek theologians of the *logos*, for whom the whole wealth of the Word of God could best be understood only when brought in touch with the achievements of secular science and philosophy. There is, we may conclude, no necessary antithesis between secular learning and a high theology of the Word, even though, as we know, that antithesis is frequently postulated by champions of one or the other. The situation is as often as not quite the reverse: the higher the theology of the Word, the more open that theology is likely to be to learning in general.

THE INTERNATIONAL DIMENSION

In a variety of ways it is possible to see the Reformed tradition as absolutely central to what New College has been and to what it is. The commitment to learning begins the list, but it does not end there by any means. The international dimension which is such a key to its identity, and which has been so effectively highlighted by Andrew Ross in his contribution to this volume, also stems directly from the religious roots of the institution. The Reformed churches world-wide have historically provided our great numbers of overseas students and alumni/ae, and this is still broadly true of the overseas student body today. It is primarily because the Christian churches and their theologies generally have become less sectarian and more ecumenical, and not because the Divinity Faculty itself has changed so much, that we now find students from a greater variety of religious backgrounds coming from abroad to study with us. The undergraduate population in both the Divinity and the Religious Studies streams is admittedly in a different category, but changes here have their root in government policy for the expansion of higher education much more than in any purported sea-change in the institution. Even at the undergraduate level, one must recognise also that many of the developments of recent years have resulted from changes in the self-perception of the different churches and in their perception of other communions; it has become appropriate for a Catholic student, for example, to study Reformed theology, just as it has become appropriate for the Reformed tradition to open up to the riches of the Catholic tradition.

If it has been chiefly the Reformed family of churches world-wide that has made possible the extensive international contacts which have always been so much a feature of New College, then it is also the international make-up of the Reformed tradition that has preserved Edinburgh theology, along with Scottish theology generally, from becoming small-minded and self-enclosed. One of the most useful functions performed by Scottish theology over the past century and more has been to act as a kind of clearing-house for theological ideas, mediating movements in continental Protestant theology to much of the English-speaking world. It is still as surprising as it is notorious that, as late as the 1960s, in certain even of the leading English universities it was difficult to find a theologian who took an active interest in many of the central movements in twentieth-century continental thought, whereas in Scottish universities, which have long been essentially outward-looking, such theological interests were the norm. If the negative side of this is that all too often Scottish theological students have had too little sense of the greatness of their own tradition, the positive is that they have received a great deal from others.

Although Chalmers' mid-nineteenth-century dream of a new university on the Mound proved impracticable in the end, many of the other goals set were indeed achieved. For 150 years, New College has stood at the centre of the Scottish theological tradition, contributing immensely through teaching and research to Scottish Christianity and Scottish society. On the scholarly level, many of its professors and lecturers have stood at the forefront of their fields, not only on the national scene but internationally as well. Finally, the extensive overseas connections which have evolved over the years and been so important for the history and character of both College and Faculty, have helped to make this relatively small institution in a small country a place of learning commanding international respect and recognition.

WORSHIP

One further factor of importance in this context, and which has scarcely been mentioned thus far, is that from the beginning New College has been a worshipping community. One can say with complete confidence that daily worship has been one of the real constants in its history. That worship has at times been informal, or individual, and at others highly organised, involving many people and a great deal of effort, but it has continued all the same, and has been an important source of personal vision and vocation for the vast majority of those who have worked and studied here. For staff and students, overwhelmed at times with new ideas or with the strains of having to use them in lectures or seminars or essays, times of worship have provided a centre of calm for reflection and renewal. If all theology proceeds from a personal and communal commitment expressed in doxology, then New College could never have been what it is without the worship that has daily taken place here. And while in recent years, moves towards ecumenism have meant that liturgical voices other than the Reformed have been heard – some of them for the very first time, as, for example, in the weekly Mass held since 1993 and sponsored jointly by the Faculty's Worship Committee and the Catholic Chaplaincy to the University – most worship at New College continues to be broadly Reformed in character, in the daily prayers and the weekly Lord's Supper.

In many ways, tensions between New College as a Church community and as the Faculty of Divinity within the modern University come to their clearest focus here, at the point of worship, and here too some of the most creative possibilities which can emerge from these tensions are also seen. It is important, for example, that ministerial candidates for the Church of Scotland and other denominations share in worship not only with friends who have no such career ambitions, but also with those who worship differently, or with those who find it difficult to worship, or even worship a different God. Perhaps one of the gains of such experience is a recognition on the part of each that any given theology or tradition is intended only to mediate the mystery of God, and not to be the mystery itself; one recognises the limitations of one's own way by recognising the strengths of others. Such an approach finds a fitting home in a Reformed context, for here the classical ecclesiological *semper reformanda* theme means that one can never presume to have the perfect church, the perfect theology, or the perfect mode of worship, but always and only something provisional and approximate, something that must be ever open to change even to be what it is.

In such ways, we see that the Reformed tradition is able to accommodate those recent developments in the life of New College which superficially seems a threat to it. In a number of further ways, the Reformed tradition can also be seen to bring specific positive strengths to the new situation that we face, and resources upon which we might well draw in the years to come. To these we now turn.

BIBLICAL SCHOLARSHIP

New College is rightly distinguished for its tradition of biblical scholarship, in keeping with that acknowledgment of Scripture as the supreme standard and rule of faith which is basic to Reformed theology. Under the inspiration of this conviction, the New College curriculum was from the beginning centred on the systematic study of the Bible in its original languages. It might even be possible to speak of the strength of its biblical scholarship as the major contribution made by New College as a Free and United Free Church institution to the combined Faculty from the 1930s down to the present day. If the whole of theology is drawn primarily from the Bible, then exegesis, and not just general study of biblical history and theology, naturally assumes central place in the theological curriculum, and if exegesis has central place, then the need for appropriate linguistic tools and precision is clear. From a contemporary vantage-point, the linguistic requirements made of students during the nineteenth and much of the twentieth centuries were such as to make the soul shudder, but they were then basic to the theological education offered, and indeed at its very centre. One must add, however, that these were not seen as an end in themselves, but were harnessed to serve a greater purpose in theological exposition. The importance of such exegetical biblical study in the New College curriculum from the beginning was signalled by the early appointment of full professors in the disciplines of Old and New Testament, which was at the time an innovation in Scotland and perhaps in the British Isles. Thus one of the great strengths of New College historically has been the high standards in biblical scholarship which developed initially, and have continued to evolve ever since, under the influence of the Reformed Christian faith.

Early exegesis of the Bible at New College was undoubtedly conservative, for it took place under the auspices of mid-nineteenth-century Scottish Calvinism, but it would be wrong to think of it as straightforwardly designed to support the dictates of a narrowly-conceived theology. Scottish theology in the mid-nineteenth century was indeed strongly Calvinist, and nowhere more than at New College in the 1850s, but it was also a theology closely allied with the philosophical tradition deriving from the eighteenth-century Scottish presbyter and philosopher Thomas Reid, the Scottish philosophy of 'common-sense'. This was an enormously influential movement at the time, not only in Scotland, but also in the United States and, in places, on the European continent. Common-sense, it was held, dictated that truth of any kind, to be truth, must exist not just in the mind of the subject, but in the world of events and objects and history. The opposition of the early biblical scholars at New College to the growing Germanic tendency to distance history from faith, the Bible from revelation, and, as often as not, scholarship from religion, was not something that was philosophically unreflective on their part. According to the common-sense tradition, much of the biblical scholarship which emerged from the Enlightenment, and which finally won the day even in Scotland as early as the late nineteenth century, resulted from a bad case of the idealist philosophical tail wagging the common-sense dog. It was an assessment of Enlightenment biblical scholarship which perhaps still has something to be said for it, for it has re-emerged in different ways at New College in the work of two of our contemporaries, Professors John McIntyre and John O'Neill.

No one familiar with the present curriculum or student body, or even the inclinations of current ministerial candidates studying at Edinburgh, can seriously place hand on heart and say that the study of the Bible, in the original languages or not, still stands at the heart of the education on offer. It is certainly true that our strong tradition of biblical exegesis continues, and that it is much more alive and well here than at most universities in the United Kingdom, but demographic changes in the student body, developments in the biblical disciplines themselves, and wider theological movements affecting the perceived source and content of religious faith and practice have combined to render the study of sacred Scripture something peripheral to too many students' experience. That this is a tragedy of immense proportions in such a place as New College is clear, but it may be appropriate to suggest that one of the ways in which the trend might be reversed could be a creative, thoughtful re-appropriation of the centrality of Scripture in the Reformed tradition – a move which would be quite in keeping with the identity of New College as one of the great centres of learning within that tradition.

A CEREBRAL THEOLOGY?

Faith, John Calvin teaches, is a species of knowledge, and it is Christian faith seen in this way which underlies so much of the long and venerable tradition of what we might call 'cerebral Christianity' in Scotland. While today's preference might seem to be for a more muscular variety of belief, complete with wellie boots on and sleeves rolled up, generations past have been literally 'schooled' in the faith through the teaching of Bible, Catechism and Confession, together with the work of the preachers and the theologians. Our new appreciation for the distinctiveness of the varieties of Christianity practised in the non-western world ought also to alert us to the fact that there is a distinctive variety nearer home, which is also to be taken seriously. But appearances can be deceptive, for just as popular Christianity in the Scottish Reformed tradition is deeply concerned with ethics and piety, in keeping with the strong Reformed emphasis on sanctification, so also is its academic theology. The tale is sometimes told differently, as if the dark days before the development of distinct departments dealing with such things were characterised by toilsome book-learning without so much as a pastoral glance at the harsh realities of life lived by most humanity. Yet Scottish theology at its heart has always been pastorally engaged, a theology in which the question of purity of doctrine has been balanced by a proper concern for the individual and the world, and most especially, for the church to which all Christian theology ultimately belongs and which it serves. All the best Edinburgh theology has its home in this tradition, a tradition which is, once again, part of the Reformed Christian heritage.

One of the great examples of this tendency in Scottish theology, and perhaps the greatest in the history of theology in Edinburgh, is Hugh Ross Mackintosh, a man of international stature in his day as Professor of Systematic Theology at New College (1904–36). One of Mackintosh's achievements was to mediate the German theology in which he had been schooled (the great Wilhelm Hermann, the Marburg teacher of Karl Barth and Rudolf Bultmann, was a friend and particular influence) to the English-speaking world. Mackintosh was responsible (with A. B. Macauley) for the translation of the final volume of Albrecht Ritschl's *The Christian Doctrine of Justification and Reconciliation* (1900), while together with James S. Stewart, he edited and translated the English version of Friedrich Schleiermacher's *The Christian Faith* (1928). In a succession of writings, and especially in his final work, *Types of Modern Theology* (1937, posthumously), he offered a careful exposition and critique of the broad trends of modern continental Protestant theology, including, crucially, the early theology of Karl Barth. Mackintosh was, however, much more than a disciple either of the Ritschlians *via* Hermann or of Barth, though he recognised their undoubted genius. What one discovers in Mackintosh is a theology which reflects continental influences, but which is also entirely distinctive. One might characterise it as less theoretically pure than the German sources upon which he drew, and yet at the same time as more theologically profound, precisely because it was a great deal more pastorally informed, less inclined to violent swings in one direction or other against any theology or theologian, and infinitely more intelligible and so useful to the Church. The Scottish theological tradition, with one or two major exceptions, is a moderating one, while Mackintosh, who lived through an age of extremes and extremists, serves as one of its best representatives. It is a pity that his work is not better known, and better emulated today.

What we may say, however, is that the place of New College in Scottish theology and in Reformed theology has, on the whole, preserved it from what might otherwise have become a merely cerebral scholasticism, and a Calvinist scholasticism at that. It is just this that constitutes one of its great strengths, both past and present. If many of the most exciting developments in the Faculty in recent years have been in the field of Practical Theology, the basis for this was laid long before in the best of the traditions of Scottish theology, and theology in Edinburgh. There is once again a lesson for us here, for in Scotland a purely cerebral theology, developed without reference to church or society, and conceived in isolation from the wider sources of theological learning and religious experience, will always be on alien soil.

OPENNESS

The Reformed tradition is also an extremely diverse one, which from the beginning has been characterised by a variety of confessions of faith and ecclesiastical polities. Its history, furthermore, is one of surprising theological conflict amid the stresses and strains imposed on all but the narrowest of Christian sects in modern times. Insofar as one may speak of a theological tradition at New College, or even of a New College tradition, therefore, one must also admit to the wide range of positions it must embrace, ranging from Principal Cunningham's strict Calvinist orthodoxy to what sometimes appears as the present theological free-for-all. Even more, Divinity in Edinburgh in recent decades has opened up to much more than the Reformed tradition. The presence at New College of staff and students who are not only not Reformed, but also not Christian by their own profession, naturally raises the question whether the days of seeing New College as a predominantly

Reformed theological institution are past, and the days of complete post-modern diversity have arrived.

At this point, it is tempting to have recourse to one of two extremes: either to engage in a certain amount of hand-wringing at the prospect of such a loss of identity, or else to look forward with anticipation to the great revolution when the past will be overthrown and happily forgotten in a secular utopia. But an alternative vision of the present situation and of our future prospect is possible, one which much more closely corresponds to the facts of the recent history of the Faculty of Divinity than do these others. First of all, it is undeniable that it was scholars with a broadly Reformed theological perspective who were responsible for opening the Faculty to the new discipline of Religious Studies, to the presence of a Roman Catholic as a professor of systematic theology, and to the secular world. It would be quite mistaken to understand all of this as if it had been something simply forced upon a recalcitrant institution slowly losing its older identity, or as if the latter must see it all as a threat to its very existence. Rather, it is from its place within the Reformed tradition that New College has reached out to embrace such things, and it is quite appropriate to see it all as an expression of its own sense of identity as such.

Perhaps the most important single figure in these developments in recent decades has been John McIntyre, Professor of Divinity (1956–86), Dean of the Faculty and Principal of New College (1968–74), and acting Principal and Vice-Chancellor of the University of Edinburgh (1973–4 and 1979). McIntyre has been one of the most outstanding administrators in the history of New College. It was under his leadership that the first Roman Catholic to hold a teaching post in a theological faculty in the Scottish universities since the Reformation was appointed. Noel Dermot O'Donoghue (lecturer in Divinity, subsequently Systematic Theology, 1971–88) was originally appointed with a view to strengthening the emerging Religious Studies programme pioneered by McIntyre, but in the event, Religious Studies came to be centred more on comparative religion than on the kind of philosophical theology taught by O'Donoghue, and he eventually found his home within the Divinity curriculum. However this may be, his appointment was followed in 1979, during McIntyre's second period as acting Principal of the University, by the more controversial appearance at New College of James P. Mackey as successor to T. F. Torrance in the newly re-named Thomas Chalmers Chair of Theology.

We can gain an insight into the thinking behind such development from McIntyre's 1968 opening lecture for the academic session, which bore the title, 'The Open-ness of Theology', subsequently published in the *New College Bulletin.*[1] Standing against that movement in modern theology which attempts to emphasise its exclusiveness, its radical differentiation from all other forms of human knowledge and endeavour, and to recall it to its foundation in revelation and in Scripture alone, McIntyre argues that theology must essentially be open, so that its categories of analysis and discourse are shared with the contemporary world, and specifically the scholarly world. Thus theology must be open to philosophy, our understanding of the church to sociological ideas, our notion of the spiritual life to modern psychological insights, and so on. The secular and the sacred, therefore, cannot finally be isolated from one another – and it is basic to McIntyre's claim that the lines of influence must be free to move in both directions – in such a way as to preserve theology from any supposed capitulation to the secular world.

To begin with, according to McIntyre, the future of theology as part of the world of discourse within the university is at stake here; if its categories and methods are not open, then theology can have no place within it. More than this, however, theology is a discipline which is never actually able to close itself off from the world. Whether we like it or not, it has historically always been open to the common conceptual currency of the times and places in which it has been written. To attempt to escape such a situation in the present is really to live an illusion, and in so doing to abdicate our responsibility, not only to our subject, but in a more important sense to the church and to the world also. It is not just that a closed theology can have no place in the modern university, but that it has no final place in the sphere of faith and Christian witness either. Against the strong tendencies towards exclusivism in twentieth-century theology, which for much of our century have actually defined theology as something discontinuous with other learned disciplines, McIntyre argues that the future of theology – the only future it can have – lies in its opening up to the common currency of modern ideas and values, so that it can both belong legitimately within the contemporary world, and, where necessary, offer a critique of what it finds there.

Such liberalism in the approach to the study of theology is not unique to McIntyre, or foreign to Scottish Reformed thought, for it stands in

[1] *NCB* 4 (1968), 6–22.

an older tradition deriving from, among others, W. P. Paterson and John Baillie, his predecessors in the chair of Divinity at Edinburgh in this century. It finds fitting expression, too, in the opening up of Reformed theology to other branches of Christian thought, for the situation between church and world is paralleled by that existing between church and church. The likely result of both movements, whether towards the wider Christian tradition or towards the world, we must frankly admit to be liable to cause alarm to a certain kind of theological reactionary. It is also likely to initiate a wave of secularity in theology, at least in the short term. Nevertheless, it is only thus that theology itself can speak or that it will be spoken of with authority and integrity, and only thus that it will survive and grow. Over time, as McIntyre himself suggests in the lecture mentioned, a balance will have to be found and the inevitable distortions resolved, but for the present we have no alternative to such openness, with all its attendant risks and confusions.

Thus, the role of the Reformed tradition in shaping the theology in Edinburgh has been anything but restrictive. The character of Reformed Christianity has made possible the remarkably outward-looking approach to theology so characteristic of Edinburgh. This is an approach which today finds fitting expression in the new initiatives in the study of non-western Christianity, in ecumenism, in the study of other faiths, and in the attempt to draw together theological research with analogous work in the social sciences, in philosophy, literature, and so on. Through all of this, we can see that it is possible to speak, not only of a Reformed heritage in the older New College tradition, but of Reformed theology as offering us resources today for facing the future. It may even only be as we open up to such things as non-western Christianity and to the wider realm of human learning in the Arts and Sciences that our theology will again achieve the coherence and integrity which all contemporary theology seeks, but which so little of it seems able to find. And if this does happen, if the New College tradition of acting as a 'clearing-house' for theological ideas repeats itself in the future, then not a little of this will be due to our Reformed roots, and to the distinctive shape which the history of Reformed theology in this institution has assumed.

Although the role of New College as a training ground for future clergy had become decreasingly central to its role in recent years, we may still say that the prevailing atmosphere within which studies are undertaken remains that of Scottish theology, and Reformed theology.

As I have tried to show, furthermore, many of the great strengths of the Scottish Reformed tradition lead naturally in the direction of the new initiatives undertaken in recent years. In the long term, one must hope that these developments will in turn lead to a strengthening of what is distinctive in Scottish theology and in the history of Edinburgh Divinity, as new methods, new courses, new ideas and new student populations prove themselves over the years. It is at times a risky venture, but also one that we need to see both as consistent with the past and as filled with promise and potential for the future.

Bibliography

Adams, D. L. (1885), *Our Universities and Theological Study* (Edinburgh)

Alexander, W. L. (1847), *A Discourse of the Qualities and Worth of Thomas Chalmers, D.D.* (Edinburgh)

Alexander, W. L., tr. (1861–72), *History of the Development of the Doctrine of the Person of Christ*, by I. A. Dorner, 5 vols (Edinburgh)

Alexander, W. L., ed. (1870), *A Cyclopaedia of Biblical Literature*, by John Kitto, 3rd edn, 3 vols (Edinburgh)

Alexander, W. L. (1888), *A System of Biblical Theology*, 2 vols (Edinburgh)

Alexander, W. M. (1902), *Demonic Possession in the New Testament* (Edinburgh)

Alexander, W. M. (1929), 'The Resurrection of our Lord', *Evangelical Quarterly* 1, 156–8

Anderson, G. W. (1959), *A Critical Introduction to the Old Testament* (London); 2nd edn, 1994

Anderson, G. W. (1966), *The History and Religion of Israel* (London)

Anderson, G. W. (1974), 'Two Scottish Semitists', in *Edinburgh Congress Volume (Supplem. to Vetus Testamentum* XXVIII; Leiden), ix–xix

Anderson, H. (1964), *Jesus and Christian Origins: A Commentary on Modern Viewpoints* (New York)

Anderson, H. (1968), *Jesus* (Englewood Cliffs)

Anderson, H. (1976), *The Gospel of Mark* (New Century Bible Commentary; London)

Anderson, H. (1985), '3 Maccabees: A New Translation and Introduction', '4 Maccabees: A New Translation and Introduction', in *The Old Testament Pseudepigrapha*, J. H. Charlesworth, ed. (London), II, 509–64

Anderson, W. S. (1994), *A Guide to the Free Church of Scotland College and Offices* (Edinburgh)

Ashton, J. (1991), *Understanding the Fourth Gospel* (Oxford)

Auld, A. G. (1980), *Joshua, Moses and the Land* (Edinburgh)

Auld, A. G. (1984), *Joshua, Judges and Ruth* (Daily Study Bible; Edinburgh)

Auld, A. G. (1986A), *Amos* (Old Testament Guides; Sheffield)

Auld, A. G. (1986B), *Kings* (Daily Study Bible; Edinburgh)

Auld, A. G., ed. (1993), *Understanding Poets and Prophets: Essays in Honour of George Wishart Anderson* (Sheffield)

Auld, A. G. (1994), *Kings without Privilege: David and Moses in the Story of the Bible's Kings* (Edinburgh)

Auld, A. G. and M. Steiner (1995), *Jerusalem to 200 BCE* (Cambridge)

Badcock, G. D., ed. (1996), *Theology After the Storm: Selected Writings of John McIntyre* (Grand Rapids)

Baillie Commission (1946), *God's Will for Church and Nation* (London)

Baillie, D. M. (1948), *God Was in Christ* (London)

Baillie, D. M. (1957), *The Theology of the Sacraments* (London)

Baillie, J. (1929), *The Place of Jesus Christ in Modern Christianity* (Edinburgh)

Baillie, J. (1929), *The Interpretation of Religion* (Edinburgh)

Baillie, J. (1936), *A Diary of Private Prayer* (London)

Baillie, J. (1962), *The Sense of the Presence of God* (London)

Balla, P. (1994), 'Challenges to New Testament Theology: An Attempt to Justify the Enterprise' (Ph.D., University of Edinburgh)

Barbour, G. F. (1923), *The Life of Alexander Whyte* (London)

Barbour, R. A. S. (1972), *Traditio-Historical Criticism of the Gospels* (London)

Barbour, R. A. S. (1972–3), 'Jesus of Nazareth – History and Myth'. *Aberdeen University Review* 45, 19–31

Barr, A. (1938), *A Diagram of Synoptic Relationships* (Edinburgh); ed. with introd. by James Barr, 1995

Barr, J. (1961), *The Semantics of Biblical Language* (London)

Barr, J. (1962), *Biblical Words for Time* (London)

Barr, J. (1993), *Biblical Faith and Natural Theology* (Gifford Lectures; Oxford)

Baxter, P. (1993), 'Deism and Development: Disruptive Forces in Scottish Natural Theology', in Brown and Fry (1993), 98–112

Beaton, D. (1929), *Some Noted Ministers of the Northern Highlands* (Inverness)

Bigg, C. (1901), *A Critical and Exegetical Commentary on the Epistles of St Peter and St Jude* (Edinburgh)

Black, A. (1824), *On the Progressive Diffusion of Divine Knowledge: A Sermon, Preached before the Very Reverend The Synod of Aberdeen, on Tuesday, April 13, 1824* (Aberdeen)

Black, A. (1856), *The Exegetical Study of the Original Scriptures considered in connexion with the Training of Theological Students in a Letter to the Rev. Thomas McCrie, D.D. LL.D., Moderator of the Free Church of Scotland* (Edinburgh)

Black, M. (1946, 1967), *An Aramaic Approach to the Gospels and Acts* (1946, 3rd edn 1967; Oxford)

Blackie, J. S. (1843), *On Subscription to Articles of Faith: A Plea for the Liberties of the Scottish Universities; with Special Reference to the Free Church Professors* (Edinburgh)

Blaikie, W. G. (1849), *Six Lectures Addressed to the Working Classes on the Improvement of their Temporal Condition* (Edinburgh)

Blaikie, W. G. (1865), *Heads and Hands in the World of Labour* (Edinburgh)

Blaikie, W. G. (1867A), *Better Days for Working People* (London)

Blaikie, W. G. (1867B), *Counsel and Cheer for the Battle of Life* (London)

Blaikie, W. G. (1873), *For the Work of the Ministry* (London)

Blaikie. W. G. (1901), *Recollections of a Busy Life* (London)

Boardman, P. (1978), *The Worlds of Patrick Geddes* (London)

Boston, T. (1720), *Human Nature in its Fourfold State* (Edinburgh)

Boston, T. (1848–52), *The Complete Works*, 12 vols (Aberdeen)

Boston, T. (1852), *Memoirs of the Life, Times and Writings* (Aberdeen)

Brown, D. (1872), *Life of John Duncan, LL.D.* (Edinburgh)

Brown, S. J. (1978), 'The Disruption and Urban Poverty: Thomas Chalmers and the West Port Operation in Edinburgh, 1844–7', in *RSCHS* 20:1, 65–89

Brown, S. J. (1982), *Thomas Chalmers and the Godly Commonwealth in Scotland* (Oxford)

Brown, S. J. (1994), 'The Social Ideal of the Church of Scotland During the 1930s', in Morton (1994), 14–31

Brown, S. J., and M. Fry, eds (1993), *Scotland in the Age of the Disruption* (Edinburgh)

Brown, T. (1893), *Annals of the Disruption*, 2nd edn (Edinburgh)

Bruce, R. (1591), *Sermons Preached in the Kirk of Edinburgh* (Edinburgh)

Brunton, A. (1818), *Sermons and Lectures* (Edinburgh)

Brunton, A. (1822), *Outlines of Persian Grammar* (Edinburgh)

Brunton, A. (1814), *Extracts from the Old Testament. With Outlines of Hebrew, Chaldee and Syriac Grammar* (Edinburgh); 3rd edn 1831

Brunton, A. (1848), *Forms for Public Worship in the Church of Scotland* (Edinburgh)

Buchanan, J. (1849), *A Letter to the Office-bearers and Members of the Free Church of Scotland, on the College Question* (Edinburgh)

Buchanan, J. (1855), *Faith in God and Modern Atheism Compared*, 2 vols (Edinburgh)

Buchanan, J. (1864), *Analogy, Considered as a Guide to Truth* (Edinburgh)

Buchanan, J. (1867), *The Doctrine of Justification* (Cunningham Lectures; Edinburgh)

Buchanan, R. (1852), *The Ten Years' Conflict*, 2 vols (Glasgow)

Burleigh, J. H. S. (1949), *The City of God: A Study of St Augustine's Philosophy* (London)

Burleigh, J. H. S., tr. and ed. (1950), *Augustine: Earlier Writings* (Library of Christian Classics VI; London)

Burleigh, J. H. S. (1960), *A Church History of Scotland* (London)

Burnett, J. H., *et al.*, eds (1986), *The University Portraits, Second Series* (Edinburgh)

Burrell, S. A. (1961), review of Burleigh (1960), in *Church History* 30, 245–6

Cairns, D. S. (1925), *Life and Times of Alexander Robertson MacEwen, D.D.* (London)

Cairns, J. (1881), *Unbelief in the Eighteenth Century* (Edinburgh)

Cameron, D. (1919), *A First Hebrew Reader* (Edinburgh)

Cameron, N. M. de S., organ. ed., D. F. Wright, D. C. Lachman, D. E. Meek, gen. eds (1993), *Dictionary of Scottish History and Theology* (Edinburgh)

Cameron, P. S. (1984), *Violence and the Kingdom: The Interpretation of Matthew 11:12*, 2nd edn (Arbeiten zum Neuen Testament und Judentum, 5: Frankfurt)

Cameron, P. S. (1994), *Heretic* (Sydney)

Campbell, A. V. (1978), *Medicine, Health and Justice: The Problem of Priorities* (Edinburgh)

Campbell, A. V. (1981), *Rediscovering Pastoral Care* (London)

Campbell, A. V. (1984), *Moderated Love: A Theology of Professional Care* (London)

Campbell, J. McLeod (1873A), *Reminiscences and Reflections* (London)

Campbell, J. McLeod (1873B), *Responsibility for the Gift of Eternal Life* (London)

Campbell, J. McLeod (1886), *The Nature of the Atonement*, '6th edn' (London)

Campbell, J. McLeod (1996), *The Nature of the Atonement*, introd. by J. B. Torrance (Edinburgh)

Campbell, W. S. (1991), 'Romans III as a Key to the Structure and Thought of Romans', in K. P. Donfried (ed.), *The Romans Debate*, revd edn (Edinburgh), 251–64

Candlish, R. S. (1849), *College Extension in the Free Church of Scotland*, 2nd edn (Edinburgh)

Chalmers, T. (1833), *On the Power, Wisdom and Goodness of God as Manifested in the Adaptation of External Nature to the Moral and Intellectual Constitution of Man*, 2 vols (London)

[Chalmers, T.] (1847), 'Morrell's Modern Philosophy', *North British Review* VI, 271–331

Chalmers, T. (1849), *Institutes of Theology*, 2 vols (Edinburgh)

Charlesworth, J. H. (1973), *The Odes of Solomon* (Oxford)

Charlesworth, J. H., ed. (1983–5), *The Old Testament Pseudepigrapha*, 2 vols (Garden City, NY)

Charteris, A. H. (1863), *Life of the Revd. James Robertson, D.D.* (Edinburgh)

Charteris, A. H. (1880), *Canonicity: A Collection of Early Testimonies to the Canonical Books of the New Testament based om Kirchhofer's 'Quellensammlung'* (Edinburgh and London)

Charteris, A. H. (1882), *The New Testament Scriptures: Their Claims, History, and Authority* (Croall Lectures; London)

Charteris, A. H. (1897), *The Present State of Biblical Criticism as regards The New Testament. The Introductory Lecture of Session 1896–97* (Edinburgh)

Cheyne, A. C. (1983), *The Transforming of the Kirk: Victorian Scotland's Religious Revolution* (Edinburgh)

Cheyne, A. C. (1985), 'In Memoriam: the Very Revd John Henderson Seaforth Burleigh, M.A., B.D., B.Litt., D.D.', in *RSCHS* 32:2, 101–2

Cheyne, A. C., ed. (1985), *The Practical and the Pious: Essays on Thomas Chalmers (1780–1843)* (Edinburgh)

Cheyne, A. C. (1986), 'Hugh Watt', in Burnett (1986), 206–8

Cheyne, A. C. (1993), *The Ten Years' Conflict and the Disruption: An Overview* (Edinburgh)

Clements, R. E. (1965), *Prophecy and Covenant* (London)

Clements, R. E. (1967), *Abraham and David* (London)

Clements, R. E. (1968A), 'The Meaning of Ritual Acts in Israelite Religion', in *Eucharistic Theology Then and Now* (London), 1–14

Clements, R. E. (1968B), *God's Chosen People* (London)

Collins, G. N. M. (1944), *Donald Maclean D.D.* (Edinburgh)

Collins, G. N. M. (1951), *John Macleod D.D.* (Edinburgh)

Colvin, H. (1978), *A Biographical Dictionary of British Architects 1600–1840* (London)

Crawford, T. J. (1866), *The Fatherhood of God* (Edinburgh)

Crawford, T. J. (1871), *The Doctrine of Holy Scripture Respecting the Atonement* (Edinburgh)

Crosfield, P. (1992), *Coates Hall, A Short History 1892–1992* (Edinburgh)

Cunningham, W. (1848), *Inaugural Lecture, addressed to the Theological Students of the Free Church of Scotland* (Edinburgh)

[Cunningham, W., *et al.*] (1851), *Inauguration of the New College of the Free Church, Edinburgh, November 1850, with Introductory Lectures on Theology, Philosophy, and Natural Science* (London)

Cunningham, W. (1862A), *Historical Theology*, 2 vols (Edinburgh)

Cunningham, W. (1862B), *The Reformers and the Theology of the Reformation* (Edinburgh)

Cunningham, W. (1878), *Theological Lectures* (London)

Curtis, W. A. (1940), *Qui vos audit, me audit (Luc. X.xvi): A Farewell Address on March 15, 1940, in the Martin Hall, New College, Edinburgh, before Communion, at the close of the Winter Session* (Edinburgh)

Curtis, W. A. (1943), *Jesus Christ the Teacher: A Study of His Method and Message Based Mainly on the Earlier Gospels* (London)

Darlow, T. H. (1925), *William Robertson Nicoll. Life and Letters* (London)

Davidson, A. B. (1861), *Outline of Hebrew Accentuation* (London)

Davidson, A. B. (1862), *A Commentary, Grammatical and Exegetical, on the Book of Job* (London)

Davidson, A. B. (1874), *An Introductory Hebrew Grammar* (Edinburgh)

Davidson, A. B. (1894), *Hebrew Syntax* (Edinburgh)

Davidson, A. B. (1902), *The Called of God* (Edinburgh)

Davidson, A. B. (1903), *Old Testament Prophecy*, ed. J. A. Paterson (Edinburgh)

Davidson, A. B. (1904), *The Theology of the Old Testament,* ed. S. D. F. Salmond (Edinburgh)

Davidson, A. B. (1993), *Introductory Hebrew Grammar*, 27th edn, revd J. D. Martin (Edinburgh)

Davidson, A. B. (1994), *Introductory Hebrew Grammar: Syntax*, 4th edn, revd J. C. L. Gibson (Edinburgh)

Davidson, F., ed. (1954), *The New Bible Commentary*, 2nd edn (London)

Davidson, R. (1973), *Genesis 1–11* (Cambridge Bible Commentaries; Cambridge)

Davie, G. (1961), *The Democratic Intellect; Scotland and her Universities in the Nineteenth Century* (Edinburgh)

Dempster, J. A. H. (1992), *The T & T Clark Story* (Bishop Auckland)

Dickson, D. and J. Durham (1886), *The Sum of Saving Knowledge*, ed. J. Macpherson (Edinburgh)

Dobie, J. (1895), [A Collation of Ethiopic MS. 50 in Paris, Bibl. Nat., of IV Esdras] (Leipzig)

Dobschütz, E. von (1910), *The Eschatology of the Gospels* (London)

Dods, M. (d. 1838) (1828), *Remarks on the Bible, in a Letter to the Corresponding Board* (Edinburgh)

Dods, M. (1877), *Revelation and Inspiration: the Historical Books of Scripture. A Sermon*, 3rd edn (Glasgow)

Dods, M. (1883), *Christ's Sacrifice and Ours* (Edinburgh)

Dods, M. (1888), *An Introduction to the New Testament* (Theological Educator; London)

Dods, M. (1889A), *Recent Progress in Theology* (Inaugural Lecture; Edinburgh)

Dods, M. (1889B), *Genesis* (Expositor's Bible; London)

Dods, M. (1889C), *The First Epistle to the Corinthians* (Expositor's Bible; London)

Dods, M. (1891), *The Gospel of John*, 2 vols (Expositor's Bible; London)

Dods, M. (1894), 'The Trustworthiness of the Gospels', in Rainy (1894), 71–111

Dods, M. (1897), *The Gospel according to John*, in *Expositor's Greek Testament* I (London)

Dods, M. (1904), 'Did Christ rise from the Dead?', in *Questions of Faith: A Series of Lectures on the Creed*, ed. P. Carnegie Simpson (London), 75–102

Dods, M. (1910), *The Epistle to the Hebrews*, in *Expositor's Greek Testament* IV (London)

Dods, M. (d. 1935), ed. (1910), *Early Letters of Marcus Dods (1850–1864)* (London)

Dowden, J. (1912), *The Bishops of Scotland* (Glasgow)

Dowden, J. (1922), *The Scottish Commission Office 1764*, ed. H. A. Wilson (Oxford)

Drummond, A. L. and J. Bulloch (1975), *The Church in Victorian Scotland 1843–1874* (Edinburgh)

Duff, A. (1840), *India and India Mission*, 2nd edn (Edinburgh)

Duke, J. A. (1932), *The Columban Church* (Edinburgh)

Duncan, J. (1851), 'The Theology of the Old Testament', in *Cunningham* (1851), 121–42

Dunlop, A. (1846), 'Memoir of Dr. Welsh', in *Sermons by the late Revd. David Welsh, D.D.* (Edinburgh)

Dunlop, A. I. (1988), *The Kirks of Edinburgh* (Scottish Record Soc. n.s. 15–16; Edinburgh)

Duns, J. (1859), 'Memoir' of John Fleming, in Fleming, *The Lithology of Edinburgh* (Edinburgh), i–civ

Duthie, C. S. (1955), *God in His World* (London)

Duthie, C. S. (1968), *Outline of Christian Belief* (London)

Edwards, S. J., Jr. (1960), 'Marcus Dods: with Special Reference to his Teaching Ministry' (Ph.D., University of Edinburgh)

Elliott, J. K. and I. A. Moir (1995), *Manuscripts and the Text of the New Testament: An Introduction for English Readers* (Edinburgh)

Ellis, E. E. (1957), *Paul's Use of the Old Testament* (Edinburgh)

Elwell, W. A. (1970), 'Aspects of the Quest of the Historical Jesus in the Works of William Manson and James M. Robinson' (Ph.D., University of Edinburgh)

Escott, H. (1960), *A History of Scottish Congregationalism* (Glasgow)

Fergusson, D. (1992), *Bultmann* (London)

Fergusson, D., ed. (1993A), *Christ, Church and Society: Essays on John Baillie and Donald Baillie* (Edinburgh)

Fergusson, D. (1993B), 'John Baillie: Orthodox Liberal', in Fergusson (1993A), 123–53

Finlayson, R. A. (1955), *The Cross in the Experience of our Lord* (London)

Finlayson, R. A. (1959), 'Contemporary Ideas of Inspiration', in C. F. H. Henry (ed.), *Revelation and the Bible* (London), 219–34

Fisher, E. (1645), *Marrow of Modern Divinity* (London)

Flint, R. (1877), *Theism* (Edinburgh)

Flint, R. (1893), *History of the Philosophy of History* (Edinburgh)

Flint, R. (1894), *Socialism* (London)

Forbes, J. (1645), *Instructiones Historico-Theologicae de Doctrina Christiana* (Amsterdam)

Forrester, D. B. (1980), 'Divinity in Use and Practice', in *SJT* 33, 1–11

Forrester, D. B. (1985), *Christianity and the Future of Welfare* (London)

Forrester, D. B. (1988), *Theology and Politics* (Oxford)

Forrester, D. B. (1991), 'Priorities for Social Theology Today', in Northcott (1991), 26–34

Forrester, D. B. (1993A), 'God's Will in a Time of Crisis', in Fergusson (1993A), 221–33

Forrester, D. B. (1993B), 'The Church of Scotland and Public Policy', in *Scottish Affairs* 4, 67–82

Forrester, D. B. and D. Skene, eds (1988), *Just Sharing: A Christian Approach to the Distribution of Wealth, Income and Benefits* (London)

Fraser, A. Campbell (1905), *Biographia Philosophica*, 2nd edn (Edinburgh)

Fraser, J. (1721), *Meditations on Several Subjects in Divinity* (Edinburgh)

Fraser, J. (1749), *A Treatise on Justifying Faith* (Edinburgh)

Garland, D., ed. (1990), *Justice, Guilt and Forgiveness in the Penal System* (CTPI Occasional Paper 18; Edinburgh)

Gibson, J. (1850), *Extension of Divinity Halls* (Glasgow)

Gibson, J. C. L. (1971–82), *Textbook of Syrian Semitic Inscriptions*, 3 vols (Oxford)

Gibson, J. C. L. (1978), *Canaanite Myths and Legends*, 2nd edn (Edinburgh)

Gibson, J. C. L. (1981–2), *Genesis*, 2 vols (Daily Study Bible; Edinburgh)

Gibson, J. C. L. (1985), *Job* (Daily Study Bible; Edinburgh)

Gibson, J. C. L., ed. (1981–6), *Daily Study Bible: Old Testament*, 24 vols (Edinburgh)

Gibson, J. C. L. (1994), see Davidson, A. B. (1994)

Gifford, J., *et al.* (1984), *Edinburgh* (Buildings of Scotland; Harmondsworth)

Gill, R. (1975), *The Social Context of Theology. A Methodological Enquiry* (London)

Gill, R. (1977), *Theology and Social Structure* (London)

Gill, R. (1981), *Prophecy and Praxis: The Social Function of the Churches* (London)

Goddard, H. L. (1953), 'The Contribution of George Smeaton 1814–1889 to Theological Thought' (Ph.D., University if Edinburgh)

Goertz, H.-J. (1993), *Thomas Müntzer: Apocalyptic, Mystic and Revolutionary*, Eng. tr. ed. P. C. Matheson (Edinburgh)

Goldie, F. (1976), *A Short History of the Episcopal Church*, 2nd edn (Edinburgh)

Goold, W. H., ed. (1850–5), *Works of John Owen*, 24 vols (Edinburgh)

Gordon, A. (1912), *The Life of Archibald Hamilton Charteris* (London)

Gordon, M. M. (1869), *The Home Life of Sir David Brewster* (Edinburgh)

Gow, I. (1984), 'William Playfair' in N. Allen (ed.), *Scottish Pioneers of the Greek Revival* (Edinburgh), 43–55

Gowan, A. L. (1890), *The City of the Lord* (London)

Grant, A. (1884), *The Story of the University of Edinburgh During its First Three Hundred Years*, 2 vols (London)

Gray, A. (1850), *The College Question* (Perth)

Gunn, G. S. (1964), *This Gospel of the Kingdom: Dilemmas in Evangelism*, ed. N. W. Porteous (London)

Hanna, W. (1849–52), *Memoirs of Dr Chalmers*, 4 vols (Edinburgh)

Hayman, A. P. (1973), *The Disputation of Sergius the Stylite against a Jew* (Louvain)

Hayman, A. P. (1991), 'Numbers' in *The Old Testament in Syriac according to the Peshitta Version*, I/2 (Leiden)

Hazlett, W. I. P., ed. (1993), *Traditions of Theology in Glasgow 1450–1990* (Edinburgh)

Henderson, G. D., ed. (1937), *The Scots Confession, 1560* (Edinburgh)

Hendry, G. S. (1960), *The Westminster Confession for Today* (London)

Heppe, H. (1950), *Reformed Dogmatics*, tr. G. T. Thomson (London)

Heron, A. (1977), *Two Churches – One Love: Interchurch Marriage between Protestant and Roman Catholic* (Dublin)

Heron, A. (1980), *A Century of Protestant Theology* (Guildford)

Heron, A., ed. (1982), *The Westminster Confession in the Church Today* (Edinburgh)

Heron, A. (1983), *Table and Tradition: Towards an Ecumenical Understanding of the Eucharist* (Edinburgh)

Hewart, E. G. K. (1960), *Vision and Achievement, 1796–1956* (London)

Hilton, B. (1988), *The Age of Atonement: The Influence of Evangelicalism on Social and Economic Thought, 1785–1865* (Oxford)

Innes, A. T. (1902), 'Biographical Introduction' in Davidson, A. B. (1902), 1–58

[Jolly, J.] (1880), *Memorials of the Rev. William Tasker* (Edinburgh)

Kee, A. (1982), *Constantine versus Christ* (London)

Kee, A. (1990), *Marx and the Failure of Liberation Theology* (London)

Kee, A. (1991), *From Bad Faith to Good News: Reflections on Good Friday and Easter* (London)

Kennedy, A. R. S. (1901A), *Leviticus and Numbers* (Century Bible; Edinburgh)

Kennedy, A. R. S. (1901B), *The Second Book of Moses called Exodus* (Temple Bible; London)

Kennedy, A. R. S. (1902), *The Book of Joshua and the Book of Judges* (Temple Bible; London)

Kennedy, A. R. S. (1905), *Samuel* (Century Bible; Edinburgh)

Kennedy, A. R. S. (1928), *The Book of Ruth* (London)

Kennedy, H. A. A. (1895), *Sources of New Testament Greek, or the Influence of the Septuagint on the Vocabulary of the New Testament* (Edinburgh)

Kennedy, H. A. A. (1904), *St Paul's Conceptions of the Last Things* (London)

Kennedy, H. A. A. (1913), *St Paul and the Mystery-Religions* (London)

Kennedy, H. A. A. (1919A), *Philo's Contribution to Religion* (London)

Kennedy, H. A. A. (1919B), *The Theology of the Epistles* (Duckworth's Studies in Theology; London)

Kennedy H. A. A. (1920), *Vital Forces of the Early Church* (London)

Kennedy, J. (1889), *Introduction to Biblical Hebrew* (London)

Kennedy, J. (1898), *Studies in Hebrew Synonyms* (London)

Kerr, F. (1986), *Theology after Wittgenstein* (Oxford)

Kerr, F., ed. with David Nicholls (1991), *John Henry Newman: Reason, Rhetoric and Romanticism* (Bristol)

Kinnear, M. A. (1996), 'Scottish New Testament Scholarship and the Atonement c.1845–1920' (Ph.D., University of Edinburgh)

Knight, W. (1903), *Some Nineteenth-Century Scotsmen; being Personal Recollections* (Edinburgh)

Knox, J. (1846–64), *Works*, ed. D. Laing, 6 vols (Edinburgh)

Laidlaw, J., ed. (1901), *Robert Bruce's Sermons on the Sacrament* (Edinburgh)

Lamb, J. A., ed. (1956), *The Fasti of the United Free Church of Scotland* (Edinburgh)

Lamb, J. A. (1962), *The Psalms in Christian Worship* (London)

Lamont, D. (1934), *Christ and the World of Thought* (Edinburgh)

Lamont, D. (1943), *The Restoration of the Soul* (London)

Landreth, P. (1876), *The United Presbyterian Divinity Hall* (Edinburgh)

Lee, R. (1843), *The Querist. Not Bishop Berkeley* (Glasgow)

Lee, R. (1851), *Thou art Peter: A Discourse on Papal Infallibility and the Causes of the Late Conversions to Romanism* (Edinburgh)

Lee, R. (1857), *What Christianity Teaches respecting The Body* (Edinburgh)

Lee, R. (1863), *A Presbyterian Prayer-Book* (Edinburgh)

Lefébure, M., ed. (1982), *Conversations on Counselling between a Doctor and a Priest: Dialogue and Trinity* (Edinburgh)

Lewis A. E. (1986), 'The Authority and Artistry of Alec Cheyne', in *NCN* 2, 3

Lewis, A. E. (1987), 'The Burial of God: Rupture and Resumption as the Story of Salvation', in *SJT* 40, 335–62

Lewis, A. E. (forthcoming), *Easter Saturday*

Longenecker, R. N. (1964), *Paul, Apostle of Liberty* (New York)

Luscombe, Edward (1994), *A Seminary of Learning. Edinburgh Theological College 1810–1994* (Edinburgh)

MacCormack, B. (1995), *Karl Barth's Critically Realistic Dialectical Theology: Its Genesis and Development, 1909–1936* (Oxford)

McDonald, J. I. H. (1980), *Kerygma and Didache: The Articulation and Structure of the Earliest Christian Message* (SNTS Monograph Series; Cambridge)

McDonald, J. I. H. (1989), *The Resurrection: Narrative and Belief* (London)

McDonald, J. I. H. (1993), *Biblical Interpretation and Christian Ethics* (Cambridge)

McDonald, J. I. H. (1995), *Christian Values: Theory and Practice in Christian Ethics Today* (Edinburgh)

McDonald, L. M. (1988), *The Formation of the Christian Biblical Canon* (Nashville, TN)

MacEwen, A. R. (1877), 'Memoir' [of father], in *Sermons, by Alexander MacEwen, M.A., D.D.* (Glasgow), ix–lvi

MacEwen, A. R. (1895), *Life and Letters of John Cairns* (London)

MacEwen, A. R. (1900), *The Erskines* (Famous Scots; Edinburgh)

MacEwen, A. R. (1909), *Antoinette Bourignon, Quietist* (London)

MacEwen, A. R. (1913–18), *History of the Church of Scotland*, 2 vols (London)

MacEwen, J. S. (1961), *The Faith of John Knox* (London)

McIntyre, J. (1954), *St Anselm and his Critics* (Edinburgh)

McIntyre, J. (1962), *On the Love of God* (London)

McIntyre, J. (1966), *The Shape of Christology* (London)

McIntyre, J. (1979), 'Thomas Forsyth Torrance', in *NCB* 10, 1–2

McIntyre, J. (1987), *Faith, Theology and Imagination* (Edinburgh)

McIntyre, J. (1992), *The Shape of Soteriology: Studies in the Doctrine of the Death of Christ* (Edinburgh)

Mackay, J. R. (1910), 'The Promise and Vow, Taken by Members of the Westminster Assembly', in *Princeton Theological Review* 8, 389–400

Mackay, J. R. (1911), *The Inquisition: the Reformation: the Counter-Reformation* (Inverness)

Mackay, J. R. (1913), 'Conscience and the Atonement', in *Princeton Theological Review* 11, 603–29

Mackay, J. R. (1914), *Armageddon: Two Discourses on the Great European War* (Inverness)

Mackay, J. R. (1931A), 'Positive Reasons for Believing that the Bible is the Word of God', in *Evangelical Quarterly* 3, 17–32

Mackay, J. R. (1931B), 'Isaiah lii 13 – liii 12; An Analysis', in *Evangelical Quarterly* 3, 307–11

Mackey, J. P. (1962), *The Modern Theology of Tradition* (London)

Mackey, J. P. (1979), *Jesus the Man and the Myth* (London)

Mackey, J. P. (1983), *The Christian Experience of God as Trinity* (London)

Mackey, J. P., ed. (1986), *Religious Imagination* [to mark the Retirement of Professor John McIntyre] (Edinburgh)

Mackey, J. P. (1987), *Modern Theology* (Oxford)

Mackey, J. P., ed. (1989), *An Introduction to Celtic Christianity* (Edinburgh)

Mackey, J. P. (1994), *Power and Christian Ethics* (Cambridge)

Mackinnon, J. (1920), *The Social and Industrial History of Scotland from the Earliest Times to the Union* (London)

Mackinnon, J. (1921), *The Social and Industrial History of Scotland from the Union to the Present Time* (London)

Mackinnon, J. (1925–30), *Luther and the Reformation*, 4 vols (London)

Mackinnon, J. (1931), *The Historic Jesus* (London)

Mackinnon, J. (1933), *The Gospel in the Early Church* (London)

Mackinnon, J. (1936A), *Calvin and the Reformation* (London)

Mackinnon, J. (1936B), *From Christ to Constantine* (London)

Mackinnon, J. (1939), *The Origins of the Reformation* (London)

Mackinnon, J. (1906–41), *A History of Modern Liberty*, 4 vols (London)

Mackintosh, H. R. (1907), 'Memoir' [of John Laidlaw] in Laidlaw, *Studies in the Parables* (Edinburgh), 1–47

Mackintosh, H. R. (1912), *The Doctrine of the Person of Jesus Christ* (Edinburgh)

Mackintosh, H. R. (1921), *The Divine Initiative* (London)

Mackintosh, H. R. (1929), *The Christian Apprehension of God* (London)

Mackintosh, H. R. (1937), *Types of Modern Theology* (London)

McLaren, K. D. (1914), *Memoir of the Very Reverend Professor Charteris D.D., LL.D.* (London and Edinburgh)

Maclean, A. J. (1910), *The Ancient Church Orders* (Cambridge)

Maclean, D. (1931) *The Counter-Reformation in Scotland, 1560–1930* (London)

MacLeod, D. (1993), 'Thomas Chalmers and Pauperism', in Brown and Fry, eds (1993), 63–76

MacLeod, J. (1943), *Scottish Theology* (Edinburgh)

MacLeod, N. (1854), *The Earnest Student; Being the Memorials of John Mackintosh* (Edinburgh)

MacMillan, K. and P., eds (1988), 'Reminiscences of the Revd Alexander Ross, 1830–1919', unpublished typescript, New College Library, Edinburgh.

McNaughton, W. D. (1993), *The Scottish Congregational Ministry from 1794 to 1993* (Glasgow)

McPherson, A., ed. (1974), *History of the Free Presbyterian Church of Scotland 1893–1970* (Inverness)

Manson, W. (1918), *Christ's View of the Kingdom of God. A Study in Jewish Apocalyptic and in the Mind of Jesus Christ* (Bruce Lectures, London)

Manson, W. (1923), *The Incarnate Glory* (London)

Manson, W. (1930), *The Gospel of Luke* (Moffatt New Testament Commentary; London)

Manson, W. (1943), *Jesus the Messiah: The Synoptic Tradition of the Revelation of God in Christ: with special reference to Form-Criticism* (Cunningham Lectures, London)

Manson, W. (1951), *The Epistle to the Hebrews: An Historical and Theological Reconsideration* (Baird Lectures, London)

Manson, W. (1967), *Jesus and the Christian*, ed. Thomas F. Torrance (London)

Marx, K. (1965), *Capital* (Moscow)

Matheson, P. C. (1972), *Cardinal Contarini at Regensburg* (Oxford)

Matheson, P. C. (1981), *The Third Reich and the Christian Churches* (Edinburgh)

Matheson, P. C., tr. and ed. (1988), *The Collected Works of Thomas Müntzer* (Edinburgh)

Matheson, P. C. (1993), *The Finger of God in the Disruption: Scottish Principles and New Zealand Realities* (Alexandra, NZ)

Matheson, P. C. (1994), *Argula von Grumbach: A Woman's Voice in the Reformation* (Edinburgh)

Mealand, D. L. (1980), *Poverty and Expectation in the Gospels* (London)

Mechie, S. (1956), *Trinity College, Glasgow, 1856–1956* (Glasgow)

Mechie, S. (1960–2), 'Education for the Ministry in Scotland since the Reformation, I, II' in *RSCHS* 14, 115–33, 161–78

Mechie, S. (1963–5), 'Education for the Ministry in Scotland since the Reformation, III' in *RSCHS* 15, 1–20

Miller, G. T. (1990), *Piety and Intellect: the Aims and Purposes of Ante-Bellum Theological Education* (Atlanta)

Mitchell, A. F. (1886), *Catechisms of the Second Reformation* (London)

Mitchell, A. (1907), *A Short History of the Church in Scotland* (London)

Mitchell, A. (1914), *Biographical Studies in Scottish Church History* (Milwaukee)

Moir, I. A. (1956), *'Codex Climaci rescriptus graecus': A Study of Portions of the Greek New Testament comprising the Underwriting of Part of a Palimpsest in the Library of Westminster College, Cambridge (MS. Gregory 1561, L)* (Texts and Studies, n.s.II; Cambridge)

Moir, I. A. (1995), see Elliott, J. K., and I. A. Moir (1995)

Morgan, R. *et al.* (1992), *Penal Policy: The Way Forward* (CTPI Occasional Paper 27; Edinburgh)

Morton, A. R., ed. (1994), *God's Will in a Time of Crisis: A Colloquium Celebrating the 50th Anniversary of the Baillie Commission* (CTPI Occasional Paper 31; Edinburgh)

Murray, I. H., ed. (1980), *Diary of Kenneth A. MacRae* (Edinburgh)

Myklebust, O. G. (1955–7), *The Study of Missions in Theological Education,* 2 vols (Oslo)

Needham, N. R. (1991), *The Doctrine of Holy Scripture in the Free Church Fathers* (Edinburgh)

Newlands, G. (1980), *The Theology of the Love of God* (London)

Nicol, H. S. (1930), *David Bruce Nicol: A Memoir* (Aberdeen)

Nicoll, W. R. (1921), *Princes of the Church* (London)

Northcott, M. S., ed. (1991), *Vision and Prophecy: The Tasks of Social Theology Today* (CTPI Occasional Paper 23; Edinburgh)

O'Donoghue, N. (1979), *Heaven in Ordinarie* (Edinburgh)

O'Donoghue, N. (1981), *Something Understood: Reflections on the Future of Academic Theology* (Edinburgh)

O'Donoghue, N. (1983), *The Holy Mountain: Approaches to the Mystery of Prayer* (Dublin)

O'Donoghue, N. (1987), *Aristocracy of the Soul: Patrick of Ireland* (Wilmington, DL)

O'Neill, J. C. (1980), *Messiah: Six Lectures on the Ministry of Jesus* (Cunningham Lectures; Cambridge)

O'Neill, J. C. (1987–8), 'A Sketch Map of the New Testament' (Inaugural Lecture), *Expository Times* 99, 199–205

O'Neill, J. C. (1995), *Who Did Jesus Think He Was?* (Leiden)

Orr, J. (1893), *The Christian View of God and the World* (Edinburgh)

Orr, J. (1897A), *The Ritschlian Theology and the Evangelical Faith* (London)

Orr, J. (1897B), *The Christian View of God and the World* (Edinburgh)

Page, R. (1985), *Ambiguity and the Presence of God* (London)

Page, R. (1991), *The Incarnation of Freedom and Love* (London)

Page, R., et al. (1991), *The Animal Kingdom and the Kingdom of God* (CTPI Occasional Paper 26; Edinburgh)

Paterson, W. P. (1912), *The Rule of Faith* (London)

Paterson, W. P., ed. (1915), *German Culture: The Contribution of the Germans to Knowledge, Literature, Art and Life* (London)

Paterson, W. P. and D. Watson, eds (1918), *Social Evils and Problems* (Church of Scotland Commission on the War; Edinburgh)

Paton, W. (1923), *Alexander Duff: Pioneer of Missionary Education* (London)

Patrick, J. (1898), *The Conservative Reaction in New Testament Criticism* (Edinburgh)

Pfleiderer, O. (1894), *Philosophy and Development of Religion: being The Gifford Lectures delivered before the University of Edinburgh 1894*, 2 vols (Edinburgh and London)

Pinkerton, R. M. and William J. Windram (1983), *Mylne's Court. Three Hundred Years of Lawnmarket Heritage* (Edinburgh)

Porteous, N. W. (1952), see Welch, A. C. (1952)

Porteous, N. W. (1964A), 'Theology in Church and University', in *NCB* 1:2, 9–17

Porteous, N. W. (1964B), see Gunn, G. S. (1964)

Porteous, N. W. (1965), *Daniel* (Old Testament Library, London); 2nd edn 1979

Porteous, N. W. (1967), *Living the Mystery* (Oxford)

Provan, I. (1988), *Hezekiah and the Book of Kings: A Contribution to the Debate about the Composition of the Deuteronomistic History* (Berlin)

Provan, I. (1991), *Lamentations* (New Century Bible Commentary; London)

Provan, I. (1995), *1 and 2 Kings* (New International Bible Commentary; Peabody, MA)

Rad, G. von (1953), *Studies in Deuteronomy*, tr. D. G. M. Stalker (London)

Rad, G. von (1962–5), *Old Testament Theology*, 2 vols, tr. D. G. M. Stalker (Edinburgh)

Rainy, R. and J. Mackenzie (1871), *Life of William Cunningham* (London)

Rainy, R. (1872), *Three Lectures on the Church of Scotland* (Edinburgh)

Rainy, R., et al. (1894), *The Supernatural in Christianity, with Special Reference to Statements in the recent Gifford Lectures* [=Pfleiderer (1894)] (Edinburgh)

Rainy, R. (1902), *The Ancient Catholic Church* (Edinburgh)

Rankin, O. S. (1936), *Israel's Wisdom Literature* (Kerr Lectures; Edinburgh)

Rankin, O. S. (1956), *Jewish Religious Polemic of Early and Later Centuries* (Edinburgh)

Rawlins, C. L., ed. (1987), *The Diaries of William Paterson Paterson* (Edinburgh)

Reid, H. M. B. (1904), *A Scottish School of Theology* (Inaugural Lecture; Glasgow)

Reid, J. K. S., tr. and ed. (1964), *Concerning the Eternal Predestination of God*, by John Calvin (London)

Rice, D. T. and P. McIntyre (1957), *The University Portraits* (Edinburgh)

Riesen, R. A. (1979), '"Higher Criticism" in the Free Church Fathers', in *RSCHS* 20:2, 119–42.

Roberts, J. D. (1974), *A Black Political Theology* (Philadelphia)

Rollock, R. (1844–9), *Select Works*, ed. W. M. Gunn, 2 vols (Edinburgh)

Ross, A., with John Durkan (1961), *Early Scottish Libraries* (Glasgow)

Ross, A. C. (1986), *John Philip (1755–1851): Missions, Race and Politics in South Africa* (Aberdeen)

Ross, A. C. (1944), *A Vision Betrayed: The Jesuits in Japan and China, 1542–1742* (Edinburgh)

Rupp, G. (1953), *The Righteousness of God: Luther Studies* (London)

Rutherford, S. (1655), *The Covenant of Life Opened* (Edinburgh)

Rutherford, S. (1863), *Letters*, 2 vols, ed. A. A. Bonar (Edinburgh)

Rutherford, S. (1877), *Fourteen Communion Sermons*, ed. A. A. Bonar (Glasgow)

Saint Quintin, G. (1956), *The History of Glenalmond* (Edinburgh)

Schleiermacher, F. (1928), *The Christian Faith*, Eng. tr. ed. H. R. Mackintosh and J. S. Stewart (Edinburgh)

Scorgie, G. (1989), *A Call for Continuity: The Theological Contribution of James Orr* (Macon, GA)

Scott, C. A. A. (1932), *Christianity according to St Paul* (Cambridge)

[Seeley, J. R.] (1865), *Ecce Homo* (London)

Sell, A. P. F. (1987), *Defending and Declaring the Faith. Some Scottish Examples, 1860–1920* (Exeter)

Shaw, D., ed. (1967), *Reformation and Revolution: Essays Presented to the Very Revd. Principal Emeritus Hugh Watt, D.D., D.Litt. on the 60th. Anniversary of his Ordination* (Edinburgh)

Shaw, D. W. D. (1968), *Who is God?* (London)

Shaw, D. W. D. (1978), *The Dissuaders: Three Explanations of Religion* (London)

Shaw, D. W. D. (1988), 'Theology in the University – a Contemporary Scottish Perspective', in *SJT* 41, 217–31

Simpson, M. C. T. (1990), *A Catalogue of the Library of the Revd James Nairn* (Edinburgh)

Simpson, P. C. (1909), *The Life of Principal Rainy*, 2 vols (London)

Skinner, J. (1922), *Prophecy and Religion* (Cambridge)

Small, A. H., *et al.* (1944), *Women's Missionary College, St. Colm's Edinburgh. Memories of Fifty Years 1894–1944* (Edinburgh)

Small, R. L. (1967), 'An Appreciation [of Hugh Watt]', in Shaw, D. (1967), 11–16

Smeaton, G. (1853), *The Necessary Harmony between Doctrine and Spiritual Life; being An Introductory Lecture, delivered on the 9th November, 1853, to the Free Church Students attending the Divinity Hall at Aberdeen* (Aberdeen)

Smeaton, G. (1854), *The Basis of Christian Doctrine in Divine Fact, with Particular Reference to the Modern Realistic Development of Theology: being An Introductory Lecture, delivered at the Opening of the Free Church Divinity Hall, Aberdeen, on Tuesday, 7th November, 1854* (Aberdeen)

Smeaton, G. (1868), *The Doctrine of the Atonement, as Taught by Christ Himself; or, The Sayings of Jesus on the Atonement Exegetically Expounded and Classified* (Edinburgh)

Smeaton, G. (1870), *The Doctrine of the Atonement, as Taught by the Apostles; or, The Sayings of the Apostles Exegetically Expounded. With Historical Appendix* (Edinburgh)

Smeaton, G. (1889), *The Doctrine of the Holy Spirit*, 2nd edn (Cunningham Lectures; Edinburgh)

Smith, D. C. (1987), *Passive Obedience and Prophetic Protest: Social Criticism in the Scottish Church 1830–1945* (New York)

Smith, J. C. and W. Wallace, eds (1903), *Robert Wallace; Life and Last Leaves* (London)

Smout, T. C. (1986), *A Century of the Scottish People* (London)

Stalker, D. M. G. (1953, 1962–5), see Rad, G. von

Stalker, D. M. G. (1968), *Ezekiel* (Torch Bible Commentary; London)

Stevenson, W. (1874), *The Legends and Commemorative Celebrations of St. Kentigern, his Friends and Disciples* (Edinburgh)

Stewart, A. and J. K. Cameron (1910), *The Free Church of Scotland 1843–1910* (Edinburgh)

Stewart, J. S. (1933), *The Life and Teaching of Jesus Christ* (Bible Class Handbook, Edinburgh)

Stewart, J. S. (1935), *A Man in Christ: The Vital Elements of St Paul's Religion* (Cunningham Lectures; London)

Stewart, J. S. (1946), *Heralds of God* (Warrack Lectures; London)

Stewart, J. S. (1956), *Thine is the Kingdom* (Duff Missionary Lectures; London)

Stewart, M. (1972), *Training in Mission – St Colm's College* (Edinburgh)

Story, R. H. (1870), *Life and Remains of Robert Lee, D.D., F.R.S.E.: Professor of Biblical Criticism and Antiquities in the University of Edinburgh*, 2 vols (London)

The Story of the Scottish Congregational Theological Hall 1811–1911 (Edinburgh, 1911)

Templeton, D. A. (1988), *Re-exploring Paul's Imagination: A Cynical Laywoman's Guide to Paul of Tarsus* (Eilsbrunn)

Templeton, E. (1991), *God's February; a Life of Archie Craig* (London)

Templeton, E. (1993), *The Strangeness of God* (London)

Torrance, D. W. and T. F. Torrance, eds (1959–72), *Calvin's New Testament Commentaries*, 12 vols (Edinburgh)

Torrance, I. R. (1990), 'A Bibliography of the Writings of Thomas F. Torrance 1941–1989', in *SJT* 43, 225–62

Torrance, J. B. and R. Walls (1992), *John Duns Scotus: Doctor of the Church* (Edinburgh)

Torrance, J. B. (1995), Introduction to Campbell (1996)

Torrance, T. F. (1948), *The Doctrine of Grace in the Apostolic Fathers* (Edinburgh)

Torrance, T. F. (1952), *Calvin's Doctrine of Man* (London)

Torrance, T. F. (1956), *Kingdom and Church: A Study in the Theology of the Reformation* (Edinburgh)

Torrance, T. F., ed. (1958A), *Calvin's Tracts*, tr. H. Beveridge, 3 vols (London)

Torrance, T. F., tr. and ed. (1958B), *The Mystery of the Lord's Supper* by Robert Bruce (London)

Torrance, T. F. (1959), *The School of Faith* (London)

Torrance, T. F. (1959–60), *Conflict and Agreement in the Church*, 2 vols (London)

Torrance, T. F. (1965), *Theology in Reconstruction* (London)

Torrance, T. F. (1969), *Theological Science* (London)

Torrance, T. F. (1988), *The Hermeneutics of John Calvin* (London)

Tracy, D. (1983), 'The Foundations of Practical Theology', in D. Browning (ed.), *Practical Theology: The Emerging Field in Theology, Church and World* (San Francisco), 61–82.

Troeltsch, E. (1931), *The Social Teaching of the Christian Churches*, 2 vols (London)

Turner, A. L., ed. (1933), *History of the University of Edinburgh 1883–1933* (Edinburgh)

Vanhoozer, K. (1990), *Biblical Narrative in the Philosophy of Paul Ricoeur: A Study in Hermeneutics and Theology* (Cambridge)

Walker, J. (1872), *The Theology and Theologians of Scotland* (Edinburgh)

Wallace, R. (1899), *George Buchanan* (Famous Scots; Edinburgh)

Warfield, B. B. (1893), *An Introduction to the Textual Criticism of the New Testament* (London)

Waterman, A. M. C. (1991), *Revolution, Economics and Religion: Christian Political Economy 1798–1833* (Cambridge)

Watt, H. (1927), *Representative Churchmen of Twenty Centuries* (London)

Watt, H. (1943A), *Published Writings of Thomas Chalmers: A Descriptive List* (Edinburgh)

Watt, H. (1943B), *Thomas Chalmers and the Disruption* (Edinburgh)

Watt, H. (1946A), *New College, Edinburgh: A Centenary History* (Edinburgh)

Watt, H. (1946B), *Recalling the Scottish Covenants* (London)

Watt, H. (1950), *John Knox in Controversy* (London)

Weir, G. A. (1969), 'Tatian's Diatessaron and the Old Syriac Gospel: the Evidence of the MS Chester Beatty 709' (Ph.D., University of Edinburgh)

Welch, A. C. (1901), *Anselm and His Work* (Edinburgh)

Welch, A. C. (1912), *The Religion of Israel under the Kingdom* (Kerr Lectures; Edinburgh)

Welch, A. C. (1913), *The Story of Joseph* (Edinburgh)

Welch, A. C. (1939), *The Work of the Chronicler* (Schweich Lectures; London)

Welch, A. C. (1952), *Kings and Prophets of Israel*, ed. N. W. Porteous, with memoir by G. S. Gunn (London)

Welsh, D. (1825), *Account of the Life and Writings of J. Brown, M.D.* (Edinburgh)

Welsh, D. (1844), *Elements of Church History*, I: *Comprising the External History of the Church during the First Three Centuries* (Edinburgh)

Whaling, F. (1986), *Christian Theology and World Religions: A Global Approach* (Basingstoke)

Whyte, A. (1909), *Former Principals of the New College, Edinburgh* (Inaugural Address; London)

Wilcox, M. (1965), *The Semitisms of Acts* (Oxford)

Wilson, W. and R. Rainy (1880), *Memorials of Robert Smith Candlish, D.D.* (Edinburgh)

Wood, C. (1991), *The End of Punishment: Christian Perspectives on the Crisis in Criminal Justice* (Edinburgh)

Wood, J. D. (1958), *The Interpretation of the Bible: A Historical Introduction* (London)

Wood, J. D. (1963), *The Sermon on the Mount and its Application* (London)

Wood, J. D. (1966), *Job and the Human Situation* (London)

Wright, D. F., tr. and ed. (1972), *Common Places of Martin Bucer* (Appleford)

Wright, D. F. (1983), 'Ecclesiastical History', in *NCB* 14, 25–6

Wright, D. F., assisted by I. M. Campbell and J. C. L. Gibson, eds (1988), *The Bible in Scottish Life and Literature* (Edinburgh)

Wright, D. F., ed. (1994), *Martin Bucer: Reforming Church and Community* (Cambridge)

Wyon, O. (1953), *The Three Windows. The Story of Ann Hunter Small* (London)

Youngson, A. J. (1966), *The Making of Classical Edinburgh* (Edinburgh)

Zizioulas, J. (1985), *Being as Communion: Studies in Personhood and the Church* (London)

Index of Names

313

Index of Names

General Index

General Index

Scottish Ecclesiological Society 194
Scottish Episcopal Church 180, 217, 247, 249–50
  Edinburgh Theological College (Coates Hall) 57, 118, 180, 190, 217, 243, 244, 247–9, 252, 253, 256
  Theological Institute 249, 255
Scottish Girls Friendly Society xiii
Scottish Historical Review xxvii
Scottish Journal of Theology xxii, xxv, xxx, 104, 127, 192
Scottish Pastoral Association 145
Scottish Record Office 193
Scottish theology xxviii, xxix, 1–28, 230–2, 242, 277–89
Secession 21, 35, 113, 189, 194, 221, 250
Secularity 159, 162
Selly Oak Colleges 275, 276
Semitic Languages 69, 135
  see also Hebrew; Oriental Languages
Septuagint 54, 69, 85, 225
Sheffield 67
Sierra Leone 215
Signet Library 81
Sikhism 153, 158, 159
Singapore 203
Slavery xxx
Slovakia 203
Social Anthropology 154, 157
Social Sciences 121, 132, 140, 288
Society for Old Testament Study xii, xxvii, 57, 61, 64, 67–8, 69
Society for the Study of Theology 127
Socinianism 18, 19, 100
Sociology 140, 144, 145, 146, 154, 155, 263–4
Soteriology 129–30
  see also Atonement
South Africa 102, 203, 205–7, 212, 214, 215
South America 216
Speaker's Lectures, Oxford 64
Spirituality 132, 142, 160, 185
Spurgeon's College, London 67
St Andrew Press xxii
St Andrews College, Sydney 95, 128
St Andrews, Drygrange, *see* Roman Catholics

St Andrews, University of viii, xxix, xxx, 35, 62, 64, 68, 71, 73, 90, 92, 95, 105, 130, 145, 146, 150, 190, 208, 223, 245, 248, 261, 271, 274
St Colm's College 249, 255–6
St John's, Newfoundland (Memorial University) xxvii
Stained glass 198
Stirling, University of 152, 160
Stornoway 232
Strasbourg xxiv
Students 46–8, 203–19
  American xx–xxi, 71, 91–2, 114, 174, 178, 204, 210, 214–15, 216
  candidates for ministry 46–8, 96, 133, 135–50 *passim*, 164, 172, 178, 181, 182, 183, 184, 204, 210, 211–12, 281
  German xix, 178, 203, 208, 211, 216
  international xx–xxi, 71, 91, 163, 174, 175, 182, 203–6, 210–12, 214–16, 279–80
  Irish xxi, 42, 203, 204, 210, 217
  non-graduating xvii–xviii, 204, 206, 210, 212, 214–5, 247
  numbers of xvii–xviii, 38, 42, 49, 147, 162, 163–4, 172, 177, 182, 210, 216, 218–19, 276
  postgraduate xvii–xviii, 71, 91–2, 114, 145, 149, 209–10, 212, 215, 216, 218–19, 242, 253, 276
  women 146, 147, 203–5, 215, 217, 218, 246–7
Studies in World Christianity: Edinburgh Review of Theology and Religion xxi, 276
Studiorum Novi Testamenti Societas 89, 93
Sussex, University of xxviii, 147
Switzerland 203, 205, 210
Sydney, St Andrews College 95, 128
Synod Hall, *see* United Presbyterian Church
Syriac 54, 55, 57, 68
Systematic Theology xxix, 37, 46, 47, 60, 62, 71, 95, 108, 117–33, 145, 154, 172, 222, 245, 251, 284, 286
  see also Christian Dogmatics; Divinity

Taiwan 203, 212
Tambaram 213